Astrological Pocket Planner

Copyright © 1998 Llewellyn Publications
All rights reserved.

Printed in the United States of America
Typography property of Llewellyn Worldwide, Ltd.

ISBN: 1-56718-944-X

Cover design and illustration by Anne Marie Garrison
Designed by Susan Van Sant
Edited by Roxanna Rejali and Corrine Kenner

A special thanks to Leslie Nielsen for astrological proofreading.

Set in Eastern and Pacific Standard Times. Year 1999 ephemeris and aspect data generated by Matrix Software. Year 2000 ephemeris and aspect data generated by ACS Publications. Re-use is prohibited.

Published by
LLEWELLYN PUBLICATIONSX
P.O. Box 64383 Dept. K944-X
St. Paul, MN 55164-0383, U.S.A.

Table of Contents

Mercury Retrograde

	DATE	EST	PST		DATE	EST	PST
Mercury Retrograde	3/10	**4:07 am**	1:07 am	— Mercury Direct	4/2	**4:15 am**	1:15 am
Mercury Retrograde	7/12	**6:26 pm**	3:26 pm	— Mercury Direct	8/5	**10:20 pm**	7:20 pm
Mercury Retrograde	11/4	**9:51 pm**	6:51 pm	— Mercury Direct	11/24	**10:53 pm**	7:53 pm

Moon Void-of-Course

Times are listed in Eastern Standard Time in this table only. All other information in the *Pocket Planner* is listed in both Eastern Standard Time and Pacific Standard Time. Refer to "Time Zone Conversions" on page 7 for changing to other time zones.

Last Aspect		Moon Enters New Sign			Last Aspect		Moon Enters New Sign			Last Aspect		Moon Enters New Sign		
Date	Time	Date	Sign	Time	Date	Time	Date	Sign	Time	Date	Time	Date	Sign	Time
JANUARY					**FEBRUARY**					**MARCH**				
3	2:35 am	3	♌	5:31 am	1	4:40 pm	1	♍	8:37 pm	2	1:59 am	3	♎	1:34 pm
5	6:31 am	5	♍	10:49 am	4	1:18 am	4	♎	4:55 am	4	5:44 am	6	♏	12:23 am
7	6:07 am	7	♎	7:53 pm	6	12:22 pm	6	♏	4:06 pm	7	9:38 am	8	♐	12:47 pm
10	1:32 am	10	♏	7:48 am	9	3:01 am	9	♐	4:38 am	10	5:41 am	11	♑	12:54 am
12	7:53 am	12	♐	8:23 pm	11	3:40 pm	11	♑	4:10 pm	12	10:33 pm	13	♒	10:32 am
15	1:43 am	15	♑	7:29 am	13	10:32 pm	14	♒	12:57 am	15	10:40 am	15	♓	4:31 pm
17	10:49 am	17	♒	4:12 pm	16	4:42 am	17	♓	6:40 am	17	1:48 pm	17	♈	7:13 pm
19	5:44 pm	19	♓	10:41 pm	18	2:42 am	18	♈	10:07 am	18	8:07 pm	19	♉	8:09 pm
21	7:35 pm	22	♈	3:26 am	20	11:12 am	20	♉	12:29 pm	21	3:52 pm	21	♊	9:05 pm
24	5:26 am	24	♉	6:53 am	21	4:36 pm	22	♊	2:54 pm	23	3:11 am	23	♋	11:33 pm
26	4:44 am	26	♊	9:30 am	24	5:28 pm	24	♋	6:09 pm	25	4:46 pm	26	♌	4:22 am
28	7:52 am	28	♋	11:57 am	26	10:24 pm	26	♌	10:44 pm	27	8:46 am	28	♍	11:35 am
30	11:17 am	30	♌	3:16 pm	28	12:18 am	3/1	♍	5:05 am	30	4:03 am	30	♎	8:50 pm

Moon Void-of-Course (cont.)

APRIL

Last Aspect		Moon Enters New Sign		
Date	Time	Date	Sign	Time
1	3:39 am	2	♏	7:49 am
4	2:01 am	4	♐	8:08 pm
4	4:07 pm	6	♑	8:39 am
9	1:06 pm	9	♒	7:24 pm
12	2:02 am	12	♓	2:35 am
13	11:53 pm	14	♈	5:46 am
15	11:22 pm	16	♉	6:07 am
17	7:56 am	18	♊	5:39 am
20	6:22 am	20	♋	6:28 am
21	9:32 am	22	♌	10:06 am
23	3:58 pm	24	♍	5:05 pm
25	11:15 pm	27	♎	2:47 am
28	4:08 pm	29	♏	2:13 pm
30	11:35 am	5/2	♐	2:36 am

MAY

Last Aspect		Moon Enters New Sign		
Date	Time	Date	Sign	Time
4	5:37 am	4	♑	3:12 pm
7	1:45 am	7	♒	2:40 am
9	9:01 am	9	♓	11:16 am
10	10:51 pm	11	♈	3:54 pm
12	12:59 pm	13	♉	4:57 pm
15	7:06 am	15	♊	4:08 pm
17	10:05 am	17	♋	3:40 pm
19	2:52 pm	19	♌	5:38 pm
21	3:15 pm	21	♍	11:16 pm
23	5:37 am	24	♎	8:29 am
26	9:56 am	26	♏	8:05 pm
28	4:08 pm	29	♐	8:37 am
31	10:54 am	31	♑	9:06 pm

JUNE

Last Aspect		Moon Enters New Sign		
Date	Time	Date	Sign	Time
3	3:39 am	3	♒	8:37 am
5	1:27 pm	5	♓	6:01 pm
6	11:21 pm	8	♈	12:09 am
9	9:28 pm	10	♉	2:44 am
11	5:35 am	12	♊	2:49 am
13	10:20 pm	14	♋	2:14 am
15	11:39 pm	16	♌	3:07 am
18	4:10 am	18	♍	7:12 am
20	1:13 pm	20	♎	3:10 pm
23	12:36 am	23	♏	2:18 am
25	12:50 pm	25	♐	2:51 pm
28	3:11 pm	28	♑	3:12 am
30	11:37 am	30	♒	2:20 pm

JULY

Last Aspect		Moon Enters New Sign		
Date	Time	Date	Sign	Time
2	10:22 pm	2	♓	11:35 pm
4	2:26 am	5	♈	6:22 am
7	5:07 am	7	♉	10:22 am
9	9:09 am	9	♊	11:59 am
11	11:37 am	11	♋	12:27 pm
12	9:24 pm	13	♌	1:25 pm
14	3:54 pm	15	♍	4:39 pm
17	1:28 pm	17	♎	11:19 pm
20	4:01 am	20	♏	9:30 am
22	9:28 pm	22	♐	9:49 pm
24	4:52 am	25	♑	10:09 am
26	6:06 pm	27	♒	8:55 pm
29	3:56 am	30	♓	5:27 am

AUGUST

Last Aspect		Moon Enters New Sign		
Date	Time	Date	Sign	Time
1	11:03 am	1	♈	11:47 am
3	2:12 pm	3	♉	4:08 pm
5	4:35 pm	5	♊	6:57 pm
7	7:43 pm	7	♋	8:52 pm
9	10:01 pm	9	♌	10:55 pm
11	6:09 am	12	♍	2:22 am
13	10:31 am	14	♎	8:25 am
16	4:12 pm	16	♏	5:41 pm
19	1:07 am	19	♐	5:32 am
21	2:36 pm	21	♑	5:59 pm
23	5:13 pm	23	♒	4:49 am
26	4:31 am	26	♓	12:49 pm
28	12:41 pm	28	♈	6:09 pm
30	7:39 pm	30	♉	9:40 pm

SEPTEMBER

Last Aspect		Moon Enters New Sign		
Date	Time	Date	Sign	Time
1	11:46 pm	2	♊	12:25 am
3	9:59 am	4	♋	3:10 am
5	8:23 am	6	♌	6:29 am
7	3:31 pm	8	♍	10:57 am
9	7:34 pm	10	♎	5:16 pm
12	4:38 am	13	♏	2:09 am
15	10:24 am	15	♐	1:35 pm
17	3:06 pm	18	♑	2:13 am
20	8:04 am	20	♒	1:38 pm
22	5:38 am	22	♓	9:51 pm
24	3:27 am	25	♈	2:34 am
26	5:34 pm	27	♉	4:51 am
28	9:01 pm	29	♊	6:21 am

OCTOBER

Last Aspect		Moon Enters New Sign		
Date	Time	Date	Sign	Time
1	1:09 am	1	♋	8:32 am
3	7:53 am	3	♌	12:14 pm
5	3:15 pm	5	♍	5:40 pm
7	12:27 pm	8	♎	12:52 am
10	12:33 am	10	♏	10:01 am
11	4:42 pm	12	♐	9:18 pm
15	7:49 am	15	♑	10:03 am
17	9:59 am	17	♒	10:17 pm
20	12:53 am	20	♓	7:33 am
21	11:25 pm	22	♈	12:42 pm
24	2:05 pm	24	♉	2:26 pm
26	9:22 am	26	♊	2:34 pm
28	1:55 pm	28	♋	3:09 pm
30	4:00 pm	30	♌	5:47 pm

NOVEMBER

Last Aspect		Moon Enters New Sign		
Date	Time	Date	Sign	Time
1	8:43 pm	1	♍	11:07 pm
3	9:03 pm	4	♎	6:56 am
6	1:01 pm	6	♏	4:45 pm
8	12:57 am	9	♐	4:15 am
11	11:53 am	11	♑	5:00 pm
14	12:08 am	14	♒	5:46 am
16	10:31 am	16	♓	4:21 pm
18	4:04 pm	18	♈	10:58 pm
20	7:42 pm	21	♉	1:26 am
22	9:24 pm	23	♊	1:14 am
24	6:21 pm	25	♋	12:29 am
26	6:35 pm	27	♌	1:18 am
28	9:43 pm	29	♍	5:11 am
30	2:11 pm	12/1	♎	12:29 pm

DECEMBER

Last Aspect		Moon Enters New Sign		
Date	Time	Date	Sign	Time
3	6:04 pm	3	♏	10:36 pm
5	9:30 pm	6	♐	10:28 am
8	1:36 pm	8	♑	11:14 pm
11	2:14 am	11	♒	11:59 am
13	1:46 pm	13	♓	11:18 pm
15	7:50 pm	16	♈	7:30 am
18	5:03 am	18	♉	11:45 am
19	5:46 pm	20	♊	12:39 pm
22	4:03 am	22	♋	11:52 am
24	3:31 am	24	♌	11:32 am
26	5:07 am	26	♍	1:34 pm
28	1:52 pm	28	♎	7:15 pm
30	10:35 pm	30	♏	4:37 am

How to Use the *Pocket Planner*

by Leslie Nielsen

This handy guide contains information that can be most valuable to you as you plan your daily activities. As you read through the first few pages, you can start to get a feel for how well organized this guide is.

Read the Symbol Key on the next page, which is rather like astrological shorthand. The characteristics of the planets can give you direction in planning your strategies. Much like traffic signs that signal "go," or "stop," or even "caution," you can determine for yourself the most precipitous time to get things done.

You'll find tables that show the dates when Mercury is retrograde (Rx) or direct (D). Because Mercury deals with the exchange of information, a retrograde Mercury makes miscommunication more noticeable.

There's also a section dedicated to the times when the Moon is void-of-course (v/c). It is generally a poor time to conduct business. If you make an appointment during a void-of-course, you might save yourself a lot of aggravation by confirming the time and date later. The Moon is only void of course for seven percent of the times when business is usually conducted during a normal work day (that is, 8:00 am to 5:00 pm) Sometimes, by waiting a matter of minutes or a few hours when the Moon has left the void of course phase, you have a much better chance to make action move more smoothly. Moon voids can also be used successfully to do some inner work, such as dream therapy or personal psychology.

You'll find Moon phases, as well as each of the Moon's entries into a new sign. Times are expressed in Eastern Standard Time (in bold type) and Pacific Standard Time (in medium type). The New Moon time is generally best for beginning new activities, as the Moon is increasing in light and can offer the element of growth to your endeavor. When the Moon is Full, its illumination is greatest and we can see the results of our efforts. When it moves from Full stage back to the New stage, it can best be used to reflect on our projects. If necessary, we can make corrections at the New Moon.

Planets also change signs and afford us opportunities for new starts. You may wish take special note of the sections on "Things Ruled by the

Planets," the "Planetary Business Guide," and "Planetary Associations." The section of "Planetary Stations" will give you the information you need for knowing when a certain planet is not as open or obvious in its particular activity.

The ephemeris in the back of your *Pocket Planner* can be very helpful to you. Read the particular sign and degree of planets and asteroids. As you start to work with the ephemeris, you may notice that not all planets seem to be comfortable in the sign they are in. Think of the planets as actors, and the signs as the costumes they wear. Sometimes, costumes just itch. If you find this to be so for a certain time period, you may choose to delay your plans for a time or be more creative with the energies at hand.

As you turn to the daily pages, you'll find information about the Moon's sign, phase, and the time it changes phase. Also, you will find times and dates when the planets and asteroids change sign and either go retrograde or direct, major holidays, a three-month calendar, and room to enter your appointments.

This guide is a powerful tool. Make the most of it!

Symbol Key

Planets:	⊙ Sun	⚳ Ceres	♄ Saturn
	☽ Moon	⚴ Pallas	⚷ Chiron
	☿ Mercury	⚵ Juno	♅ Uranus
	♀ Venus	⚶ Vesta	♆ Neptune
	♂ Mars	♃ Jupiter	♇ Pluto
Signs:	♈ Aries	♌ Leo	♐ Sagittarius
	♉ Taurus	♍ Virgo	♑ Capricorn
	♊ Gemini	♎ Libra	♒ Aquarius
	♋ Cancer	♏ Scorpio	♓ Pisces
Aspects:	☌ Conjunction	◻ Square	☍ Opposition
	⊻ Semisextile	△ Trine	
	⚹ Sextile	⋔ Quincunx	
Motion:	℞ Retrograde	D Direct	

World Map of Time Zones

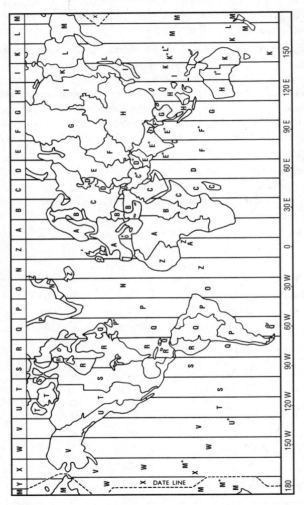

Time Zone Conversions

World Time Zones
Compared to Eastern Standard Time

( ) From Map	(Y) Subtract 7 hours	(C*) Add 8.5 hours
(S) Subtract 1 hour	(A) Add 6 hours	(D*) Add 9.5 hours
(R) EST (Used in calendar)	(B) Add 7 hours	(E*) Add 10.5 hours
(Q) Add 1 hour	(C) Add 8 hours	(F*) Add 11.5 hours
(P) Add 2 hours	(D) Add 9 hours	(I*) Add 14.5 hours
(O) Add 3 hours	(E) Add 10 hours	(K*) Add 15.5 hours
(N) Add 4 hours	(F) Add 11 hours	(L*) Add 16.5 hours
(Z) Add 5 hours	(G) Add 12 hours	(M*) Add 18 hours
(T) MST/Subtract 2 hours	(H) Add 13 hours	(P*) Add 2.5 hours
(U) PST/Subtract 3 hours	(I) Add 14 hours	(V*) Subtract 4.5 hours
(V) Subtract 4 hours	(K) Add 15 hours	
(W) Subtract 5 hours	(L) Add 16 hours	
(X) Subtract 6 hours	(M) Add 17 hours	

Planetary Stations for 1999

Eastern Standard Time in regular typeface, Pacific Standard Time in **bold typeface**.

Planet	Begin	EST	PST	End	EST	PST
Ceres	10/10/98	6:49 pm	**3:49 pm**	01/16/99	10:32 am	**7:32 am**
Vesta	12/19/98	9:31 pm	**6:31 pm**	03/23/99	11:51 pm	**8:51 pm**
Mercury	03/10/99	4:07 am	**1:07 am**	04/02/99	4:15 am	**1:15 am**
Pluto	03/13/99	10:56 am	**7:56 pm**	08/18/99	5:59 pm	**2:59 pm**
Chiron	03/15/99	5:19 pm	**2:19 pm**	07/28/99	2:30 pm	**11:30 pm**
Mars	03/18/99	8:40 am	**5:40 am**	06/04/99	1:12 am	**10:12 pm 6/3**
Juno	03/30/99	1:58 pm	**10:58 am**	07/22/99	12:48 pm	**9:48 am 7/21**
Neptune	05/06/99	1:33 pm	**10:33 am**	10/13/99	5:01 pm	**2:01 pm**
Uranus	05/21/99	1:43 pm	**10:43 am**	10/22/99	10:34 pm	**7:34 pm**
Mercury	7/12/99	6:26 pm	**3:26 pm**	08/05/99	10:20 pm	**7:20 pm**
Venus	07/29/99	8:41 pm	**5:41 pm**	09/10/99	7:25 pm	**4:25 pm**
Jupiter	08/24/99	8:46 pm	**5:46 pm**	12/20/99	10:23 am	**7:23 am**
Saturn	08/29/99	7:09 pm	**4:09 pm**	01/11/00	11:03 pm	**8:03 pm**
Mercury	11/04/99	9:51 pm	**6:51 pm**	11/24/99	10:53 pm	**7:53 pm**
Pallas	12/15/99	5:56 pm	**2:56 pm**	03/07/00	1:08 pm	**10:08 am**

1 Friday
2nd ♊
) enters ♋ **3:16 am** 12:16 am
Full Moon **9:50 pm** 6:50 pm

New Year's Day • Kwanzaa ends

2 Saturday
3rd ♋
♀ enters ♊ **3:44 pm** 12:44 pm
) v/c 11:35 pm

3 Sunday
3rd ♋
) v/c **2:35 am**
) enters ♌ **5:31 am** 2:31 am

December 1998								January 1999							February 1999					
S	M	T	W	T	F	S		S	M	T	W	T	F	S	S	M	T	W	T	F	S
		1	2	3	4	5							1	2		1	2	3	4	5	6
6	7	8	9	10	11	12		3	4	5	6	7	8	9	7	8	9	10	11	12	13
13	14	15	16	17	18	19		10	11	12	13	14	15	16	14	15	16	17	18	19	20
20	21	22	23	24	25	26		17	18	19	20	21	22	23	21	22	23	24	25	26	27
27	28	29	30	31				24	25	26	27	28	29	30	28						
								31													

Eastern Standard Time in bold type
Pacific Standard Time in medium type

4 Monday
3rd ♌
♀ enters ♒ **11:25 am** 8:25 am

5 Tuesday
3rd ♌
☽ v/c **6:31 am** 3:31 am
☽ enters ♍ **10:49 am** 7:49 am

6 Wednesday
3rd ♍
☿ enters ♑ **9:03 pm** 6:03 pm

7 Thursday
3rd ♍
☽ v/c **6:07 am** 3:07 am
♅ enters ♐ **3:16 pm** 12:16 pm
☽ enters ♎ **7:53 pm** 4:53 pm

Eastern Standard Time in bold type
Pacific Standard Time in medium type

8 Friday
3rd ♎

9 Saturday
3rd ♎
4th Quarter **9:21 am** 6:21 am
☽ v/c 10:32 pm

10 Sunday
4th ♎
☽ v/c **1:32 am**
☽ enters ♏ **7:48 am** 4:48 am

December 1998						
S	M	T	W	T	F	S
		1	2	3	4	5
6	7	8	9	10	11	12
13	14	15	16	17	18	19
20	21	22	23	24	25	26
27	28	29	30	31		

January 1999						
S	M	T	W	T	F	S
					1	2
3	4	5	6	7	8	9
10	11	12	13	14	15	16
17	18	19	20	21	22	23
24	25	26	27	28	29	30
31						

February 1999						
S	M	T	W	T	F	S
	1	2	3	4	5	6
7	8	9	10	11	12	13
14	15	16	17	18	19	20
21	22	23	24	25	26	27
28						

11 Monday
4th ♏

12 Tuesday
4th ♏
☽ v/c	**7:53 am**	4:53 am
☽ enters ♐	**8:23 pm**	5:23 pm

13 Wednesday
4th ♐

14 Thursday
4th ♐
☽ v/c		10:43 pm

Eastern Standard Time in bold type
Pacific Standard Time in medium type

15 Friday

4th ♐
☽ v/c	**1:43 am**	
⚷ enters ♐	**7:12 am**	4:12 am
☽ enters ♑	**7:29 am**	4:29 am

Birthday of Martin Luther King, Jr.

16 Saturday

4th ♑
☿ D	**10:32 am**	7:32 am

17 Sunday

4th ♑
New Moon	**10:47 am**	7:47 am
☽ enters ♒	**4:12 pm**	1:12 pm

December 1998						
S	M	T	W	T	F	S
		1	2	3	4	5
6	7	8	9	10	11	12
13	14	15	16	17	18	19
20	21	22	23	24	25	26
27	28	29	30	31		

January 1999						
S	M	T	W	T	F	S
					1	2
3	4	5	6	7	8	9
10	11	12	13	14	15	16
17	18	19	20	21	22	23
24	25	26	27	28	29	30
31						

February 1999						
S	M	T	W	T	F	S
	1	2	3	4	5	6
7	8	9	10	11	12	13
14	15	16	17	18	19	20
21	22	23	24	25	26	27
28						

18 Monday
1st ≈

Birthday of Martin Luther King, Jr. (Observed)

---

19 Tuesday
1st ≈
☽ v/c   **5:44 pm**   2:44 pm
☽ enters ♓   **10:41 pm**   7:41 pm

---

20 Wednesday
1st ♓
☉ enters ≈   **7:38 am**   4:38 am

Sun enters Aquarius

---

21 Thursday
1st ♓
☽ v/c   **7:35 pm**   4:35 pm

Eastern Standard Time in bold type
Pacific Standard Time in medium type

22 Friday
1st ♓
☽ enters ♈   **3:26 am** 12:26 am

23 Saturday
1st ♈

24 Sunday
1st ♈
☽ v/c   **5:26 am** 2:26 am
☽ enters ♉   **6:53 am** 3:53 am
2nd Quarter **2:16 pm** 11:16 am

December 1998						
S	M	T	W	T	F	S
		1	2	3	4	5
6	7	8	9	10	11	12
13	14	15	16	17	18	19
20	21	22	23	24	25	26
27	28	29	30	31		

January 1999						
S	M	T	W	T	F	S
					1	2
3	4	5	6	7	8	9
10	11	12	13	14	15	16
17	18	19	20	21	22	23
24	25	26	27	28	29	30
31						

February 1999						
S	M	T	W	T	F	S
	1	2	3	4	5	6
7	8	9	10	11	12	13
14	15	16	17	18	19	20
21	22	23	24	25	26	27
28						

Eastern Standard Time in bold type
Pacific Standard Time in medium type

25 Monday
2nd ♉

26 Tuesday
2nd ♉
☿ enters ≈　**4:32 am**　1:32 am
☽ v/c　**4:44 am**　1:44 am
♂ enters ♏　**6:59 am**　3:59 am
☽ enters ♊　**9:30 am**　6:30 am

27 Wednesday
2nd ♊

28 Thursday
2nd ♊
☽ v/c　**7:52 am**　4:52 am
♀ enters ♓　**11:16 am**　8:16 am
☽ enters ♋　**11:57 am**　8:57 am

Eastern Standard Time in bold type
Pacific Standard Time in medium type

29 Friday
2nd ⊙

30 Saturday
2nd ⊙
☽ v/c **11:17 am** 8:17 am
♀ enters Ⅱ **12:55 pm** 9:55 am
☽ enters ♌ **3:16 pm** 12:16 pm

31 Sunday
2nd ♌
Full Moon **11:07 am** 8:07 am

Lunar Eclipse 11° ♌ 25'

	January 1999					
S	M	T	W	T	F	S
					1	2
3	4	5	6	7	8	9
10	11	12	13	14	15	16
17	18	19	20	21	22	23
24	25	26	27	28	29	30
31						

	February 1999					
S	M	T	W	T	F	S
	1	2	3	4	5	6
7	8	9	10	11	12	13
14	15	16	17	18	19	20
21	22	23	24	25	26	27
28						

	March 1999					
S	M	T	W	T	F	S
	1	2	3	4	5	6
7	8	9	10	11	12	13
14	15	16	17	18	19	20
21	22	23	24	25	26	27
28	29	30	31			

1 Monday

3rd ♌
☽ v/c **4:40 pm** 1:40 pm
☽ enters ♍ **8:37 pm** 5:37 pm

2 Tuesday

3rd ♍

Imbolc

3 Wednesday

3rd ♍
♀ enters ♈ **9:53 pm** 6:53 pm
☽ v/c 10:18 pm

4 Thursday

3rd ♍
☽ v/c **1:18 am**
☽ enters ♎ **4:55 am** 1:55 am

Eastern Standard Time in bold type
Pacific Standard Time in medium type

5 Friday
3rd ♎

6 Saturday
3rd ♎
☽ v/c   **12:22 pm** 9:22 am
☽ enters ♏ **4:06 pm** 1:06 pm

7 Sunday
3rd ♏

January 1999						
S	M	T	W	T	F	S
					1	2
3	4	5	6	7	8	9
10	11	12	13	14	15	16
17	18	19	20	21	22	23
24	25	26	27	28	29	30
31						

February 1999						
S	M	T	W	T	F	S
	1	2	3	4	5	6
7	8	9	10	11	12	13
14	15	16	17	18	19	20
21	22	23	24	25	26	27
28						

March 1999						
S	M	T	W	T	F	S
	1	2	3	4	5	6
7	8	9	10	11	12	13
14	15	16	17	18	19	20
21	22	23	24	25	26	27
28	29	30	31			

8 Monday
3rd ♏
4th Quarter **6:58 am** 3:58 am

9 Tuesday
4th ♏
☽ v/c **3:01 am** 12:01 am
☽ enters ♐ **4:38 am** 1:38 am

10 Wednesday
4th ♐

11 Thursday
4th ♐
☽ v/c **3:40 pm** 12:40 pm
☽ enters ♑ **4:10 pm** 1:10 pm

Eastern Standard Time in bold type
Pacific Standard Time in medium type

12 Friday

4th ♑
♃ enters ♈ **8:21 pm** 5:21 pm
☿ enters ♓ **10:27 am** 7:27 am

13 Saturday

4th ♑
☽ enters ♒ 9:57 pm
☽ v/c **10:32 pm** 7:32 pm

14 Sunday

4th ♒
☽ enters ♒ **12:57 am**

Valentine's Day

January 1999						
S	M	T	W	T	F	S
					1	2
3	4	5	6	7	8	9
10	11	12	13	14	15	16
17	18	19	20	21	22	23
24	25	26	27	28	29	30
31						

February 1999						
S	M	T	W	T	F	S
	1	2	3	4	5	6
7	8	9	10	11	12	13
14	15	16	17	18	19	20
21	22	23	24	25	26	27
28						

March 1999						
S	M	T	W	T	F	S
	1	2	3	4	5	6
7	8	9	10	11	12	13
14	15	16	17	18	19	20
21	22	23	24	25	26	27
28	29	30	31			

15 Monday
4th ≈
New Moon   10:40 pm

Washington's Birthday (Observed)

16 Tuesday
4th ≈
New Moon   **1:40 am**
☽ v/c   **4:42 am**   1:42 am
☽ enters ♓ **6:40 am**   3:40 am

Solar Eclipse 27° ≈ 08'

17 Wednesday
1st ♓
☽ v/c   11:42 pm

Ash Wednesday

18 Thursday
1st ♓
☽ v/c   **2:42 am**
☽ enters ♈ **10:07 am**   7:07 am
☉ enters ♓ **9:47 pm**   6:47 pm

Sun enters Pisces

Eastern Standard Time in bold type
          Pacific Standard Time in medium type

19 Friday
1st ♈

20 Saturday
1st ♈
☽ v/c   **11:12 am** 8:12 am
☽ enters ♉   **12:29 pm** 9:29 am

21 Sunday
1st ♉
♀ enters ♈   **3:49 pm** 12:49 pm
☽ v/c   **4:36 pm** 1:36 pm

January 1999						
S	M	T	W	T	F	S
					1	2
3	4	5	6	7	8	9
10	11	12	13	14	15	16
17	18	19	20	21	22	23
24	25	26	27	28	29	30
31						

February 1999						
S	M	T	W	T	F	S
	1	2	3	4	5	6
7	8	9	10	11	12	13
14	15	16	17	18	19	20
21	22	23	24	25	26	27
28						

March 1999						
S	M	T	W	T	F	S
	1	2	3	4	5	6
7	8	9	10	11	12	13
14	15	16	17	18	19	20
21	22	23	24	25	26	27
28	29	30	31			

Eastern Standard Time in bold type
Pacific Standard Time in medium type

Llewellyn's 1999 Pocket Planner and Ephemeris

22 Monday
1st ♉
☽ enters ♊ **2:54 pm** 11:54 am
2nd Quarter **9:43 pm** 6:43 pm

Washington's Birthday

23 Tuesday
2nd ♊

24 Wednesday
2nd ♊
☽ v/c **5:28 pm** 2:28 pm
☽ enters ♋ **6:09 pm** 3:09 pm

25 Thursday
2nd ♋

Eastern Standard Time in bold type
Pacific Standard Time in medium type

26 Friday

2nd ♋
☽ v/c   **10:24 pm** 7:24 pm
☽ enters ♌ **10:44 pm** 7:44 pm

27 Saturday

2nd ♌
☽ v/c   9:18 pm

28 Sunday

2nd ♌
☽ v/c   **12:18 am**
♄ enters ♉ **8:26 pm** 5:26 pm

February 1999						
S	M	T	W	T	F	S
	1	2	3	4	5	6
7	8	9	10	11	12	13
14	15	16	17	18	19	20
21	22	23	24	25	26	27
28						

March 1999						
S	M	T	W	T	F	S
	1	2	3	4	5	6
7	8	9	10	11	12	13
14	15	16	17	18	19	20
21	22	23	24	25	26	27
28	29	30	31			

April 1999						
S	M	T	W	T	F	S
				1	2	3
4	5	6	7	8	9	10
11	12	13	14	15	16	17
18	19	20	21	22	23	24
25	26	27	28	29	30	

Eastern Standard Time in bold type
Pacific Standard Time in medium type

1 Monday
2nd ♌
☽ enters ♍ **5:05 am** 2:05 am
Full Moon   10:59 pm
☽ v/c   10:59 pm

Purim begins

2 Tuesday
3rd ♍
Full Moon   **1:59 am**
☽ v/c   **1:59 am**
☿ enters ♈ **5:50 pm** 2:50 pm

Purim ends

3 Wednesday
3rd ♍
☽ enters ♎ **1:34 pm** 10:34 am

4 Thursday
3rd ♎
☽ v/c   **5:44 pm** 2:44 pm

Eastern Standard Time in bold type
Pacific Standard Time in medium type

5 Friday
3rd ♎︎
☽ enters ♏︎   9:23 pm

6 Saturday
3rd ♎︎
☽ enters ♏︎ **12:23 am**

7 Sunday
3rd ♏︎
☽ v/c   **9:38 am**   6:38 am

February 1999						
S	M	T	W	T	F	S
	1	2	3	4	5	6
7	8	9	10	11	12	13
14	15	16	17	18	19	20
21	22	23	24	25	26	27
28						

March 1999						
S	M	T	W	T	F	S
	1	2	3	4	5	6
7	8	9	10	11	12	13
14	15	16	17	18	19	20
21	22	23	24	25	26	27
28	29	30	31			

April 1999						
S	M	T	W	T	F	S
					1	2	3
4	5	6	7	8	9	10
11	12	13	14	15	16	17
18	19	20	21	22	23	24
25	26	27	28	29	30	

Eastern Standard Time in bold type
Pacific Standard Time in medium type

8 Monday
3rd ♏
☽ enters ♐ **12:47 pm** 9:47 am

9 Tuesday
3rd ♐

10 Wednesday
3rd ♐
4th Quarter **3:41 am** 12:41 am
☽ v/c **5:41 am** 2:41 am
☿ R **4:07 am** 1:07 am
☽ enters ♑ 9:54 pm

11 Thursday
4th ♐
☽ enters ♑ **12:54 am**

Eastern Standard Time in bold type
Pacific Standard Time in medium type

12 Friday
4th ♑
☽ v/c   **10:33 pm**   7:33 pm

13 Saturday
4th ♑
☽ enters ♒ **10:32 am**   7:32 am
♇ ℞   **10:56 am**   7:56 am

14 Sunday
4th ♒

February 1999						
S	M	T	W	T	F	S
	1	2	3	4	5	6
7	8	9	10	11	12	13
14	15	16	17	18	19	20
21	22	23	24	25	26	27
28						

March 1999						
S	M	T	W	T	F	S
	1	2	3	4	5	6
7	8	9	10	11	12	13
14	15	16	17	18	19	20
21	22	23	24	25	26	27
28	29	30	31			

April 1999						
S	M	T	W	T	F	S
				1	2	3
4	5	6	7	8	9	10
11	12	13	14	15	16	17
18	19	20	21	22	23	24
25	26	27	28	29	30	

Eastern Standard Time in bold type
Pacific Standard Time in medium type

15 Monday

4th ≈

☽ v/c	**10:40 am**	7:40 am
☽ enters ♓	**4:31 pm**	1:31 pm
♀ ℞	**5:19 pm**	2:19 pm

16 Tuesday

4th ♓

17 Wednesday

4th ♓

☿ enters ♓	**4:23 am**	1:23 am
New Moon	**1:48 pm**	10:48 am
☽ v/c	**1:48 pm**	10:48 am
☽ enters ♈	**7:13 pm**	4:13 pm

St. Patrick's Day

18 Thursday

1st ♈

♀ enters ♉	**4:59 am**	1:59 am
♂ ℞	**8:40 am**	5:40 am
☽ v/c	**8:07 pm**	5:07 pm

Eastern Standard Time in bold type
Pacific Standard Time in medium type

19 Friday
1st ♈
☽ enters ♉ **8:09 pm** 5:09 pm

---

20 Saturday
1st ♉
☉ enters ♈ **8:46 pm** 5:46 pm

Sun enters Aries • Spring Equinox • 8:46 pm EST/5:46 pm PST

---

21 Sunday
1st ♉
☽ v/c **3:52 pm** 12:52 pm
☽ enters ♊ **9:05 pm** 6:05 pm

February 1999						
S	M	T	W	T	F	S
	1	2	3	4	5	6
7	8	9	10	11	12	13
14	15	16	17	18	19	20
21	22	23	24	25	26	27
28						

March 1999						
S	M	T	W	T	F	S
	1	2	3	4	5	6
7	8	9	10	11	12	13
14	15	16	17	18	19	20
21	22	23	24	25	26	27
28	29	30	31			

April 1999						
S	M	T	W	T	F	S
					1	2	3
4	5	6	7	8	9	10
11	12	13	14	15	16	17
18	19	20	21	22	23	24
25	26	27	28	29	30	

22 Monday
1st ♊

23 Tuesday
1st ♊
☽ v/c   **3:11 pm** 12:11 pm
☽ enters ♋ **11:33 pm** 8:33 pm
⚸ D   **11:51 pm** 8:51 pm

24 Wednesday
1st ♋
2nd Quarter **5:18 am** 2:18 am

25 Thursday
2nd ♋
☽ v/c   **4:46 pm** 1:46 pm

Eastern Standard Time in bold type
Pacific Standard Time in medium type

26 Friday
2nd ♌
☽ enters ♌ **4:22 am** 1:22 am

27 Saturday
2nd ♌
☽ v/c **8:46 am** 5:46 am

28 Sunday
2nd ♌
☽ enters ♍ **11:35 am** 8:35 am

Palm Sunday

February 1999						
S	M	T	W	T	F	S
	1	2	3	4	5	6
7	8	9	10	11	12	13
14	15	16	17	18	19	20
21	22	23	24	25	26	27
28						

March 1999						
S	M	T	W	T	F	S
	1	2	3	4	5	6
7	8	9	10	11	12	13
14	15	16	17	18	19	20
21	22	23	24	25	26	27
28	29	30	31			

April 1999						
S	M	T	W	T	F	S
					1	2	3
4	5	6	7	8	9	10
11	12	13	14	15	16	17
18	19	20	21	22	23	24
25	26	27	28	29	30	

Eastern Standard Time in bold type
Pacific Standard Time in medium type

29 Monday
2nd ♍

30 Tuesday
2nd ♍
☽ v/c	**4:03 am**	1:03 am
☿ ℞	**1:58 pm**	10:58 am
☽ enters ♎	**8:50 pm**	5:50 pm

31 Wednesday
2nd ♎
| Full Moon | **5:50 pm** | 2:50 pm |

Passover begins

1 Thursday
3rd ♎
| ☽ v/c | **3:39 am** | 12:39 am |

April Fool's Day

Eastern Standard Time in bold type
Pacific Standard Time in medium type

2 Friday

3rd ♎

☿ D	**4:15 am**	1:15 am
☽ enters ♏	**7:49 am**	4:49 am

Good Friday

3 Saturday

3rd ♏

☽ v/c	11:01 pm

4 Sunday

3rd ♏

☽ v/c	**2:01 am**	
☽ enters ♐	**8:08 pm**	5:08 pm

Easter • Daylight Saving Time begins at 2 AM

March 1999						
S	M	T	W	T	F	S
	1	2	3	4	5	6
7	8	9	10	11	12	13
14	15	16	17	18	19	20
21	22	23	24	25	26	27
28	29	30	31			

April 1999						
S	M	T	W	T	F	S
				1	2	3
4	5	6	7	8	9	10
11	12	13	14	15	16	17
18	19	20	21	22	23	24
25	26	27	28	29	30	

May 1999						
S	M	T	W	T	F	S
						1
2	3	4	5	6	7	8
9	10	11	12	13	14	15
16	17	18	19	20	21	22
23	24	25	26	27	28	29
30	31					

5 Monday
3rd ♐

6 Tuesday
3rd ♐
☽ v/c   **4:07 pm** 1:07 pm

7 Wednesday
3rd ♑
☽ enters ♑ **8:39 am** 5:39 am

8 Thursday
3rd ♑
4th Quarter **9:51 pm** 6:51 pm

Passover ends

    Eastern Standard Time in bold type
Pacific Standard Time in medium type

9 Friday
4th ♑
| ☽ v/c | **1:06 pm** 10:06 am |
| ☽ enters ♒ | **7:24 pm** 4:24 pm |

10 Saturday
4th ♒

11 Sunday
4th ♒
| ☽ v/c | 11:02 pm |
| ☽ enters ♓ | 11:35 pm |

Orthodox Easter

March 1999						
S	M	T	W	T	F	S
		1	2	3	4	5	6
7	8	9	10	11	12	13
14	15	16	17	18	19	20
21	22	23	24	25	26	27
28	29	30	31

April 1999						
S	M	T	W	T	F	S
				1	2	3
4	5	6	7	8	9	10
11	12	13	14	15	16	17
18	19	20	21	22	23	24
25	26	27	28	29	30

May 1999						
S	M	T	W	T	F	S
						1
2	3	4	5	6	7	8
9	10	11	12	13	14	15
16	17	18	19	20	21	22
23	24	25	26	27	28	29
30	31

Eastern Standard Time in bold type
Pacific Standard Time in medium type

12 Monday
4th ≈
☽ v/c	**2:02 am**	
☽ enters ♓	**2:35 am**	
♀ enters ♊	**8:17 am**	5:17 am

13 Tuesday
4th ♓
☽ v/c	**11:53 pm**	8:53 pm

14 Wednesday
4th ♓
☽ enters ♈	**5:46 am**	2:46 am

15 Thursday
4th ♈
New Moon	**11:22 pm**	8:22 pm
☽ v/c	**11:22 pm**	8:22 pm

Eastern Standard Time in bold type
Pacific Standard Time in medium type

16 Friday
1st ♈
☽ enters ♉   **6:07 am**   3:07 am

17 Saturday
1st ♉
☽ v/c   **7:56 am**   4:56 am
☿ enters ♈ **5:09 pm**   2:09 pm

18 Sunday
1st ♉
☽ enters ♊   **5:39 am**   2:39 am

March 1999							April 1999							May 1999						
S	M	T	W	T	F	S	S	M	T	W	T	F	S	S	M	T	W	T	F	S
	1	2	3	4	5	6					1	2	3							1
7	8	9	10	11	12	13	4	5	6	7	8	9	10	2	3	4	5	6	7	8
14	15	16	17	18	19	20	11	12	13	14	15	16	17	9	10	11	12	13	14	15
21	22	23	24	25	26	27	18	19	20	21	22	23	24	16	17	18	19	20	21	22
28	29	30	31				25	26	27	28	29	30		23	24	25	26	27	28	29
														30	31					

19 Monday
1st ♊
♀ enters ♉ **8:12 pm** 5:12 pm

20 Tuesday
1st ♊
☽ v/c **6:22 am** 3:22 am
☽ enters ♋ **6:28 am** 3:28 am
☉ enters ♉ **7:46 am** 4:46 am

Sun enters Taurus

21 Wednesday
1st ♋
☽ v/c **9:32 am** 6:32 am

22 Thursday
1st ♋
☽ enters ♌ **10:06 am** 7:06 am
2nd Quarter **2:02 pm** 11:02 am

Eastern Standard Time in bold type
Pacific Standard Time in medium type

23 Friday
2nd ♌
☽ v/c   **3:58 pm** 12:58 pm

24 Saturday
2nd ♌
☽ enters ♍ **5:05 pm** 2:05 pm

25 Sunday
2nd ♍
☽ v/c   **11:15 pm** 8:15 pm

March 1999						
S	M	T	W	T	F	S
	1	2	3	4	5	6
7	8	9	10	11	12	13
14	15	16	17	18	19	20
21	22	23	24	25	26	27
28	29	30	31			

April 1999						
S	M	T	W	T	F	S
				1	2	3
4	5	6	7	8	9	10
11	12	13	14	15	16	17
18	19	20	21	22	23	24
25	26	27	28	29	30	

May 1999						
S	M	T	W	T	F	S
						1
2	3	4	5	6	7	8
9	10	11	12	13	14	15
16	17	18	19	20	21	22
23	24	25	26	27	28	29
30	31					

26 Monday
2nd ♍
☽ enters ♎   11:47 pm

27 Tuesday
2nd ♍
☽ enters ♎ **2:47 am**

28 Wednesday
2nd ♎
☽ v/c   **4:08 pm** 1:08 pm

29 Thursday
2nd ♎
☽ enters ♏ **2:13 pm** 11:13 am

Eastern Standard Time in bold type
          Pacific Standard Time in medium type

30 Friday
2nd ♏
☽ v/c **11:35 pm** 8:35 pm
Full Moon **9:55 am** 6:55 am

1 Saturday
3rd ♏
☽ enters ♐ 11:36 pm

Beltane

2 Sunday
3rd ♏
☽ enters ♐ **2:36 am**

April 1999						
S	M	T	W	T	F	S
				1	2	3
4	5	6	7	8	9	10
11	12	13	14	15	16	17
18	19	20	21	22	23	24
25	26	27	28	29	30	

May 1999						
S	M	T	W	T	F	S
						1
2	3	4	5	6	7	8
9	10	11	12	13	14	15
16	17	18	19	20	21	22
23	24	25	26	27	28	29
30	31					

June 1999						
S	M	T	W	T	F	S
		1	2	3	4	5
6	7	8	9	10	11	12
13	14	15	16	17	18	19
20	21	22	23	24	25	26
27	28	29	30			

3 Monday
3rd ♐

4 Tuesday
3rd ♐
☽ v/c   **5:37 am**   2:37 am
☽ enters ♑   **3:12 pm** 12:12 pm

5 Wednesday
3rd ♑
♂ enters ♎   **4:32 pm**   1:32 pm

6 Thursday
3rd ♑
♆ ℞   **1:33 pm** 10:33 am
☽ v/c   10:45 pm
☽ enters ♒   11:40 pm

Eastern Standard Time in bold type
          Pacific Standard Time in medium type

7 Friday

3rd ♑
☽ v/c	**1:45 am**	
☽ enters ♒	**2:40 am**	

8 Saturday

3rd ♒
♀ enters ♋	**11:28 am**	8:28 am
4th Quarter	**12:28 pm**	9:28 am
☿ enters ♉	**4:22 pm**	1:22 pm

9 Sunday

4th ♒
☽ v/c	**9:01 am**	6:01 am
☽ enters ♓	**11:16 am**	8:16 am

Mother's Day

April 1999							May 1999							June 1999						
S	M	T	W	T	F	S	S	M	T	W	T	F	S	S	M	T	W	T	F	S
				1	2	3							1			1	2	3	4	5
4	5	6	7	8	9	10	2	3	4	5	6	7	8	6	7	8	9	10	11	12
11	12	13	14	15	16	17	9	10	11	12	13	14	15	13	14	15	16	17	18	19
18	19	20	21	22	23	24	16	17	18	19	20	21	22	20	21	22	23	24	25	26
25	26	27	28	29	30		23	24	25	26	27	28	29	27	28	29	30			
							30	31												

Eastern Standard Time in bold type
Pacific Standard Time in medium type

10 Monday
4th ♓
☽ v/c   **10:51 pm** 7:51 pm

11 Tuesday
4th ♓
☽ enters ♈ **3:54 pm** 12:54 pm

12 Wednesday
4th ♈

13 Thursday
4th ♈
♀ enters ♋ **8:56 am** 5:56 am
☽ enters ♉ **4:57 pm** 1:57 pm
☽ v/c   **12:59 pm** 9:59 am

Eastern Standard Time in bold type
Pacific Standard Time in medium type

14 Friday
4th ♉

15 Saturday
4th ♉

New Moon	**7:06 am**	4:06 am
☽ v/c	**7:06 am**	4:06 am
☽ enters ♊	**4:08 pm**	1:08 pm

16 Sunday
1st ♊

April 1999							May 1999							June 1999					
S	M	T	W	T	F	S	S	M	T	W	T	F	S	S	M	T	W	T	F	S
				1	2	3							1			1	2	3	4	5
4	5	6	7	8	9	10	2	3	4	5	6	7	8	6	7	8	9	10	11	12
11	12	13	14	15	16	17	9	10	11	12	13	14	15	13	14	15	16	17	18	19
18	19	20	21	22	23	24	16	17	18	19	20	21	22	20	21	22	23	24	25	26
25	26	27	28	29	30		23	24	25	26	27	28	29	27	28	29	30			
							30	31												

Eastern Standard Time in bold type
Pacific Standard Time in medium type

Llewellyn's 1999 Pocket Planner and Ephemeris

17 Monday
1st ♊
☽ v/c **10:05 am** 7:05 am
☽ enters ♋ **3:40 pm** 12:40 pm

18 Tuesday
1st ♋

19 Wednesday
1st ♋
☽ v/c **2:52 pm** 11:52 am
☽ enters ♌ **5:38 pm** 2:38 pm

20 Thursday
1st ♌

Eastern Standard Time in bold type
Pacific Standard Time in medium type

21 Friday

1st ♌

☉ enters ♊ **6:52 am** 3:52 am
♅ R **1:43 pm** 10:43 am
☽ v/c **3:15 pm** 12:15 pm
☽ enters ♍ **11:16 pm** 8:16 pm
2nd Quarter 9:35 pm

Sun enters Gemini

22 Saturday

2nd ♍
2nd Quarter **12:35 am**

23 Sunday

2nd ♍
☽ v/c **5:37 am** 2:37 am
☿ enters ♊ **4:22 pm** 1:22 pm

April 1999						
S	M	T	W	T	F	S
				1	2	3
4	5	6	7	8	9	10
11	12	13	14	15	16	17
18	19	20	21	22	23	24
25	26	27	28	29	30	

May 1999						
S	M	T	W	T	F	S
						1
2	3	4	5	6	7	8
9	10	11	12	13	14	15
16	17	18	19	20	21	22
23	24	25	26	27	28	29
30	31					

June 1999						
S	M	T	W	T	F	S
		1	2	3	4	5
6	7	8	9	10	11	12
13	14	15	16	17	18	19
20	21	22	23	24	25	26
27	28	29	30			

Eastern Standard Time in bold type
Pacific Standard Time in medium type

24 Monday
2nd ♍
☽ enters ♎ **8:29 am** 5:29 am

25 Tuesday
2nd ♎

26 Wednesday
2nd ♎
☽ v/c **9:56 am** 6:56 am
☽ enters ♏ **8:05 pm** 5:05 pm

27 Thursday
2nd ♏

Eastern Standard Time in bold type
Pacific Standard Time in medium type

---

28 Friday
2nd ♏
☽ v/c   **4:08 pm**   1:08 pm

---

29 Saturday
2nd ♏
☽ enters ♐   **8:37 am**   5:37 am
♅ enters ♐   **6:54 pm**   3:54 pm
Full Moon   10:40 pm

---

30 Sunday
3rd ♐
Full Moon   **1:40 am**

April 1999						
S	M	T	W	T	F	S
				1	2	3
4	5	6	7	8	9	10
11	12	13	14	15	16	17
18	19	20	21	22	23	24
25	26	27	28	29	30	

May 1999						
S	M	T	W	T	F	S
						1
2	3	4	5	6	7	8
9	10	11	12	13	14	15
16	17	18	19	20	21	22
23	24	25	26	27	28	29
30	31					

June 1999						
S	M	T	W	T	F	S
		1	2	3	4	5
6	7	8	9	10	11	12
13	14	15	16	17	18	19
20	21	22	23	24	25	26
27	28	29	30			

---

31 Monday
3rd ♐
| ☽ v/c | 10:54 am | 7:54 am |
| ☽ enters ♑ | 9:06 pm | 6:06 pm |

Memorial Day

1 Tuesday
3rd ♑

2 Wednesday
3rd ♑

3 Thursday
3rd ♑
☽ v/c	**3:39 am**	12:39 am
☽ enters ≈	**8:37 am**	5:37 am
♂ D		10:12 pm

Eastern Standard Time in bold type
Pacific Standard Time in medium type

4 Friday

3rd ≈
♂ D   **1:12 am**

5 Saturday

3rd ≈
☽ v/c   **1:27 pm** 10:27 am
♀ enters ♌   **4:25 pm** 1:25 pm
☽ enters ♓   **6:01 pm** 3:01 pm

6 Sunday

3rd ♓
☿ enters ♋   **7:18 pm** 4:18 pm
4th Quarter **11:21 pm** 8:21 pm
☽ v/c   **11:21 pm** 8:21 pm

May 1999						
S	M	T	W	T	F	S
						1
2	3	4	5	6	7	8
9	10	11	12	13	14	15
16	17	18	19	20	21	22
23	24	25	26	27	28	29
30	31					

June 1999						
S	M	T	W	T	F	S
		1	2	3	4	5
6	7	8	9	10	11	12
13	14	15	16	17	18	19
20	21	22	23	24	25	26
27	28	29	30			

July 1999						
S	M	T	W	T	F	S
				1	2	3
4	5	6	7	8	9	10
11	12	13	14	15	16	17
18	19	20	21	22	23	24
25	26	27	28	29	30	31

7 Monday
4th ♓
☽ enters ♈   9:09 pm

8 Tuesday
4th ♓
☽ enters ♈ **12:09 am**

9 Wednesday
4th ♈
☽ v/c   **9:28 pm**   6:28 pm
☽ enters ♉   11:44 pm

10 Thursday
4th ♈
☽ enters ♉ **2:44 am**

Eastern Standard Time in bold type
Pacific Standard Time in medium type

11 Friday

4th ♉
☽ v/c   **5:35 am**   2:35 am
☽ enters ♊   11:49 pm

12 Saturday

4th ♉
☽ enters ♊   **2:49 am**

13 Sunday

4th ♊
New Moon   **2:03 pm** 11:03 am
⚹ enters ♐   **7:58 pm**   4:58 pm
☽ v/c   **10:20 pm**   7:20 pm
☽ enters ♋   11:14 pm

May 1999						
S	M	T	W	T	F	S
						1
2	3	4	5	6	7	8
9	10	11	12	13	14	15
16	17	18	19	20	21	22
23	24	25	26	27	28	29
30	31					

June 1999						
S	M	T	W	T	F	S
		1	2	3	4	5
6	7	8	9	10	11	12
13	14	15	16	17	18	19
20	21	22	23	24	25	26
27	28	29	30			

July 1999						
S	M	T	W	T	F	S
				1	2	3
4	5	6	7	8	9	10
11	12	13	14	15	16	17
18	19	20	21	22	23	24
25	26	27	28	29	30	31

14 Monday
1st ♊
☽ enters ♋ **2:14 am**

15 Tuesday
1st ♋
☽ v/c **11:39 pm** 8:39 pm

16 Wednesday
1st ♋
☽ enters ♌ **3:07 am** 12:07 am

17 Thursday
1st ♌

18 Friday

1st ♌
☽ v/c   **4:10 am** 1:10 am
☽ enters ♍ **7:12 am** 4:12 am

19 Saturday

1st ♍

20 Sunday

1st ♍
2nd Quarter **1:13 pm** 10:13 am
☽ v/c   **1:13 pm** 10:13 am
☽ enters ♎ **3:10 pm** 12:10 pm

Father's Day

May 1999						
S	M	T	W	T	F	S
						1
2	3	4	5	6	7	8
9	10	11	12	13	14	15
16	17	18	19	20	21	22
23	24	25	26	27	28	29
30	31					

June 1999						
S	M	T	W	T	F	S
		1	2	3	4	5
6	7	8	9	10	11	12
13	14	15	16	17	18	19
20	21	22	23	24	25	26
27	28	29	30			

July 1999						
S	M	T	W	T	F	S
					1	2	3
4	5	6	7	8	9	10
11	12	13	14	15	16	17
18	19	20	21	22	23	24
25	26	27	28	29	30	31

21 Monday
2nd ♎︎
☉ enters ♋︎ **2:49 pm** 11:49 am
♀ enters ♊︎ **4:44 pm** 1:44 pm

Sun enters Cancer • Summer Solstice • Litha • 2:49 pm EST • 11:49 am PST

22 Tuesday
2nd ♎︎
☽ v/c   9:36 pm
☽ enters ♏︎   11:18 pm

23 Wednesday
2nd ♎︎
☽ v/c   **12:36 am**
☽ enters ♏︎ **2:18 am**
⚷ enters ♍︎ **6:22 am** 3:22 am

24 Thursday
2nd ♏︎

25 Friday
2nd ♏
☽ v/c **12:50 pm** 9:50 am
☽ enters ♐ **2:51 pm** 11:51 am

26 Saturday
2nd ♐
☿ enters ♌ **10:39 am** 7:39 am

27 Sunday
2nd ♐

		May 1999				
S	M	T	W	T	F	S
						1
2	3	4	5	6	7	8
9	10	11	12	13	14	15
16	17	18	19	20	21	22
23	24	25	26	27	28	29
30	31					

		June 1999				
S	M	T	W	T	F	S
		1	2	3	4	5
6	7	8	9	10	11	12
13	14	15	16	17	18	19
20	21	22	23	24	25	26
27	28	29	30			

		July 1999				
S	M	T	W	T	F	S
					1	2	3
4	5	6	7	8	9	10
11	12	13	14	15	16	17
18	19	20	21	22	23	24
25	26	27	28	29	30	31

28 Monday

2nd ✗

☽ v/c	**3:11 am**	12:11 am
☽ enters ♑	**3:12 am**	12:12 am
♃ enters ♉	**4:27 am**	1:27 am
Full Moon	**4:38 pm**	1:38 pm

29 Tuesday

3rd ♑

30 Wednesday

3rd ♑

☽ v/c	**11:37 am**	8:37 am
☽ enters ≈	**2:20 pm**	11:20 am

1 Thursday

3rd ≈

Eastern Standard Time in bold type
Pacific Standard Time in medium type

2 Friday

3rd ≈
☽ v/c   **10:22 pm** 7:22 pm
☽ enters ♓ **11:35 pm** 8:35 pm

3 Saturday

3rd ♓
☽ v/c   11:26 pm

4 Sunday

3rd ♓
☽ v/c   **2:26 am**
♂ enters ♏ **11:00 pm** 8:00 pm

Independence Day

June 1999						
S	M	T	W	T	F	S
		1	2	3	4	5
6	7	8	9	10	11	12
13	14	15	16	17	18	19
20	21	22	23	24	25	26
27	28	29	30			

July 1999						
S	M	T	W	T	F	S
				1	2	3
4	5	6	7	8	9	10
11	12	13	14	15	16	17
18	19	20	21	22	23	24
25	26	27	28	29	30	31

August 1999						
S	M	T	W	T	F	S
1	2	3	4	5	6	7
8	9	10	11	12	13	14
15	16	17	18	19	20	21
22	23	24	25	26	27	28
29	30	31				

5 Monday

3rd ♓
☽ enters ♈ **6:22 am** 3:22 am

6 Tuesday

3rd ♈
4th Quarter **6:57 am** 3:57 am

7 Wednesday

4th ♈
☽ v/c **5:07 am** 2:07 am
☽ enters ♉ **10:22 am** 7:22 am

8 Thursday

4th ♉

Eastern Standard Time in bold type
Pacific Standard Time in medium type

9 Friday

4th ♉
| ☽ v/c | **9:09 am** | 6:09 am |
| ☽ enters ♊ | **11:59 am** | 8:59 am |

10 Saturday

4th ♊

11 Sunday

4th ♊
| ☽ v/c | **11:37 am** | 8:37 am |
| ☽ enters ♋ | **12:27 pm** | 9:27 am |

June 1999								July 1999								August 1999					
S	M	T	W	T	F	S		S	M	T	W	T	F	S		S	M	T	W	T	F	S
		1	2	3	4	5						1	2	3		1	2	3	4	5	6	7
6	7	8	9	10	11	12		4	5	6	7	8	9	10		8	9	10	11	12	13	14
13	14	15	16	17	18	19		11	12	13	14	15	16	17		15	16	17	18	19	20	21
20	21	22	23	24	25	26		18	19	20	21	22	23	24		22	23	24	25	26	27	28
27	28	29	30					25	26	27	28	29	30	31		29	30	31				

Eastern Standard Time in bold type
Pacific Standard Time in medium type

12 Monday
4th ♋
♀ enters ♍	**10:18 am**	7:18 am
☿ R	**6:26 pm**	3:26 pm
New Moon	**9:24 pm**	6:24 pm
☽ v/c	**9:24 pm**	6:24 pm

13 Tuesday
1st ♋
☽ enters ♌	**1:25 pm**	10:25 am

14 Wednesday
1st ♌
☽ v/c	**3:54 pm**	12:54 pm

15 Thursday
1st ♌
☽ enters ♍	**4:39 pm**	1:39 pm

Eastern Standard Time in bold type
Pacific Standard Time in medium type

16 Friday
1st ♍

17 Saturday
1st ♍
☽ v/c **1:28 pm** 10:28 am
☽ enters ♎ **11:19 pm** 8:19 pm

18 Sunday
1st ♎

June 1999						
S	M	T	W	T	F	S
		1	2	3	4	5
6	7	8	9	10	11	12
13	14	15	16	17	18	19
20	21	22	23	24	25	26
27	28	29	30			

July 1999						
S	M	T	W	T	F	S
				1	2	3
4	5	6	7	8	9	10
11	12	13	14	15	16	17
18	19	20	21	22	23	24
25	26	27	28	29	30	31

August 1999						
S	M	T	W	T	F	S
1	2	3	4	5	6	7
8	9	10	11	12	13	14
15	16	17	18	19	20	21
22	23	24	25	26	27	28
29	30	31				

19 Monday
1st ♎

20 Tuesday
1st ♎
2nd Quarter **4:01 am** 1:01 am
☽ v/c **4:01 am** 1:01 am
☽ enters ♏ **9:30 am** 6:30 am

21 Wednesday
2nd ♏
♀ enters ♌ 9:40 pm
☿ D 9:48 pm

22 Thursday
2nd ♏
♀ enters ♌ **12:40 am**
☿ D **12:48 am**
☽ v/c **9:28 pm** 6:28 pm
☽ enters ♐ **9:49 pm** 6:49 pm
☉ enters ♌ 10:44 pm

Sun enters Leo (PST)

Eastern Standard Time in bold type
Pacific Standard Time in medium type

23 Friday
2nd ♐
☉ enters ♌ **1:44 am**

Sun enters Leo (EST)

---

24 Saturday
2nd ♐
☽ v/c   **4:52 am** 1:52 am

---

25 Sunday
2nd ♐
☽ enters ♑ **10:09 am** 7:09 am

June 1999						
S	M	T	W	T	F	S
		1	2	3	4	5
6	7	8	9	10	11	12
13	14	15	16	17	18	19
20	21	22	23	24	25	26
27	28	29	30			

July 1999						
S	M	T	W	T	F	S
					1	2	3
4	5	6	7	8	9	10
11	12	13	14	15	16	17
18	19	20	21	22	23	24
25	26	27	28	29	30	31

August 1999						
S	M	T	W	T	F	S
1	2	3	4	5	6	7
8	9	10	11	12	13	14
15	16	17	18	19	20	21
22	23	24	25	26	27	28
29	30	31				

Eastern Standard Time in bold type
Pacific Standard Time in medium type

26 Monday

2nd ♑
☽ v/c   **6:06 pm** 3:06 pm

27 Tuesday

2nd ♑
☽ enters ♒   **8:55 pm** 5:55 pm

28 Wednesday

2nd ♒
Full Moon   **6:25 am** 3:25 am
☿ D   **2:30 pm** 11:30 am

Lunar Eclipse 4° ♒ 58'

29 Thursday

3rd ♒
☽ v/c   **3:56 am** 12:56 am
♀ R⬩   **8:41 pm** 5:41 pm

Eastern Standard Time in bold type
Pacific Standard Time in medium type

30 Friday
3rd ≈
☽ enters ♓ **5:28 am** 2:28 am

31 Saturday
3rd ♓
☿ enters ♋ **1:44 pm** 10:44 am

1 Sunday
3rd ♓
☽ v/c **11:03 am** 8:03 am
☽ enters ♈ **11:47 am** 8:47 am

Lammas

July 1999						
S	M	T	W	T	F	S
					1	2	3
4	5	6	7	8	9	10
11	12	13	14	15	16	17
18	19	20	21	22	23	24
25	26	27	28	29	30	31

August 1999						
S	M	T	W	T	F	S
1	2	3	4	5	6	7
8	9	10	11	12	13	14
15	16	17	18	19	20	21
22	23	24	25	26	27	28
29	30	31				

September 1999						
S	M	T	W	T	F	S
				1	2	3	4
5	6	7	8	9	10	11
12	13	14	15	16	17	18
19	20	21	22	23	24	25
26	27	28	29	30		

2 Monday
3rd ♈

3 Tuesday
3rd ♈
☽ v/c   **2:12 pm** 11:12 am
☽ enters ♉   **4:08 pm** 1:08 pm

4 Wednesday
3rd ♉
4th Quarter **12:26 pm** 9:26 am

5 Thursday
4th ♉
☽ v/c   **4:35 pm** 1:35 pm
☽ enters ♊   **6:57 pm** 3:57 pm
☿ D   **10:20 pm** 7:20 pm

Eastern Standard Time in bold type
Pacific Standard Time in medium type

6 Friday
4th ♊
☽ v/c   **7:43 pm** 4:43 pm

7 Saturday
4th ♊
☽ enters ♋ **8:52 pm** 5:52 pm

8 Sunday
4th ♋

July 1999						
S	M	T	W	T	F	S
				1	2	3
4	5	6	7	8	9	10
11	12	13	14	15	16	17
18	19	20	21	22	23	24
25	26	27	28	29	30	31

August 1999						
S	M	T	W	T	F	S
1	2	3	4	5	6	7
8	9	10	11	12	13	14
15	16	17	18	19	20	21
22	23	24	25	26	27	28
29	30	31				

September 1999						
S	M	T	W	T	F	S
			1	2	3	4
5	6	7	8	9	10	11
12	13	14	15	16	17	18
19	20	21	22	23	24	25
26	27	28	29	30		

9 Monday

4th ♋
| ☽ v/c | **10:01 pm** | 7:01 pm |
| ☽ enters ♌ | **10:55 pm** | 7:55 pm |

10 Tuesday

4th ♌
| ☿ enters ♌ | **11:25 pm** | 8:25 pm |

11 Wednesday

4th ♌
New Moon	**6:09 am**	3:09 am
☽ v/c	**6:09 am**	3:09 am
☽ enters ♍	**11:22 pm**	

Solar Eclipse 18° ♌ 21'

12 Thursday

1st ♌
| ☽ enters ♍ | 2:22 am | |

13 Friday
1st ♍
☽ v/c   **10:31 am**   7:31 am

14 Saturday
1st ♍
☽ enters ♎   **8:25 am**   5:25 am

15 Sunday
1st ♎
♀ enters ♌   **9:11 am**   6:11 am

July 1999						
S	M	T	W	T	F	S
					1	2	3
4	5	6	7	8	9	10
11	12	13	14	15	16	17
18	19	20	21	22	23	24
25	26	27	28	29	30	31

August 1999						
S	M	T	W	T	F	S
1	2	3	4	5	6	7
8	9	10	11	12	13	14
15	16	17	18	19	20	21
22	23	24	25	26	27	28
29	30	31				

September 1999						
S	M	T	W	T	F	S
			1	2	3	4
5	6	7	8	9	10	11
12	13	14	15	16	17	18
19	20	21	22	23	24	25
26	27	28	29	30		

16 Monday
1st ♎︎
☽ v/c **4:12 pm** 1:12 pm
☽ enters ♏︎ **5:41 pm** 2:41 pm

17 Tuesday
1st ♏︎

18 Wednesday
1st ♏︎
♀ enters ♋︎ **1:22 pm** 10:22 am
♇ D **5:59 pm** 2:59 pm
2nd Quarter **8:48 pm** 5:48 pm
☽ v/c 10:07 pm

19 Thursday
2nd ♏︎
☽ v/c **1:07 am**
☽ enters ♐︎ **5:32 am** 2:32 am

Eastern Standard Time in bold type
Pacific Standard Time in medium type

20 Friday
2nd ♐

21 Saturday
2nd ♐
☽ v/c   **2:36 pm** 11:36 am
☽ enters ♑   **5:59 pm** 2:59 pm

22 Sunday
2nd ♑

July 1999						
S	M	T	W	T	F	S
				1	2	3
4	5	6	7	8	9	10
11	12	13	14	15	16	17
18	19	20	21	22	23	24
25	26	27	28	29	30	31

August 1999						
S	M	T	W	T	F	S
1	2	3	4	5	6	7
8	9	10	11	12	13	14
15	16	17	18	19	20	21
22	23	24	25	26	27	28
29	30	31				

September 1999						
S	M	T	W	T	F	S
			1	2	3	4
5	6	7	8	9	10	11
12	13	14	15	16	17	18
19	20	21	22	23	24	25
26	27	28	29	30		

23 Monday
2nd ♑
| ☉ enters ♍ | **8:51 am** | 5:51 am |
| ☽ v/c | **5:13 pm** | 2:13 pm |

Sun enters Virgo

24 Tuesday
2nd ♒
| ☽ enters ♒ | **4:49 am** | 1:49 am |
| ♃ Rℵ | **8:46 pm** | 5:46 pm |

25 Wednesday
2nd ♒

26 Thursday
2nd ♒
☽ v/c	**4:31 am**	1:31 am
☽ enters ♓	**12:49 pm**	9:49 am
Full Moon	**6:48 pm**	3:48 pm

27 Friday
3rd ♓
♆ enters ♎ **7:14 pm** 4:14 pm

28 Saturday
3rd ♓
☽ v/c 12:41 pm 9:41 am
☽ enters ♈ **6:09 pm** 3:09 pm

29 Sunday
3rd ♈
♄ ℞ **7:09 pm** 4:09 pm

July 1999						
S	M	T	W	T	F	S
					1	2	3
4	5	6	7	8	9	10
11	12	13	14	15	16	17
18	19	20	21	22	23	24
25	26	27	28	29	30	31

August 1999						
S	M	T	W	T	F	S
1	2	3	4	5	6	7
8	9	10	11	12	13	14
15	16	17	18	19	20	21
22	23	24	25	26	27	28
29	30	31				

September 1999						
S	M	T	W	T	F	S
			1	2	3	4
5	6	7	8	9	10	11
12	13	14	15	16	17	18
19	20	21	22	23	24	25
26	27	28	29	30		

30 Monday

3rd ♈

♅ enters ♐	**4:15 am**	1:15 am
☽ v/c	**7:39 pm**	4:39 pm
☽ enters ♉	**9:40 pm**	6:40 pm

31 Tuesday

3rd ♉

☿ enters ♍	**10:15 am**	7:15 am

1 Wednesday

3rd ♉

☽ v/c	**11:46 pm**	8:46 pm
☽ enters ♊		9:25 pm

2 Thursday

3rd ♉

☽ enters ♊	**12:25 am**	
♂ enters ♐	**2:29 pm**	11:29 am
4th Quarter	**5:18 pm**	2:18 pm

Eastern Standard Time in bold type
Pacific Standard Time in medium type

3 Friday
4th ♊
☽ v/c   **9:59 am**   6:59 am

4 Saturday
4th ♊
☽ enters ♋   **3:10 am** 12:10 am

5 Sunday
4th ♋
☽ v/c   **8:23 am**   5:23 am

August 1999						
S	M	T	W	T	F	S
1	2	3	4	5	6	7
8	9	10	11	12	13	14
15	16	17	18	19	20	21
22	23	24	25	26	27	28
29	30	31				

September 1999						
S	M	T	W	T	F	S
			1	2	3	4
5	6	7	8	9	10	11
12	13	14	15	16	17	18
19	20	21	22	23	24	25
26	27	28	29	30		

October 1999						
S	M	T	W	T	F	S
					1	2
3	4	5	6	7	8	9
10	11	12	13	14	15	16
17	18	19	20	21	22	23
24	25	26	27	28	29	30
31						

6 Monday
4th ⊚
☽ enters ♌ **6:29 am** 3:29 am

Labor Day

7 Tuesday
4th ♌
☽ v/c **3:31 pm** 12:31 pm

8 Wednesday
4th ♌
☽ enters ♍ **10:57 am** 7:57 am

9 Thursday
4th ♍
New Moon **5:03 pm** 2:03 pm
☽ v/c **7:34 pm** 4:34 pm

Eastern Standard Time in bold type
Pacific Standard Time in medium type

10 Friday
1st ♍
☽ enters ♎ **5:16 pm** 2:16 pm
♀ D **7:25 pm** 4:25 pm

Rosh Hashanah begins

11 Saturday
1st ♎

12 Sunday
1st ♎
☽ v/c **4:38 am** 1:38 am
☽ enters ♏ 11:09 pm

Rosh Hashanah ends

August 1999						
S	M	T	W	T	F	S
1	2	3	4	5	6	7
8	9	10	11	12	13	14
15	16	17	18	19	20	21
22	23	24	25	26	27	28
29	30	31				

September 1999						
S	M	T	W	T	F	S
			1	2	3	4
5	6	7	8	9	10	11
12	13	14	15	16	17	18
19	20	21	22	23	24	25
26	27	28	29	30		

October 1999						
S	M	T	W	T	F	S
					1	2
3	4	5	6	7	8	9
10	11	12	13	14	15	16
17	18	19	20	21	22	23
24	25	26	27	28	29	30
31						

13 Monday
1st ♎
☽ enters ♏ **2:09 am**

14 Tuesday
1st ♏

15 Wednesday
1st ♏
☽ v/c **10:24 am** 7:24 am
☽ enters ♐ **1:35 pm** 10:35 am

16 Thursday
1st ♐
☿ enters ♎ **7:53 am** 4:53 am

Eastern Standard Time in bold type
Pacific Standard Time in medium type

17 Friday
1st ♐
☽ v/c   **3:06 pm** 12:06 pm
2nd Quarter **3:06 pm** 12:06 pm
☽ enters ♑   11:13 pm

18 Saturday
2nd ♐
☽ enters ♑ **2:13 am**

19 Sunday
2nd ♑

Yom Kippur begins

August 1999						
S	M	T	W	T	F	S
1	2	3	4	5	6	7
8	9	10	11	12	13	14
15	16	17	18	19	20	21
22	23	24	25	26	27	28
29	30	31				

September 1999						
S	M	T	W	T	F	S
			1	2	3	4
5	6	7	8	9	10	11
12	13	14	15	16	17	18
19	20	21	22	23	24	25
26	27	28	29	30		

October 1999						
S	M	T	W	T	F	S
					1	2
3	4	5	6	7	8	9
10	11	12	13	14	15	16
17	18	19	20	21	22	23
24	25	26	27	28	29	30
31						

Eastern Standard Time in bold type
Pacific Standard Time in medium type

20 Monday

2nd ♑

| ☽ v/c | **8:04 am** | 5:04 am |
| ☽ enters ♒ | **1:38 pm** | 10:38 am |

Yom Kippur ends

21 Tuesday

2nd ♒

22 Wednesday

2nd ♒

| ☽ v/c | **5:38 am** | 2:38 am |
| ☽ enters ♓ | **9:51 pm** | 6:51 pm |

23 Thursday

2nd ♓

| ☉ enters ♎ | **6:31 am** | 3:31 am |
| ☿ enters ♐ | **7:15 am** | 4:15 am |

Sun enters Libra • Fall Equinox • Mabon • 6:31 am EST • 3:31 am PST

Eastern Standard Time in bold type
Pacific Standard Time in medium type

24 Friday

2nd ♓
☽ v/c   **3:27 am** 12:27 am
☽ enters ♈   11:34 pm

Sukkot begins

25 Saturday

2nd ♓
☽ enters ♈ **2:34 am**
Full Moon   **5:51 am** 2:51 am

26 Sunday

3rd ♈
☽ v/c   **5:34 pm** 2:34 pm

August 1999						
S	M	T	W	T	F	S
1	2	3	4	5	6	7
8	9	10	11	12	13	14
15	16	17	18	19	20	21
22	23	24	25	26	27	28
29	30	31				

September 1999						
S	M	T	W	T	F	S
			1	2	3	4
5	6	7	8	9	10	11
12	13	14	15	16	17	18
19	20	21	22	23	24	25
26	27	28	29	30		

October 1999						
S	M	T	W	T	F	S
					1	2
3	4	5	6	7	8	9
10	11	12	13	14	15	16
17	18	19	20	21	22	23
24	25	26	27	28	29	30
31						

Eastern Standard Time in bold type
Pacific Standard Time in medium type

27 Monday
3rd ♈
☽ enters ♉ **4:51 am** 1:51 am
♀ enters ♍ **11:20 am** 8:20 am

28 Tuesday
3rd ♉
☽ v/c **9:01 pm** 6:01 pm

29 Wednesday
3rd ♉
☽ enters ♊ **6:21 am** 3:21 am

30 Thursday
3rd ♊
☽ v/c 10:09 pm

Eastern Standard Time in bold type
Pacific Standard Time in medium type

1 Friday
3rd ♊
☽ v/c **1:09 am**
☽ enters ♋ **8:32 am** 5:32 am
4th Quarter **11:03 pm** 8:03 pm

2 Saturday
4th ♋

Sukkot ends

3 Sunday
4th ♋
☽ v/c **7:53 am** 4:53 am
☽ enters ♌ **12:14 pm** 9:14 am

September 1999						
S	M	T	W	T	F	S
			1	2	3	4
5	6	7	8	9	10	11
12	13	14	15	16	17	18
19	20	21	22	23	24	25
26	27	28	29	30		

October 1999						
S	M	T	W	T	F	S
					1	2
3	4	5	6	7	8	9
10	11	12	13	14	15	16
17	18	19	20	21	22	23
24	25	26	27	28	29	30
31						

November 1999						
S	M	T	W	T	F	S
	1	2	3	4	5	6
7	8	9	10	11	12	13
14	15	16	17	18	19	20
21	22	23	24	25	26	27
28	29	30				

4 Monday
4th ♌
☿ enters ♏︎   9:12 pm

5 Tuesday
4th ♌
☿ enters ♏︎   **12:12 am**
☽ v/c   **3:15 pm** 12:15 pm
☽ enters ♍   **5:40 pm** 2:40 pm

6 Wednesday
4th ♍

7 Thursday
4th ♍
♀ enters ♍ **11:51 am** 8:51 am
☽ v/c   **12:27 pm** 9:27 am
☽ enters ♎   9:52 pm

Eastern Standard Time in bold type
Pacific Standard Time in medium type

8 Friday
4th ♍
☽ enters ♎ **12:52 am**

9 Saturday
4th ♎
New Moon **6:34 am** 3:34 am
☽ v/c 9:33 pm

10 Sunday
1st ♎
☽ v/c **12:33 am**
☽ enters ♏ **10:01 am** 7:01 am

September 1999						
S	M	T	W	T	F	S
			1	2	3	4
5	6	7	8	9	10	11
12	13	14	15	16	17	18
19	20	21	22	23	24	25
26	27	28	29	30		

October 1999						
S	M	T	W	T	F	S
					1	2
3	4	5	6	7	8	9
10	11	12	13	14	15	16
17	18	19	20	21	22	23
24	25	26	27	28	29	30
31						

November 1999						
S	M	T	W	T	F	S
	1	2	3	4	5	6
7	8	9	10	11	12	13
14	15	16	17	18	19	20
21	22	23	24	25	26	27
28	29	30				

Eastern Standard Time in bold type
Pacific Standard Time in medium type

11 Monday
1st ♏
☽ v/c   **4:42 pm** 1:42 pm

Columbus Day

12 Tuesday
1st ♏
☽ enters ♐   **9:18 pm** 6:18 pm

13 Wednesday
1st ♐
♆ D   **5:01 pm** 2:01 pm

14 Thursday
1st ♐

    Eastern Standard Time in bold type
Pacific Standard Time in medium type

15 Friday
1st ♐
☽ v/c   **7:49 am** 4:49 am
☽ enters ♑ **10:03 am** 7:03 am

16 Saturday
1st ♑
♂ enters ♑ **8:35 pm** 5:35 pm

17 Sunday
1st ♑
2nd Quarter **9:59 am** 6:59 am
☽ v/c   **9:59 am** 6:59 am
♀ enters ♌ **1:56 pm** 10:56 am
☽ enters ≈ **10:17 pm** 7:17 pm

September 1999						
S	M	T	W	T	F	S
			1	2	3	4
5	6	7	8	9	10	11
12	13	14	15	16	17	18
19	20	21	22	23	24	25
26	27	28	29	30		

October 1999						
S	M	T	W	T	F	S
					1	2
3	4	5	6	7	8	9
10	11	12	13	14	15	16
17	18	19	20	21	22	23
24	25	26	27	28	29	30
31						

November 1999						
S	M	T	W	T	F	S
	1	2	3	4	5	6
7	8	9	10	11	12	13
14	15	16	17	18	19	20
21	22	23	24	25	26	27
28	29	30				

18 Monday
2nd ≈

19 Tuesday
2nd ≈
☽ v/c   9:53 pm

20 Wednesday
2nd ≈
☽ v/c   **12:53 am**
☽ enters ♓   **7:33 am**   4:33 am

21 Thursday
2nd ♓
☽ v/c   **11:25 pm**   8:25 pm

22 Friday

2nd ♓︎
☽ enters ♈︎ **12:42 pm** 9:42 am
♅ D **10:34 pm** 7:34 pm
♃ enters ♈︎ 9:49 pm

23 Saturday

2nd ♈︎
♃ enters ♈︎ **12:49 am**
☉ enters ♏︎ **3:52 pm** 12:52 pm

Sun enters Scorpio

24 Sunday

2nd ♈︎
☽ v/c **2:05 pm** 11:05 am
☽ enters ♉︎ **2:26 pm** 11:26 am
Full Moon **4:03 pm** 1:03 pm

September 1999						
S	M	T	W	T	F	S
			1	2	3	4
5	6	7	8	9	10	11
12	13	14	15	16	17	18
19	20	21	22	23	24	25
26	27	28	29	30		

October 1999						
S	M	T	W	T	F	S
					1	2
3	4	5	6	7	8	9
10	11	12	13	14	15	16
17	18	19	20	21	22	23
24	25	26	27	28	29	30
31						

November 1999						
S	M	T	W	T	F	S
	1	2	3	4	5	6
7	8	9	10	11	12	13
14	15	16	17	18	19	20
21	22	23	24	25	26	27
28	29	30				

Eastern Standard Time in bold type
Pacific Standard Time in medium type

25 Monday
3rd ♉
⚳ enters ♏ **5:07 am** 2:07 am

26 Tuesday
3rd ♉
☽ v/c   **9:22 am** 6:22 am
☽ enters ♊ **2:34 pm** 11:34 am

27 Wednesday
3rd ♊

28 Thursday
3rd ♊
☽ v/c   **1:55 pm** 10:55 am
☽ enters ♋ **3:09 pm** 12:09 pm

     Eastern Standard Time in bold type
Pacific Standard Time in medium type

29 Friday
3rd ♋

30 Saturday
3rd ♋
☿ enters ♐	**3:08 pm**	12:08 pm
☽ v/c	**4:00 pm**	1:00 pm
☽ enters ♌	**5:47 pm**	2:47 pm

31 Sunday
3rd ♌
| 4th Quarter | **7:04 am** | 4:04 am |

Samhain • Halloween • Daylight Saving Time ends at 2 AM

September 1999	October 1999	November 1999
S M T W T F S	S M T W T F S	S M T W T F S
1 2 3 4	1 2	1 2 3 4 5 6
5 6 7 8 9 10 11	3 4 5 6 7 8 9	7 8 9 10 11 12 13
12 13 14 15 16 17 18	10 11 12 13 14 15 16	14 15 16 17 18 19 20
19 20 21 22 23 24 25	17 18 19 20 21 22 23	21 22 23 24 25 26 27
26 27 28 29 30	24 25 26 27 28 29 30	28 29 30
	31	

1 Monday

4th ♌
☽ v/c	**8:43 pm**	5:43 pm
☽ enters ♍	**11:07 pm**	8:07 pm

2 Tuesday

4th ♍

General Election Day

3 Wednesday

4th ♍
☽ v/c	**9:03 pm**	6:03 pm

4 Thursday

4th ♍
☽ enters ♎	**6:56 am**	3:56 am
☿ R	**9:51 pm**	6:51 pm

Eastern Standard Time in bold type
Pacific Standard Time in medium type

5 Friday
4th ♎

6 Saturday
4th ♎
☽ v/c   **1:01 pm** 10:01 am
☽ enters ♏,   **4:45 pm** 1:45 pm

7 Sunday
4th ♏,
☽ v/c   9:57 pm
New Moon **10:53 pm** 7:53 pm

October 1999						
S	M	T	W	T	F	S
					1	2
3	4	5	6	7	8	9
10	11	12	13	14	15	16
17	18	19	20	21	22	23
24	25	26	27	28	29	30
31						

November 1999						
S	M	T	W	T	F	S
	1	2	3	4	5	6
7	8	9	10	11	12	13
14	15	16	17	18	19	20
21	22	23	24	25	26	27
28	29	30				

December 1999						
S	M	T	W	T	F	S
			1	2	3	4
5	6	7	8	9	10	11
12	13	14	15	16	17	18
19	20	21	22	23	24	25
26	27	28	29	30	31	

8 Monday

1st ♏
☽ v/c   **12:57 am**
♀ enters ♎   **9:19 pm** 6:19 pm

9 Tuesday

1st ♏
☽ enters ♐   **4:15 am** 1:15 am
☿ enters ♏   **3:12 pm** 12:12 pm

10 Wednesday

1st ♐

11 Thursday

1st ♐
☽ v/c   **11:53 am** 8:53 am
☽ enters ♑   **5:00 pm** 2:00 pm

Veterans' Day

Eastern Standard Time in bold type
Pacific Standard Time in medium type

12 Friday
1st ♑

13 Saturday
1st ♑
☽ v/c   9:08 pm

14 Sunday
1st ♑
☽ v/c   **12:08 am**
☽ enters ♒   **5:46 am**   2:46 am

October 1999						
S	M	T	W	T	F	S
					1	2
3	4	5	6	7	8	9
10	11	12	13	14	15	16
17	18	19	20	21	22	23
24	25	26	27	28	29	30
31						

November 1999						
S	M	T	W	T	F	S
	1	2	3	4	5	6
7	8	9	10	11	12	13
14	15	16	17	18	19	20
21	22	23	24	25	26	27
28	29	30				

December 1999						
S	M	T	W	T	F	S
			1	2	3	4
5	6	7	8	9	10	11
12	13	14	15	16	17	18
19	20	21	22	23	24	25
26	27	28	29	30	31	

Eastern Standard Time in bold type
Pacific Standard Time in medium type

15 Monday
1st ≈

16 Tuesday
1st ≈
☽ v/c **10:31 am** 7:31 am
2nd Quarter **4:04 am** 1:04 am
☽ enters ♓ **4:21 pm** 1:21 pm

17 Wednesday
2nd ♓

18 Thursday
2nd ♓
☽ v/c **4:04 pm** 1:04 pm
☽ enters ♈ **10:58 pm** 7:58 pm

Eastern Standard Time in bold type
Pacific Standard Time in medium type

19 Friday
2nd ♈

20 Saturday
2nd ♈
☽ v/c   **7:42 pm** 4:42 pm
☽ enters ♉   10:26 pm

21 Sunday
2nd ♈
☽ enters ♉   **1:26 am**

October 1999						
S	M	T	W	T	F	S
					1	2
3	4	5	6	7	8	9
10	11	12	13	14	15	16
17	18	19	20	21	22	23
24	25	26	27	28	29	30
31						

November 1999						
S	M	T	W	T	F	S
	1	2	3	4	5	6
7	8	9	10	11	12	13
14	15	16	17	18	19	20
21	22	23	24	25	26	27
28	29	30				

December 1999						
S	M	T	W	T	F	S
			1	2	3	4
5	6	7	8	9	10	11
12	13	14	15	16	17	18
19	20	21	22	23	24	25
26	27	28	29	30	31	

22 Monday

2nd ♉
☉ enters ♐ **1:25 pm** 10:25 am
☽ v/c **9:24 pm** 6:24 pm
☽ enters ♊ 10:14 pm
Full Moon 11:04 pm

Sun enters Sagittarius

23 Tuesday

2nd ♉
☽ enters ♊ **1:14 am**
Full Moon **2:04 am**

24 Wednesday

3rd ♊
☽ v/c **6:21 pm** 3:21 pm
☿ D **10:53 pm** 7:53 pm
☽ enters ♋ 9:29 pm

25 Thursday

3rd ♊
☽ enters ♋ **12:29 am**
♂ enters ≈ 10:56 pm

Thanksgiving Day

Eastern Standard Time in bold type
Pacific Standard Time in medium type

26 Friday
3rd ♋
♂ enters ♒ **1:56 am**
☽ v/c **6:35 pm** 3:35 pm
☽ enters ♌ 10:18 pm

27 Saturday
3rd ♋
☽ enters ♌ **1:18 am**

28 Sunday
3rd ♌
☽ v/c **9:43 pm** 6:43 pm

October 1999						
S	M	T	W	T	F	S
					1	2
3	4	5	6	7	8	9
10	11	12	13	14	15	16
17	18	19	20	21	22	23
24	25	26	27	28	29	30
31						

November 1999						
S	M	T	W	T	F	S
	1	2	3	4	5	6
7	8	9	10	11	12	13
14	15	16	17	18	19	20
21	22	23	24	25	26	27
28	29	30				

December 1999						
S	M	T	W	T	F	S
			1	2	3	4
5	6	7	8	9	10	11
12	13	14	15	16	17	18
19	20	21	22	23	24	25
26	27	28	29	30	31	

Eastern Standard Time in bold type
Pacific Standard Time in medium type

29 Monday
3rd ♌
☽ enters ♍ **5:11 am** 2:11 am
4th Quarter **6:19 pm** 3:19 pm

30 Tuesday
4th ♍
☽ v/c **2:11 pm** 11:11 am

1 Wednesday
4th ♍
☽ enters ♎ **12:29 pm** 9:29 am

2 Thursday
4th ♎

Eastern Standard Time in bold type
Pacific Standard Time in medium type

3 Friday
4th ♎
| ☽ v/c | **6:04 pm** | 3:04 pm |
| ☽ enters ♏ | **10:36 pm** | 7:36 pm |

4 Saturday
4th ♏

Chanukkah begins

5 Sunday
4th ♏
| ♀ enters ♏ | **5:41 pm** | 2:41 pm |
| ☽ v/c | **9:30 pm** | 6:30 pm |

November 1999						
S	M	T	W	T	F	S
	1	2	3	4	5	6
7	8	9	10	11	12	13
14	15	16	17	18	19	20
21	22	23	24	25	26	27
28	29	30				

December 1999						
S	M	T	W	T	F	S
			1	2	3	4
5	6	7	8	9	10	11
12	13	14	15	16	17	18
19	20	21	22	23	24	25
26	27	28	29	30	31	

January 2000						
S	M	T	W	T	F	S
						1
2	3	4	5	6	7	8
9	10	11	12	13	14	15
16	17	18	19	20	21	22
23	24	25	26	27	28	29
30	31					

6 Monday
4th ♏
☽ enters ♐ **10:28 am** 7:28 am

7 Tuesday
4th ♐
New Moon **5:32 pm** 2:32 pm

8 Wednesday
1st ♐
☽ v/c **1:36 pm** 10:36 am
☽ enters ♑ **11:14 pm** 8:14 pm

9 Thursday
1st ♑

Eastern Standard Time in bold type
Pacific Standard Time in medium type

10 Friday
1st ♑
✳ enters ♑ **2:09 pm** 11:09 am
☿ enters ♐ **9:09 pm** 6:09 pm
☽ v/c   11:14 pm

11 Saturday
1st ♑
☽ v/c   **2:14 am**
☽ enters ♒ **11:59 am** 8:59 am

Chanukkah ends

12 Sunday
1st ♒

November 1999						
S	M	T	W	T	F	S
	1	2	3	4	5	6
7	8	9	10	11	12	13
14	15	16	17	18	19	20
21	22	23	24	25	26	27
28	29	30				

December 1999						
S	M	T	W	T	F	S
			1	2	3	4
5	6	7	8	9	10	11
12	13	14	15	16	17	18
19	20	21	22	23	24	25
26	27	28	29	30	31	

January 2000						
S	M	T	W	T	F	S
						1
2	3	4	5	6	7	8
9	10	11	12	13	14	15
16	17	18	19	20	21	22
23	24	25	26	27	28	29
30	31					

13 Monday
1st ≈
☽ v/c **1:46 pm** 10:46 am
☽ enters ♓ **11:18 pm** 8:18 pm

14 Tuesday
1st ♓
♀ enters ♎ 9:16 pm

15 Wednesday
1st ♓
♀ enters ♎ **12:16 am**
☿ Rℵ **5:56 pm** 2:56 pm
2nd Quarter **7:50 pm** 4:50 pm
☽ v/c **7:50 pm** 4:50 pm

16 Thursday
2nd ♓
☽ enters ♈ **7:30 am** 4:30 am

Eastern Standard Time in bold type
Pacific Standard Time in medium type

17 Friday
2nd ♈

18 Saturday
2nd ♈
☽ v/c **5:03 am** 2:03 am
☽ enters ♉ **11:45 am** 8:45 am

19 Sunday
2nd ♉
☽ v/c **5:46 pm** 2:46 pm

November 1999						
S	M	T	W	T	F	S
	1	2	3	4	5	6
7	8	9	10	11	12	13
14	15	16	17	18	19	20
21	22	23	24	25	26	27
28	29	30				

December 1999						
S	M	T	W	T	F	S
			1	2	3	4
5	6	7	8	9	10	11
12	13	14	15	16	17	18
19	20	21	22	23	24	25
26	27	28	29	30	31	

January 2000						
S	M	T	W	T	F	S
						1
2	3	4	5	6	7	8
9	10	11	12	13	14	15
16	17	18	19	20	21	22
23	24	25	26	27	28	29
30	31					

Eastern Standard Time in bold type
Pacific Standard Time in medium type

20 Monday

2nd ♉
♃ D   **10:23 am**   7:23 am
☽ enters ♊ **12:39 pm**   9:39 am
♦ enters ♐   **8:55 pm**   5:55 pm

21 Tuesday

2nd ♊
☉ enters ♑   11:44 pm

Sun enters Capricorn (PST) • Winter Solstice • Yule • 11:44 pm PST

22 Wednesday

2nd ♊
☉ enters ♑   **2:44 am**
☽ v/c   **4:03 am**   1:03 am
☽ enters ♋ **11:52 am**   8:52 am
Full Moon   **12:31 pm**   9:31 am

Sun enters Capricorn (EST) • Winter Solstice • Yule • 2:44 am EST

23 Thursday

3rd ♋

Eastern Standard Time in bold type
Pacific Standard Time in medium type

24 Friday
3rd ♋
☽ v/c **3:31 am** 12:31 am
☽ enters ♌ **11:32 am** 8:32 am

Christmas Eve

25 Saturday
3rd ♌

Christmas Day

26 Sunday
3rd ♌
☽ v/c **5:07 am** 2:07 am
☽ enters ♍ **1:34 pm** 10:34 am

Kwanzaa begins

November 1999						
S	M	T	W	T	F	S
	1	2	3	4	5	6
7	8	9	10	11	12	13
14	15	16	17	18	19	20
21	22	23	24	25	26	27
28	29	30				

December 1999						
S	M	T	W	T	F	S
			1	2	3	4
5	6	7	8	9	10	11
12	13	14	15	16	17	18
19	20	21	22	23	24	25
26	27	28	29	30	31	

January 2000						
S	M	T	W	T	F	S
						1
2	3	4	5	6	7	8
9	10	11	12	13	14	15
16	17	18	19	20	21	22
23	24	25	26	27	28	29
30	31					

27 Monday
3rd ♍

28 Tuesday
3rd ♍
☽ v/c   **1:52 pm** 10:52 am
☽ enters ♎   **7:15 pm** 4:15 pm

29 Wednesday
3rd ♎
4th Quarter   **9:05 am** 6:05 am

30 Thursday
4th ♎
☽ v/c   **10:35 pm** 7:35 pm
♀ enters ♐   **11:54 pm** 8:54 pm
☿ enters ♑   10:48 pm

31 Friday
4th ♎
☿ enters ♑   **1:48 am**
☽ enters ♏   **4:37 am** 1:37 am

New Year's Eve

Eastern Standard Time in bold type
Pacific Standard Time in medium type

	3 Monday	10 Monday	17 Monday	24 Monday
				31 Monday
	4 Tuesday	11 Tuesday	18 Tuesday	25 Tuesday
	5 Wednesday	12 Wednesday	19 Wednesday	26 Wednesday
	6 Thursday	13 Thursday	20 Thursday	27 Thursday
	7 Friday	14 Friday	21 Friday	28 Friday
1 Saturday	8 Saturday	15 Saturday	22 Saturday	29 Saturday
2 Sunday	9 Sunday	16 Sunday	23 Sunday	30 Sunday

February 2000

	7 Monday	14 Monday	21 Monday	28 Monday
1 Tuesday	8 Tuesday	15 Tuesday	22 Tuesday	29 Tuesday
2 Wednesday	9 Wednesday	16 Wednesday	23 Wednesday	
3 Thursday	10 Thursday	17 Thursday	24 Thursday	
4 Friday	11 Friday	18 Friday	25 Friday	
5 Saturday	12 Saturday	19 Saturday	26 Saturday	
6 Sunday	13 Sunday	20 Sunday	27 Sunday	

	6 Monday	13 Monday	20 Monday	27 Monday
	7 Tuesday	14 Tuesday	21 Tuesday	28 Tuesday
1 Wednesday	8 Wednesday	15 Wednesday	22 Wednesday	29 Wednesday
2 Thursday	9 Thursday	16 Thursday	23 Thursday	30 Thursday
3 Friday	10 Friday	17 Friday	24 Friday	31 Friday
4 Saturday	11 Saturday	18 Saturday	25 Saturday	
5 Sunday	12 Sunday	19 Sunday	26 Sunday	

April 2000

	3 Monday	10 Monday	17 Monday	24 Monday
	4 Tuesday	11 Tuesday	18 Tuesday	25 Tuesday
	5 Wednesday	12 Wednesday	19 Wednesday	26 Wednesday
	6 Thursday	13 Thursday	20 Thursday	27 Thursday
	7 Friday	14 Friday	21 Friday	28 Friday
1 Saturday	8 Saturday	15 Saturday	22 Saturday	29 Saturday
2 Sunday	9 Sunday	16 Sunday	23 Sunday	30 Sunday

1 Monday	8 Monday	15 Monday	22 Monday	29 Monday
2 Tuesday	9 Tuesday	16 Tuesday	23 Tuesday	30 Tuesday
3 Wednesday	10 Wednesday	17 Wednesday	24 Wednesday	31 Wednesday
4 Thursday	11 Thursday	18 Thursday	25 Thursday	
5 Friday	12 Friday	19 Friday	26 Friday	
6 Saturday	13 Saturday	20 Saturday	27 Saturday	
7 Sunday	14 Sunday	21 Sunday	28 Sunday	

June 2000

	5 Monday	12 Monday	19 Monday	26 Monday
	6 Tuesday	13 Tuesday	20 Tuesday	27 Tuesday
	7 Wednesday	14 Wednesday	21 Wednesday	28 Wednesday
1 Thursday	8 Thursday	15 Thursday	22 Thursday	29 Thursday
2 Friday	9 Friday	16 Friday	23 Friday	30 Friday
3 Saturday	10 Saturday	17 Saturday	24 Saturday	
4 Sunday	11 Sunday	18 Sunday	25 Sunday	

July 2000

	3 Monday	10 Monday	17 Monday	24 Monday
				31 Monday
	4 Tuesday	11 Tuesday	18 Tuesday	25 Tuesday
	5 Wednesday	12 Wednesday	19 Wednesday	26 Wednesday
	6 Thursday	13 Thursday	20 Thursday	27 Thursday
	7 Friday	14 Friday	21 Friday	28 Friday
1 Saturday	8 Saturday	15 Saturday	22 Saturday	29 Saturday
2 Sunday	9 Sunday	16 Sunday	23 Sunday	30 Sunday

August 2000

	7 Monday	14 Monday	21 Monday	28 Monday
1 Tuesday	8 Tuesday	15 Tuesday	22 Tuesday	29 Tuesday
2 Wednesday	9 Wednesday	16 Wednesday	23 Wednesday	30 Wednesday
3 Thursday	10 Thursday	17 Thursday	24 Thursday	31 Thursday
4 Friday	11 Friday	18 Friday	25 Friday	
5 Saturday	12 Saturday	19 Saturday	26 Saturday	
6 Sunday	13 Sunday	20 Sunday	27 Sunday	

	4 Monday	11 Monday	18 Monday	25 Monday
	5 Tuesday	12 Tuesday	19 Tuesday	26 Tuesday
	6 Wednesday	13 Wednesday	20 Wednesday	27 Wednesday
	7 Thursday	14 Thursday	21 Thursday	28 Thursday
1 Friday	8 Friday	15 Friday	22 Friday	29 Friday
2 Saturday	9 Saturday	16 Saturday	23 Saturday	30 Saturday
3 Sunday	10 Sunday	17 Sunday	24 Sunday	

October 2000

	2 Monday	9 Monday	16 Monday	23 Monday / 30 Monday
	3 Tuesday	10 Tuesday	17 Tuesday	24 Tuesday / 31 Tuesday
	4 Wednesday	11 Wednesday	18 Wednesday	25 Wednesday
	5 Thursday	12 Thursday	19 Thursday	26 Thursday
	6 Friday	13 Friday	20 Friday	27 Friday
	7 Saturday	14 Saturday	21 Saturday	28 Saturday
1 Sunday	8 Sunday	15 Sunday	22 Sunday	29 Sunday

	6 Monday	13 Monday	20 Monday	27 Monday
	7 Tuesday	14 Tuesday	21 Tuesday	28 Tuesday
1 Wednesday	8 Wednesday	15 Wednesday	22 Wednesday	29 Wednesday
2 Thursday	9 Thursday	16 Thursday	23 Thursday	30 Thursday
3 Friday	10 Friday	17 Friday	24 Friday	
4 Saturday	11 Saturday	18 Saturday	25 Saturday	
5 Sunday	12 Sunday	19 Sunday	26 Sunday	

December 2000

	4 Monday	11 Monday	18 Monday	25 Monday
	5 Tuesday	12 Tuesday	19 Tuesday	26 Tuesday
	6 Wednesday	13 Wednesday	20 Wednesday	27 Wednesday
	7 Thursday	14 Thursday	21 Thursday	28 Thursday
1 Friday	8 Friday	15 Friday	22 Friday	29 Friday
2 Saturday	9 Saturday	16 Saturday	23 Saturday	30 Saturday
3 Sunday	10 Sunday	17 Sunday	24 Sunday	31 Sunday

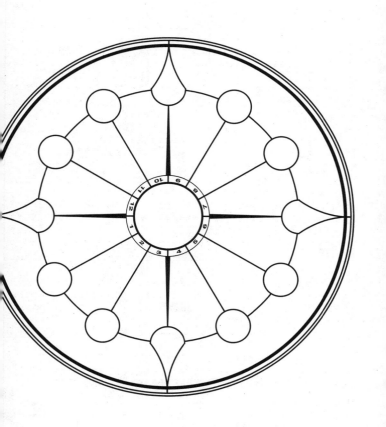

JANUARY 1999

1 FRIDAY
2:06 am
3:30 am
5:02 am
5:07 am
6:30 am
7:51 am
4:08 pm
6:21 pm
9:27 pm
9:44 pm
9:50 pm
12:30 pm
2:02 pm
2:07 pm
4:51 pm
1:08 pm
3:21 pm
6:27 pm
6:44 pm
6:50 pm

2 SATURDAY
1:10 am
3:24 am
4:15 am
7:28 am
11:31 am
8:10 am
10:11 am
12:24 pm
1:15 pm
4:28 pm
8:31 pm
9:01 pm
11:35 pm

3 SUNDAY
2:39 am
4:06 am
4:47 am
3:27 am
5:04 am
7:40 am
1:11 am
7:47 am
10:11 am
12:27 pm
12:43 pm
2:04 pm
4:28 pm
8:31 pm
11:43 pm

4 MONDAY
12:27 am
12:52 am
5:14 am
4:26 am
4:25 pm
5:12 pm
6:22 pm
8:19 pm
9:15 pm
1:26 am
2:14 am
5:30 am
1:25 pm
2:12 pm
3:22 pm
5:19 pm
6:15 pm

5 TUESDAY
4:59 am
5:36 am
6:31 am
6:32 am
10:23 am
10:24 am
10:57 am
1:05 pm
1:19 pm
1:59 am
2:36 am
3:31 am
3:32 am
7:23 am
7:24 am
7:57 am

6 WEDNESDAY
2:39 am
4:06 am
7:47 am
3:27 am
3:43 am
5:04 pm
7:40 pm
9:01 pm
11:35 pm
1:06 am
4:47 am
12:27 pm
12:43 pm
2:04 pm
4:28 pm
11:43 pm

7 THURSDAY
2:43 am
3:18 am
3:30 am
6:07 am
1:43 am
3:03 am
3:41 am
6:28 am
7:06 am
7:55 am
10:28 pm
11:00 pm
12:18 pm
12:30 pm
3:07 pm
12:03 am
12:41 am
3:28 am
4:06 am
4:55 am
7:28 am
8:00 pm

8 FRIDAY
5:05 am
2:23 am
6:23 am
2:05 am
1:23 am
3:23 pm
2:43 pm
12:24 am
1:46 am
3:56 am
4:41 am
5:31 am

9 SATURDAY
9:21 am
1:16 pm
4:10 pm
5:03 pm
6:22 pm
6:21 am
10:16 am
1:10 pm
2:03 pm
3:22 pm

10 SUNDAY
1:32 am
4:56 am
6:45 am
6:22 am
10:48 am
7:48 pm
1:56 am
3:45 am
5:22 am
7:40 am
9:23 pm
10:23 pm
11:57 pm

11 MONDAY
12:23 am
1:23 am
2:57 am
7:08 am
8:51 am
4:08 am
5:51 am
10:04 am
10:12 am

12 TUESDAY
1:04 am
1:12 am
6:15 am
7:53 am
2:16 pm
6:59 pm
9:27 pm
11:24 pm
12:40 am
3:15 am
4:53 am
5:10 am
11:16 pm
3:59 pm
4:09 pm
6:27 pm
8:24 pm
10:21 pm

13 WEDNESDAY
1:21 am
5:43 am
3:24 am
4:46 am
6:56 am
7:37 am
7:41 am
8:15 am
8:42 pm
2:43 am
12:24 pm
1:46 pm
3:56 pm
4:37 pm
4:41 pm
5:15 pm
5:42 pm

14 THURSDAY
1:56 am
2:15 am
4:02 am
7:14 am
8:15 pm
3:00 pm
8:56 am
11:15 am
1:02 pm
2:04 pm
4:14 pm
5:15 pm

15 FRIDAY
1:43 am
6:13 am
7:29 am
6:58 am
10:34 am
11:12 am
3:13 pm
4:29 pm
5:58 pm
7:34 pm
8:12 pm
10:54 pm

16 SATURDAY
1:54 am
6:05 am
11:10 am
12:16 pm
8:36 pm
3:05 pm
8:10 pm
9:16 pm
5:36 pm

17 SUNDAY
5:47 am
6:15 am
9:09 am
10:47 am
10:49 am
11:19 am
2:59 pm
6:02 pm
7:19 pm
2:47 pm
3:15 pm
6:09 pm
7:47 pm
7:49 pm
11:59 pm
3:02 pm
4:19 pm

18 MONDAY
3:56 am
9:59 am
2:06 pm
6:59 am
11:06 am
10:36 pm
11:11 pm
11:57 pm

19 TUESDAY
1:36 am
2:11 am
2:57 am
7:53 am
8:59 am
1:51 am
1:54 am
1:59 am
2:38 am
3:04 am
4:55 pm
5:39 pm
4:53 am
5:59 am
10:51 am
10:54 am
10:59 am
11:38 am
12:04 pm
1:55 pm
2:39 pm

20 WEDNESDAY
5:44 am
9:34 am
9:57 am
12:49 pm
12:57 pm
1:51 pm
8:04 pm
2:44 pm
6:34 pm
6:57 pm
9:49 pm
9:57 pm
10:51 pm
12:58 am
5:04 pm

21 THURSDAY
7:25 am
12:19 pm
2:30 pm
3:17 pm
7:35 pm
8:05 pm
10:42 pm
4:25 am
9:19 am
11:30 am
12:17 pm
4:35 pm
5:05 pm
7:42 pm
9:20 pm
11:20 pm
11:28 pm

22 FRIDAY
12:20 pm
2:20 pm
2:28 pm
5:51 pm
6:39 pm
6:39 pm
6:54 pm
6:57 pm
8:21 pm
12:22 am
2:51 am
3:22 am
3:39 am
3:39 am
3:54 am
3:57 am
5:21 am
9:28 am

23 SATURDAY
12:28 am
3:09 am
9:09 am
11:55 am
7:28 am
12:09 pm
8:55 pm
9:21 pm
9:52 pm
11:25 pm

24 SUNDAY
12:21 pm
12:52 pm
2:25 pm
5:26 pm
6:07 pm
9:34 pm
10:59 pm
2:16 pm
2:59 pm
3:07 pm
7:11 pm
7:59 pm
12:08 am
1:50 am
6:16 am
9:04 am
12:57 am

25 MONDAY
3:44 am
7:57 am
9:39 am
12:30 pm
11:21 pm
12:44 pm
4:57 pm
6:39 pm
9:30 pm
8:21 pm

26 TUESDAY
3:19 am
3:43 am
4:04 am
4:42 am
4:44 am
5:15 am
8:57 am
9:34 am
10:52 am
12:26 pm
12:54 pm
2:28 pm
8:41 pm
12:19 pm
12:43 pm
1:04 pm
1:42 pm
2:15 pm
5:57 pm
6:34 pm
7:09 pm
7:52 pm
9:26 pm
9:54 pm
11:28 pm
5:41 pm
11:08 pm

27 WEDNESDAY
2:08 pm
6:23 am
6:56 am
10:25 am
10:27 am
2:04 pm
3:23 am
3:56 am
7:25 am
7:27 am
11:04 am

28 THURSDAY
5:11 am
6:27 am
7:40 am
7:52 am
9:09 pm
9:52 pm
9:55 pm
11:25 pm
2:11 am
3:27 am
4:40 am
4:52 am

29 FRIDAY
8:17 am
11:40 am
12:01 pm
1:30 pm
3:31 pm
5:51 pm
7:17 pm
5:17 am
8:40 am
9:01 am
10:30 am
12:12 pm
12:31 pm
4:17 pm

30 SATURDAY
3:08 pm
4:50 pm
9:16 pm
3:57 pm
12:08 am
1:50 am
6:16 am
9:04 am
12:57 am
11:25 am

31 SUNDAY
2:25 am
3:16 am
4:54 am
10:22 am
11:17 am
12:44 pm
3:17 pm
6:22 pm
6:53 pm
7:04 pm
8:25 pm
10:15 pm
12:16 am
1:54 am
7:22 am
8:17 am
9:44 am
12:17 pm
3:22 pm
3:53 pm
4:04 pm
5:26 pm
7:15 pm
6:03 pm
8:47 pm
11:07 pm
1:31 pm
5:37 pm
7:15 pm
8:44 pm
10:11 pm
3:03 am
5:47 am
8:07 am
10:31 am
2:37 pm
4:15 pm
5:44 pm
7:11 pm

JANUARY 1999

☽ Last Aspect day	EST / hr:mn / PST		asp	☽ Ingress sign	day	EST / hr:mn / PST	
31	**9:58 pm**	6:58 pm	⚹ ♄	♋	1	**3:16 am**	12:16 am
2		11:35 pm	☍ ♀	♌	3	**5:31 am**	2:31 am
3	**2:35 am**		☍ ♀	♌	3	**5:31 am**	2:31 am
5	**6:31 am**	3:31 am	△ ☿	♍	5	**10:49 am**	7:49 am
7	**6:07 am**	3:07 am	☍ ♃	♎	7	**7:53 pm**	4:53 pm
9		10:32 pm	☍ ♄	♏	10	**7:48 am**	4:48 am
10	**1:32 am**		☍ ♄	♏	10	**7:48 am**	4:48 am
12	**7:53 am**	4:53 am	△ ♃	♐	12	**8:23 pm**	5:23 pm
14		10:43 pm	△ ♄	♑	15	**7:29 am**	4:29 am
15	**1:43 am**		△ ♄	♑	15	**7:29 am**	4:29 am

☽ Last Aspect day	EST / hr:mn / PST		asp	☽ Ingress sign	day	EST / hr:mn / PST	
17	**10:49 am**	7:49 am	□ ♄	♒	17	**4:12 pm**	1:12 pm
19	**5:44 pm**	2:44 pm	△ ♂	♓	19	**10:41 pm**	7:41 pm
21	**7:35 pm**	4:35 pm	☌ ♃	♈	22	**3:26 am**	2:26 am
24	**5:26 am**	2:26 am	☍ ♂	♉	24	**6:53 am**	3:53 am
26	**4:44 am**	1:44 am	□ ♀	♊	26	**9:30 am**	6:30 am
28	**7:52 am**	4:52 am	⚹ ♄	♋	28	**11:57 am**	8:57 am
30	**11:17 am**	8:17 am	□ ♄	♌	30	**3:16 pm**	12:16 pm

☽ Phases & Eclipses phase	day	EST / hr:mn / PST	
Full Moon	1	**9:50 pm**	6:50 pm
4th Quarter	9	**9:21 am**	6:21 am
New Moon	17	**10:47 am**	7:47 am
2nd Quarter	24	**2:16 pm**	11:16 am
Full Moon	31	**11:07 am**	8:07 am
●	31	11° ♌ 20'	

Planet Ingress		day	EST / hr:mn / PST	
⚵	♊	2	**3:44 pm**	12:44 pm
♀	♒	4	**11:25 am**	8:25 am
☿	♑	6	**9:03 pm**	6:03 pm
⚷	♐	7	**3:16 pm**	12:16 pm
⚵	♐	15	**7:12 am**	4:12 am
☉	♒	20	**7:38 am**	4:38 am
☿	♒	26	**4:32 am**	1:32 am
♂	♏	26	**6:59 am**	3:59 am
♀	♓	28	**11:16 am**	8:16 am
⚳	♊	30	**12:55 pm**	9:55 am

Planetary Motion		day	EST / hr:mn / PST	
⚳	D	16	**10:32 am**	7:32 am

DATE		SID.TIME	SUN	MOON	NODE	MERCURY	VENUS	MARS	JUPITER	SATURN	URANUS	NEPTUNE	PLUTO	CERES	PALLAS	JUNO	VESTA	CHIRON
F	1	6:40:49	10 ♑ 06	24 ♊ 58	22 ♌ ℞ 53	21 ♐ 16	25 ♑ 23	18 ♎ 23	21 ♓ 56	26 ♈ 46	10 ♒ 57	01 ♒ 04	09 ♐ 07	00 ♊ ℞ 11	19 ♓ 58	25 ♏ 50	21 ♌ ℞ 54	29 ♏ 16
S	2	6:44:46	11 07	09 ♋ 32	22 47	22 40	26 38	18 53	22 05	26 47	11 01	01 06	09 09	00 05	20 13	26 08	21 48	29 23
S	3	6:48:42	12 08	23 50	22 41	24 05	27 53	19 22	22 14	26 47	11 04	01 08	09 11	29 ♉ 59	20 28	26 26	21 42	29 29
M	4	6:52:39	13 09	07 ♌ 47	22 38	25 31	29 09	19 51	22 23	26 48	11 07	01 10	09 13	29 54	20 43	26 44	21 35	29 36
T	5	6:56:35	14 10	21 19	22 D 36	26 58	00 ♒ 24	20 21	22 33	26 48	11 10	01 12	09 15	29 49	20 58	27 01	21 28	29 42
W	6	7:00:32	15 12	04 ♍ 25	22 36	28 25	01 39	20 50	22 42	26 49	11 13	01 14	09 17	29 44	21 13	27 19	21 21	29 48
T	7	7:04:28	16 13	17 09	22 37	29 52	02 54	21 18	22 52	26 50	11 17	01 17	09 19	29 40	21 29	27 36	21 13	29 55
F	8	7:08:25	17 14	29 33	22 38	01 ♑ 21	04 09	21 47	23 01	26 51	11 20	01 19	09 21	29 36	21 45	27 54	21 04	00 ♐ 01
S	9	7:12:22	18 15	11 ♎ 42	22 ℞ 40	02 50	05 24	22 15	23 11	26 52	11 23	01 21	09 23	29 33	22 01	28 11	20 56	00 07
S	10	7:16:18	19 16	23 39	22 40	04 19	06 39	22 44	23 21	26 53	11 26	01 23	09 25	29 30	22 17	28 28	20 46	00 13
M	11	7:20:15	20 17	05 ♏ 32	22 39	05 49	07 55	23 12	23 31	26 55	11 30	01 26	09 27	29 27	22 34	28 45	20 37	00 19
T	12	7:24:11	21 18	17 23	22 36	07 20	09 10	23 40	23 41	26 56	11 33	01 28	09 29	29 25	22 50	29 02	20 27	00 25
W	13	7:28:08	22 20	29 19	22 32	08 51	10 25	24 07	23 51	26 57	11 36	01 30	09 31	29 23	23 07	29 18	20 16	00 31
T	14	7:32:04	23 21	11 ♐ 21	22 27	10 22	11 40	24 35	24 02	26 59	11 40	01 32	09 32	29 22	23 24	29 35	20 05	00 37
F	15	7:36:01	24 22	23 34	22 22	11 54	12 55	25 02	24 12	27 01	11 43	01 35	09 34	29 21	23 41	29 52	19 54	00 43
S	16	7:39:57	25 23	05 ♑ 59	22 18	13 27	14 10	25 29	24 23	27 03	11 46	01 37	09 36	29 21	23 58	00 ♐ 08	19 42	00 49
S	17	7:43:54	26 24	18 38	22 14	15 00	15 25	25 56	24 34	27 05	11 50	01 39	09 38	29 D 20	24 16	00 24	19 30	00 54
M	18	7:47:51	27 25	01 ♒ 31	22 12	16 33	16 40	26 23	24 44	27 07	11 53	01 41	09 40	29 21	24 34	00 41	19 18	01 00
T	19	7:51:47	28 26	14 37	22 D 11	18 07	17 55	26 49	24 55	27 09	11 57	01 44	09 41	29 22	24 51	00 57	19 05	01 05
W	20	7:55:44	29 27	27 57	22 11	19 42	19 10	27 16	25 07	27 11	12 00	01 46	09 43	29 23	25 09	01 12	18 52	01 11
T	21	7:59:40	00 ♒ 28	11 ♓ 27	22 12	21 17	20 25	27 42	25 18	27 14	12 04	01 48	09 45	29 24	25 28	01 28	18 38	01 16
F	22	8:03:37	01 30	25 09	22 14	22 52	21 40	28 07	25 29	27 16	12 07	01 51	09 46	29 26	25 46	01 44	18 25	01 21
S	23	8:07:33	02 31	09 ♈ 01	22 15	24 29	22 55	28 33	25 40	27 19	12 11	01 53	09 48	29 29	26 04	01 59	18 11	01 27
S	24	8:11:30	03 32	23 01	22 ℞ 16	26 06	24 10	28 58	25 52	27 21	12 14	01 55	09 49	29 31	26 23	02 15	17 56	01 32
M	25	8:15:26	04 33	07 ♉ 09	22 16	27 43	25 25	29 23	26 03	27 24	12 17	01 57	09 51	29 35	26 42	02 30	17 42	01 37
T	26	8:19:23	05 34	21 23	22 15	29 21	26 40	29 48	26 15	27 27	12 21	02 00	09 53	29 38	27 01	02 45	17 27	01 42
W	27	8:23:20	06 35	05 ♊ 40	22 13	01 ♒ 00	27 54	00 ♏ 12	26 27	27 30	12 24	02 02	09 54	29 42	27 20	03 00	17 12	01 46
T	28	8:27:16	07 36	19 57	22 11	02 39	29 09	00 36	26 39	27 33	12 28	02 04	09 56	29 46	27 39	03 15	16 57	01 51
F	29	8:31:13	08 37	04 ♋ 10	22 09	04 19	00 ♓ 24	01 00	26 51	27 36	12 31	02 06	09 57	29 51	27 58	03 30	16 42	01 56
S	30	8:35:09	09 38	18 15	22 07	05 59	01 39	01 24	27 03	27 40	12 35	02 09	09 58	29 56	28 18	03 44	16 27	02 00
S	31	8:39:06	10 38	02 ♌ 09	22 05	07 41	02 54	01 47	27 15	27 43	12 38	02 11	10 00	00 ♊ 02	28 38	03 58	16 11	02 05

EPHEMERIS CALCULATED FOR 12 MIDNIGHT GREENWICH MEAN TIME. ALL OTHER DATA AND FACING ASPECTARIAN PAGE IN **EASTERN STANDARD TIME (BOLD)** AND PACIFIC STANDARD TIME (REGULAR).

FEBRUARY 1999

1 MONDAY

☿ ⚹ ♇	**4:11 am**	1:11 am
☽ ⚻ ♃	**4:18 pm**	1:18 pm
☽ △ ♄	**4:40 pm**	1:40 pm
☽ ⚻ ⚴	**7:20 pm**	4:20 pm
☉ ☌ ♅	**8:59 pm**	5:59 pm
☽ □ ⚳	**9:03 pm**	6:03 pm
☽ □ ⚷		9:44 pm
☽ ⚻ ♆		9:46 pm
☽ ⚹ ♂		10:29 pm

2 TUESDAY

☽ □ ⚷	**12:44 am**	
☽ ⚻ ♆	**12:46 am**	
☽ ⚹ ♂	**1:29 am**	
☽ □ ⚵	**4:56 am**	1:56 am
☽ ☍ ♀	**7:42 am**	4:42 am
☽ □ ♇	**3:09 pm**	12:09 pm
♆ ⚹ ⚷	**3:43 pm**	12:43 pm
☿ ☌ ♅	**7:04 pm**	4:04 pm
☽ ⚻ ♅	**8:17 pm**	5:17 pm
☽ ⚻ ☿	**8:28 pm**	5:28 pm
☽ ⚻ ☉	**10:10 pm**	7:10 pm
☽ ⚺ ⚶		9:59 pm
♃ ⚺ ♄		10:40 pm

3 WEDNESDAY

☽ ⚺ ⚶	**12:59 am**	
♃ ⚺ ♄	**1:40 am**	
☿ ☌ ☉		9:20 pm
☽ ⚻ ♄		10:02 pm
☽ ☍ ♃		10:18 pm
☿ ☍ ⚶		10:59 pm
☉ ☍ ⚶		11:57 pm

4 THURSDAY

☿ ☌ ☉	**12:20 am**	
☽ ⚻ ♄	**1:02 am**	
☽ ☍ ♃	**1:18 am**	
☿ ☍ ⚶	**1:59 am**	
☉ ☍ ⚶	**2:57 am**	
☽ ☍ ⚴	**5:07 am**	2:07 am
☽ △ ⚳	**5:53 am**	2:53 am
☽ △ ♆	**9:29 am**	6:29 am
☽ ⚹ ⚷	**9:35 am**	6:35 am
☽ ⚺ ♂	**11:48 am**	8:48 am
☽ ⚹ ⚵	**2:47 pm**	11:47 am
☽ ⚻ ♀	**11:03 pm**	8:03 pm
☽ ⚹ ♇		9:36 pm

5 FRIDAY

☽ ⚹ ♇	**12:36 am**	
☽ △ ♅	**6:11 am**	3:11 am
☽ ⚹ ⚶	**9:38 am**	6:38 am
☽ △ ☉	**1:09 pm**	10:09 am
♀ □ ♇	**2:32 pm**	11:32 am
☽ △ ☿	**3:47 pm**	12:47 pm
⚳ ⚹ ⚴		9:59 pm

6 SATURDAY

⚳ ⚹ ⚴	**12:59 am**	
☽ ☍ ♄	**12:22 pm**	9:22 am
☽ ⚻ ♃	**1:23 pm**	10:23 am
☽ ⚻ ⚳	**5:45 pm**	2:45 pm
☽ ⚻ ⚴	**6:03 pm**	3:03 pm
☽ □ ♆	**9:01 pm**	6:01 pm
☽ ⚺ ⚷	**9:16 pm**	6:16 pm
☽ ☌ ♂		10:05 pm

7 SUNDAY

☽ ☌ ♂	**1:05 am**	
☽ ⚺ ⚵	**3:28 am**	12:28 am
☽ ⚺ ♇	**12:34 pm**	9:34 am
☽ △ ♀	**5:52 pm**	2:52 pm
☽ □ ♅	**6:31 pm**	3:31 pm
☽ □ ⚶	**8:26 pm**	5:26 pm
♀ ⚺ ♅		9:25 pm

8 MONDAY

♀ ⚺ ♅	**12:25 am**	
☽ □ ☉	**6:58 am**	3:58 am
♀ ⚻ ⚶	**2:36 pm**	11:36 am
☽ □ ☿	**2:39 pm**	11:39 am
☽ ⚻ ♄		10:15 pm

9 TUESDAY

☽ ⚻ ♄	**1:15 am**	
☽ △ ♃	**3:01 am**	12:01 am
☽ ☍ ⚳	**7:01 am**	4:01 am
☽ △ ⚴	**8:24 am**	5:24 am
☽ ⚹ ♆	**9:45 am**	6:45 am
☽ ☌ ⚷	**10:08 am**	7:08 am
☽ ⚺ ♂	**3:24 pm**	12:24 pm
☽ ☌ ⚵	**5:06 pm**	2:06 pm
☽ ☌ ♇		10:08 pm

10 WEDNESDAY

☽ ☌ ♇	**1:08 am**	
☽ ⚹ ♅	**7:12 am**	4:12 am
☽ △ ⚶	**7:30 am**	4:30 am
☽ □ ♀	**1:10 pm**	10:10 am
♅ ☍ ⚶	**7:03 pm**	4:03 pm
☽ ⚹ ☉		9:35 pm

11 THURSDAY

☽ ⚹ ☉	**12:35 am**	
♆ ⚹ ⚴	**11:13 am**	8:13 am
☽ ⚹ ☿	**12:59 pm**	9:59 am
☽ △ ♄	**1:15 pm**	10:15 am
☿ ⚹ ♄	**2:49 pm**	11:49 am
☽ □ ♃	**3:40 pm**	12:40 pm
☽ ⚻ ⚳	**7:13 pm**	4:13 pm
☽ ⚺ ♆	**9:17 pm**	6:17 pm
☽ □ ⚴	**9:33 pm**	6:33 pm
☽ ⚺ ⚷	**9:45 pm**	6:45 pm

12 FRIDAY

☽ ⚹ ♂	**4:07 am**	1:07 am
⚴ △ ⚷	**5:56 am**	2:56 am
☽ ⚺ ⚵	**5:10 am**	2:10 am
☿ ⚺ ♃	**9:07 am**	6:07 am
☽ ⚺ ♇	**11:56 am**	8:56 am
☽ ⚻ ⚶	**4:46 pm**	1:46 pm
☽ ⚺ ♅	**5:55 pm**	2:55 pm

13 SATURDAY

☽ ⚹ ♀	**5:37 am**	2:37 am
☿ □ ⚳	**10:34 am**	7:34 am
☽ ⚺ ☉	**3:06 pm**	12:06 □m
☿ ⚺ ♆	**9:54 pm**	6:54 pm
☽ □ ♄	**10:32 pm**	7:32 pm
☽ ⚹ ♃		10:27 pm
☿ □ ⚷		10:39 pm

14 SUNDAY

☽ ⚹ ♃	**1:27 am**	
☿ □ ⚷	**1:39 am**	
☽ △ ⚳	**4:34 am**	1:34 am
☽ ☌ ♆	**5:56 am**	2:56 am
☽ ⚹ ⚷	**6:28 am**	3:28 am
☽ ⚺ ☿	**7:13 am**	4:13 am
☽ ⚹ ⚴	**7:37 am**	4:37 am
☿ ⚺ ⚴	**10:39 am**	7:39 am
☽ □ ♂	**1:36 pm**	10:36 am
☽ ⚹ ⚵	**2:06 pm**	11:06 am
☽ ⚹ ♇	**7:42 pm**	4:42 pm
☽ ☍ ⚶	**11:10 pm**	8:10 pm
☽ ☌ ♅		10:32 pm

15 MONDAY

☽ ☌ ♅	**1:32 am**	
☽ ⚺ ♀	**5:51 pm**	2:51 pm
☽ ☌ ☉		10:40 pm

16 TUESDAY

☽ ☌ ☉	**1:40 am**	
☽ ⚹ ♄	**4:42 am**	1:42 am
☽ ⚺ ♃	**8:01 am**	5:01 am
☽ □ ⚳	**10:49 am**	7:49 am
☽ ⚺ ♆	**11:33 am**	8:33 am
☽ □ ⚷	**12:06 pm**	9:06 am
☿ △ ♂	**12:41 pm**	9:41 am
☿ □ ⚵	**1:34 pm**	10:34 am
☽ ⚺ ⚴	**2:26 pm**	11:26 am
☽ △ ♂	**7:51 pm**	4:51 pm
☽ □ ⚵	**7:54 pm**	4:54 pm
☽ ☌ ☿	**8:46 pm**	5:46 pm
☽ □ ♇		9:34 pm
☽ ⚻ ⚶		11:55 pm

17 WEDNESDAY

☽ □ ♇	**12:34 am**	
☽ ⚻ ⚶	**2:55 am**	
♂ ⚺ ⚵	**3:26 am**	12:26 am
☽ ⚺ ♅	**6:18 am**	3:18 am
☉ ⚹ ♄	**10:13 pm**	7:13 pm
☿ □ ♇		10:59 pm
☽ ☌ ♀		11:42 pm

18 THURSDAY

☿ □ ♇	**1:59 am**	
☽ ☌ ♀	**2:42 am**	
☽ ⚺ ♄	**8:30 am**	5:30 am
☽ ⚺ ☉	**9:13 am**	6:13 am
☽ ☌ ♃	**12:14 pm**	9:14 am
☽ ⚹ ⚳	**2:49 pm**	11:49 am
☽ ⚹ ♆	**2:58 pm**	11:58 am
☿ ⚻ ⚶	**3:03 pm**	12:03 pm
☽ △ ⚷	**3:32 pm**	12:32 pm
☽ ☌ ⚴	**6:59 pm**	3:59 pm
☽ △ ⚵	**11:37 pm**	8:37 pm
☽ ⚻ ♂	**11:55 pm**	8:55 pm

19 FRIDAY

♆ △ ⚳	**3:27 am**	12:27 am
☽ △ ♇	**3:33 am**	12:33 am
☽ △ ⚶	**4:58 am**	1:58 am
☽ ⚺ ☿	**7:14 am**	4:14 am
☽ ⚹ ♅	**9:18 am**	6:18 am
☿ ⚺ ♅		9:13 pm

20 SATURDAY

☿ ⚺ ♅	**12:13 am**	
☽ ⚺ ♀	**9:55 am**	6:55 am
☽ ☌ ♄	**11:12 am**	8:12 am
☉ ⚺ ♃	**2:58 pm**	11:58 am
☽ ⚺ ♃	**3:23 pm**	12:23 pm
☽ ⚹ ☉	**3:25 pm**	12:25 pm
☽ □ ♆	**5:25 pm**	2:25 pm
☽ ⚺ ⚳	**5:52 pm**	2:52 pm
☽ ⚻ ⚷	**6:01 pm**	3:01 pm
☽ ⚺ ⚴	**10:38 pm**	7:38 pm
♀ ⚺ ♄		10:49 pm
☽ ⚻ ⚵		11:32 pm

21 SUNDAY

♀ ⚺ ♄	**1:49 am**	
☽ ⚻ ⚵	**2:32 am**	
☽ ☍ ♂	**3:08 am**	12:08 am
☽ ⚻ ♇	**5:52 am**	2:52 am
☽ □ ⚶	**6:27 am**	3:27 am
⚳ ☍ ⚷	**6:47 am**	3:47 am
☽ □ ♅	**11:46 am**	8:46 am
☽ ⚹ ☿	**4:36 pm**	1:36 pm
☉ ⚺ ♆	**8:44 pm**	5:44 pm

22 MONDAY

☉ □ ⚷	**5:44 am**	2:44 am
☉ □ ⚳	**10:40 am**	7:40 am
☽ ⚺ ♄	**1:54 pm**	10:54 am
☽ ⚹ ♀	**5:05 pm**	2:05 pm
♇ △ ⚶	**6:10 pm**	3:10 pm
☽ ⚹ ♃	**6:39 pm**	3:39 pm
☽ △ ♆	**7:59 pm**	4:59 pm
☽ ☍ ⚷	**8:37 pm**	5:37 pm
☽ ☌ ⚳	**9:05 pm**	6:05 pm
☽ □ ☉	**9:43 pm**	6:43 pm
☽ ⚹ ⚴		11:31 pm

23 TUESDAY

☽ ⚹ ⚴	**2:31 am**	
☽ ☍ ⚵	**5:43 am**	2:43 am
☽ ⚻ ♂	**6:37 am**	3:37 am
☽ ⚹ ⚶	**8:18 am**	5:18 am
☽ ☍ ♇	**8:32 am**	5:32 am
☽ △ ♅	**2:41 pm**	11:41 am
♀ ☌ ♃	**2:48 pm**	11:48 am
☽ □ ☿		11:22 pm

24 WEDNESDAY

☽ □ ☿	**2:22 am**	
♀ ⚹ ♆	**3:23 am**	12:23 am
♀ △ ⚷	**10:49 am**	7:49 am
☽ ⚹ ♄	**5:28 pm**	2:28 pm
☽ □ ♃	**10:51 pm**	7:51 pm
☽ ⚻ ♆	**11:29 pm**	8:29 pm
☽ ⚻ ⚷		9:08 pm
♀ ⚹ ⚳		9:13 pm
☽ ⚺ ⚳		10:18 pm
☽ □ ♀		10:23 pm

25 THURSDAY

☽ ⚻ ⚷	**12:08 am**	
♀ ⚹ ⚳	**12:13 am**	
☽ ⚺ ⚳	**1:18 am**	
☽ □ ♀	**1:23 am**	
☽ △ ☉	**5:09 am**	2:09 am
☽ □ ⚴	**7:29 am**	4:29 am
☽ ⚻ ⚵	**9:55 am**	6:55 am
☽ △ ♂	**11:06 am**	8:06 am
☽ ⚺ ⚶	**11:13 am**	8:13 am
☽ ⚻ ♇	**12:14 pm**	9:14 am
♂ □ ⚶	**2:32 pm**	11:32 am
☽ ⚻ ♅	**6:43 pm**	3:43 pm

26 FRIDAY

☽ △ ☿	**1:15 pm**	10:15 am
♃ ⚹ ♆	**7:26 pm**	4:26 pm
☽ □ ♄	**10:24 pm**	7:24 pm

27 SATURDAY

☽ ☍ ♆	**4:22 am**	1:22 am
☽ △ ♃	**4:30 am**	1:30 am
☽ △ ⚷	**5:01 am**	2:01 am
☽ ⚹ ⚳	**7:02 am**	4:02 am
☉ ⚺ ⚴	**7:21 am**	4:21 am
☽ △ ♀	**11:32 am**	8:32 am
☽ △ ⚴	**2:03 pm**	11:03 am
⚵ △ ⚶	**2:16 pm**	11:16 am
☽ ⚻ ☉	**2:23 pm**	11:23 am
☽ ☌ ⚶	**3:35 pm**	12:35 pm
☽ △ ⚵	**3:37 pm**	12:37 pm
☽ □ ♂	**5:04 pm**	2:04 pm
☽ △ ♇	**5:26 pm**	2:26 pm
☽ ☍ ♅		9:18 pm

28 SUNDAY

☽ ☍ ♅	**12:18 am**	
☉ ⚻ ⚶	**3:57 am**	12:57 am
☉ □ ⚵	**9:13 am**	6:13 am
♃ △ ⚷	**3:04 pm**	12:04 pm
♂ ⚺ ♇	**6:26 pm**	3:26 pm
☽ ⚻ ☿		10:31 pm
♀ ☌ ⚴		11:13 pm
♀ △ ⚶		11:24 pm
⚴ △ ⚶		11:43 pm

Eastern Standard Time in bold type
Pacific Standard Time in medium type

FEBRUARY 1999

☽ Last Aspect day	EST / hr:mn / PST		asp	☽ Ingress sign	day	EST / hr:mn / PST	
1	**4:40 pm**	1:40 pm	△ ♄	♍	1	**8:37 pm**	5:37 pm
3		10:18 pm	☍ ♃	♎	4	**4:55 am**	1:55 am
4	**1:18 am**		☍ ♃	♎	4	**4:55 am**	1:55 am
6	**12:22 pm**	9:22 am	☍ ♄	♏	6	**4:07 pm**	1:07 pm
9	**3:01 am**	12:01 am	△ ♃	♐	9	**4:38 am**	1:38 am
11	**3:40 pm**	12:40 pm	□ ♃	♑	11	**4:10 pm**	1:10 pm
13	**10:32 pm**	7:32 pm	□ ♄	♒	13		9:57 pm
13	**10:32 pm**	7:32 pm	□ ♄	♒	14	**12:57 am**	
16	**4:42 am**	1:42 am	⚹ ♄	♓	16	**6:40 am**	3:40 am
17		11:42 pm	☌ ♀	♈	18	**10:07 am**	7:07 am
18	**2:42 am**		☌ ♀	♈	18	**10:07 am**	7:07 am
20	**11:12 am**	8:12 am	☌ ♄	♉	20	**12:29 pm**	9:29 am
21	**4:36 pm**	1:36 pm	⚹ ☿	♊	22	**2:54 pm**	11:54 am
24	**5:28 pm**	2:28 pm	⚹ ♄	♋	24	**6:09 pm**	3:09 pm
26	**10:24 pm**	7:24 pm	□ ♄	♌	26	**10:44 pm**	7:44 pm
27		9:18 pm	☍ ♅	♍	1	**5:05 am**	2:05 am
28	**12:18 am**		☍ ♅	♍	1	**5:05 am**	2:05 am

☽ Phases & Eclipses phase	day	EST / hr:mn / PST	
4th Quarter	8	**6:58 am**	3:58 am
New Moon	15		10:40 pm
New Moon	16	**1:40 am**	
●	16	27° ♒ 08'	
2nd Quarter	22	**9:43 pm**	6:43 pm

Planet Ingress		day	EST / hr:mn / PST	
♀	♈	3	**9:53 pm**	6:53 pm
☿	♓	12	**10:27 am**	7:27 am
♃	♈	12	**8:21 pm**	5:21 pm
☉	♓	18	**9:47 pm**	6:47 pm
♀	♈	21	**3:49 pm**	12:49 pm
♄	♉	28	**8:29 pm**	5:29 pm

Planetary Motion	day	EST / hr:mn / PST

DATE		SID.TIME	SUN	MOON	NODE	MERCURY	VENUS	MARS	JUPITER	SATURN	URANUS	NEPTUNE	PLUTO	CERES	PALLAS	JUNO	VESTA	CHIRON
M	1	8:43:02	11 ♒ 39	15 ♌ 47	22 ♌ D 04	09 ♒ 23	04 ♓ 08	02 ♏ 11	27 ♓ 27	27 ♈ 47	12 ♒ 42	02 ♒ 13	10 ♐ 01	00 ♊ 07	28 ♓ 57	04 ♐ 13	15 ♌ ℞ 55	02 ♐ 09
T	2	8:46:59	12 40	29 07	22 04	11 05	05 23	02 33	27 39	27 50	12 45	02 16	10 03	00 13	29 17	04 27	15 40	02 14
W	3	8:50:55	13 41	12 ♍ 08	22 04	12 49	06 38	02 56	27 52	27 54	12 49	02 18	10 04	00 20	29 37	04 41	15 24	02 18
T	4	8:54:52	14 42	24 50	22 05	14 33	07 52	03 18	28 04	27 58	12 52	02 20	10 05	00 27	29 58	04 54	15 08	02 22
F	5	8:58:49	15 43	07 ♎ 15	22 06	16 17	09 07	03 40	28 16	28 02	12 56	02 22	10 06	00 34	00 ♈ 18	05 08	14 52	02 26
S	6	9:02:45	16 44	19 26	22 07	18 03	10 21	04 01	28 29	28 06	12 59	02 24	10 08	00 42	00 38	05 21	14 36	02 30
S	7	9:06:42	17 44	01 ♏ 27	22 07	19 49	11 36	04 23	28 42	28 10	13 03	02 27	10 09	00 49	00 59	05 34	14 20	02 34
M	8	9:10:38	18 45	13 21	22 07	21 36	12 50	04 43	28 54	28 14	13 06	02 29	10 10	00 58	01 20	05 48	14 04	02 38
T	9	9:14:35	19 46	25 13	22 ℞ 08	23 24	14 05	05 04	29 07	28 18	13 10	02 31	10 11	01 06	01 41	06 00	13 48	02 42
W	10	9:18:31	20 47	07 ♐ 09	22 08	25 12	15 19	05 24	29 20	28 22	13 13	02 33	10 12	01 15	02 01	06 13	13 32	02 45
T	11	9:22:28	21 47	19 12	22 D 08	27 00	16 34	05 44	29 33	28 27	13 17	02 35	10 13	01 24	02 23	06 26	13 17	02 49
F	12	9:26:24	22 48	01 ♑ 27	22 08	28 49	17 48	06 03	29 46	28 31	13 20	02 38	10 14	01 34	02 44	06 38	13 01	02 52
S	13	9:30:21	23 49	13 58	22 08	00 ♓ 39	19 02	06 22	29 59	28 36	13 24	02 40	10 15	01 44	03 05	06 50	12 46	02 55
S	14	9:34:18	24 49	26 46	22 09	02 29	20 17	06 41	00 ♈ 12	28 40	13 27	02 42	10 16	01 54	03 27	07 02	12 30	02 59
M	15	9:38:14	25 50	09 ♒ 54	22 09	04 19	21 31	06 59	00 26	28 45	13 31	02 44	10 17	02 04	03 48	07 14	12 15	03 02
T	16	9:42:11	26 51	23 21	22 ℞ 10	06 09	22 45	07 17	00 39	28 50	13 34	02 46	10 18	02 15	04 10	07 25	12 00	03 05
W	17	9:46:07	27 51	07 ♓ 06	22 10	07 59	23 59	07 35	00 52	28 55	13 38	02 48	10 19	02 26	04 32	07 37	11 46	03 08
T	18	9:50:04	28 52	21 05	22 09	09 48	25 14	07 51	01 06	29 00	13 41	02 50	10 20	02 37	04 54	07 48	11 31	03 10
F	19	9:54:00	29 52	05 ♈ 16	22 09	11 37	26 28	08 08	01 19	29 05	13 44	02 53	10 21	02 49	05 16	07 59	11 17	03 13
S	20	9:57:57	00 ♓ 53	19 33	22 08	13 25	27 42	08 24	01 33	29 10	13 48	02 55	10 21	03 01	05 38	08 09	11 03	03 16
S	21	10:01:53	01 54	03 ♉ 53	22 07	15 12	28 56	08 40	01 46	29 15	13 51	02 57	10 22	03 13	06 00	08 20	10 49	03 18
M	22	10:05:50	02 54	18 12	22 06	16 57	00 ♈ 10	08 55	02 00	29 21	13 54	02 59	10 23	03 26	06 22	08 30	10 36	03 20
T	23	10:09:47	03 54	02 ♊ 26	22 D 05	18 40	01 24	09 10	02 13	29 26	13 58	03 01	10 24	03 38	06 45	08 40	10 23	03 23
W	24	10:13:43	04 55	16 32	22 05	20 20	02 38	09 24	02 27	29 31	14 01	03 03	10 24	03 51	07 07	08 50	10 10	03 25
T	25	10:17:40	05 55	00 ♋ 30	22 05	21 57	03 51	09 37	02 41	29 37	14 04	03 05	10 25	04 05	07 30	09 00	09 58	03 27
F	26	10:21:36	06 56	14 17	22 06	23 31	05 05	09 51	02 55	29 43	14 08	03 07	10 25	04 18	07 53	09 09	09 46	03 29
S	27	10:25:33	07 56	27 54	22 06	25 00	06 19	10 03	03 08	29 48	14 11	03 09	10 26	04 32	08 16	09 18	09 34	03 31
S	28	10:29:29	08 56	11 ♌ 19	22 ℞ 07	26 25	07 33	10 15	03 22	29 54	14 14	03 11	10 26	04 46	08 38	09 27	09 23	03 33

EPHEMERIS CALCULATED FOR 12 MIDNIGHT GREENWICH MEAN TIME. ALL OTHER DATA AND FACING ASPECTARIAN PAGE IN **EASTERN STANDARD TIME (BOLD)** AND PACIFIC STANDARD TIME (REGULAR).

MARCH 1999

1 MONDAY
☽ ⚻ ☿ **1:31 am**
♀ ☌ ☿ **2:13 am**
♀ △ ⚶ **2:24 am**
☿ △ ⚶ **2:43 am**
☽ △ ♄ **5:08 am** 2:08 am
☉ □ ♇ **7:04 am** 4:04 am
☉ △ ♂ **9:50 am** 6:50 am
☽ ⚻ ♆ **11:03 am** 8:03 am
☽ □ ⚷ **11:43 am** 8:43 am
☽ ⚻ ♃ **12:03 pm** 9:03 am
♀ △ ⚵ **1:13 pm** 10:13 am
☽ □ ⚳ **2:42 pm** 11:42 am
☽ ⚺ ⚶ **9:48 pm** 6:48 pm
☽ ⚻ ♀ **10:40 pm** 7:40 pm
☽ □ ⚵ **11:12 pm** 8:12 pm
☽ ⚻ ♀ 9:08 pm
☽ □ ♇ 9:30 pm
☽ ✶ ♂ 9:56 pm
☽ ☍ ☉ 10:59 pm

2 TUESDAY
☽ ⚻ ♀ **12:08 am**
☽ □ ♇ **12:30 am**
☽ ✶ ♂ **12:56 am**
☽ ☍ ☉ **1:59 am**
♀ △ ♇ **3:59 am** 12:59 am
☽ ⚻ ♅ **7:51 am** 4:51 am
♀ ⚻ ♂ **9:36 am** 6:36 am
☿ ⚺ ♄ **10:34 pm** 7:34 pm
♀ △ ⚵ 11:12 pm

3 WEDNESDAY
♀ △ ⚵ **2:12 am**
☽ ⚻ ♄ **2:06 pm** 11:06 am
☽ ☍ ☿ **3:18 pm** 12:18 pm
☽ △ ♆ **7:57 pm** 4:57 pm
☽ ✶ ⚷ **8:36 pm** 5:36 pm
☽ ☍ ♃ **9:56 pm** 6:56 pm
☽ △ ⚳ 9:46 pm

4 THURSDAY
☽ △ ⚳ **12:46 am**
☽ ✶ ⚶ **6:16 am** 3:16 am
☽ ✶ ⚵ **9:05 am** 6:05 am
☽ ☍ ♀ **9:46 am** 6:46 am
☽ ✶ ♇ **9:51 am** 6:51 am
☽ ⚺ ♂ **11:03 am** 8:03 am
♇ △ ♀ **12:30 pm** 9:30 am
☽ ☍ ♀ **3:47 pm** 12:47 pm
☽ ⚻ ☉ **4:27 pm** 1:27 pm
☽ △ ♅ **5:44 pm** 2:44 pm

5 FRIDAY
☉ ⚺ ♅ **8:50 am** 5:50 am
♀ ✶ ♅ **12:04 pm** 9:04 am
☽ ☍ ♄ 10:25 pm
♀ ⚺ ☉ 10:56 pm

6 SATURDAY
☽ ☍ ♄ **1:25 am**
♀ ⚺ ☉ **1:56 am**
☽ ⚻ ☿ **6:11 am** 3:11 am
☽ □ ♆ **7:08 am** 4:08 am
☽ ⚺ ⚷ **7:45 am** 4:45 am
☽ ⚻ ♃ **10:13 am** 7:13 am
☽ ⚻ ⚳ **1:16 pm** 10:16 am
☽ □ ⚶ **4:57 pm** 1:57 pm
☽ ⚺ ⚵ **9:11 pm** 6:11 pm
☽ ⚺ ♇ **9:23 pm** 6:23 pm
☽ ⚻ ♀ **11:17 pm** 8:17 pm
☽ ☌ ♂ **11:18 pm** 8:18 pm
♂ ⚻ ♀ 9:05 pm

7 SUNDAY
♂ ⚻ ♀ **12:05 am**
☽ □ ♅ **5:44 am** 2:44 am
☿ ✶ ♆ **5:47 am** 2:47 am
☽ △ ☉ **9:38 am** 6:38 am
☽ ⚻ ♀ **10:18 am** 7:18 am
♇ ☌ ⚵ **5:02 pm** 2:02 pm
☿ △ ⚷ 10:17 pm

8 MONDAY
☿ △ ⚷ **1:17 am**
☽ ⚻ ♄ **2:22 pm** 11:22 am
☽ ✶ ♆ **7:46 pm** 4:46 pm
☽ ☌ ⚷ **8:19 pm** 5:19 pm
☽ △ ☿ **8:43 pm** 5:43 pm
☽ △ ♃ **11:57 pm** 8:57 pm

9 TUESDAY
☽ ☍ ⚳ **3:11 am** 12:11 am
☽ △ ⚶ **4:52 am** 1:52 am
☽ ☌ ♇ **9:57 am** 6:57 am
☽ ☌ ⚵ **10:20 am** 7:20 am
☽ ⚺ ♂ **12:28 pm** 9:28 am
☽ △ ♀ **1:56 pm** 10:56 am
☽ ✶ ♅ **6:33 pm** 3:33 pm

10 WEDNESDAY
☽ □ ☉ **3:41 am** 12:41 am
☽ △ ♀ **5:41 am** 2:41 am
☽ △ ♄ 11:58 pm

11 THURSDAY
☽ △ ♄ **2:58 am**
⚳ ✶ ⚶ **7:40 am** 4:40 am
☽ ⚺ ♆ **7:51 am** 4:51 am
☽ ⚺ ⚷ **8:17 am** 5:17 am
☽ □ ☿ **8:41 am** 5:41 am
☽ □ ♃ **12:57 pm** 9:57 am
☽ ⚻ ⚶ **4:00 pm** 1:00 pm
☽ ⚻ ⚳ **4:16 pm** 1:16 pm
☽ ⚺ ♇ **9:27 pm** 6:27 pm
☽ ⚺ ⚵ **10:17 pm** 7:17 pm
☽ ✶ ♂ 9:17 pm

12 FRIDAY
☽ ✶ ♂ **12:17 am**
☽ □ ♀ **3:14 am** 12:14 am
☿ △ ⚷ **4:36 am** 1:36 am
☽ ⚺ ♅ **5:55 am** 2:55 am
☿ ✶ ♆ **6:29 pm** 3:29 pm
☽ ✶ ☉ **7:28 pm** 4:28 pm
☽ □ ♀ **10:33 pm** 7:33 pm

13 SATURDAY
☽ □ ♄ **12:59 pm** 9:59 am
☽ ✶ ☿ **4:26 pm** 1:26 pm
☽ ☌ ♆ **5:12 pm** 2:12 pm
☽ ✶ ⚷ **5:31 pm** 2:31 pm
☽ ✶ ♃ **10:56 pm** 7:56 pm
☽ ☍ ⚶ 9:22 pm
☽ △ ⚳ 11:15 pm

14 SUNDAY
☽ ☍ ⚶ **12:22 am**
☽ △ ⚳ **2:15 am**
☽ ✶ ♇ **5:51 am** 2:51 am
☽ ✶ ⚵ **7:01 am** 4:01 am
☽ □ ♂ **8:46 am** 5:46 am
☽ ✶ ♀ **1:01 pm** 10:01 am
☽ ☌ ♅ **1:59 pm** 10:59 am

15 MONDAY
☽ ⚺ ☉ **6:47 am** 3:47 am
☽ ✶ ♀ **10:40 am** 7:40 am
☽ ✶ ♄ **7:13 pm** 4:13 pm
☽ ⚺ ☿ **7:47 pm** 4:47 pm
☽ ⚺ ♆ **10:50 pm** 7:50 pm
☽ □ ⚷ **11:02 pm** 8:02 pm
♅ ✶ ♀ 9:57 pm

16 TUESDAY
♅ ✶ ♀ **12:57 am**
☽ ⚺ ♃ **5:01 am** 2:01 am
☿ ⚺ ♄ **5:03 am** 2:03 am
☽ ⚻ ⚶ **5:10 am** 2:10 am
☽ □ ⚳ **8:18 am** 5:18 am
☽ □ ♇ **10:33 am** 7:33 am
♃ △ ⚶ **11:53 am** 8:53 am
☽ □ ⚵ **11:57 am** 8:57 am
☽ △ ♂ **1:26 pm** 10:26 am
☽ ⚺ ♅ **6:22 pm** 3:22 pm
☽ ⚺ ♀ **6:50 pm** 3:50 pm

17 WEDNESDAY
☽ ☌ ☉ **1:48 pm** 10:48 am
☽ ⚺ ♀ **6:20 pm** 3:20 pm
☽ ☌ ☿ **7:44 pm** 4:44 pm
☽ ⚺ ♄ **10:11 pm** 7:11 pm
☽ ✶ ♆ 10:19 pm
☽ △ ⚷ 10:25 pm

18 THURSDAY
☽ ✶ ♆ **1:19 am**
☽ △ ⚷ **1:25 am**
☿ ⚺ ♀ **4:44 am** 1:44 am
☽ △ ⚶ **7:06 am** 4:06 am
☽ ☌ ♃ **7:58 am** 4:58 am
☽ ✶ ⚳ **11:19 am** 8:19 am
☽ △ ♇ **12:26 pm** 9:26 am
☽ △ ⚵ **2:00 pm** 11:00 am
☽ ⚻ ♂ **3:14 pm** 12:14 pm
☽ ✶ ♅ **8:07 pm** 5:07 pm
☽ ☌ ♀ **9:49 pm** 6:49 pm

19 FRIDAY
☿ ☌ ☉ **2:14 pm** 11:14 am
☽ ⚺ ☿ **5:52 pm** 2:52 pm
☽ ⚺ ☉ **6:22 pm** 3:22 pm
♆ ✶ ⚷ **7:43 pm** 4:43 pm
♀ ☌ ♄ **9:05 pm** 6:05 pm
☽ ☌ ♄ **11:26 pm** 8:26 pm
☽ ☌ ♀ **11:38 pm** 8:38 pm
☽ □ ♆ 11:14 pm
☽ ⚻ ⚷ 11:14 pm

20 SATURDAY
☽ □ ♆ **2:14 am**
☽ ⚻ ⚷ **2:14 am**
☽ □ ⚶ **7:44 am** 4:44 am
☽ ⚺ ♃ **9:32 am** 6:32 am
☽ ⚺ ⚳ **1:04 pm** 10:04 am
☽ ⚻ ♇ **1:09 pm** 10:09 am
☽ ⚻ ⚵ **2:55 pm** 11:55 am
☽ ☍ ♂ **3:54 pm** 12:54 pm
♇ ☍ ⚳ **4:54 pm** 1:54 pm
☽ □ ♅ **8:59 pm** 5:59 pm
☽ ⚺ ♀ **11:57 pm** 8:57 pm

21 SUNDAY
♀ ⚻ ⚷ **7:16 am** 4:16 am
♀ □ ♆ **8:15 am** 5:15 am
☽ ✶ ☿ **3:52 pm** 12:52 pm
☽ ✶ ☉ **10:52 pm** 7:52 pm
☽ ⚺ ♄ 9:50 pm

22 MONDAY
☽ ⚺ ♄ **12:50 am**
☽ ☍ ⚷ **3:15 am** 12:15 am
☽ △ ♆ **3:23 am** 12:23 am
☽ ⚺ ♀ **5:05 am** 2:05 am
☽ ✶ ⚶ **8:52 am** 5:52 am
☽ ✶ ♃ **11:37 am** 8:37 am
☽ ☍ ♇ **2:28 pm** 11:28 am
☽ ☌ ⚳ **3:30 pm** 12:30 pm
☽ ☍ ⚵ **4:28 pm** 1:28 pm
☽ ⚻ ♂ **5:10 pm** 2:10 pm
☽ △ ♅ **10:43 pm** 7:43 pm

23 TUESDAY
☽ ✶ ♀ **3:06 am** 12:06 am
☉ ⚺ ♄ **7:07 am** 4:07 am
☽ □ ☿ **3:11 pm** 12:11 pm
♀ □ ⚶ 11:07 pm

24 WEDNESDAY
♀ □ ⚶ **2:07 am**
☽ ✶ ♄ **3:53 am** 12:53 am
☽ □ ☉ **5:18 am** 2:18 am
☽ ⚻ ⚷ **5:57 am** 2:57 am
☽ ⚻ ♆ **6:13 am** 3:13 am
☽ ⚺ ⚶ **11:50 am** 8:50 am
☽ ✶ ♀ **12:45 pm** 9:45 am
☉ △ ⚷ **2:10 pm** 11:10 am
☽ □ ♃ **3:38 pm** 12:38 pm
⚳ ☍ ⚵ **5:22 pm** 2:22 pm
☽ ⚻ ♇ **5:42 pm** 2:42 pm
☉ ✶ ♆ **6:20 pm** 3:20 pm
☽ ⚻ ⚵ **7:56 pm** 4:56 pm
☽ ⚺ ⚳ **7:59 pm** 4:59 pm
☽ △ ♂ **8:17 pm** 5:17 pm
☽ ⚻ ♅ 11:30 pm

25 THURSDAY
☽ ⚻ ♅ **2:30 am**
☽ □ ♀ **8:35 am** 5:35 am
☽ △ ☿ **4:46 pm** 1:46 pm

26 FRIDAY
♀ ⚺ ♃ **5:26 am** 2:26 am
☽ □ ♄ **9:24 am** 6:24 am
☽ △ ⚷ **10:59 am** 7:59 am
☽ ☍ ♆ **11:26 am** 8:26 am
☽ △ ☉ **2:41 pm** 11:41 am
☽ ☌ ⚶ **5:17 pm** 2:17 pm
♂ ⚻ ⚳ **7:27 pm** 4:27 pm
♀ ⚻ ♇ **9:03 pm** 6:03 pm
☽ △ ♃ **10:13 pm** 7:13 pm
☽ △ ♇ **11:21 pm** 8:21 pm
☽ □ ♀ **11:34 pm** 8:34 pm
☽ □ ♂ 10:41 pm
☽ △ ⚵ 10:49 pm

27 SATURDAY
☽ □ ♂ **1:41 am**
☽ △ ⚵ **1:49 am**
☽ ✶ ⚳ **3:08 am** 12:08 am
☽ ☍ ♅ **8:46 am** 5:46 am
☽ △ ♀ **4:46 pm** 1:46 pm
♀ ☍ ♂ **8:53 pm** 5:53 pm
☽ ⚻ ☿ **9:03 pm** 6:03 pm
♀ ⚻ ⚵ 9:24 pm
☉ △ ⚶ 11:07 pm

28 SUNDAY
♀ ⚻ ⚵ **12:24 am**
☉ △ ⚶ **2:07 am**
☽ △ ♄ **5:20 pm** 2:20 pm
☽ □ ⚷ **6:23 pm** 3:23 pm
☽ ⚻ ♆ **7:01 pm** 4:01 pm
☽ ⚺ ⚶ 10:08 pm

29 MONDAY
☽ ⚺ ⚶ **1:08 am**
☽ ⚻ ☉ **3:01 am** 12:01 am
♀ ⚺ ⚳ **3:39 am** 12:39 am
☽ ⚻ ♃ **7:14 am** 4:14 am
☽ □ ♇ **7:16 am** 4:16 am
♃ △ ♇ **8:54 am** 5:54 am
☽ ✶ ♂ **9:12 am** 6:12 am
☽ □ ⚵ **9:56 am** 6:56 am
☽ □ ⚳ **12:44 pm** 9:44 am
☽ △ ♀ **1:25 pm** 10:25 am
☽ ⚻ ♅ **5:16 pm** 2:16 pm

30 TUESDAY
☽ ⚻ ♀ **3:22 am** 12:22 am
☽ ☍ ☿ **4:03 am** 1:03 am
☿ ⚺ ♀ **3:58 pm** 12:58 pm

31 WEDNESDAY
☽ ⚻ ♄ **3:20 am** 12:20 am
☽ ✶ ⚷ **3:45 am** 12:45 am
☽ △ ♆ **4:37 am** 1:37 am
♀ □ ♅ **7:13 am** 4:13 am
☉ △ ♇ **8:58 am** 5:58 am
☽ ✶ ⚶ **11:04 am** 8:04 am
☽ ✶ ♇ **5:07 pm** 2:07 pm
☽ ☍ ☉ **5:50 pm** 2:50 pm
☽ ☍ ♃ **6:17 pm** 3:17 pm
☽ ⚺ ♂ **6:25 pm** 3:25 pm
☽ ✶ ⚵ **7:54 pm** 4:54 pm
♂ ⚻ ♃ **10:22 pm** 7:22 pm
☉ ⚻ ♂ 9:10 pm
☽ △ ⚳ 9:25 pm
☉ ☌ ♃ 10:10 pm

Eastern Standard Time in bold type
Pacific Standard Time in medium type

MARCH 1999

EPHEMERIS CALCULATED FOR 12 MIDNIGHT GREENWICH MEAN TIME. ALL OTHER DATA AND FACING ASPECTARIAN PAGE IN EASTERN STANDARD TIME (BOLD) AND PACIFIC STANDARD TIME (REGULAR).

D Last Aspect / D Ingress

D Last Aspect EST / hr:m / PST	asp	D Ingress sign day EST / hr:m / PST
1:59 am	⊙□♇	♋ 3 1:34 pm 10:34 am
5:44 am	△♄	♌ 3 1:34 am 10:34 am
2:44 pm	△♃	♍ 5 9:23 pm
5:44 am 2:44 pm	□♀	♎ 8 6:23 am
9:38 am	□♇	♏ 10 12:47 pm 9:47 am
5:41 am 2:41 am	△♄	✶ 10 ♐ 12:54 am 9:54 am
5:41 am 2:41 am	△♃	♑ 12 10:32 am 7:32 am
12:10:33 pm 7:33 pm	✶♀	♒ 15 4:31 am 1:31 pm
15:10:40 am 7:40 am	✶♇	♒ 15 4:31 am 1:31 pm
17 1:48 pm 10:48 am	⊙♂	♓ 17 7:13 pm 4:13 pm

D Last Aspect / D Ingress (continued)

D Last Aspect EST / hr:m / PST	asp	D Ingress sign day EST / hr:m / PST
18 8:07 pm 5:07 pm	⊙♂	♈ 19 8:09 pm 5:09 pm
		♉ 21 9:05 pm 6:09 pm
21 3:52 pm 12:52 pm	✶♃	♊ 23 11:33 pm 8:33 pm
23 3:11 pm 12:11 pm	□♇	♋ 25 4:22 am 1:22 am
25 5:46 am 2:46 am	□♃	♌ 28 11:35 am 8:35 am
27 8:46 am 5:46 am	✶♀	♍ 30 8:50 pm 5:50 pm
30 4:03 am 1:03 am	⊙□	

Planetary Motion

day	EST / hr:m / PST
☿ R. 2	5:50 pm 2:50 pm
☿ R. 13	4:23 am 1:23 am
♃ R. 18	4:59 am 1:59 am
♄ R. 20	8:46 pm 5:46 pm

D Phases & Eclipses

phase	day	EST / hr:m / PST
Full Moon	2	1:59 am 10:59 pm
4th Quarter	10	3:41 am 12:41 am
New Moon	17	1:48 pm 10:48 am
2nd Quarter	24	5:18 am 2:18 am
Full Moon	31	5:50 pm 2:50 pm

Ephemeris data table for March 1999 — columns: DATE, SID. TIME, SUN, MOON, NODE, MERCURY, VENUS, MARS, JUPITER, SATURN, URANUS, NEPTUNE, PLUTO, CERES, PALLAS, JUNO, VESTA, CHIRON — daily rows M 1 through W 31.

APRIL 1999

1 THURSDAY
☉⚻♂	**12:10 am**	
☽△⚳	**12:25 am**	
☉☌♃	**1:10 am**	
☽△♅	**3:39 am**	12:39 am
☽⚻♀	**5:47 am**	2:47 am
♄⚻⚷	**1:20 pm**	10:20 am
☽⚻☿	**1:45 pm**	10:45 am
☽☍♀	**3:59 pm**	12:59 pm
☉△⚵	**7:15 pm**	4:15 pm

2 FRIDAY
☽⚺⚷	**2:47 pm**	11:47 am
☽☍♄	**3:06 pm**	12:06 pm
☽□♆	**3:54 pm**	12:54 pm
☽□⚶	**10:45 pm**	7:45 pm

3 SATURDAY
☽⚺♇	**4:34 am**	1:34 am
☽☌♂	**5:04 am**	2:04 am
☽⚻♃	**7:04 am**	4:04 am
☽⚺⚵	**7:25 am**	4:25 am
☽⚻☉	**10:43 am**	7:43 am
☽⚻⚳	**1:51 pm**	10:51 am
☽□♅	**3:36 pm**	12:36 pm
♃△⚵	**11:07 pm**	8:07 pm
☽☍♀		9:15 pm
☽△☿		11:01 pm

4 SUNDAY
☽☍♀	**12:15 am**	
☽△☿	**2:01 am**	
☽⚻♀	**6:16 am**	3:16 am
♂⚺♇	**11:04 am**	8:04 am
☿⚹♀	**9:29 pm**	6:29 pm

5 MONDAY
☽☌⚷	**3:02 am**	12:02 am
☽⚻♄	**4:09 am**	1:09 am
☽⚹♆	**4:26 am**	1:26 am
☽△⚶	**11:41 am**	8:41 am
☽⚺♂	**4:33 pm**	1:33 pm
☽☌♇	**5:05 pm**	2:05 pm
☉⚹⚳	**7:11 pm**	4:11 pm
☽☌⚵	**7:52 pm**	4:52 pm
☽△♃	**8:54 pm**	5:54 pm
☉⚹♅	**11:56 pm**	8:56 pm

6 TUESDAY
☽☍⚳	**4:16 am**	1:16 am
☽⚹♅	**4:25 am**	1:25 am
☽△☉	**4:48 am**	1:48 am
♅△⚳	**9:40 am**	6:40 am
♄□♆	**10:07 am**	7:07 am
☽□☿	**4:07 pm**	1:07 pm
☽⚻♀	**7:35 pm**	4:35 pm
☽△♀	**9:11 pm**	6:11 pm

7 WEDNESDAY
☽⚺⚷	**3:16 pm**	12:16 pm
☽⚺♆	**4:55 pm**	1:55 pm
☽△♄	**5:11 pm**	2:11 pm
♀⚺♀	**8:12 pm**	5:12 pm
☽⚻⚶		9:28 pm

8 THURSDAY
☽⚻⚶	**12:28 am**	
☽⚹♂	**3:32 am**	12:32 am
☽⚺♇	**5:10 am**	2:10 am
☽⚺⚵	**7:45 am**	4:45 am
☽□♃	**10:11 am**	7:11 am
☽⚺♅	**4:26 pm**	1:26 pm
☽⚻⚳	**5:53 pm**	2:53 pm
☽□☉	**9:51 pm**	6:51 pm

9 FRIDAY
☽⚹☿	**5:58 am**	2:58 am
☽□♀	**10:35 am**	7:35 am
☽△♀	**1:06 pm**	10:06 am
☽⚹⚷		10:31 pm

10 SATURDAY
☽⚹⚷	**1:31 am**	
☽☌♆	**3:19 am**	12:19 am
☽□♄	**4:06 am**	1:06 am
☽☍⚶	**10:56 am**	7:56 am
☽□♂	**12:06 pm**	9:06 am
☽⚹♇	**2:46 pm**	11:46 am
☽⚹⚵	**5:01 pm**	2:01 pm
☽⚹♃	**8:38 pm**	5:38 pm
☽☌♅		10:34 pm

11 SUNDAY
☽☌♅	**1:34 am**	
☽△⚳	**4:22 am**	1:22 am
☽⚹☉	**11:02 am**	8:02 am
☽⚺☿	**4:59 pm**	1:59 pm
☽⚹♀	**8:16 pm**	5:16 pm
♂□⚶	**11:19 pm**	8:19 pm
☽□♀		11:02 pm

12 MONDAY
☽□♀	**2:02 am**	
☽□⚷	**8:05 am**	5:05 am
☽⚺♆	9:59 am	6:59 am
☽⚹♄	**11:09 am**	8:09 am
☽△♂	**4:57 pm**	1:57 pm
☽⚻⚶	**5:31 pm**	2:31 pm
☽□♇	**8:29 pm**	5:29 pm
☽□⚵	**10:22 pm**	7:22 pm
☽⚺♃		11:54 pm

13 TUESDAY
☽⚺♃	**2:54 am**	
☽⚺♅	**6:40 am**	3:40 am
☽□⚳	**10:31 am**	7:31 am
☽⚺☉	**7:10 pm**	4:10 pm
☽☌☿	**11:53 pm**	8:53 pm
☽⚺♀		10:31 pm

14 WEDNESDAY
☽⚺♀	**1:31 am**	
☽⚹♀	**9:45 am**	6:45 am
☽△⚷	**10:44 am**	7:44 am
☽⚹♆	**12:43 pm**	9:43 am
☽⚺♄	**2:12 pm**	11:12 am
☽⚻♂	**6:09 pm**	3:09 pm
☽△⚶	**8:14 pm**	5:14 pm
♀☍⚷	**9:39 pm**	6:39 pm
☽△♇	**10:28 pm**	7:28 pm
☽△⚵		9:01 pm

15 THURSDAY
☽△⚵	**12:01 am**	
☽☌♃	**5:22 am**	2:22 am
☽⚹♅	**8:12 am**	5:12 am
☽⚹⚳	**12:58 pm**	9:58 am
♀△♆	**11:20 pm**	8:20 pm
☽☌☉	**11:22 pm**	8:22 pm
☿⚺♀		9:22 pm

16 FRIDAY
☿⚺♀	**12:22 am**	
☽☌♀	**3:30 am**	12:30 am
☽⚺☿	**3:37 am**	12:37 am
☽⚻⚷	**10:45 am**	7:45 am
☽□♆	**12:52 pm**	9:52 am
☽⚺♀	**1:59 pm**	10:59 am
☽☌♄	**2:40 pm**	11:40 am
☽☍♂	**5:04 pm**	2:04 pm
☽□⚶	**8:37 pm**	5:37 pm
☽⚻♇	**10:14 pm**	7:14 pm
☽⚻⚵	**11:32 pm**	8:32 pm
♀⚺♄	**11:54 pm**	8:54 pm

17 SATURDAY
☽⚺♃	**5:49 am**	2:49 am
☽□♅	**7:56 am**	4:56 am
☽⚺⚳	**1:44 pm**	10:44 am
♀⚻♂	**9:39 pm**	6:39 pm
☽⚺☉		11:11 pm

18 SUNDAY
☽⚺☉	**2:11 am**	
☽⚺♀	**4:28 am**	1:28 am
☽⚹☿	**6:36 am**	3:36 am
☽☍⚷	**10:09 am**	7:09 am
☽△♆	**12:29 pm**	9:29 am
☽⚺♄	**2:42 pm**	11:42 am
☽⚻♂	**3:38 pm**	12:38 pm
☽☌♀	**5:37 pm**	2:37 pm
☽⚹⚶	**8:54 pm**	5:54 pm
☽☍♇	**9:55 pm**	6:55 pm
☽☍⚵	**10:59 pm**	7:59 pm

19 MONDAY
☽⚹♃	**6:32 am**	3:32 am
☽△♅	**8:00 am**	5:00 am
☽☌⚳	**3:09 pm**	12:09 pm
♂☍♄	**8:45 pm**	5:45 pm

20 TUESDAY
☿△⚷	**4:38 am**	1:38 am
☽⚹☉	**6:22 am**	3:22 am
☽⚹♀	**6:48 am**	3:48 am
☽⚻⚷	**10:59 am**	7:59 am
☽□☿	**11:35 am**	8:35 am
☽⚻♆	**1:40 pm**	10:40 am
☽△♂	**3:44 pm**	12:44 pm
☽⚹♄	**4:23 pm**	1:23 pm
☉☌♀	**5:37 pm**	2:37 pm
♀⚹⚶	**6:57 pm**	3:57 pm
☽⚺⚶	**11:07 pm**	8:07 pm
☽⚺♀	**11:26 pm**	8:26 pm
☽⚻♇	**11:30 pm**	8:30 pm
♀☍♇		9:05 pm
☽⚻⚵		9:17 pm

21 WEDNESDAY
♀☍♇	**12:05 am**	
☽⚻⚵	**12:17 am**	
♀☍⚵	**8:50 am**	5:50 am
☽□♃	**9:32 am**	6:32 am
☽⚻♅	**10:19 am**	7:19 am
☿⚹♆	**12:52 pm**	9:52 am
☽⚺⚳	**7:14 pm**	4:14 pm
♇△⚶	**11:35 pm**	8:35 pm
☿⚻♂		11:31 pm

22 THURSDAY
☿⚻♂	**2:31 am**	
☽□♀	**12:15 pm**	9:15 am
☽□☉	**2:02 pm**	11:02 am
☽△⚷	**2:43 pm**	11:43 am
☽☍♆	**5:49 pm**	2:49 pm
☽□♂	**6:36 pm**	3:36 pm
☽△☿	**8:44 pm**	5:44 pm
☽□♄	**9:12 pm**	6:12 pm
☉⚻⚷	**10:53 pm**	7:53 pm
☿⚺♄		11:08 pm
⚵△⚶		11:49 pm

23 FRIDAY
☿⚺♄	**2:08 am**	
⚵△⚶	**2:49 am**	
☽△♇	**4:11 am**	1:11 am
☽△⚵	**4:37 am**	1:37 am
☽☌⚶	**4:40 am**	1:40 am
☽⚹♀	**9:17 am**	6:17 am
♃⚹♅	**11:55 am**	8:55 am
☽☍♅	**3:54 pm**	12:54 pm
☽△♃	**3:58 pm**	12:58 pm
♂□♆	**10:12 pm**	7:12 pm
☽⚹⚳		11:55 pm

24 SATURDAY
☽⚹⚳	**2:55 am**	
☉☍♂	**12:37 pm**	9:37 am
☉□♆	**6:17 pm**	3:17 pm
☽△♀	**9:23 pm**	6:23 pm
☽□⚷	**9:42 pm**	6:42 pm
☽⚹♂		9:29 pm
☽⚻♆		10:16 pm
☽△☉		10:51 pm

25 SUNDAY
☽⚹♂	**12:29 am**	
☽⚻♆	**1:16 am**	
☽△☉	**1:51 am**	
☽△♄	**5:22 am**	2:22 am
♀⚻⚷	**5:32 am**	2:32 am
♇☌⚵	**7:08 am**	4:08 am
☽⚻☿	**10:43 am**	7:43 am
☽□⚵	**12:03 pm**	9:03 am
☽□♇	**12:05 pm**	9:05 am
☽⚺⚶	**1:38 pm**	10:38 am
☿△⚵	**9:56 pm**	6:56 pm
☿△♇	**11:13 pm**	8:13 pm
☽□♀	**11:15 pm**	8:15 pm
☽⚻♅		9:35 pm
☽⚻♃		10:39 pm

26 MONDAY
☽⚻♅	**12:35 am**	
☽⚻♃	**1:39 am**	
☽□⚳	**1:51 pm**	10:51 am
♀△♅	**1:55 pm**	10:55 am
☿△⚶	**5:50 pm**	2:50 pm
♂☍♀	**10:10 pm**	7:10 pm

27 TUESDAY
☉☌♄	**6:04 am**	3:04 am
♀⚹♃	**7:18 am**	4:18 am
☽⚹⚷	**7:18 am**	4:18 am
☽⚺♂	**8:44 am**	5:44 am
☽⚻♀	**9:29 am**	6:29 am
☽△♆	**11:18 am**	8:18 am
☽⚻♄	**4:09 pm**	1:09 pm
☽⚻☉	**4:55 pm**	1:55 pm
☽⚹⚵	**9:44 pm**	6:44 pm
☽⚹♇	**10:22 pm**	7:22 pm
☽⚹⚶		10:09 pm

28 WEDNESDAY
☽⚹⚶	**1:09 am**	
☽☍☿	**4:38 am**	1:38 am
☽△♅	**11:27 am**	8:27 am
☽☍♃	**1:37 pm**	10:37 am
☽△♀	**4:08 pm**	1:08 pm
☽△⚳		11:56 pm

29 THURSDAY
☽△⚳	**2:56 am**	
♆□♀	**10:44 am**	7:44 am
♂⚺⚷	**5:41 pm**	2:41 pm
☽☌♂	**6:30 pm**	3:30 pm
☽⚺⚷	**6:31 pm**	3:31 pm
☉⚻⚵	**9:40 pm**	6:40 pm
☽□♆	**10:56 pm**	7:56 pm
☽☍♀	**11:25 pm**	8:25 pm

30 FRIDAY
☽☍♄	**4:30 am**	1:30 am
☽⚺⚵	**8:46 am**	5:46 am
☽☍☉	**9:55 am**	6:55 am
☽⚺♇	**10:05 am**	7:05 am
☉⚻♇	**11:57 am**	8:57 am
☿⚹♅	**1:07 pm**	10:07 am
☽□⚶	**2:13 pm**	11:13 am
☽□♅	**11:35 pm**	8:35 pm
☽⚻☿		10:06 pm
☽⚻♃		11:53 pm

Eastern Standard Time in bold type
Pacific Standard Time in medium type

APRIL 1999

☽ Last Aspect			☽ Ingress		
day	EST / hr:mn / PST	asp	sign day	EST / hr:mn / PST	
1	3:39 am 12:39 am	△♀	♏ 2	7:49 am 4:49 am	
2			♐ 4	8:08 am 5:08 am	
3	2:01 am	△♂	♐ 4	8:08 am 5:08 am	
4	3:31 pm 12:31 pm	△♄	♐ 4	8:08 am 5:08 am	
6	4:07 pm 1:07 pm	□♀	♑ 6	8:39 am 5:39 am	
6	1:06 pm 10:06 am	□♂	♒ 9	7:24 am 4:24 am	
11			♓ 11	11:35 am	
12	2:02 am	△♀	♈ 12	2:35 am	
13	11:53 pm 8:53 pm	△♄	♉ 14	5:46 am 2:46 am	
15	11:22 pm 8:22 pm	□♂	♊ 16	6:07 am 3:07 am	
17	7:56 am 4:56 am	□♀	♋ 18	5:39 am 2:39 am	

☽ Last Aspect			☽ Ingress		
day	EST / hr:mn / PST	asp	sign day	EST / hr:mn / PST	
20	6:22 am 3:22 am	✶⊙	♌ 20	6:28 am 3:28 am	
21	9:32 am 6:32 am	△♀	♍ 22	10:06 am 7:06 am	
23	3:58 pm 12:58 pm	□♂	♎ 24	5:05 pm 2:05 pm	
25	11:15 pm 8:15 pm	□♀	♏ 27	2:47 am	
28	4:08 pm 1:08 pm	△♀	♐ 29	2:13 pm 11:13 am	
31	11:35 pm 8:35 pm	△♄	♑ 2	2:36 am	

Planet Ingress			
	day	EST / hr:mn / PST	
♀ ♊	12	9:51 pm 6:51 pm	
☿ ♉	17	11:22 pm 8:22 pm	
☿ ♉	22	2:02 pm 11:02 am	
⊙ ♉	20	9:55 pm 6:55 pm	

☽ Phases & Eclipses			
phase	day	EST / hr:mn / PST	
4th Quarter	8	9:51 pm 6:51 pm	
New Moon	15	11:22 pm 8:22 pm	
2nd Quarter	22	2:02 pm 11:02 am	
Full Moon	30	9:55 pm 6:55 pm	

Planet Ingress (Planetary Motion)			
		day	EST / hr:mn / PST
☿ D	2	4:15 am 1:15 am	

Planet Ingress			
	day	EST / hr:mn / PST	
♀ ☐	8	8:17 am 5:17 am	
☿ ♉	17	5:09 pm 2:09 pm	
☿ ♉	22	5:12 pm	
⊙ ♉	20	7:46 am 4:46 am	

EPHEMERIS CALCULATED FOR 12 MIDNIGHT GREENWICH MEAN TIME. ALL OTHER DATA AND FACING ASPECTARIAN PAGE IN **EASTERN STANDARD TIME (BOLD)** AND PACIFIC STANDARD TIME (REGULAR).

MAY 1999

1 SATURDAY

☽ ⚻ ☿	**1:06 am**	
☽ ⚻ ♃	**2:53 am**	
☽ ⚻ ♀	**10:36 am**	7:36 am
☿ ☌ ♃	**4:59 pm**	1:59 pm
☽ ⚻ ⚳	**5:14 pm**	2:14 pm

2 SUNDAY

☽ ⚺ ♂	**5:06 am**	2:06 am
☽ ☌ ⚷	**6:37 am**	3:37 am
☽ ⚹ ♆	**11:26 am**	8:26 am
☽ ⚻ ♀	**2:20 pm**	11:20 am
☽ ⚻ ♄	**5:41 pm**	2:41 pm
☽ ☌ ⚵	**8:28 pm**	5:28 pm
☽ ☌ ♇	**10:32 pm**	7:32 pm

3 MONDAY

☽ ⚻ ☉	**3:52 am**	12:52 am
☽ △ ⚶	**4:04 am**	1:04 am
☉ □ ⚶	**7:09 am**	4:09 am
☽ ⚹ ♅	**12:17 pm**	9:17 am
☽ △ ♃	**4:43 pm**	1:43 pm
☽ △ ☿	**11:01 pm**	8:01 pm

4 TUESDAY

☽ ☍ ♀	**5:37 am**	2:37 am
☽ ☍ ⚳	**7:55 am**	4:55 am
☽ ⚹ ♂	**3:55 pm**	12:55 pm
☽ ⚺ ⚷	**6:50 pm**	3:50 pm
☽ ⚺ ♆	**11:58 pm**	8:58 pm

5 WEDNESDAY

☽ △ ♀	**5:16 am**	2:16 am
☽ △ ♄	**6:48 am**	3:48 am
☽ ⚺ ⚵	**8:01 am**	5:01 am
☽ ⚺ ♇	**10:49 am**	7:49 am
☽ ⚻ ⚶	**5:42 pm**	2:42 pm
♀ ☌ ⚳	**6:01 pm**	3:01 pm
☽ △ ☉	**9:27 pm**	6:27 pm
☽ ⚺ ♅		9:32 pm

6 THURSDAY

☽ ⚺ ♅	**12:32 am**	
☽ □ ♃	**5:58 am**	2:58 am
☽ □ ☿	**8:26 pm**	5:26 pm
☽ ⚻ ⚳	**9:36 pm**	6:36 pm
☽ ⚻ ♀	**11:24 pm**	8:24 pm
☽ □ ♂		10:45 pm

7 FRIDAY

☽ □ ♂	**1:45 am**	
☽ ⚹ ⚷	**5:51 am**	2:51 am
♄ ⚻ ⚵	**6:29 am**	3:29 am
☿ ⚹ ⚳	**6:55 am**	3:55 am
♀ ⚻ ⚵	**8:52 am**	5:52 am
♄ ☌ ♀	**11:06 am**	8:06 am
☽ ☌ ♆	**11:08 am**	8:08 am
☉ □ ♅	**12:24 pm**	9:24 am
☽ ⚹ ⚵	**5:59 pm**	2:59 pm
☽ □ ♄	**6:17 pm**	3:17 pm
☽ □ ♀	**6:29 pm**	3:29 pm
♀ △ ♂	**7:53 pm**	4:53 pm
☽ ⚹ ♇	**9:25 pm**	6:25 pm

8 SATURDAY

☿ ☍ ♂	**4:51 am**	1:51 am
☽ ☍ ⚶	**5:23 am**	2:23 am
☽ ☌ ♅	**10:40 am**	7:40 am
☽ □ ☉	**12:28 pm**	9:28 am
☽ ⚹ ♃	**4:49 pm**	1:49 pm
☿ ⚹ ♀		9:35 pm

9 SUNDAY

☿ ⚹ ♀	**12:35 am**	
☽ △ ⚳	**8:18 am**	5:18 am
☽ △ ♂	**9:01 am**	6:01 am
☿ ⚻ ⚷	**12:16 pm**	9:16 am
☽ △ ♀	**1:28 pm**	10:28 am
☽ □ ⚷	**1:57 pm**	10:57 am
☽ ⚹ ☿	**2:14 pm**	11:14 am
♀ ⚻ ⚷	**6:59 pm**	3:59 pm
☽ ⚺ ♆	**7:11 pm**	4:11 pm
♂ △ ⚳	**9:46 pm**	6:46 pm
☽ □ ⚵		9:48 pm
☽ ⚹ ♄		11:24 pm

10 MONDAY

☽ □ ⚵	**12:48 am**	
☽ ⚹ ♄	**2:24 am**	
☽ ⚹ ♀	**4:03 am**	1:03 am
☽ □ ♇	**4:41 am**	1:41 am
☽ ⚻ ⚶	**1:19 pm**	10:19 am
☽ ⚺ ♅	**5:08 pm**	2:08 pm
♇ ⚻ ♀	**9:27 pm**	6:27 pm
☽ ⚹ ☉	**10:51 pm**	7:51 pm
☽ ⚺ ♃	**11:41 pm**	8:41 pm
☿ □ ♆		11:07 pm

11 TUESDAY

☿ □ ♆	**2:07 am**	
☽ ⚻ ♂	**12:41 pm**	9:41 am
☉ ⚺ ♃	**2:12 pm**	11:12 am
☽ □ ⚳	**2:41 pm**	11:41 am
☽ △ ⚷	**6:07 pm**	3:07 pm
☽ □ ♀	**10:20 pm**	7:20 pm
☽ ⚹ ♆	**11:13 pm**	8:13 pm
☽ ⚺ ☿		11:22 pm

12 WEDNESDAY

☽ ⚺ ☿	**2:22 am**	
☽ △ ⚵	**3:43 am**	12:43 am
☽ ⚺ ♄	**6:22 am**	3:22 am
☽ △ ♇	**7:57 am**	4:57 am
☽ ⚺ ♀	**9:10 am**	6:10 am
♀ ⚻ ♆	**9:44 am**	6:44 am
☿ ⚻ ⚵	**11:47 am**	8:47 am
☽ △ ⚶	**5:05 pm**	2:05 pm
☽ ⚹ ♅	**7:39 pm**	4:39 pm
☽ ☌ ♃		11:30 pm

13 THURSDAY

☽ ☌ ♃	**2:30 am**	
☽ ⚺ ☉	**4:26 am**	1:26 am
☿ ☌ ♄	**10:37 am**	7:37 am
☽ ☍ ♂	**12:59 pm**	9:59 am
☽ ⚹ ⚳	**5:10 pm**	2:10 pm
☽ ⚻ ⚷	**6:49 pm**	3:49 pm
☿ ⚻ ♇	**8:13 pm**	5:13 pm
☽ □ ♆	**11:52 pm**	8:52 pm
☽ ⚹ ♀		11:51 pm

14 FRIDAY

☽ ⚹ ♀	**2:51 am**	
☽ ⚻ ⚵	**3:29 am**	12:29 am
☽ ☌ ♄	**7:04 am**	4:04 am
☽ ⚻ ♇	**8:06 am**	5:06 am
☽ ☌ ☿	**9:52 am**	6:52 am
♀ ⚻ ⚵	**10:15 am**	7:15 am
☽ ☌ ♀	**10:53 am**	7:53 am
☽ □ ⚶	**5:52 pm**	2:52 pm
☽ □ ♅	**7:25 pm**	4:25 pm
☿ ☌ ♀	**7:54 pm**	4:54 pm
☽ ⚺ ♃		11:44 pm

15 SATURDAY

☽ ⚺ ♃	**2:44 am**	
☽ ☌ ☉	**7:06 am**	4:06 am
☽ ⚻ ♂	**11:27 am**	8:27 am
☽ ⚺ ⚳	**5:38 pm**	2:38 pm
☽ ☍ ⚷	**5:45 pm**	2:45 pm
⚳ ⚻ ⚷	**9:15 pm**	6:15 pm
☽ △ ♆	**10:57 pm**	7:57 pm
☽ ☍ ⚵		10:55 pm

16 SUNDAY

☽ ☍ ⚵	**1:55 am**	
☽ ⚺ ♀	**5:34 am**	2:34 am
☽ ⚺ ♄	**6:31 am**	3:31 am
☽ ☍ ♇	**7:04 am**	4:04 am
☽ ⚺ ♀	**11:26 am**	8:26 am
☽ ⚺ ☿	**4:00 pm**	1:00 pm
☽ ⚹ ⚶	**5:55 pm**	2:55 pm
☽ △ ♅	**6:33 pm**	3:33 pm
♀ ⚹ ♄	**8:24 pm**	5:24 pm
♀ ⚻ ♇		11:11 pm
☽ ⚹ ♃		11:38 pm

17 MONDAY

♀ ⚻ ♇	**2:11 am**	
☽ ⚹ ♃	**2:38 am**	
☿ □ ⚶	**8:28 am**	5:28 am
☽ ⚺ ☉	**9:39 am**	6:39 am
☽ △ ♂	**10:05 am**	7:05 am
☿ □ ♅	**10:55 am**	7:55 am
☉ ⚻ ♂	**3:06 pm**	12:06 pm
☽ ⚻ ⚷	**5:06 pm**	2:06 pm
☽ ☌ ⚳	**6:34 pm**	3:34 pm
☽ ⚻ ♆	**10:42 pm**	7:42 pm
♅ ☍ ⚶		9:45 pm
☽ ⚻ ⚵		10:06 pm

18 TUESDAY

♅ ☍ ⚶	**12:45 am**	
☽ ⚻ ⚵	**1:06 am**	
☽ ⚹ ♄	**7:00 am**	4:00 am
☽ ⚻ ♇	**7:06 am**	4:06 am
☽ ☌ ♀	**9:29 am**	6:29 am
☽ ⚹ ♀	**1:23 pm**	10:23 am
♄ ⚻ ♇	**3:16 pm**	12:16 pm
☽ ⚻ ♅	**7:13 pm**	4:13 pm
☽ ⚺ ⚶	**7:38 pm**	4:38 pm
☽ ⚹ ☿		9:40 pm

19 WEDNESDAY

☽ ⚹ ☿	**12:40 am**	
☽ □ ♃	**4:32 am**	1:32 am
☽ □ ♂	**10:54 am**	7:54 am
☽ ⚹ ☉	**2:52 pm**	11:52 am
☽ △ ⚷	**6:54 pm**	3:54 pm
☽ ⚺ ⚳	**10:15 pm**	7:15 pm
☽ ☍ ♆		10:07 pm
☽ △ ⚵		11:54 pm

20 THURSDAY

☽ ☍ ♆	**1:07 am**	
☽ △ ⚵	**2:54 am**	
☿ ⚺ ♃	**5:24 am**	2:24 am
☽ △ ♇	**10:02 am**	7:02 am
☽ □ ♄	**10:30 am**	7:30 am
☽ ⚺ ♀	**5:08 pm**	2:08 pm
☽ □ ♀	**6:47 pm**	3:47 pm
☽ ☍ ♅	**11:10 pm**	8:10 pm
☽ ☌ ⚶		9:52 pm

21 FRIDAY

☽ ☌ ⚶	**12:52 am**	
☽ △ ♃	**10:04 am**	7:04 am
☽ □ ☿	**3:04 pm**	12:04 pm
☽ ⚹ ♂	**3:15 pm**	12:15 pm
☿ ⚻ ♂	**4:07 pm**	1:07 pm
☉ ☍ ⚷	**9:19 pm**	6:19 pm
☽ □ ⚷		9:19 pm
☽ □ ☉		9:35 pm

22 SATURDAY

☽ □ ⚷	**12:19 am**	
☽ □ ☉	**12:35 am**	
♀ ⚹ ♀	**4:58 am**	1:58 am
☽ ⚹ ⚳	**6:02 am**	3:02 am
☽ ⚻ ♆	**7:16 am**	4:16 am
☽ □ ⚵	**8:18 am**	5:18 am
☽ □ ♇	**4:45 pm**	1:45 pm
☽ △ ♄	**5:55 pm**	2:55 pm

23 SUNDAY

☽ △ ♀	**4:25 am**	1:25 am
☽ ⚹ ♀	**5:37 am**	2:37 am
☽ ⚻ ♅	**6:55 am**	3:55 am
☽ ⚺ ⚶	**10:13 am**	7:13 am
☽ ⚻ ♃	**7:30 pm**	4:30 pm
♆ ⚻ ⚳	**7:47 pm**	4:47 pm
♀ ⚻ ♅	**8:51 pm**	5:51 pm
☿ ☍ ⚷	**9:07 pm**	6:07 pm
☽ ⚺ ♂	**11:16 pm**	8:16 pm

24 MONDAY

⚳ ⚻ ⚵	**4:22 am**	1:22 am
☽ ⚹ ⚷	**9:15 am**	6:15 am
☽ △ ☿	**11:59 am**	8:59 am
☽ △ ☉	**2:45 pm**	11:45 am
☽ △ ♆	**4:53 pm**	1:53 pm
☽ ⚹ ⚵	**4:58 pm**	1:58 pm
☽ □ ⚳	**5:39 pm**	2:39 pm
♆ ⚹ ⚵	**9:14 pm**	6:14 pm
☽ ⚹ ♇		11:45 pm

25 TUESDAY

☽ ⚹ ♇	**2:45 am**	
☽ ⚻ ♄	**4:41 am**	1:41 am
☿ ☌ ☉	**1:22 pm**	10:22 am
☿ ☍ ⚵	**1:36 pm**	10:36 am
☉ ☍ ⚵	**1:52 pm**	10:52 am
☿ △ ♆	**3:12 pm**	12:12 pm
☽ ⚻ ♀	**5:29 pm**	2:29 pm
☉ △ ♆	**5:33 pm**	2:33 pm
☽ △ ♅	**5:38 pm**	2:38 pm
♅ □ ♀	**9:12 pm**	6:12 pm
☽ □ ♀	**9:58 pm**	6:58 pm
☽ ⚹ ⚶	**10:46 pm**	7:46 pm
☿ ⚺ ⚳		10:36 pm

26 WEDNESDAY

☿ ⚺ ⚳	**1:36 am**	
☽ ☍ ♃	**7:46 am**	4:46 am
☽ ☌ ♂	**9:56 am**	6:56 am
♀ ⚺ ⚶	**11:10 am**	8:10 am
☽ ⚺ ⚷	**8:31 pm**	5:31 pm

27 THURSDAY

☽ ⚺ ⚵	**3:40 am**	12:40 am
☽ □ ♆	**4:39 am**	1:39 am
☉ ⚺ ⚳	**5:30 am**	2:30 am
☽ △ ⚳	**7:39 am**	4:39 am
☽ ⚻ ☉	**7:45 am**	4:45 am
☽ ⚻ ☿	**1:09 pm**	10:09 am
☽ ⚺ ♇	**2:38 pm**	11:38 am
☽ ☍ ♄	**5:21 pm**	2:21 pm
☿ ☍ ♇	**9:08 pm**	6:08 pm

28 FRIDAY

☽ □ ♅	**5:54 am**	2:54 am
☽ ☍ ♀	**8:19 am**	5:19 am
☽ □ ⚶	**12:54 pm**	9:54 am
☿ ⚺ ♄	**1:04 pm**	10:04 am
☽ △ ♀	**4:08 pm**	1:08 pm
☽ ⚻ ♃	**9:17 pm**	6:17 pm
☽ ⚺ ♂	**9:54 pm**	6:54 pm

29 SATURDAY

☽ ☌ ⚷	**8:41 am**	5:41 am
☽ ☌ ⚵	**3:07 pm**	12:07 pm
☽ ⚹ ♆	**5:10 pm**	2:10 pm
☽ ⚻ ⚳	**10:27 pm**	7:27 pm
♂ ☍ ♃	**11:17 pm**	8:17 pm
☽ ☍ ☉		10:40 pm

30 SUNDAY

☽ ☍ ☉	**1:40 am**	
☽ ☌ ♇	**3:06 am**	12:06 am
☽ ⚻ ♄	**6:35 am**	3:35 am
☽ ☍ ☿	**3:22 pm**	12:22 pm
☽ ⚹ ♅	**6:28 pm**	3:28 pm
☉ ☍ ♇	**7:04 pm**	4:04 pm
☽ ⚻ ♀	**11:29 pm**	8:29 pm

31 MONDAY

☽ △ ⚶	**3:19 am**	12:19 am
♀ □ ♂	**6:52 am**	3:52 am
☿ △ ♅	**8:28 am**	5:28 am
☽ ⚹ ♂	**10:07 am**	7:07 am
☽ ⚻ ♀	**10:26 am**	7:26 am
☽ △ ♃	**10:54 am**	7:54 am
♀ □ ♃	**5:00 pm**	2:00 pm
☽ ⚺ ⚷	**8:48 pm**	5:48 pm
☽ ⚺ ⚵		11:26 pm

Eastern Standard Time in bold type
Pacific Standard Time in medium type

MAY 1999

D Last Aspect			D Ingress		
day	EST / hr:m / PST		sign	day	EST / hr:m / PST
30	11:35 am	8:35 am	♈ ♂	2	11:36 am
30	11:35 am	8:35 am	✕⁷	2	2:36 am
	5:37 am	2:37 am	♐	4	3:12 pm 12:12 pm
	10:45 pm		≈	6	11:40 pm
	1:45 am		⌘	9	11:16 am 8:16 am
	6:01 am		♈	11	3:54 pm 12:54 pm
	9:01 am		♉	13	4:57 pm 1:57 pm
	10:51 pm 7:51 pm		Ⅱ	15	4:08 pm 1:08 pm
13	12:59 pm 9:59 am		♋	17	3:40 pm 12:40 pm
15	7:06 am 4:06 am				
17	10:05 am 7:05 am				

D Last Aspect		D Ingress		
day EST / hr:m / PST	asp	sign day	asp	EST / hr:m / PST
19 2:52 pm 11:52 am	✶⊙	♌ 19 5:38 pm		2:38 pm
21 3:15 pm 12:15 pm	✶♂	♍ 21 11:16 pm		8:16 pm
23 5:37 am 2:37 am	✶♂	♎ 24 8:29 am		5:29 am
26 9:56 am 6:56 am	♂♀	♏ 26 8:05 pm		5:05 pm
28 4:09 pm 1:09 pm	♂♂	♐ 29 8:37 am		5:37 am
31 10:54 am	△♃	✕⁷ 31 9:06 pm		6:06 pm

D Phases & Eclipses		
phase	day	EST / hr:m / PST
4th Quarter	8	12:29 pm 9:28 am
New Moon	15	7:06 am 4:06 am
2nd Quarter		9:35 pm
2nd Quarter	22	12:35 am
Full Moon	22	9:35 pm
Full Moon	30	1:40 am

Planet Ingress		
	day	EST / hr:m / PST
♂ ♎	5	4:32 pm 1:32 pm
♀ ⊗	8	11:28 am 8:28 am
♀ ⊗	9	4:23 pm 1:23 pm
♀ ⊗	13	8:56 am 5:56 am
⊙ Ⅱ	21	6:52 am 3:52 am
♀ Ⅱ	23	4:22 pm 1:22 pm
♀ ✕⁷	29	6:54 pm 3:54 pm

Planetary Motion		
	day	EST / hr:m / PST
♆ R	6	1:33 pm 10:33 am
♅ R	21	1:43 pm 10:43 am

DATE	SID. TIME	SUN	MOON	NODE	MERCURY	VENUS	MARS	JUPITER	SATURN	URANUS	NEPTUNE	PLUTO	CERES	PALLAS	JUNO	VESTA	CHIRON
S 1	14:33:55	10 ♉ 11	14 ♍ 20	18 ♋ R, 16	16 ♉ 59	21 Ⅱ 20	01 ♏ R, 46	18 ♈ 17	07 ♉ 33	16 ≈ 37	04 ≈ 05	09 ✕⁷ R, 54	25 Ⅱ 00	04 ♉ 58	09 ♈ R, 11	12 ♌ 05	02 ✕⁷ R, 05
S 2	14:37:52	11	09	18	02	23	01 R, 40	18	07	16	04	09	25	05	09	12	01
M 3	14:41:49	12	07	17	20	24	01	18	07	16	04	09	25	05	08	12	01
T 4	14:45:45	13	06	17	33	25	00	18	07	16	04	09	26	05	08	13	01
W 5	14:49:42	14	59	17	22	26	00	18	07	16	04	09	27	04	08	13	01
T 6	14:53:38	15	59	17	24	27	00	19	07	16	04 R,	09	28	04	07	13	01
F 7	14:57:35	16	26	17	25	28	29	19	07	16	04	09	28	04	07	13	01
S 8	15:01:31	17	17 D	17 D	26	00 ⌘ 12	28	19	07	16	04	09	28	04	06	14	01
S 9	15:05:28	17	56	17 R,	25	14	28	20	08	16	04	09	29	04	06	14	00
M 10	15:09:25	18	52	17	25	29	27	20	08	16	04	09	00 ⊗ 00	03	06	14	00
T 11	15:13:21	19	49	17	22	44	28	20	08	16	04	09	01	03	06	14	00
W 12	15:17:18	20	46	17	17	03	29	20	08	16	04	09	02	03	06	15	00
T 13	15:21:14	21	17 ♉ 00	17	11	21	00 ⌘ 49	21	08	16	04	09	03	02	05	15	00
F 14	15:25:11	22	22	17	03	46	02	21	08	16	04	09	04	02	05	15	00
S 15	15:29:07	23	29	16 R,	55	09	03	21	08	16	04	09	05	02	04	15	00
S 16	15:33:04	24	40	16	48	34	05	21	09	16	04	09	06	02	04	16	00
M 17	15:37:00	25	35	16	42	04 Ⅱ 02	06	22	09	16	04	09	07	01	04	16	00
T 18	15:40:57	26	38	16	38	31	07	22	09	16 R,	04	09	08	01	03	16	00
W 19	15:44:54	27	29	16	36	03	09	22	09	16	04	09	09	01	03	17	00
T 20	15:48:50	28	15	16 D	37	37	10	23	09	16	04	09	10	01	03	17	00
F 21	15:52:47	29	46	16	37	12	11	23	09	16	04	09	11	00	02	17	00
S 22	15:56:43	00 Ⅱ 26	16	42	49	12	23	09	16	04	09	12	00	02	17	00	00
S 23	16:00:40	01	26	16	56	09 ⌘ 22	13	24	10	16	04	09	13	00	02	18	00
M 24	16:04:36	02	24	16	58	14	14	24	10	16	04	09	15	00	01	18	00
T 25	16:08:33	03	16	16	52	55	16	24	10	16	04	09	16	00	01	19	00
W 26	16:12:29	04	17	16	39	37	17	25	10	16	04	09	17	00	01	19	00
T 27	16:16:26	05	23	16	23	49	18	25	10	16	04	09	18	00	00	19	00
F 28	16:20:23	06	11 ♉ 23	16	08	00 Ⅱ 11	20	25	10	16	04	09	19	00	00	20	00
S 29	16:24:19	07	27	16	15	23	21	24	10	16	04	09	20	00	00	20	00
S 30	16:28:16	08	05 ✕⁷ 09	15	08	13	23	24	10	16	04	09	22	00	41	20	00 ✕⁷ 00
M 31	16:32:12	09	17	15	07	15	24	24	10	16	04	09	23	00	24	20	29 ♏ 56

EPHEMERIS CALCULATED FOR 12 MIDNIGHT GREENWICH MEAN TIME. ALL OTHER DATA AND FACING ASPECTARIAN PAGE IN **EASTERN STANDARD TIME (BOLD)** AND PACIFIC STANDARD TIME (REGULAR).

JUNE 1999

1 TUESDAY

☽ ⚺ ⚵	**2:26 am**	
☽ ⚺ ♆	**5:30 am**	2:30 am
☽ ☍ ⚳	**12:59 pm**	9:59 am
☽ ⚺ ♇	**3:15 pm**	12:15 pm
☽ ⚻ ☉	**7:11 pm**	4:11 pm
☽ △ ♄	**7:25 pm**	4:25 pm
☉ ⚺ ♄	**10:27 pm**	7:27 pm
☿ ⚺ ♀	**11:42 pm**	8:42 pm

2 WEDNESDAY

☽ ⚺ ♅	**6:30 am**	3:30 am
☽ △ ♀	**1:59 pm**	10:59 am
☽ ⚻ ☿	**4:16 pm**	1:16 pm
☽ ⚻ ⚶	**5:02 pm**	2:02 pm
☿ ⚹ ⚶	**9:35 pm**	6:35 pm
☽ □ ♂	**9:44 pm**	6:44 pm
☽ □ ♃	**11:40 pm**	8:40 pm

3 THURSDAY

☽ ☍ ♀	**3:39 am**	12:39 am
☽ ⚹ ⚷	**7:59 am**	4:59 am
☽ ⚹ ⚵	**12:46 pm**	9:46 am
☽ ☌ ♆	**4:45 pm**	1:45 pm
☿ △ ♂		9:29 pm
♇ ⚻ ⚳		10:34 pm
☽ ⚹ ♇		11:09 pm
☽ ⚻ ⚳		11:10 pm

4 FRIDAY

☿ △ ♂	**12:29 am**	
♇ ⚻ ⚳	**1:34 am**	
☽ ⚹ ♇	**2:09 am**	
☽ ⚻ ⚳	**2:10 am**	
☽ □ ♄	**6:51 am**	3:51 am
☽ △ ☉	**10:59 am**	7:59 am
☿ ⚹ ♃	**4:07 pm**	1:07 pm
☽ ☌ ♅	**4:57 pm**	1:57 pm
☽ □ ♀		11:32 pm

5 SATURDAY

☽ □ ♀	**2:32 am**	
☽ ☍ ⚶	**4:50 am**	1:50 am
♀ △ ⚷	**5:25 am**	2:25 am
☽ △ ♂	**7:38 am**	4:38 am
☽ ⚹ ♃	**10:23 am**	7:23 am
☽ △ ☿	**1:27 pm**	10:27 am
☽ □ ⚷	**5:06 pm**	2:06 pm
☽ ⚻ ♀	**6:09 pm**	3:09 pm
☽ □ ⚵	**9:02 pm**	6:02 pm
☽ ⚺ ♆		10:41 pm

6 SUNDAY

☽ ⚺ ♆	**1:41 am**	
☽ □ ♇	**10:33 am**	7:33 am
☽ △ ⚳	**12:34 pm**	9:34 am
☿ ⚻ ⚷	**12:35 pm**	9:35 am
☽ ⚹ ♄	**3:36 pm**	12:36 pm
☽ □ ☉	**11:21 pm**	8:21 pm
☽ ⚺ ♅		9:34 pm
♀ △ ⚵		10:31 pm

7 MONDAY

☽ ⚺ ♅	**12:34 am**	
♀ △ ⚵	**1:31 am**	
☿ ⚻ ⚵	**11:14 am**	8:14 am
☽ ⚹ ♀	**11:43 am**	8:43 am
☽ ⚻ ⚶	**1:20 pm**	10:20 am
☽ ⚻ ♂	**2:33 pm**	11:33 am
☉ △ ♅	**4:14 pm**	1:14 pm
☽ ⚺ ♃	**5:48 pm**	2:48 pm
☽ △ ⚷	**11:01 pm**	8:01 pm
☿ ⚺ ♀	**11:49 pm**	8:49 pm
☽ △ ⚵		11:09 pm

8 TUESDAY

☽ △ ⚵	**2:09 am**	
☽ △ ♀	**4:26 am**	1:26 am
☽ □ ☿	**4:47 am**	1:47 am
☽ ⚹ ♆	**7:15 am**	4:15 am
☽ △ ♇	**3:29 pm**	12:29 pm
☽ □ ⚳	**7:08 pm**	4:08 pm
☽ ⚺ ♄	**8:44 pm**	5:44 pm
☿ ⚻ ♆	**10:51 pm**	7:51 pm

9 WEDNESDAY

☽ ⚹ ♅	**4:38 am**	1:38 am
☽ ⚹ ☉	**7:17 am**	4:17 am
♂ ⚹ ⚶	**4:52 pm**	1:52 pm
☽ ⚺ ♀	**4:54 pm**	1:54 pm
☽ ☍ ♂	**5:57 pm**	2:57 pm
☽ △ ⚶	**5:59 pm**	2:59 pm
♀ ☍ ♆	**7:51 pm**	4:51 pm
☽ ☌ ♃	**9:28 pm**	6:28 pm
☽ ⚻ ⚷		10:27 pm

10 THURSDAY

☽ ⚻ ⚷	**1:27 am**	
☽ ⚻ ⚵	**3:55 am**	12:55 am
☽ □ ♆	**9:21 am**	6:21 am
☽ □ ♀	**10:19 am**	7:19 am
☽ ⚹ ☿	**2:15 pm**	11:15 am
☽ ⚻ ♇	**5:05 pm**	2:05 pm
☽ ⚹ ⚳	**10:05 pm**	7:05 pm
☽ ☌ ♄	**10:30 pm**	7:30 pm

11 FRIDAY

☽ □ ♅	**5:35 am**	2:35 am
♂ ⚻ ♀	**5:45 am**	2:45 am
☽ ⚺ ☉	**11:28 am**	8:28 am
☿ ⚻ ♇	**1:44 pm**	10:44 am
♄ ⚹ ⚳	**5:43 pm**	2:43 pm
☽ ⚻ ♂	**6:38 pm**	3:38 pm
☽ ☌ ♀	**6:59 pm**	3:59 pm
☽ □ ⚶	**7:38 pm**	4:38 pm
☽ ⚺ ♃	**10:21 pm**	7:21 pm
☽ ☍ ⚷		10:22 pm

12 SATURDAY

☽ ☍ ⚷	**1:22 am**	
☽ ☍ ⚵	**3:20 am**	12:20 am
☽ △ ♆	**9:10 am**	6:10 am
☽ ⚹ ♀	**1:22 pm**	10:22 am
☽ ☍ ♇	**4:40 pm**	1:40 pm
☽ ⚺ ☿	**8:10 pm**	5:10 pm
☽ ⚺ ♄	**10:25 pm**	7:25 pm
☽ ⚺ ⚳	**11:02 pm**	8:02 pm

13 SUNDAY

☽ △ ♅	**4:59 am**	1:59 am
☽ ☌ ☉	**2:03 pm**	11:03 am
☿ ⚹ ♄	**5:47 pm**	2:47 pm
☽ △ ♂	**6:22 pm**	3:22 pm
☽ ⚺ ♀	**7:59 pm**	4:59 pm
☽ ⚹ ⚶	**8:16 pm**	5:16 pm
☽ ⚹ ♃	**10:20 pm**	7:20 pm
☽ ⚻ ⚷		9:35 pm
☽ ⚻ ⚵		11:09 pm

14 MONDAY

☽ ⚻ ⚷	**12:35 am**	
☽ ⚻ ⚵	**2:09 am**	
☿ ☌ ⚳	**6:30 am**	3:30 am
☽ ⚻ ♆	**8:37 am**	5:37 am
☽ ⚺ ♀	**4:08 pm**	1:08 pm
☽ ⚻ ♇	**4:13 pm**	1:13 pm
♀ △ ♇	**5:30 pm**	2:30 pm
☽ ⚹ ♄	**10:32 pm**	7:32 pm
☽ ☌ ⚳		9:16 pm
☽ ☌ ☿		10:52 pm

15 TUESDAY

☽ ☌ ⚳	**12:16 am**	
☽ ☌ ☿	**1:52 am**	
☽ ⚻ ♅	**4:54 am**	1:54 am
♀ □ ⚶	**10:17 am**	7:17 am
☽ ⚺ ☉	**5:47 pm**	2:47 pm
☽ □ ♂	**7:19 pm**	4:19 pm
☽ ⚺ ⚶	**10:12 pm**	7:12 pm
☽ ⚹ ♀	**10:18 pm**	7:18 pm
☽ □ ♃	**11:39 pm**	8:39 pm
☽ △ ⚷		10:10 pm
☽ △ ⚵		11:24 pm

16 WEDNESDAY

☽ △ ⚷	**1:10 am**	
☽ △ ⚵	**2:24 am**	
☿ ⚻ ♅	**5:58 am**	2:58 am
☽ ☍ ♆	**9:46 am**	6:46 am
☽ △ ♇	**5:48 pm**	2:48 pm
☽ ☌ ♀	**9:18 pm**	6:18 pm
☉ △ ♂	**9:22 pm**	6:22 pm
☽ □ ♄		9:59 pm

17 THURSDAY

☽ □ ♄	**12:59 am**	
☽ ⚺ ⚳	**4:03 am**	1:03 am
☽ ☍ ♅	**7:19 am**	4:19 am
☽ ⚺ ☿	**10:31 am**	7:31 am
☽ ⚹ ♂	**11:26 pm**	8:26 pm
☽ ⚹ ☉		10:05 pm

18 FRIDAY

☽ ⚹ ☉	**1:05 am**	
☽ ☌ ⚶	**3:29 am**	12:29 am
☽ □ ♀	**4:01 am**	1:01 am
☽ △ ♃	**4:10 am**	1:10 am
☽ □ ⚷	**4:52 am**	1:52 am
☽ □ ⚵	**5:45 am**	2:45 am
♃ ⚺ ♀	**10:12 am**	7:12 am
☽ ⚻ ♆	**2:16 pm**	11:16 am
☽ □ ♇	**10:53 pm**	7:53 pm
♀ ☍ ⚷		9:37 pm

19 SATURDAY

♀ ☍ ⚷	**12:37 am**	
☽ ⚺ ♀	**6:46 am**	3:46 am
☽ △ ♄	**7:10 am**	4:10 am
☽ ⚹ ⚳	**11:55 am**	8:55 am
♀ □ ♄	**1:22 pm**	10:22 am
☽ ⚻ ♅	**1:27 pm**	10:27 am
♀ ☍ ⚵	**2:50 pm**	11:50 am
♃ △ ⚶	**7:35 pm**	4:35 pm
⚶ □ ⚷	**8:09 pm**	5:09 pm
♃ ⚻ ⚷	**8:43 pm**	5:43 pm
☽ ⚹ ☿	**11:58 pm**	8:58 pm

20 SUNDAY

☉ ⚻ ⚷	**3:28 am**	12:28 am
☉ ⚹ ♃	**5:29 am**	2:29 am
☽ ⚺ ♂	**7:41 am**	4:41 am
⚵ □ ⚶	**9:05 am**	6:05 am
☉ ⚻ ⚵	**9:16 am**	6:16 am
☉ ⚹ ⚶	**9:33 am**	6:33 am
☽ ⚹ ⚷	**12:26 pm**	9:26 am
☽ ⚻ ♃	**12:43 pm**	9:43 am
☽ ⚹ ⚵	**12:52 pm**	9:52 am
☽ ⚺ ⚶	**1:03 pm**	10:03 am
☽ □ ☉	**1:13 pm**	10:13 am
☽ △ ♀	**2:06 pm**	11:06 am
♃ ⚻ ⚵	**6:10 pm**	3:10 pm
☽ △ ♆	**10:38 pm**	7:38 pm

21 MONDAY

♅ ⚻ ⚳	**7:02 am**	4:02 am
☽ ⚹ ♇	**7:47 am**	4:47 am
☉ ⚺ ♀	**12:43 pm**	9:43 am
☽ ⚻ ♄	**5:11 pm**	2:11 pm
☽ ⚹ ♀	**8:44 pm**	5:44 pm
☽ △ ♅	**11:14 pm**	8:14 pm
☽ □ ⚳	**11:52 pm**	8:52 pm

22 TUESDAY

♂ ⚺ ⚵	**3:01 pm**	12:01 pm
⚵ ☌ ⚷	**5:14 pm**	2:14 pm
☽ □ ☿	**5:37 pm**	2:37 pm
☽ ☌ ♂	**7:31 pm**	4:31 pm
☽ ⚺ ⚵	**11:07 pm**	8:07 pm
☽ ⚺ ⚷	**11:10 pm**	8:10 pm
☽ ☍ ♃		9:36 pm
☽ ⚹ ⚶		11:09 pm

23 WEDNESDAY

☽ ☍ ♃	**12:36 am**	
☽ ⚹ ⚶	**2:09 am**	
☽ ⚻ ♀	**3:47 am**	12:47 am
☽ △ ☉	**5:22 am**	2:22 am
♀ ☍ ♅	**7:15 am**	4:15 am
☽ □ ♆	**9:56 am**	6:56 am
☿ □ ♂	**3:52 pm**	12:52 pm
☽ ⚺ ♇	**7:24 pm**	4:24 pm

24 THURSDAY

☽ ☍ ♄	**5:41 am**	2:41 am
☽ □ ♅	**11:15 am**	8:15 am
☽ □ ♀	**1:27 pm**	10:27 am
☽ △ ⚳	**2:19 pm**	11:19 am
☿ △ ⚵	**6:47 pm**	3:47 pm
☿ △ ⚷	**10:49 pm**	7:49 pm
♂ ⚺ ⚵	**11:35 pm**	8:35 pm

25 FRIDAY

☽ ⚺ ♂	**9:14 am**	6:14 am
☽ ☌ ⚵	**10:54 am**	7:54 am
☽ ☌ ⚷	**11:26 am**	8:26 am
☽ △ ☿	**12:50 pm**	9:50 am
☉ ⚻ ♆	**1:23 pm**	10:23 am
☽ ⚻ ♃	**2:00 pm**	11:00 am
♀ ⚺ ⚳	**2:51 pm**	11:51 am
☽ □ ⚶	**4:53 pm**	1:53 pm
☽ ☍ ♀	**7:02 pm**	4:02 pm
☽ ⚹ ♆	**10:26 pm**	7:26 pm
☽ ⚻ ☉	**11:15 pm**	8:15 pm

26 SATURDAY

☿ □ ♃	**3:22 am**	12:22 am
☽ ☌ ♇	**7:55 am**	4:55 am
☽ ⚻ ♄	**6:48 pm**	3:48 pm
☽ ⚹ ♅	**11:43 pm**	8:43 pm

27 SUNDAY

☽ ⚻ ⚳	**5:12 am**	2:12 am
☽ △ ♀	**6:30 am**	3:30 am
☽ ⚺ ⚵	**10:37 pm**	7:37 pm
☽ ⚹ ♂	**10:59 pm**	7:59 pm
☽ ⚺ ⚷	**11:35 pm**	8:35 pm

28 MONDAY

☽ △ ♃	**3:11 am**	12:11 am
☽ ⚻ ☿	**6:59 am**	3:59 am
☽ △ ⚶	**7:22 am**	4:22 am
☽ ⚻ ♀	**9:58 am**	6:58 am
☽ ⚺ ♆	**10:34 am**	7:34 am
☿ ⚺ ⚶	**2:38 pm**	11:38 am
☽ ☍ ☉	**4:38 pm**	1:38 pm
☽ ⚺ ♇	**7:53 pm**	4:53 pm
♆ △ ♀	**11:23 pm**	8:23 pm

29 TUESDAY

☽ △ ♄	**7:09 am**	4:09 am
☽ ⚺ ♅	**11:22 am**	8:22 am
☽ ☍ ⚳	**7:06 pm**	4:06 pm
☽ ⚻ ♀	**10:13 pm**	7:13 pm

30 WEDNESDAY

☿ ☍ ♆	**4:13 am**	1:13 am
☉ ⚻ ♇	**8:54 am**	5:54 am
☽ ⚹ ⚵	**9:17 am**	6:17 am
☽ ⚹ ⚷	**10:35 am**	7:35 am
☽ □ ♂	**11:37 am**	8:37 am
☽ □ ♃	**3:05 pm**	12:05 pm
☽ ⚻ ⚶	**8:27 pm**	5:27 pm
☽ ☌ ♆	**9:23 pm**	6:23 pm
☽ ☍ ☿	**10:41 pm**	7:41 pm
☽ △ ♀	**11:26 pm**	8:26 pm

Eastern Standard Time in bold type
Pacific Standard Time in medium type

JUNE 1999

☽ Last Aspect day	EST / hr:mn / PST	asp	☽ Ingress sign day	EST / hr:mn / PST
3	**3:39 am** 12:39 am	☍ ♀	♒ 3	**8:37 am** 5:37 am
5	**1:27 pm** 10:27 am	△ ☿	♓ 5	**6:01 pm** 3:01 pm
6	**11:21 pm** 8:21 pm	□ ☉	♈ 7	9:09 pm
6	**11:21 pm** 8:21 pm	□ ☉	♈ 8	**12:09 am**
9	**9:28 pm** 6:28 pm	☌ ♃	♉ 9	11:44 pm
9	**9:28 pm** 6:28 pm	☌ ♃	♉ 10	**2:44 am**
11	**5:35 am** 2:35 am	□ ♅	♊ 11	11:49 pm
11	**5:35 am** 2:35 am	□ ♅	♊ 12	**2:49 am**
13	**10:20 pm** 7:20 pm	⚹ ♃	♋ 13	11:14 pm
13	**10:20 pm** 7:20 pm	⚹ ♃	♋ 14	**2:14 am**
15	**11:39 pm** 8:39 pm	□ ♃	♌ 16	**3:07 am** 12:07 am
18	**4:10 am** 1:10 am	△ ♃	♍ 18	**7:12 am** 4:12 am
20	**1:13 pm** 10:13 am	□ ☉	♎ 20	**3:10 pm** 12:10 pm
22	9:36 pm	☍ ♃	♏ 22	11:18 pm
23	**12:36 am**	☍ ♃	♏ 23	**2:18 am**
25	**12:50 pm** 9:50 am	△ ☿	♐ 25	**2:51 pm** 11:51 am
28	**3:11 am** 12:11 am	△ ♃	♑ 28	**3:12 am** 12:12 am
30	**11:37 am** 8:37 am	□ ♂	♒ 30	**2:20 pm** 11:20 am

☽ Phases & Eclipses phase	day	EST / hr:mn / PST
4th Quarter	6	**11:21 pm** 8:21 pm
New Moon	13	**2:03 pm** 11:03 am
2nd Quarter	20	**1:13 pm** 10:13 am
Full Moon	28	**4:38 pm** 1:38 pm

Planet Ingress	day	EST / hr:mn / PST
♀ ♌	5	**4:25 pm** 1:25 pm
☿ ♋	6	**7:18 pm** 4:18 pm
⚵ ♐	13	**7:58 pm** 4:58 pm
♀ ♊	21	**4:44 pm** 1:44 pm
☉ ♋	21	**2:49 pm** 11:49 am
⚶ ♍	23	**6:22 am** 3:22 am
☿ ♌	26	**10:39 am** 7:39 am
♃ ♉	28	**4:27 am** 1:27 am

Planetary Motion	day	EST / hr:mn / PST
♂ D	3	10:12 pm
♂ D	4	**1:12 am**

DATE		SID.TIME	SUN	MOON	NODE	MERCURY	VENUS	MARS	JUPITER	SATURN	URANUS	NEPTUNE	PLUTO	CERES	PALLAS	JUNO	VESTA	CHIRON
T	1	16:36:09	10 ♊ 05	28 ♐ 57	14 ♌ R 53	17 ♊ 42	25 ♋ 04	24 ♎ R 31	24 ♈ 59	11 ♉ 03	16 ♒ R 45	04 ♒ R 12	09 ♐ R 06	07 ♋ 38	19 ♉ 39	02 ♐ R 44	21 ♌ 23	29 ♏ R 51
W	2	16:40:05	11 02	10 ♑ 57	14 46	19 49	26 05	24 29	25 12	11 10	16 45	04 11	09 05	08 03	20 08	02 31	21 44	29 47
T	3	16:44:02	12 00	23 04	14 42	21 55	27 06	24 27	25 24	11 17	16 44	04 11	09 03	08 28	20 37	02 17	22 06	29 43
F	4	16:47:58	12 57	05 ♒ 19	14 D 41	23 59	28 06	24 27	25 36	11 24	16 43	04 10	09 01	08 54	21 07	02 04	22 28	29 39
S	5	16:51:55	13 55	17 48	14 41	26 01	29 07	24 D 27	25 48	11 31	16 43	04 09	09 00	09 19	21 36	01 51	22 50	29 34
S	6	16:55:52	14 52	00 ♓ 32	14 43	28 01	00 ♌ 06	24 28	26 00	11 38	16 42	04 08	08 58	09 45	22 06	01 38	23 12	29 30
M	7	16:59:48	15 49	13 36	14 R 44	29 59	01 06	24 30	26 11	11 44	16 41	04 07	08 56	10 10	22 35	01 25	23 34	29 26
T	8	17:03:45	16 47	27 04	14 43	01 ♋ 54	02 05	24 32	26 23	11 51	16 41	04 06	08 55	10 36	23 05	01 13	23 56	29 22
W	9	17:07:41	17 44	10 ♈ 57	14 41	03 47	03 04	24 36	26 35	11 58	16 40	04 05	08 53	11 02	23 34	01 00	24 19	29 18
T	10	17:11:38	18 42	25 17	14 37	05 38	04 02	24 40	26 46	12 05	16 39	04 04	08 52	11 27	24 04	00 48	24 41	29 14
F	11	17:15:34	19 39	10 ♉ 01	14 31	07 26	05 00	24 44	26 57	12 11	16 38	04 03	08 50	11 53	24 33	00 36	25 04	29 10
S	12	17:19:31	20 36	25 04	14 23	09 12	05 58	24 50	27 09	12 18	16 37	04 02	08 48	12 19	25 03	00 24	25 27	29 06
S	13	17:23:27	21 34	10 ♊ 16	14 15	10 55	06 55	24 56	27 20	12 24	16 36	04 01	08 47	12 45	25 33	00 12	25 50	29 02
M	14	17:27:24	22 31	25 27	14 08	12 36	07 51	25 03	27 31	12 31	16 35	04 00	08 45	13 11	26 03	00 00	26 13	28 58
T	15	17:31:21	23 28	10 ♋ 27	14 02	14 14	08 47	25 11	27 42	12 37	16 34	03 59	08 44	13 37	26 33	29 ♏ 49	26 37	28 55
W	16	17:35:17	24 26	25 08	13 D 58	15 49	09 43	25 19	27 53	12 44	16 33	03 58	08 42	14 02	27 03	29 38	27 00	28 51
T	17	17:39:14	25 23	09 ♌ 23	13 55	17 22	10 38	25 28	28 04	12 50	16 32	03 57	08 41	14 28	27 33	29 27	27 24	28 47
F	18	17:43:10	26 20	23 10	13 55	18 53	11 33	25 38	28 15	12 57	16 30	03 55	08 39	14 54	28 03	29 16	27 48	28 44
S	19	17:47:07	27 18	06 ♍ 30	13 56	20 20	12 27	25 49	28 25	13 03	16 29	03 54	08 37	15 20	28 33	29 06	28 12	28 40
S	20	17:51:03	28 15	19 25	13 R 57	21 45	13 20	26 00	28 36	13 09	16 28	03 53	08 36	15 47	29 03	28 55	28 36	28 37
M	21	17:55:00	29 12	01 ♎ 59	13 57	23 08	14 13	26 11	28 46	13 15	16 26	03 52	08 34	16 13	29 33	28 46	29 00	28 33
T	22	17:58:56	00 ♋ 09	14 16	13 56	24 27	15 05	26 24	28 57	13 21	16 25	03 50	08 33	16 39	00 ♊ 03	28 36	29 24	28 30
W	23	18:02:53	01 07	26 21	13 54	25 44	15 57	26 37	29 07	13 27	16 24	03 49	08 31	17 05	00 33	28 26	29 48	28 27
T	24	18:06:50	02 04	08 ♏ 18	13 49	26 58	16 48	26 50	29 17	13 33	16 22	03 48	08 30	17 31	01 03	28 17	00 ♍ 13	28 24
F	25	18:10:46	03 01	20 11	13 43	28 09	17 38	27 04	29 27	13 39	16 21	03 47	08 29	17 57	01 34	28 08	00 38	28 21
S	26	18:14:43	03 58	02 ♐ 03	13 36	29 17	18 27	27 19	29 37	13 45	16 19	03 45	08 27	18 24	02 04	28 00	01 02	28 18
S	27	18:18:39	04 56	13 56	13 28	00 ♌ 22	19 16	27 35	29 47	13 51	16 17	03 44	08 26	18 50	02 34	27 52	01 27	28 15
M	28	18:22:36	05 53	25 54	13 22	01 24	20 04	27 51	29 56	13 56	16 16	03 42	08 24	19 16	03 05	27 44	01 52	28 12
T	29	18:26:32	06 50	07 ♑ 56	13 16	02 23	20 52	28 07	00 ♉ 06	14 02	16 14	03 41	08 23	19 42	03 35	27 36	02 17	28 09
W	30	18:30:29	07 47	20 06	13 13	03 19	21 38	28 24	00 15	14 08	16 13	03 40	08 22	20 09	04 06	27 28	02 42	28 06

EPHEMERIS CALCULATED FOR 12 MIDNIGHT GREENWICH MEAN TIME. ALL OTHER DATA AND FACING ASPECTARIAN PAGE IN **EASTERN STANDARD TIME (BOLD)** AND PACIFIC STANDARD TIME (REGULAR).

JULY 1999

1 THURSDAY

☽ ⚹ ♇	**6:26 am**	3:26 am
☽ ⚻ ☉	**8:16 am**	5:16 am
☽ □ ♄	**5:55 pm**	2:55 pm
☽ ☌ ♅	**9:26 pm**	6:26 pm
♆ ⚻ ⚴	**10:14 pm**	7:14 pm

2 FRIDAY

☿ ⚹ ♀	**6:22 am**	3:22 am
☽ ⚻ ⚳	**7:07 am**	4:07 am
☽ ☍ ♀	**11:39 am**	8:39 am
☽ □ ⚵	**6:13 pm**	3:13 pm
☽ □ ⚷	**7:47 pm**	4:47 pm
☽ △ ♂	**10:22 pm**	7:22 pm
☽ ⚹ ♃		9:59 pm

3 SATURDAY

☽ ⚹ ♃	**12:59 am**	
☽ ⚺ ♆	**6:15 am**	3:15 am
☽ ☍ ⚴	**7:25 am**	4:25 am
☽ □ ♀	**10:41 am**	7:41 am
☽ ⚻ ☿	**11:09 am**	8:09 am
☽ □ ♇	**2:58 pm**	11:58 am
☽ △ ☉	**9:16 pm**	6:16 pm
☽ ⚹ ♄		11:26 pm

4 SUNDAY

☽ ⚹ ♄	**2:26 am**	
☽ ⚺ ♅	**5:17 am**	2:17 am
☽ △ ⚳	**4:34 pm**	1:34 pm
☽ ⚻ ♀	**10:05 pm**	7:05 pm
☽ △ ⚵		9:51 pm
☽ △ ⚷		11:36 pm

5 MONDAY

☽ △ ⚵	**12:51 am**	
☽ △ ⚷	**2:36 am**	
☽ ⚻ ♂	**6:33 am**	3:33 am
☽ ⚺ ♃	**8:18 am**	5:18 am
☽ ⚹ ♆	**12:37 pm**	9:37 am
☽ ⚻ ⚴	**3:35 pm**	12:35 pm
☽ ⚹ ♀	**7:02 pm**	4:02 pm
☽ △ ☿	**7:51 pm**	4:51 pm
☽ △ ♇	**8:54 pm**	5:54 pm

6 TUESDAY

☽ □ ☉	**6:57 am**	3:57 am
☽ ⚺ ♄	**8:12 am**	5:12 am
☽ ⚹ ♅	**10:27 am**	7:27 am
☽ □ ⚳	**10:59 pm**	7:59 pm
♀ □ ⚵	**11:25 pm**	8:25 pm
☿ △ ♇		9:25 pm
☉ ⚹ ♄		11:48 pm

7 WEDNESDAY

☿ △ ♇	**12:25 am**	
☉ ⚹ ♄	**2:48 am**	
☽ ⚻ ⚵	**4:49 am**	1:49 am
☽ △ ♀	**5:07 am**	2:07 am
☽ ⚻ ⚷	**6:39 am**	3:39 am
☽ ☍ ♂	**11:50 am**	8:50 am
☽ ☌ ♃	**12:43 pm**	9:43 am
☽ □ ♆	**4:13 pm**	1:13 pm
♇ ☍ ♀	**7:11 pm**	4:11 pm
☽ △ ⚴	**8:44 pm**	5:44 pm
☽ ⚻ ♇		9:06 pm
☽ ⚺ ♀		9:18 pm
☽ □ ☿		9:49 pm

8 THURSDAY

☽ ⚻ ♇	**12:06 am**	
☽ ⚺ ♀	**12:18 am**	
☽ □ ☿	**12:49 am**	
☉ ⚻ ♅	**8:17 am**	5:17 am
☽ ☌ ♄	**11:14 am**	8:14 am
☽ □ ♅	**12:59 pm**	9:59 am
☽ ⚹ ☉	**1:19 pm**	10:19 am
♀ □ ⚷	**1:53 pm**	10:53 am
☽ ⚹ ⚳		11:38 pm

9 FRIDAY

☽ ⚹ ⚳	**2:38 am**	
☽ ☍ ⚵	**6:24 am**	3:24 am
☽ ☍ ⚷	**8:19 am**	5:19 am
☽ □ ♀	**9:09 am**	6:09 am
☿ ⚹ ♀	**12:32 pm**	9:32 am
☽ ⚻ ♂	**2:38 pm**	11:38 am
☽ ⚺ ♃	**2:44 pm**	11:44 am
☽ △ ♆	**5:33 pm**	2:33 pm
♂ ☍ ♃	**8:22 pm**	5:22 pm
☽ □ ⚴	**11:29 pm**	8:29 pm
☽ ☍ ♇		10:12 pm
☽ ⚹ ☿		11:56 pm

10 SATURDAY

☽ ☍ ♇	**1:12 am**	
☽ ⚹ ☿	**2:56 am**	
☽ ☌ ♀	**3:13 am**	12:13 am
☽ ⚺ ♄	**12:22 pm**	9:22 am
☽ △ ♅	**1:41 pm**	10:41 am
☽ ⚺ ☉	**5:28 pm**	2:28 pm

11 SUNDAY

☽ ⚺ ⚳	**4:41 am**	1:41 am
☽ ⚻ ⚵	**6:42 am**	3:42 am
☽ ⚻ ⚷	**8:42 am**	5:42 am
☽ ⚹ ♀	**11:37 am**	8:37 am
☽ ⚹ ♃	**3:36 pm**	12:36 pm
☽ △ ♂	**4:20 pm**	1:20 pm
☽ ⚻ ♆	**5:53 pm**	2:53 pm
☽ ⚹ ⚴		10:23 pm
☽ ⚻ ♇		10:33 pm

12 MONDAY

☽ ⚹ ⚴	**1:23 am**	
☽ ⚻ ♇	**1:33 am**	
☽ ⚺ ☿	**3:47 am**	12:47 am
☽ ⚺ ♀	**5:23 am**	2:23 am
♇ □ ⚴	**6:57 am**	3:57 am
☽ ⚹ ♄	**1:07 pm**	10:07 am
☽ ⚻ ♅	**2:04 pm**	11:04 am
☽ ☌ ☉	**9:24 pm**	6:24 pm

13 TUESDAY

☽ ☌ ⚳	**6:59 am**	3:59 am
☽ △ ⚵	**7:21 am**	4:21 am
☽ △ ⚷	**9:29 am**	6:29 am
☽ ⚺ ♀	**2:27 pm**	11:27 am
☽ □ ♃	**5:06 pm**	2:06 pm
⚳ △ ⚵	**5:50 pm**	2:50 pm
☽ □ ♂	**6:47 pm**	3:47 pm
☽ ☍ ♆	**6:56 pm**	3:56 pm
♂ □ ♆	**11:52 pm**	8:52 pm
☽ △ ♇		11:55 pm

14 WEDNESDAY

☽ △ ♇	**2:55 am**	
☽ ⚺ ⚴	**4:23 am**	1:23 am
☽ ☌ ☿	**5:10 am**	2:10 am
☽ ⚹ ♀	**8:50 am**	5:50 am
☽ □ ♄	**3:18 pm**	12:18 pm
☽ ☍ ♅	**3:54 pm**	12:54 pm
☿ ⚺ ⚴	**11:33 pm**	8:33 pm

15 THURSDAY

☽ ⚺ ☉	**3:26 am**	12:26 am
☽ □ ⚵	**10:03 am**	7:03 am
☽ ⚺ ⚳	**11:31 am**	8:31 am
☽ □ ⚷	**12:23 pm**	9:23 am
☽ ☌ ♀	**7:38 pm**	4:38 pm
☽ △ ♃	**9:01 pm**	6:01 pm
☽ ⚻ ♆	**10:24 pm**	7:24 pm
☽ ⚹ ♂	**11:55 pm**	8:55 pm

16 FRIDAY

☽ □ ♇	**6:55 am**	3:55 am
☽ ⚺ ☿	**8:37 am**	5:37 am
☽ ☌ ⚴	**10:21 am**	7:21 am
⚳ △ ⚷	**12:55 pm**	9:55 am
☽ □ ♀	**3:26 pm**	12:26 pm
☽ △ ♄	**8:30 pm**	5:30 pm
☽ ⚻ ♅	**8:43 pm**	5:43 pm

17 SATURDAY

☽ ⚹ ☉	**1:28 pm**	10:28 am
☽ ⚹ ⚵	**4:09 pm**	1:09 pm
☽ ⚹ ⚷	**6:41 pm**	3:41 pm
☽ ⚹ ⚳	**7:48 pm**	4:48 pm
♄ □ ♅	**10:58 pm**	7:58 pm

18 SUNDAY

☽ ⚺ ♀	**4:26 am**	1:26 am
☽ ⚻ ♃	**4:31 am**	1:31 am
☽ △ ♆	**5:22 am**	2:22 am
♀ △ ♃	**8:06 am**	5:06 am
☽ ⚺ ♂	**9:01 am**	6:01 am
☽ ⚹ ♇	**2:31 pm**	11:31 am
☽ ⚹ ☿	**2:49 pm**	11:49 am
☽ ⚺ ⚴	**8:21 pm**	5:21 pm
☿ △ ♇	**11:32 pm**	8:32 pm
☉ △ ⚵		9:50 pm
☽ △ ♀		11:08 pm

19 MONDAY

☉ △ ⚵	**12:50 am**	
☽ △ ♀	**2:08 am**	
☽ △ ♅	**5:08 am**	2:08 am
☽ ⚻ ♄	**5:24 am**	2:24 am
♀ ⚻ ♆	**9:26 am**	6:26 am
☽ ⚺ ⚵		10:51 pm

20 TUESDAY

☽ ⚺ ⚵	**1:51 am**	
☽ □ ☉	**4:01 am**	1:01 am
☽ ⚺ ⚷	**4:32 am**	1:32 am
☽ □ ⚳	**8:00 am**	5:00 am
☉ △ ⚷	**10:33 am**	7:33 am
☽ ☍ ♃	**3:31 pm**	12:31 pm
☽ □ ♆	**3:44 pm**	12:44 pm
☽ ⚹ ♀	**4:41 pm**	1:41 pm
☽ ☌ ♂	**9:54 pm**	6:54 pm
☽ □ ☿	**11:20 pm**	8:20 pm
☽ ⚺ ♇		10:23 pm

21 WEDNESDAY

☽ ⚺ ♇	**1:23 am**	
☽ ⚹ ⚴	**9:53 am**	6:53 am
♃ □ ♆	**10:55 am**	7:55 am
☿ □ ♂	**3:07 pm**	12:07 pm
☽ ⚻ ♀	**4:16 pm**	1:16 pm
☽ □ ♅	**4:29 pm**	1:29 pm
☽ ☍ ♄	**5:16 pm**	2:16 pm
♅ △ ♀	**8:54 pm**	5:54 pm

22 THURSDAY

☽ ☌ ⚵	**1:59 pm**	10:59 am
☽ ☌ ⚷	**4:41 pm**	1:41 pm
♄ ⚺ ♀	**6:22 pm**	3:22 pm
☽ △ ☉	**9:28 pm**	6:28 pm
☽ △ ⚳	**10:39 pm**	7:39 pm

23 FRIDAY

☽ ⚹ ♆	**3:59 am**	12:59 am
☽ ⚻ ♃	**4:27 am**	1:27 am
☽ □ ♀	**6:34 am**	3:34 am
☽ △ ☿	**8:44 am**	5:44 am
☽ ⚺ ♂	**12:46 pm**	9:46 am
☽ ☌ ♇	**1:49 pm**	10:49 am
☉ ☌ ⚳	**11:45 pm**	8:45 pm
☽ □ ⚴		9:52 pm

24 SATURDAY

☽ □ ⚴	**12:52 am**	
☽ ⚹ ♅	**4:52 am**	1:52 am
☽ ⚻ ♄	**6:10 am**	3:10 am
☽ ☍ ♀	**7:37 am**	4:37 am
☿ ⚺ ♀	**12:34 pm**	9:34 am
♂ ⚺ ♇	**3:22 pm**	12:22 pm
☽ ⚺ ⚵		11:28 pm

25 SUNDAY

☽ ⚺ ⚵	**2:28 am**	
☽ ⚺ ⚷	**5:03 am**	2:03 am
☽ ⚻ ⚳	**1:17 pm**	10:17 am
☽ ⚻ ☉	**2:59 pm**	11:59 am
☽ ⚺ ♆	**4:06 pm**	1:06 pm
☽ △ ♃	**5:10 pm**	2:10 pm
☽ ⚻ ☿	**5:35 pm**	2:35 pm
☽ △ ♀	**7:44 pm**	4:44 pm
☿ □ ♃	**11:44 pm**	8:44 pm
☽ ⚺ ♇		10:48 pm

26 MONDAY

☽ ⚺ ♇	**1:48 am**	
☽ ⚹ ♂	**3:13 am**	12:13 am
☉ ☍ ♆	**4:32 am**	1:32 am
☿ ☌ ☉	**10:48 am**	7:48 am
☽ △ ⚴	**2:58 pm**	11:58 am
☽ ⚺ ♅	**4:21 pm**	1:21 pm
☽ △ ♄	**6:06 pm**	3:06 pm
☿ ☍ ♆	**7:49 pm**	4:49 pm
☉ □ ♃	**9:06 pm**	6:06 pm
☽ ⚻ ♀	**9:51 pm**	6:51 pm

27 TUESDAY

☿ ☌ ⚳	**12:54 pm**	9:54 am
☽ ⚹ ⚵	**1:36 pm**	10:36 am
☽ ⚹ ⚷	**3:58 pm**	12:58 pm
♅ ⚻ ⚴		9:52 pm
☽ ☍ ☿		9:59 pm
☽ ☍ ⚳		11:07 pm
☽ ☌ ♆		11:32 pm

28 WEDNESDAY

♅ ⚻ ⚴	**12:52 am**	
☽ ☍ ☿	**12:59 am**	
☽ ☍ ⚳	**2:07 am**	
☽ ☌ ♆	**2:32 am**	
☽ □ ♃	**4:06 am**	1:06 am
☽ ☍ ☉	**6:25 am**	3:25 am
☽ ⚻ ♀	**6:39 am**	3:39 am
♀ ⚺ ☉	**9:38 am**	6:38 am
☽ ⚹ ♇	**11:57 am**	8:57 am
♆ ☍ ⚳	**1:06 pm**	10:06 am
☽ □ ♂	**3:39 pm**	12:39 pm
☽ ☌ ♅		10:50 pm
☽ ⚻ ⚴		11:52 pm

29 THURSDAY

☽ ☌ ♅	**1:50 am**	
☽ ⚻ ⚴	**2:52 am**	
☽ □ ♄	**3:56 am**	12:56 am
☽ △ ♀	**9:45 am**	6:45 am
☽ □ ⚵	**10:35 pm**	7:35 pm
☽ □ ⚷		9:42 pm

30 FRIDAY

☽ □ ⚷	**12:42 am**	
☽ ⚻ ☿	**6:44 am**	3:44 am
☽ ⚺ ♆	**10:44 am**	7:44 am
♄ △ ⚴	**12:09 pm**	9:09 am
☽ ⚻ ⚳	**12:27 pm**	9:27 am
☽ ⚹ ♃	**12:44 pm**	9:44 am
☽ ☍ ♀	**2:53 pm**	11:53 am
☽ ⚻ ☉	**7:00 pm**	4:00 pm
☽ □ ♇	**7:51 pm**	4:51 pm
♃ □ ⚳	**10:20 pm**	7:20 pm
☽ △ ♂		10:37 pm

31 SATURDAY

☽ △ ♂	**1:37 am**	
☉ △ ♇	**6:28 am**	3:28 am
☽ ⚺ ♅	**9:04 am**	6:04 am
☽ ⚹ ♄	**11:28 am**	8:28 am
☽ ☍ ⚴	**12:14 pm**	9:14 am
☽ □ ♀	**7:05 pm**	4:05 pm

Eastern Standard Time in bold type
Pacific Standard Time in medium type

JULY 1999

EPHEMERIS CALCULATED FOR 12 MIDNIGHT GREENWICH MEAN TIME. ALL OTHER DATA AND FACING ASPECTARIAN PAGE IN **EASTERN STANDARD TIME (BOLD)** AND PACIFIC STANDARD TIME (REGULAR).

D Last Aspect / D Ingress (first set)

D Last Aspect day	EST / hr:mn / PST	asp	D Ingress sign day	EST / hr:mn / PST
2	10:22 am 7:22 am	△♂	✶ 2	11:35 am 8:35 am
4	2:26 am	✶♄	♈ 4	6:22 am 3:22 am
5	5:07 am 2:07 am	□♀	♉ 5	6:22 am 3:22 am
9	9:09 am 6:09 am	□♀	♊ 7	10:22 am 7:22 am
11	11:37 am 8:37 am		♋ 9	11:59 am 8:59 am
12	8:24 am 5:24 am	♂♀	♌ 11	12:27 pm 9:27 am
13	3:54 am 12:54 am		♍ 13	1:25 pm 10:25 am
17	1:28 am 10:28 am		♎ 15	5:39 pm 1:39 pm
20	4:01 am 1:01 am		♏ 17	11:19 pm 8:19 pm
			♐ 20	9:30 am 6:30 am

D Last Aspect / D Ingress (second set)

D Last Aspect day	EST / hr:mn / PST	asp	D Ingress sign day	EST / hr:mn / PST
22	9:28 am	△⊙	♐ 22	9:49 pm 6:49 pm
24	4:52 am 1:52 am	✶♀	♑ 25	10:09 am 7:09 am
26	6:06 pm 3:06 pm		♒ 27	8:55 pm 5:55 pm
29	3:56 am 12:56 am	□♃	♓ 30	5:27 am 2:27 am

Phases & Eclipses

phase	day	EST / hr:mn / PST
4th Quarter	6	6:57 am 3:57 am
New Moon	12	9:24 am 6:24 am
2nd Quarter	20	4:01 am 1:01 am
Full Moon	28	6:25 am 3:25 am
	28	4° ♒ 58'

Planet Ingress

	day	EST / hr:mn / PST
♂ ♏	4	11:00 pm 8:00 pm
♀ ♍	12	10:18 am 7:18 am
♀ ♌	22	12:40 am
⊙ ♌	23	1:44 am
♀ ℞	31	1:44 pm 10:44 pm

Planetary Motion

	day	EST / hr:mn / PST
♀ ℞	12	6:26 pm 3:26 pm
✶	21	9:48 pm
♀	22	12:48 am
♂	28	2:30 pm 11:30 am
♀ ℞	29	8:41 pm 5:41 pm

Ephemeris Table

DATE	SID.TIME	SUN	MOON	NODE	MERCURY	VENUS	MARS	JUPITER	SATURN	URANUS	NEPTUNE	PLUTO	CERES	PALLAS	JUNO	VESTA	CHIRON
1 T	18:34:25	08♋		02	04♋	22♌	28♎	24♈	14♉	13♒	03♒	08♐	20♏	04♊	17♉	03♍	28♏
2 F	18:38:22	09 42		01		23	29	28	00	14	35	03	08	21	05	18	04	27
3 S	18:42:19	10				24	29	18		14	24	03	08	21	06	18	05	27
4 S	18:46:15	11 36	10♓28	15	06	24			00	14	36	03	08	21	06	19	06	27
5 M	18:50:12	12 33	23 39	17	07	25		57	01	14	35	03	08	22	06	20	08	27
6 T	18:54:08	13 30	07♈	17	08	25			01	14	45	03	08	23	07	20	10	27
7 W	18:58:05	14	20	17	09	26			01	14	50	03	08	23	07	21	11	27
8 T	19:02:01	15	03♉58	13	10	27			01	14	55	03	08	24	08	22	12	27
9 F	19:05:58	16	17	13	11	27		20	02	14	00	03	08	24	08	22	14	27
10 S	19:09:54	17	01♊19	13	12	28			02	14	05	03	08	25	09	23	15	27
11 S	19:13:51	18	14	10	16	29		04	02	15	05	03	08	25	09	24	17	27
12 M	19:17:48	19	28	08	18	29			02	15	40	03	08	26	10	24	18	27
13 T	19:21:44	20	11♋48	06	20	01		37	02	15	44	03	08	26	10	25	19	27
14 W	19:25:41	21	25	05	21	02			02	15	48	03	08	27	11	26	21	27
15 T	19:29:37	22	09♌36	03	23	03			02	15	52	03	08	27	12	26	22	27
16 F	19:33:34	23	23	01	24	04			03	15	56	03	08	28	12	27	24	27
17 S	19:37:30	24	07♍	00	26	05		32	03	16	00	03	08	28	13	28	25	27
18 S	19:41:27	24 57	20	58	57	24		52	03	16	04	03	08	00	14	28	26	27
19 M	19:45:23	25 54	04♎	54	54	25			03	16	11	03	08	00	14	29	28	27
20 T	19:49:20	26 51	17	48	49	26			03	16	15	03	08	01	15	29	29	27
21 W	19:53:17	27 48	01♏	46	46	27		43	03	16	19	03	07	01	16	00♋	01♎	27
22 T	19:57:13	28 46	14	46	43	28			03	16	23	03	07	02	16	00	02	27
23 F	20:01:10	29 43	27	26	00	01			03	16	28	03	07	02	17	01	04	27
24 S	20:05:06	00♌41	10♐	24	01	02		53	03	16	32	03	07	03	18	01	05	27 D
25 S	20:09:03	01 38	23	22	02	03			03	16	36	03	07	03	18	02	06	27
26 M	20:12:59	02 35	06♑	20	04	04			03	16	40	02	07	04	19	02	08	27
27 T	20:16:56	03 33	18	00	05	06		20	03	16	44	02	07	04	19	03	09	27
28 W	20:20:52	04 30	00♒	58	07	08			03	17	48	02	07	05	20	03	10	27
29 T	20:24:49	05 27	11	56	09	10	05♏ ℞		03	17	53	02	07	05	20	04	12	27
30 F	20:28:45	06 25	23	56					03	17	58	02	07	06	21	04	13	26
31 S	20:32:42	07 22	05♓	56					03	18	58	02	07	06	21	05	14	26

AUGUST 1999

1 SUNDAY

5:22 am / 2:22 am · 7:14 am / 4:14 am · 11:03 am / 8:03 am · 4:45 pm / 1:45 pm · 7:05 pm / 4:05 pm · 8:21 pm / 5:21 pm · 8:33 pm / 5:33 pm · 10:23 pm · 10:36 pm

2 MONDAY

1:23 am · 1:36 am · 4:52 am / 1:52 am · 9:13 am / 6:13 am · 2:13 pm / 11:13 am · 4:52 pm / 1:52 pm · 7:17 pm / 4:17 pm

3 TUESDAY

2:07 am · 10:10 am / 7:10 am · 11:46 am / 8:46 am · 2:12 pm / 11:12 am · 8:50 pm / 5:50 pm · 11:28 pm / 8:28 pm · 9:02 pm · 11:08 pm

4 WEDNESDAY

12:02 am · 2:08 am · 5:28 am / 2:28 am · 2:50 am · 5:35 am / 2:35 am · 8:28 am / 5:28 am · 9:24 am

5 THURSDAY

12:24 am / 12:50 am · 3:50 am / 12:50 am · 7:14 am / 4:14 am · 1:22 pm / 10:22 am · 2:44 pm / 11:44 am · 4:35 pm / 1:35 pm

6 FRIDAY

1:49 am · 2:19 am · 8:20 am / 5:20 am · 7:57 am · 6:23 am / 3:23 am · 7:03 am / 4:03 am · 7:43 am / 4:43 am · 10:50 pm / 7:50 pm

7 SATURDAY

4:16 am / 1:16 am · 11:11 am / 8:11 am · 11:54 am / 8:54 am · 1:38 pm / 10:38 am · 3:37 pm / 12:37 pm · 3:56 pm / 12:56 pm · 4:45 pm / 1:45 pm · 6:50 pm / 3:50 pm · 10:14 pm · 11:37 pm

8 SUNDAY

1:14 am · 2:37 am · 4:24 am / 1:24 am · 9:19 am / 6:19 am · 9:46 am / 6:46 am · 9:25 am · 9:47 am / 6:47 am · 10:48 pm / 7:48 pm · 11:47 pm · 8:47 pm · 9:49 pm

9 MONDAY

12:49 am · 7:51 am / 4:51 am · 3:01 am / 12:01 am · 3:51 am / 12:51 am · 5:55 am / 2:55 am · 6:49 am / 3:49 am · 10:01 am / 7:01 am

10 TUESDAY

3:16 am / 12:16 am · 3:24 am / 12:24 am

11 WEDNESDAY

6:45 am / 3:45 am · 7:56 am / 4:56 am · 12:02 pm / 9:02 am · 3:27 am / 12:27 am · 3:36 am / 12:36 am · 6:20 am / 3:20 am · 6:23 am / 3:23 am · 9:28 am / 6:28 am · 8:11 pm / 5:11 pm · 8:10 pm · 10:43 pm · 8:50 pm

12 THURSDAY

3:40 am / 12:40 am · 5:20 am / 2:20 am · 6:47 am / 3:47 am · 10:41 am / 7:41 am · 4:02 pm / 1:02 pm · 5:23 pm / 2:36 pm · 10:31 pm / 7:31 pm

13 FRIDAY

4:16 am / 1:16 am · 8:30 am / 5:30 am · 10:31 am / 7:31 am · 3:12 pm / 12:12 pm · 3:47 pm / 12:47 pm · 7:50 pm / 4:50 pm · 11:36 pm

14 SATURDAY

2:36 am · 3:45 am / 12:45 am · 4:08 am / 1:08 am · 9:26 am / 6:26 am · 12:59 pm / 9:59 am · 1:32 pm / 10:32 am · 5:23 pm / 2:23 pm · 10:53 pm / 7:53 pm

15 SUNDAY

4:41 am / 1:41 am · 11:42 am / 8:42 am · 4:06 pm / 1:06 pm · 9:08 pm / 6:08 pm · 10:40 pm / 7:40 pm · 11:50 pm

16 MONDAY

4:11 am / 1:11 am · 5:06 am / 2:06 am · 6:40 am / 3:40 am · 1:07 pm / 10:07 am · 1:14 pm / 10:14 am · 3:43 pm / 12:43 pm · 4:12 pm / 1:12 pm · 9:17 pm / 6:17 pm · 10:24 pm / 7:24 pm

17 TUESDAY

3:18 am / 12:18 am · 4:49 am / 1:49 am · 8:56 am / 5:56 am · 5:18 pm / 2:18 pm · 10:12 pm / 7:12 pm

18 WEDNESDAY

12:30 am · 11:12 am / 8:12 am · 4:17 pm / 1:17 pm · 6:13 pm / 3:13 pm · 6:59 pm / 3:59 pm · 8:41 pm / 5:41 pm · 8:48 pm / 5:48 pm · 9:52 pm · 10:07 pm · 10:40 pm

19 THURSDAY

12:52 am · 1:07 am · 1:40 am · 6:17 am / 3:17 am · 10:16 am / 7:16 am · 12:59 pm / 9:59 am · 3:31 pm / 12:31 pm · 9:10 pm / 6:10 pm · 9:46 pm

20 FRIDAY

12:46 am · 6:58 am / 3:58 am · 8:03 am / 5:03 am · 10:27 am / 7:27 am · 1:06 pm / 10:06 am · 10:40 pm / 7:40 pm · 11:50 pm

21 SATURDAY

2:50 am · 4:22 am / 1:22 am · 11:47 am / 8:47 am · 2:36 pm / 11:36 am · 6:36 pm / 3:36 pm · 9:30 pm / 6:30 pm · 10:33 pm / 7:33 pm

22 SUNDAY

3:55 am / 12:55 am · 9:24 am / 6:24 am · 3:58 pm / 12:58 pm · 8:32 pm / 5:32 pm · 9:59 pm / 6:59 pm · 10:10 pm / 7:10 pm · 11:22 pm / 8:22 pm · 10:05 pm

23 MONDAY

1:05 am · 3:55 am / 12:55 am · 5:13 pm / 2:13 pm · 5:50 pm / 2:50 pm · 6:58 pm / 3:58 pm · 10:00 pm · 10:16 pm · 11:33 pm

24 TUESDAY

1:00 am · 1:16 am · 2:33 am · 6:29 am / 3:29 am · 9:05 am / 6:05 am · 10:44 am / 7:44 am · 12:23 pm / 9:23 am · 2:20 pm / 11:20 am · 7:34 pm / 4:34 pm

25 WEDNESDAY

7:33 am / 4:33 am · 9:55 am / 6:55 am · 1:13 pm / 10:13 am · 3:33 pm / 12:33 pm · 4:41 pm / 1:41 pm

26 THURSDAY

9:17 pm · 10:04 pm · 12:17 am · 1:04 am · 1:31 am · 4:31 am / 1:31 am · 9:24 am / 6:24 am · 11:21 am / 8:21 am · 11:38 am / 8:38 am · 4:46 pm / 1:46 pm · 6:48 pm / 3:48 pm · 8:44 pm / 5:44 pm · 9:51 pm / 6:51 pm · 11:50 pm

27 FRIDAY

2:50 am · 2:04 pm / 11:04 am · 3:42 pm / 12:42 pm · 6:20 pm / 3:20 pm · 7:38 pm / 4:38 pm · 9:26 pm

28 SATURDAY

12:26 am · 4:52 am / 1:52 am · 7:35 am / 4:35 am · 12:25 pm / 9:25 am · 3:03 pm / 12:03 pm · 5:24 pm / 2:24 pm · 6:59 pm / 3:59 pm · 9:50 pm / 6:50 pm · 11:45 pm · 11:53 pm

29 SUNDAY

2:45 am · 2:53 am · 3:49 am / 12:49 am · 3:51 am / 12:51 am · 7:37 am / 4:37 am · 10:05 am / 7:05 am · 6:17 pm / 3:17 pm · 11:48 pm / 8:48 pm · 9:15 pm

30 MONDAY

12:15 am · 7:02 am / 4:02 am · 10:01 am / 7:01 am

31 TUESDAY

1:46 am / 10:46 pm · 6:42 am / 3:42 am · 6:51 am / 3:51 am · 7:39 am / 4:39 am · 9:35 am / 6:35 am · 10:41 am / 7:41 am · 9:23 pm · 10:12 pm · 12:23 am · 1:12 am · 6:02 am / 3:02 am · 9:05 am / 6:05 am · 10:21 am / 7:21 am · 10:52 am / 7:52 am · 10:55 am / 7:55 am · 9:12 pm / 6:12 pm · 10:52 pm / 7:52 pm · 11:46 pm

Eastern Standard Time in bold type
Pacific Standard Time in medium type

AUGUST 1999

☽ Last Aspect day	EST / hr:mn / PST		asp	☽ Ingress sign day	EST / hr:mn / PST	
1	**11:03 am**	8:03 am	△☿	♈ 1	**11:47 am**	8:47 am
3	**2:12 pm**	11:12 am	□☿	♉ 3	**4:08 pm**	1:08 pm
5	**4:35 pm**	1:35 pm	⚹☿	♊ 5	**6:57 pm**	3:57 pm
6	**7:43 pm**	4:43 pm	△♅	♋ 7	**8:52 pm**	5:52 pm
9	**10:01 pm**	7:01 pm	☌☿	♌ 9	**10:55 pm**	7:55 pm
11	**6:09 am**	3:09 am	☌☉	♍ 11		11:22 pm
11	**6:09 am**	3:09 am	☌☉	♍ 12	**2:22 am**	
13	**10:31 am**	7:31 am	⚹♂	♎ 14	**8:25 am**	5:25 am
16	**4:12 pm**	1:12 pm	⚹♀	♏ 16	**5:41 pm**	2:41 pm
18		10:07 pm	□♀	♐ 19	**5:32 am**	2:32 am
19	**1:07 am**		□♀	♐ 19	**5:32 am**	2:32 am
21	**2:36 pm**	11:36 am	△☉	♑ 21	**5:59 pm**	2:59 pm
23	**5:13 pm**	2:13 pm	⚹♂	♒ 23	**4:49 am**	1:49 am
26	**4:31 am**	1:31 am	□♂	♓ 26	**12:49 pm**	9:49 am
28	**12:41 pm**	9:41 am	△♂	♈ 28	**6:09 pm**	3:09 pm
30	**7:39 pm**	4:39 pm	△☿	♉ 30	**9:40 pm**	6:40 pm

☽ Phases & Eclipses phase	day	EST / hr:mn / PST	
4th Quarter	4	**12:26 pm**	9:26 am
●	11	18° ♌ 21'	
New Moon	11	**6:09 am**	3:09 am
2nd Quarter	18	**8:48 pm**	5:48 pm
Full Moon	26	**6:48 pm**	3:48 pm

Planet Ingress	day	EST / hr:mn / PST	
☿ ♌	10	**11:25 pm**	8:25 pm
♀ ♌	15	**9:11 am**	6:11 am
⚴ ♋	18	**1:22 pm**	10:22 am
☉ ♍	23	**8:51 am**	5:51 am
⚶ ♎	27	**7:14 pm**	4:14 pm
⚵ ♐	30	**4:15 am**	1:15 am
☿ ♍	31	**10:15 am**	7:15 am

Planetary Motion	day	EST / hr:mn / PST	
☿ D	5	**10:20 pm**	7:20 pm
♇ D	18	**5:59 pm**	2:59 pm
♃ R	24	**8:46 pm**	5:46 pm
♄ R	29	**7:09 pm**	4:09 pm

DATE		SID.TIME	SUN	MOON	NODE	MERCURY	VENUS	MARS	JUPITER	SATURN	URANUS	NEPTUNE	PLUTO	CERES	PALLAS	JUNO	VESTA	CHIRON
S	1	20:36:39	08 ♌ 19	20 ♓ 37	12 ♌ 58	29 ♋ R 54	05 ♍ R 03	11 ♏ 21	04 ♉ 03	16 ♉ 27	15 ♒ R 05	02 ♋ R 49	07 ♐ R 50	04 ♌ 22	20 ♊ 39	26 ♏ 22	16 ♍ 59	27 ♏ 26
M	2	20:40:35	09 17	04 ♈ 05	12 58	29 27	04 58	11 52	04 07	16 30	15 03	02 48	07 49	04 49	21 11	26 26	17 27	27 27
T	3	20:44:32	10 14	17 46	12 R 58	29 06	04 50	12 22	04 12	16 33	15 00	02 46	07 48	05 16	21 42	26 29	17 55	27 27
W	4	20:48:28	11 11	01 ♉ 40	12 58	28 49	04 39	12 53	04 16	16 35	14 58	02 45	07 48	05 42	22 14	26 33	18 23	27 28
T	5	20:52:25	12 09	15 46	12 58	28 39	04 26	13 24	04 20	16 38	14 56	02 43	07 47	06 09	22 45	26 37	18 52	27 28
F	6	20:56:21	13 06	00 ♊ 02	12 D 58	28 D 35	04 11	13 55	04 23	16 40	14 53	02 41	07 47	06 36	23 17	26 41	19 20	27 29
S	7	21:00:18	14 04	14 25	12 57	28 37	03 54	14 27	04 27	16 43	14 51	02 40	07 47	07 03	23 48	26 46	19 48	27 30
S	8	21:04:15	15 01	28 52	12 57	28 46	03 34	14 59	04 30	16 45	14 48	02 38	07 46	07 30	24 20	26 51	20 17	27 31
M	9	21:08:11	15 59	13 ♋ 19	12 57	29 02	03 12	15 31	04 34	16 47	14 46	02 37	07 46	07 57	24 52	26 56	20 46	27 32
T	10	21:12:08	16 56	27 40	12 57	29 25	02 48	16 03	04 37	16 50	14 44	02 35	07 46	08 24	25 23	27 01	21 14	27 33
W	11	21:16:04	17 54	11 ♌ 51	12 R 57	29 54	02 22	16 36	04 40	16 52	14 41	02 34	07 45	08 51	25 55	27 07	21 43	27 35
T	12	21:20:01	18 52	25 47	12 56	00 ♌ 30	01 54	17 09	04 42	16 54	14 39	02 32	07 45	09 18	26 26	27 13	22 12	27 36
F	13	21:23:57	19 49	09 ♍ 25	12 55	01 13	01 24	17 42	04 45	16 55	14 36	02 30	07 45	09 44	26 58	27 20	22 40	27 37
S	14	21:27:54	20 47	22 43	12 54	02 03	00 53	18 15	04 47	16 57	14 34	02 29	07 45	10 11	27 30	27 26	23 09	27 39
S	15	21:31:50	21 44	05 ♎ 41	12 52	02 59	00 20	18 49	04 49	16 59	14 32	02 27	07 44	10 38	28 01	27 33	23 38	27 41
M	16	21:35:47	22 42	18 19	12 51	04 01	29 ♌ 46	19 22	04 51	17 00	14 29	02 26	07 44	11 05	28 33	27 40	24 07	27 42
T	17	21:39:44	23 40	00 ♏ 40	12 49	05 10	29 11	19 56	04 53	17 02	14 27	02 24	07 44	11 32	29 04	27 47	24 36	27 44
W	18	21:43:40	24 37	12 48	12 48	06 24	28 35	20 31	04 54	17 03	14 25	02 23	07 44	11 59	29 36	27 55	25 06	27 46
T	19	21:47:37	25 35	24 47	12 D 48	07 44	27 58	21 05	04 56	17 04	14 22	02 21	07 D 44	12 26	00 ♋ 07	28 03	25 35	27 48
F	20	21:51:33	26 33	06 ♐ 40	12 49	09 10	27 21	21 40	04 57	17 05	14 20	02 20	07 44	12 53	00 39	28 11	26 04	27 50
S	21	21:55:30	27 31	18 33	12 50	10 40	26 43	22 15	04 58	17 06	14 18	02 19	07 44	13 19	01 11	28 19	26 33	27 53
S	22	21:59:26	28 28	00 ♑ 30	12 52	12 15	26 06	22 50	04 58	17 07	14 15	02 17	07 44	13 46	01 42	28 28	27 03	27 55
M	23	22:03:23	29 26	12 36	12 54	13 54	25 29	23 25	04 59	17 08	14 13	02 16	07 44	14 13	02 14	28 37	27 32	27 58
T	24	22:07:19	00 ♍ 24	24 54	12 56	15 37	24 53	24 01	04 59	17 09	14 11	02 14	07 45	14 40	02 45	28 46	28 01	28 00
W	25	22:11:16	01 22	07 ♒ 27	12 R 58	17 23	24 17	24 37	04 59	17 09	14 09	02 13	07 45	15 07	03 17	28 55	28 31	28 03
T	26	22:15:13	02 20	20 17	12 58	19 12	23 43	25 13	04 R 59	17 10	14 06	02 12	07 45	15 34	03 48	29 05	29 00	28 05
F	27	22:19:09	03 17	03 ♓ 24	12 57	21 04	23 09	25 49	04 59	17 10	14 04	02 10	07 45	16 00	04 20	29 15	29 30	28 08
S	28	22:23:06	04 15	16 49	12 55	22 57	22 37	26 25	04 58	17 11	14 02	02 09	07 46	16 27	04 51	29 25	30 00	28 11
S	29	22:27:02	05 13	00 ♈ 29	12 53	24 52	22 07	27 02	04 58	17 11	14 00	02 08	07 46	16 54	05 23	29 35	00 ♎ 29	28 14
M	30	22:30:59	06 11	14 23	12 49	26 48	21 38	27 38	04 57	17 11	13 58	02 06	07 46	17 21	05 54	29 45	00 59	28 17
T	31	22:34:55	07 09	28 26	12 46	28 45	21 11	28 15	04 56	17 R 11	13 55	02 05	07 47	17 48	06 25	29 56	01 29	28 20

EPHEMERIS CALCULATED FOR 12 MIDNIGHT GREENWICH MEAN TIME. ALL OTHER DATA AND FACING ASPECTARIAN PAGE IN **EASTERN STANDARD TIME (BOLD)** AND PACIFIC STANDARD TIME (REGULAR).

SEPTEMBER 1999

1 WEDNESDAY

☽ ☌ ♄	**2:46 am**	
☽ □ ⚳	**4:52 am**	1:52 am
☽ □ ♀	**8:29 am**	5:29 am
☿ ⚻ ♆	**11:20 am**	8:20 am
☿ ⚺ ⚶	**3:44 pm**	12:44 pm
☽ ☍ ⚷	**9:49 pm**	6:49 pm
☽ ☍ ♂	**11:46 pm**	8:46 pm
☽ ☍ ⚵		9:59 pm

2 THURSDAY

☽ ☍ ⚵	**12:59 am**	
☽ △ ♆	**3:51 am**	12:51 am
☽ △ ⚶	**4:57 am**	1:57 am
☽ □ ☿	**6:32 am**	3:32 am
☽ ⚺ ♃	**8:38 am**	5:38 am
♇ ⚻ ⚴	**10:05 am**	7:05 am
☽ ☍ ♇	**1:35 pm**	10:35 am
☽ ⚺ ⚴	**1:43 pm**	10:43 am
☽ □ ☉	**5:18 pm**	2:18 pm
☿ △ ♃	**9:37 pm**	6:37 pm
☽ △ ♅	**11:44 pm**	8:44 pm

3 FRIDAY

☽ ⚺ ♄	**5:25 am**	2:25 am
☽ ⚹ ⚳	**9:11 am**	6:11 am
☽ ⚹ ♀	**9:59 am**	6:59 am
♂ ☌ ⚵	**3:11 pm**	12:11 pm
☽ ⚻ ⚷		9:46 pm
♀ ☌ ⚳		10:29 pm

4 SATURDAY

☽ ⚻ ⚷	**12:46 am**	
♀ ☌ ⚳	**1:29 am**	
☽ ⚻ ⚵	**4:26 am**	1:26 am
☽ ⚻ ♂	**4:52 am**	1:52 am
☽ ⚻ ♆	**6:33 am**	3:33 am
☽ □ ⚶	**9:35 am**	6:35 am
☿ □ ♇	**9:57 am**	6:57 am
☽ ⚹ ♃	**11:20 am**	8:20 am
☽ ⚻ ♇	**4:27 pm**	1:27 pm
☽ ⚹ ☿	**5:30 pm**	2:30 pm
☽ ☌ ⚴	**6:31 pm**	3:31 pm
☽ ⚹ ☉	**11:56 pm**	8:56 pm
☽ ⚻ ♅		11:34 pm

5 SUNDAY

☽ ⚻ ♅	**2:34 am**	
☿ ⚹ ⚴	**3:08 am**	12:08 am
☽ ⚹ ♄	**8:23 am**	5:23 am
☽ ⚺ ♀	**12:10 pm**	9:10 am
☽ ⚺ ⚳	**1:55 pm**	10:55 am
♂ ⚹ ♆	**5:31 pm**	2:31 pm

6 MONDAY

☽ △ ⚷	**4:16 am**	1:16 am
♃ ⚻ ⚶	**7:02 am**	4:02 am
☽ △ ⚵	**8:32 am**	5:32 am
☽ ☍ ♆	**9:52 am**	6:52 am
☽ △ ♂	**10:40 am**	7:40 am
☉ ⚻ ♅	**12:50 pm**	9:50 am
☽ □ ♃	**2:39 pm**	11:39 am
☽ ⚹ ⚶	**2:57 pm**	11:57 am
☽ △ ♇	**8:03 pm**	5:03 pm
☽ ⚺ ⚴		9:08 pm

7 TUESDAY

☽ ⚺ ⚴	**12:08 am**	
☽ ⚺ ☿	**5:29 am**	2:29 am
☽ ☍ ♅	**6:13 am**	3:13 am
☽ ⚺ ☉	**7:35 am**	4:35 am
☿ ⚻ ♅	**10:36 am**	7:36 am
☽ □ ♄	**12:14 pm**	9:14 am
☽ ☌ ♀	**3:31 pm**	12:31 pm
☽ ☌ ⚳	**7:42 pm**	4:42 pm

8 WEDNESDAY

☽ □ ⚷	**8:56 am**	5:56 am
☿ ☌ ☉	**9:58 am**	6:58 am
☽ □ ⚵	**1:52 pm**	10:52 am
☽ ⚻ ♆	**2:21 pm**	11:21 am
☽ □ ♂	**5:52 pm**	2:52 pm
☽ △ ♃	**7:10 pm**	4:10 pm
☽ ⚺ ⚶	**9:43 pm**	6:43 pm
☽ □ ♇		9:58 pm

9 THURSDAY

☽ □ ♇	**12:58 am**	
☿ △ ♄	**5:51 am**	2:51 am
☽ ⚹ ⚴	**7:17 am**	4:17 am
☽ ⚻ ♅	**11:18 am**	8:18 am
☽ ☌ ☉	**5:03 pm**	2:03 pm
☽ △ ♄	**5:36 pm**	2:36 pm
♂ ⚻ ♃	**7:09 pm**	**4:09 pm**
♆ ⚹ ⚵	**7:18 pm**	4:18 pm
☽ ☌ ☿	**7:34 pm**	4:34 pm
☽ ⚺ ♀	**8:44 pm**	5:44 pm
☉ △ ♄		9:19 pm

10 FRIDAY

☉ △ ♄	**12:19 am**	
☽ ⚺ ⚳	**3:17 am**	12:17 am
☿ ⚺ ♀	**3:43 am**	12:43 am
☽ ⚹ ⚷	**3:27 pm**	12:27 pm
☽ △ ♆	**8:45 pm**	5:45 pm
☽ ⚹ ⚵	**9:13 pm**	6:13 pm
☽ ⚻ ♃		10:38 pm

11 SATURDAY

☽ ⚻ ♃	**1:38 am**	
☽ ⚹ ♂	**3:23 am**	12:23 am
☽ ☌ ⚶	**6:45 am**	3:45 am
☽ ⚹ ♇	**7:58 am**	4:58 am
☽ □ ⚴	**4:50 pm**	1:50 pm
☽ △ ♅	**6:35 pm**	3:35 pm
♀ ⚺ ☉	**7:10 pm**	4:10 pm
☽ ⚻ ♄		10:13 pm

12 SUNDAY

☽ ⚻ ♄	**1:13 am**	
☽ ⚹ ♀	**4:38 am**	1:38 am
☽ ⚺ ☉	**5:24 am**	2:24 am
☽ ⚺ ☿	**1:02 pm**	10:02 am
☽ ⚹ ⚳	**1:31 pm**	10:31 am
♇ ⚹ ⚶	**2:04 pm**	11:04 am
☿ ⚺ ⚳	**5:17 pm**	2:17 pm
☽ ⚺ ⚷		9:34 pm

13 MONDAY

☽ ⚺ ⚷	**12:34 am**	
☽ □ ♆	**5:43 am**	2:43 am
☽ ⚺ ⚵	**7:19 am**	4:19 am
♅ ⚻ ⚴	**9:44 am**	6:44 am
☽ ☍ ♃	**10:38 am**	7:38 am
☽ ⚺ ♂	**3:58 pm**	12:58 pm
☽ ⚺ ♇	**5:37 pm**	2:37 pm
☽ ⚺ ⚶	**6:47 pm**	3:47 pm

14 TUESDAY

☽ □ ♅	**4:32 am**	1:32 am
☽ △ ⚴	**5:25 am**	2:25 am
☽ ☍ ♄	**11:30 am**	8:30 am
☽ □ ♀	**3:41 pm**	12:41 pm
☽ ⚹ ☉	**9:09 pm**	6:09 pm
♂ ☌ ♇	**11:20 pm**	8:20 pm
☽ □ ⚳		11:43 pm

15 WEDNESDAY

☽ □ ⚳	**2:43 am**	
☽ ⚹ ☿	**10:24 am**	7:24 am
☽ ☌ ⚷	**12:19 pm**	9:19 am
☽ ⚹ ♆	**5:12 pm**	2:12 pm
☽ ☌ ⚵	**8:05 pm**	5:05 pm
☽ ⚻ ♃	**10:01 pm**	7:01 pm
☿ ⚹ ⚷	**11:47 pm**	8:47 pm

16 THURSDAY

☽ ☌ ♇	**5:38 am**	2:38 am
☽ ☌ ♂	**7:23 am**	4:23 am
☽ ⚹ ⚶	**9:27 am**	6:27 am
☽ ⚹ ♅	**4:37 pm**	1:37 pm
☽ ⚻ ⚴	**8:22 pm**	5:22 pm
☽ ⚻ ♄	**11:43 pm**	8:43 pm

17 FRIDAY

☽ △ ♀	**5:07 am**	2:07 am
☿ △ ♆	**8:15 am**	5:15 am
☽ □ ☉	**3:06 pm**	12:06 pm
☽ △ ⚳	**5:38 pm**	2:38 pm
☽ ⚺ ⚷		10:21 pm

18 SATURDAY

☽ ⚺ ⚷	**1:21 am**	
☽ ⚺ ♆	**5:46 am**	2:46 am
☽ □ ☿	**9:27 am**	6:27 am
☽ ⚺ ⚵	**9:56 am**	6:56 am
☽ △ ♃	**10:16 am**	7:16 am
☿ ⚹ ⚵	**1:12 pm**	10:12 am
☿ ⚻ ♃	**2:52 pm**	11:52 am
☽ ⚺ ♇	**6:17 pm**	3:17 pm
♃ ⚻ ⚵	**10:39 pm**	7:39 pm
☽ ⚺ ♂	**11:28 pm**	8:28 pm
☽ □ ⚶		9:39 pm

19 SUNDAY

☽ □ ⚶	**12:39 am**	
♂ ⚹ ⚶	**4:07 am**	1:07 am
☽ ⚺ ♅	**4:54 am**	1:54 am
☽ ☍ ⚴	**11:20 am**	8:20 am
☽ △ ♄	**11:49 am**	8:49 am
☽ ⚻ ♀	**6:38 pm**	3:38 pm
☉ ⚺ ⚳	**9:13 pm**	6:13 pm
♄ ⚹ ⚴	**9:59 pm**	6:59 pm

20 MONDAY

☽ ⚻ ⚳	**7:34 am**	4:34 am
☽ △ ☉	**8:04 am**	5:04 am
☽ ⚹ ⚷	**1:11 pm**	10:11 am
☽ ☌ ♆	**4:59 pm**	1:59 pm
☽ □ ♃	**8:57 pm**	5:57 pm
☽ ⚹ ⚵	**10:10 pm**	7:10 pm
☿ ⚹ ♇		9:11 pm

21 TUESDAY

☿ ⚹ ♇	**12:11 am**	
☽ ⚹ ♇	**5:04 am**	2:04 am
☽ △ ☿	**5:48 am**	2:48 am
☽ ⚹ ♂	**1:10 pm**	10:10 am
☽ △ ⚶	**1:28 pm**	10:28 am
☽ ☌ ♅	**2:56 pm**	11:56 am
☽ □ ♄	**9:25 pm**	6:25 pm
☽ ⚻ ⚴	**11:29 pm**	8:29 pm

22 WEDNESDAY

☽ ☍ ♀	**5:38 am**	2:38 am
☽ ☍ ⚳	**6:07 pm**	3:07 pm
☽ ⚻ ☉	**9:10 pm**	6:10 pm
♂ ⚹ ♅	**9:31 pm**	6:31 pm
☽ □ ⚷	**9:47 pm**	6:47 pm
♅ △ ⚶		9:26 pm
☽ ⚺ ♆		9:56 pm

23 THURSDAY

♅ △ ⚶	**12:26 am**	
☽ ⚺ ♆	**12:56 am**	
☽ ⚹ ♃	**4:20 am**	1:20 am
☉ ⚹ ⚷	**6:27 am**	3:27 am
☽ □ ⚵	**6:54 am**	3:54 am
☽ □ ♇	**12:23 pm**	9:23 am
☽ ⚻ ☿	**8:39 pm**	5:39 pm
☽ ⚺ ♅	**9:27 pm**	6:27 pm
☽ ⚻ ⚶	**10:18 pm**	7:18 pm
☽ □ ♂	**10:44 pm**	7:44 pm

24 FRIDAY

☿ △ ♅	**3:10 am**	12:10 am
☽ ⚹ ♄	**3:27 am**	12:27 am
☽ △ ⚴	**7:35 am**	4:35 am
☽ ⚻ ♀	**1:01 pm**	10:01 am
☿ ☌ ⚶	**4:07 pm**	1:07 pm
☉ △ ♆	**11:51 pm**	8:51 pm
☽ ⚻ ⚳		9:45 pm
☿ ⚹ ♂		10:18 pm
☽ △ ⚷		11:50 pm

25 SATURDAY

☽ ⚻ ⚳	**12:45 am**	
☿ ⚹ ♂	**1:18 am**	
☽ △ ⚷	**2:50 am**	
☽ ⚹ ♆	**5:26 am**	2:26 am
☽ ☍ ☉	**5:51 am**	2:51 am
☽ ⚺ ♃	**8:20 am**	5:20 am
☽ △ ⚵	**12:03 pm**	9:03 am
☽ △ ♇	**4:21 pm**	1:21 pm
☽ ⚹ ♅		9:49 pm

26 SUNDAY

☽ ⚹ ♅	**12:49 am**	
☽ ☍ ⚶	**3:38 am**	12:38 am
☽ △ ♂	**4:42 am**	1:42 am
☿ ⚻ ♄	**4:48 am**	1:48 am
☽ ⚺ ♄	**6:28 am**	3:28 am
☽ ☍ ☿	**6:41 am**	3:41 am
♂ ⚹ ⚶	**6:51 am**	3:51 am
☽ □ ⚴	**12:24 pm**	9:24 am
☉ ⚻ ♃	**2:30 pm**	11:30 am
☽ △ ♀	**5:34 pm**	2:34 pm

27 MONDAY

☽ △ ⚳	**4:39 am**	1:39 am
☽ ⚻ ⚷	**5:25 am**	2:25 am
☽ □ ♆	**7:36 am**	4:36 am
☽ ☌ ♃	**10:06 am**	7:06 am
☽ ⚻ ☉	**11:40 am**	8:40 am
☽ ⚻ ⚵	**2:58 pm**	11:58 am
♂ ⚻ ♄	**3:26 pm**	12:26 pm
☽ ⚻ ♇	**6:20 pm**	3:20 pm
☽ □ ♅		11:30 pm

28 TUESDAY

☽ □ ♅	**2:30 am**	
☽ ⚻ ⚶	**7:09 am**	4:09 am
☽ ☌ ♄	**7:57 am**	4:57 am
☽ ⚻ ♂	**8:50 am**	5:50 am
⚳ □ ⚷	**1:07 pm**	10:07 am
☽ ⚻ ☿	**2:21 pm**	11:21 am
☽ ⚹ ⚴	**3:43 pm**	12:43 pm
☽ □ ♀	**9:01 pm**	6:01 pm

29 WEDNESDAY

♄ ⚻ ⚶	**3:48 am**	12:48 am
☽ ☍ ⚷	**7:15 am**	4:15 am
☽ □ ⚳	**7:41 am**	4:41 am
☿ □ ⚴	**8:30 am**	5:30 am
☽ △ ♆	**9:05 am**	6:05 am
☽ ⚺ ♃	**11:16 am**	8:16 am
☽ △ ☉	**4:48 pm**	1:48 pm
☽ ☍ ⚵	**5:26 pm**	2:26 pm
♂ ⚼ ♃	**6:40 pm**	3:40 pm
☽ ☍ ♇	**7:59 pm**	4:59 pm

30 THURSDAY

☽ △ ♅	**4:05 am**	1:05 am
☉ ⚹ ⚵	**5:19 am**	2:19 am
☽ ⚺ ♄	**9:30 am**	6:30 am
☽ △ ⚶	**10:44 am**	7:44 am
☽ ☍ ♂	**1:05 pm**	10:05 am
☽ ⚺ ⚴	**7:21 pm**	4:21 pm
☽ △ ☿	**10:13 pm**	7:13 pm
☽ ⚹ ♀		10:09 pm

Eastern Standard Time in bold type
Pacific Standard Time in medium type

SEPTEMBER 1999

☽ Last Aspect day	EST / hr:mn / PST	asp	☽ Ingress sign day	EST / hr:mn / PST
1	**11:46 pm** 8:46 pm	☍♂	♊ 1	9:25 pm
1	**11:46 pm** 8:46 pm	☍♂	♊ 2	**12:25 am**
3	**9:59 am** 6:59 am	⚹♀	♋ 3	**3:10 am** 12:10 am
5	**8:23 am** 5:23 am	⚹♄	♌ 6	**6:29 am** 3:29 am
7	**3:31 pm** 12:31 pm	☌♀	♍ 8	**10:57 am** 7:57 am
9	**7:34 pm** 4:34 pm	☌☿	♎ 10	**5:16 pm** 2:16 pm
12	**4:38 am** 1:38 am	⚹♀	♏ 12	11:09 pm
12	**4:38 am** 1:38 am	⚹♀	♏ 13	**2:09 am**
15	**10:24 am** 7:24 am	⚹☿	♐ 15	**1:35 pm** 10:35 am
17	**3:06 pm** 12:06 pm	□☉	♑ 17	11:13 pm

☽ Last Aspect day	EST / hr:mn / PST	asp	☽ Ingress sign day	EST / hr:mn / PST
17	**3:06 pm** 12:06 pm	□☉	♑ 18	**2:13 am**
20	**8:04 am** 5:04 am	△☉	♒ 20	**1:38 pm** 10:38 am
22	**5:38 am** 2:38 am	☍♀	♓ 22	**9:51 pm** 6:51 pm
24	**3:27 am** 12:27 am	⚹♄	♈ 24	11:34 pm
24	**3:27 am** 12:27 am	⚹♄	♈ 25	**2:34 am**
26	**5:34 pm** 2:34 pm	△♀	♉ 27	**4:52 am** 1:52 am
28	**9:01 pm** 6:01 pm	□♀	♊ 29	**6:21 am** 3:2 1 am
30	10:09 pm	⚹♀	♋ 1	**8:32 am** 5:32 am
1	**1:09 am**	⚹♀	♋ 1	**8:32 am** 5:32 am

☽ Phases & Eclipses phase	day	EST / hr:mn / PST
4th Quarter	2	**5:18 pm** 2:18 pm
New Moon	9	**5:03 pm** 2:03 pm
2nd Quarter	17	**3:06 pm** 12:06 pm
Full Moon	25	**5:51 am** 2:51 am

Planet Ingress	day	EST / hr:mn / PST
♂ ♐	2	**2:29 pm** 11:29 am
☿ ♎	16	**7:53 am** 4:53 am
☉ ♎	23	**6:31 am** 3:31 am
⚷ ♐	23	**7:15 am** 4:15 am
⚳ ♍	27	**11:20 am** 8:20 am

Planetary Motion	day	EST / hr:mn / PST
♀ D	10	**7:25 pm** 4:25 pm

DATE		SID.TIME	SUN	MOON	NODE	MERCURY	VENUS	MARS	JUPITER	SATURN	URANUS	NEPTUNE	PLUTO	CERES	PALLAS	JUNO	VESTA	CHIRON
W	1	22:38:52	08 ♍ 07	12 ♉ 35	12 ♌ ℞ 43	00 ♍ 43	20 ♌ ℞ 47	28 ♏ 52	04 ♉ ℞ 54	17 ♌ ℞ 11	13 ♒ ℞ 53	02 ♒ ℞ 04	07 ♐ 47	18 ♌ 14	06 ♑ 57	00 ♐ 07	01 ♎ 59	28 ♏ 24
T	2	22:42:48	09 05	26 47	12 D 41	02 41	20 24	29 30	04 53	17 10	13 51	02 03	07 47	18 41	07 28	00 18	02 29	28 27
F	3	22:46:45	10 03	11 ♊ 00	12 41	04 38	20 04	00 ♐ 07	04 51	17 10	13 49	02 01	07 48	19 08	07 59	00 29	02 59	28 31
S	4	22:50:42	11 01	25 11	12 41	06 36	19 46	00 45	04 49	17 10	13 47	02 00	07 48	19 34	08 31	00 40	03 29	28 34
S	5	22:54:38	12 00	09 ♋ 18	12 42	08 33	19 30	01 22	04 47	17 09	13 45	01 59	07 49	20 01	09 02	00 52	03 59	28 38
M	6	22:58:35	12 58	23 20	12 43	10 29	19 17	02 00	04 45	17 08	13 43	01 58	07 50	20 28	09 33	01 04	04 29	28 42
T	7	23:02:31	13 56	07 ♌ 14	12 ℞ 44	12 25	19 06	02 38	04 43	17 08	13 41	01 57	07 50	20 54	10 04	01 16	04 59	28 45
W	8	23:06:28	14 54	20 58	12 43	14 20	18 58	03 17	04 40	17 07	13 39	01 56	07 51	21 21	10 35	01 28	05 29	28 49
T	9	23:10:24	15 53	04 ♍ 31	12 41	16 14	18 52	03 55	04 37	17 06	13 37	01 55	07 51	21 48	11 06	01 41	05 59	28 53
F	10	23:14:21	16 51	17 51	12 37	18 07	18 48	04 34	04 34	17 04	13 35	01 54	07 52	22 14	11 37	01 53	06 30	28 57
S	11	23:18:17	17 49	00 ♎ 56	12 32	19 59	18 47	05 13	04 31	17 03	13 33	01 53	07 53	22 41	12 08	02 06	07 00	29 01
S	12	23:22:14	18 48	13 45	12 26	21 50	18 D 48	05 52	04 27	17 02	13 32	01 52	07 54	23 07	12 39	02 19	07 30	29 06
M	13	23:26:11	19 46	26 18	12 19	23 40	18 52	06 31	04 24	17 01	13 30	01 51	07 54	23 34	13 10	02 32	08 01	29 10
T	14	23:30:07	20 44	08 ♏ 37	12 12	25 29	18 58	07 10	04 20	16 59	13 28	01 50	07 55	24 00	13 41	02 46	08 31	29 14
W	15	23:34:04	21 43	20 44	12 06	27 17	19 05	07 49	04 16	16 57	13 26	01 49	07 56	24 27	14 11	02 59	09 01	29 19
T	16	23:38:00	22 41	02 ♐ 41	12 02	29 03	19 15	08 29	04 12	16 56	13 25	01 48	07 57	24 53	14 42	03 13	09 32	29 23
F	17	23:41:57	23 40	14 34	12 D 01	00 ♎ 49	19 28	09 08	04 07	16 54	13 23	01 47	07 58	25 20	15 13	03 27	10 03	29 28
S	18	23:45:53	24 38	26 25	12 01	02 33	19 42	09 48	04 03	16 52	13 21	01 46	07 59	25 46	15 43	03 41	10 33	29 33
S	19	23:49:50	25 37	08 ♑ 21	12 02	04 17	19 58	10 28	03 58	16 50	13 20	01 45	08 00	26 13	16 13	03 55	11 04	29 38
M	20	23:53:46	26 35	20 27	12 04	05 59	20 16	11 08	03 53	16 48	13 18	01 45	08 01	26 39	16 44	04 10	11 34	29 42
T	21	23:57:43	27 34	02 ♒ 47	12 ℞ 06	07 41	20 36	11 49	03 48	16 46	13 17	01 44	08 02	27 05	17 14	04 24	12 05	29 47
W	22	0:01:39	28 33	15 26	12 07	09 21	20 58	12 29	03 43	16 43	13 15	01 43	08 03	27 31	17 44	04 39	12 36	29 52
T	23	0:05:36	29 31	28 26	12 06	11 00	21 22	13 10	03 38	16 41	13 14	01 43	08 04	27 58	18 14	04 54	13 07	29 57
F	24	0:09:33	00 ♎ 30	11 ♓ 49	12 03	12 39	21 47	13 50	03 32	16 38	13 12	01 42	08 05	28 24	18 44	05 09	13 37	00 ♐ 03
S	25	0:13:29	01 29	25 35	11 57	14 16	22 14	14 31	03 26	16 36	13 11	01 41	08 07	28 50	19 14	05 24	14 08	00 08
S	26	0:17:26	02 28	09 ♈ 42	11 50	15 53	22 43	15 12	03 21	16 33	13 10	01 41	08 08	29 16	19 44	05 39	14 39	00 13
M	27	0:21:22	03 26	24 03	11 42	17 28	23 13	15 53	03 15	16 30	13 09	01 40	08 09	29 42	20 14	05 55	15 10	00 18
T	28	0:25:19	04 25	08 ♉ 34	11 34	19 03	23 45	16 34	03 09	16 27	13 07	01 40	08 10	00 ♍ 08	20 43	06 10	15 41	00 24
W	29	0:29:15	05 24	23 08	11 27	20 37	24 18	17 15	03 02	16 24	13 06	01 39	08 12	00 34	21 13	06 26	16 12	00 29
T	30	0:33:12	06 23	07 ♊ 37	11 22	22 10	24 53	17 57	02 56	16 21	13 05	01 39	08 13	01 00	21 42	06 42	16 43	00 35

EPHEMERIS CALCULATED FOR 12 MIDNIGHT GREENWICH MEAN TIME. ALL OTHER DATA AND FACING ASPECTARIAN PAGE IN **EASTERN STANDARD TIME (BOLD)** AND PACIFIC STANDARD TIME (REGULAR).

OCTOBER 1999

1 FRIDAY
1:09 am
5:46 am 2:46 am
9:47 am 6:47 am
11:18 am 8:18 am
11:29 am 8:29 am
1:11 pm 10:11 am
4:38 pm 1:38 pm
8:53 pm 5:53 pm
10:36 pm 7:36 pm
11:03 pm 8:03 pm

2 SATURDAY
6:48 am 3:48 am
12:15 pm 9:15 am
3:41 pm 12:41 pm
6:50 pm 3:50 pm
7:29 pm 4:29 pm
9:28 pm

3 SUNDAY
12:28 am
7:06 am 4:06 am
7:53 am 4:53 am
8:01 am 5:01 am
1:53 pm 10:53 am
2:04 pm 12:04 pm
4:36 pm 1:36 pm
4:57 pm 1:57 pm
11:04 pm
11:52 pm

4 MONDAY
2:04 am
2:52 am
7:19 am 4:19 am
11:11 am 8:11 am
4:40 pm 1:40 pm
7:33 pm
10:33 pm

5 TUESDAY
2:36 am
7:30 am 4:30 am
3:15 pm 12:15 pm
7:18 pm 4:18 pm
7:46 pm 4:46 pm
7:50 pm 4:50 pm

6 WEDNESDAY
8:35 am 5:35 am
9:21 am 6:21 am
9:43 am 6:43 am
11:38 am

7 THURSDAY
7:24 am 4:24 am
12:27 pm 9:27 am
4:26 pm 1:26 pm

8 FRIDAY
1:40 am
3:29 am 12:29 am
3:51 am 12:51 am
4:31 am 1:31 am
5:14 am 2:14 am
9:41 am 6:41 am
10:05 am 7:05 am
4:43 pm 1:43 pm
6:07 pm 3:07 pm
10:16 pm

9 SATURDAY
1:16 am
6:34 am 3:34 am
6:43 am 3:43 am
8:19 am 5:19 am
12:54 pm 9:54 am
2:36 pm 11:36 am
6:22 pm 3:22 pm
7:30 pm 4:30 pm
9:33 pm
10:20 pm

10 SUNDAY
12:33 am
1:20 am

11 MONDAY
1:47 am
2:36 am
2:57 am
5:19 am 2:19 am
5:47 am 2:47 am
10:47 pm 7:47 pm

12 TUESDAY
5:23 am 2:23 am
7:45 am 4:45 am
3:13 pm 12:13 pm
4:55 pm 1:55 pm
11:59 pm 8:59 pm
9:30 pm
10:08 pm

13 WEDNESDAY
12:30 am
1:08 am
6:22 am 3:22 am
11:06 am 8:06 am
2:34 pm 11:34 am
6:44 pm 3:44 pm
10:26 pm 7:26 pm
11:20 pm 8:20 pm

14 THURSDAY
4:34 am 1:34 am
6:30 am 3:30 am
12:54 pm 9:54 am
3:54 pm 12:54 pm
11:07 pm 8:07 pm

15 FRIDAY
7:49 am 4:49 am
8:02 am 5:02 am
12:07 pm 9:07 am
1:17 pm 10:17 am
2:29 pm 11:29 am

16 SATURDAY
2:11 am
3:34 am 12:34 am
3:58 am 12:58 am
9:09 am 6:09 am
12:08 pm 9:08 am
5:01 pm 2:01 pm
6:38 pm 3:38 pm

17 SUNDAY
9:59 am 6:59 am
2:22 pm 11:22 am
7:56 pm 4:56 pm
8:44 pm 5:44 pm
10:36 pm 7:36 pm
11:38 pm 8:38 pm
11:54 pm 8:54 pm
10:25 pm

18 MONDAY
1:25 am
3:07 am 12:07 am
4:21 am 1:21 am
10:40 am 7:40 am
3:19 pm 12:19 pm
3:55 pm 12:55 pm
4:08 pm 1:08 pm
8:47 pm 5:47 pm
9:58 pm 6:58 pm
11:19 pm 8:19 pm
10:33 pm

19 TUESDAY
1:33 pm
3:39 pm 12:39 pm
11:50 pm 8:50 pm
9:53 pm
11:35 pm

20 WEDNESDAY
12:53 am
2:35 am
8:13 am 5:13 am
10:29 am 7:29 am
12:25 pm 9:25 am
12:33 pm 9:33 am
3:13 pm 12:13 pm

21 THURSDAY
11:33 pm 8:33 pm
10:46 pm
1:46 am
4:13 am 1:13 am
4:41 am 1:41 am
6:33 am 3:33 am
6:51 am 3:51 am
6:54 am 3:54 am
10:34 am 7:34 am
9:59 pm 6:59 pm
11:25 pm 8:25 pm

22 FRIDAY
10:11 am 7:11 am
10:38 am 7:38 am
12:49 pm 9:49 am
3:27 pm 12:27 pm
4:27 pm 1:27 pm
5:45 pm 2:45 pm
6:26 pm 3:26 pm
8:04 pm 5:04 pm

23 SATURDAY
3:40 am 12:40 am
7:09 am 4:09 am
10:21 am 7:21 am
11:27 am 8:27 am
11:32 am 8:32 am
1:13 pm 10:13 am
1:33 pm 10:33 am
2:04 pm 11:04 am

24 SUNDAY
5:48 am 2:48 am
1:53 pm 10:53 am
2:05 pm 11:05 am
4:03 pm 1:03 pm
5:03 pm 2:03 pm
5:30 pm 2:30 pm
6:25 pm 3:25 pm
7:25 pm 4:25 pm
7:37 pm 4:37 pm
11:59 pm 8:59 pm

25 MONDAY
4:49 am 1:49 am
4:57 am 1:57 am
7:01 am 4:01 am
9:26 am 6:26 am
11:09 am 8:09 am

26 TUESDAY
9:22 am 6:22 am
1:48 pm 10:48 am
2:55 pm 11:55 am
3:47 pm 12:47 pm
5:11 pm 2:11 pm
7:36 pm 4:36 pm
8:05 pm 5:05 pm
8:52 pm 5:52 pm
11:33 pm

27 WEDNESDAY
2:33 am
3:41 am 12:41 am
4:59 am 1:59 am
10:52 am 7:52 am
11:15 am 8:15 am
1:51 pm 10:51 am
2:29 pm 11:29 am
6:59 pm 3:59 pm
10:04 pm
11:33 pm

28 THURSDAY
1:04 am
2:33 am
8:00 am 5:00 am
12:46 pm 9:46 am
1:55 pm 10:55 am
5:53 pm 2:53 pm
6:15 pm 3:15 pm
9:14 pm 6:14 pm
11:02 pm 8:02 pm
11:57 pm 8:57 pm

29 FRIDAY
6:10 am 3:10 am
6:10 am 3:10 am
6:21 am 3:21 am
8:08 am 5:08 am
12:35 pm 9:35 am
1:36 pm 10:36 am
3:00 pm 12:00 pm
5:04 pm 2:04 pm
9:21 pm

30 SATURDAY
12:21 am
4:00 am 1:00 am
5:54 am 2:54 am
8:41 am 5:41 am
11:03 am 8:03 am
9:37 pm

31 SUNDAY
12:37 am
3:34 am 12:34 am
7:04 am 4:04 am
7:32 am 4:32 am
9:43 am 6:43 am
12:32 pm 9:32 am
4:22 pm 1:22 pm
6:36 pm 3:36 pm
7:00 pm 4:00 pm
10:21 pm 7:21 pm

Eastern Standard Time in **bold type**
Pacific Standard Time in medium type

OCTOBER 1999

☽ Last Aspect day	EST / hr:mn / PST	asp	☽ Ingress sign day	EST / hr:mn / PST
30	10:09 pm	⚹♀	♋ 1	**8:32 am** 5:32 am
1	**1:09 am**	⚹♀	♋ 1	**8:32 am** 5:32 am
3	**7:53 am** 4:53 am	□☿	♌ 3	**12:14 pm** 9:14 am
5	**3:15 pm** 12:15 pm	☌♀	♍ 5	**5:40 pm** 2:40 pm
7	**12:27 pm** 9:27 am	□♂	♎ 7	9:52 pm
7	**12:27 pm** 9:27 am	□♂	♎ 8	**12:52 am**
9	9:33 pm	⚹♂	♏ 10	**10:01 am** 7:01 am
10	**12:33 am**	⚹♂	♏ 10	**10:01 am** 7:01 am
11	**4:42 pm** 1:42 pm	☍♄	♐ 12	**9:18 pm** 6:18 pm
15	**7:49 am** 4:49 am	☌♂	♑ 15	**10:03 am** 7:0 am

☽ Last Aspect day	EST / hr:mn / PST	asp	☽ Ingress sign day	EST / hr:mn / PST
17	**9:59 am** 6:59 am	□☉	♒ 17	**10:17 pm** 7:17 pm
19	9:53 pm	△☉	♓ 20	**7:33 am** 4:33 am
20	**12:53 am**	△☉	♓ 20	**7:33 am** 4:33 am
21	**11:25 pm** 8:25 pm	△☿	♈ 22	**12:42 pm** 9:42 am
24	**2:05 pm** 11:05 am	☌♃	♉ 24	**2:26 pm** 11:26 am
26	**9:22 am** 6:22 am	☍☿	♊ 26	**2:34 pm** 11:34 am
28	**1:55 pm** 10:55 am	⚹♃	♋ 28	**3:09 pm** 12:09 pm
30	**4:00 pm** 1:00 pm	□♃	♌ 30	**5:47 pm** 2:47 pm

☽ Phases & Eclipses phase	day	EST / hr:mn / PST
4th Quarter	1	**11:03 pm** 8:03 pm
New Moon	8	**6:34 am** 3:34 am
2nd Quarter	17	**9:59 am** 6:59 am
Full Moon	24	**4:03 pm** 1:03 pm
4th Quarter	31	**7:04 am** 4:04 am

Planet Ingress	day	EST / hr:mn / PST
☿ ♏	4	9:12 pm
☿ ♏	5	**12:12 am**
♀ ♍	7	**11:51 am** 8:51 am
♂ ♑	16	**8:35 pm** 5:35 pm
♀ ♌	17	**1:56 pm** 10:56 am
♃ ♈	22	9:49 pm
♃ ♈	23	**12:49 am**
☉ ♏	23	**3:52 pm** 12:52 pm
⚶ ♏	25	**5:07 am** 2:07 am
☿ ♐	30	**3:08 pm** 12:08 pm

Planetary Motion		day	EST / hr:mn / PST
♆	D	13	**5:01 pm** 2:01 pm
♅	D	22	**10:34 pm** 7:34 pm

DATE		SID.TIME	SUN	MOON	NODE	MERCURY	VENUS	MARS	JUPITER	SATURN	URANUS	NEPTUNE	PLUTO	CERES	PALLAS	JUNO	VESTA	CHIRON
F	1	0:37:08	07 ♎ 22	21 ♊ 59	11 ♌℞ 18	23 ♎ 42	25 ♌ 28	18 ♐ 38	02 ♉℞ 49	16 ♉℞ 18	13 ♒℞ 04	01 ♒℞ 38	08 ♐ 14	01 ♍ 26	22 ♋ 11	06 ♐ 58	17 ♎ 14	00 ♐ 40
S	2	0:41:05	08 21	06 ♋ 09	11 D 16	25 13	26 06	19 20	02 43	16 15	13 03	01 38	08 16	01 52	22 40	07 14	17 45	00 46
S	3	0:45:02	09 20	20 07	11 16	26 43	26 44	20 01	02 36	16 12	13 02	01 37	08 17	02 18	23 09	07 30	18 16	00 52
M	4	0:48:58	10 19	03 ♌ 51	11 ℞ 16	28 12	27 24	20 43	02 29	16 08	13 01	01 37	08 19	02 44	23 38	07 47	18 47	00 58
T	5	0:52:55	11 18	17 24	11 16	29 41	28 04	21 25	02 22	16 05	13 00	01 37	08 20	03 10	24 07	08 03	19 18	01 04
W	6	0:56:51	12 17	00 ♍ 44	11 14	01 ♏ 09	28 46	22 07	02 15	16 01	12 59	01 36	08 21	03 35	24 35	08 20	19 50	01 10
T	7	1:00:48	13 16	13 54	11 09	02 35	29 29	22 49	02 07	15 58	12 58	01 36	08 23	04 01	25 04	08 37	20 21	01 16
F	8	1:04:44	14 16	26 52	11 02	04 01	00 ♍ 13	23 32	02 00	15 54	12 58	01 36	08 25	04 27	25 32	08 54	20 52	01 22
S	9	1:08:41	15 15	09 ♎ 38	10 53	05 26	00 58	24 14	01 53	15 50	12 57	01 36	08 26	04 52	26 00	09 11	21 23	01 28
S	10	1:12:37	16 14	22 13	10 41	06 50	01 44	24 57	01 45	15 46	12 56	01 36	08 28	05 18	26 28	09 28	21 55	01 34
M	11	1:16:34	17 13	04 ♏ 37	10 28	08 13	02 31	25 39	01 38	15 43	12 55	01 35	08 29	05 43	26 56	09 45	22 26	01 40
T	12	1:20:31	18 13	16 49	10 16	09 35	03 19	26 22	01 30	15 39	12 55	01 35	08 31	06 09	27 24	10 03	22 57	01 46
W	13	1:24:27	19 12	28 51	10 05	10 56	04 07	27 05	01 22	15 35	12 54	01 35	08 33	06 34	27 51	10 20	23 29	01 53
T	14	1:28:24	20 12	10 ♐ 46	09 56	12 16	04 56	27 48	01 14	15 30	12 54	01 D 35	08 34	06 59	28 18	10 38	24 00	01 59
F	15	1:32:20	21 11	22 35	09 50	13 35	05 47	28 31	01 06	15 26	12 53	01 35	08 36	07 24	28 46	10 56	24 31	02 06
S	16	1:36:17	22 10	04 ♑ 25	09 47	14 52	06 37	29 14	00 58	15 22	12 53	01 35	08 38	07 50	29 12	11 13	25 03	02 12
S	17	1:40:13	23 10	16 18	09 D 46	16 08	07 29	29 57	00 50	15 18	12 53	01 35	08 40	08 15	29 39	11 31	25 34	02 19
M	18	1:44:10	24 09	28 20	09 ℞ 46	17 23	08 21	00 ♑ 40	00 42	15 14	12 52	01 36	08 41	08 40	00 ♌ 06	11 50	26 06	02 25
T	19	1:48:06	25 09	10 ♒ 37	09 47	18 36	09 15	01 24	00 34	15 09	12 52	01 36	08 43	09 05	00 32	12 08	26 37	02 32
W	20	1:52:03	26 09	23 15	09 46	19 47	10 08	02 07	00 26	15 05	12 52	01 36	08 45	09 30	00 58	12 26	27 09	02 38
T	21	1:56:00	27 08	06 ♓ 16	09 44	20 57	11 03	02 51	00 18	15 00	12 52	01 36	08 47	09 54	01 24	12 44	27 40	02 45
F	22	1:59:56	28 08	19 45	09 39	22 05	11 58	03 35	00 10	14 56	12 52	01 36	08 49	10 19	01 49	13 03	28 12	02 52
S	23	2:03:53	29 08	03 ♈ 42	09 31	23 10	12 53	04 18	00 02	14 51	12 D 52	01 37	08 51	10 44	02 15	13 21	28 43	02 59
S	24	2:07:49	00 ♏ 07	18 06	09 22	24 14	13 49	05 02	29 ♈ 54	14 47	12 52	01 37	08 53	11 08	02 40	13 40	29 15	03 05
M	25	2:11:46	01 07	02 ♉ 50	09 11	25 14	14 46	05 46	29 46	14 42	12 52	01 37	08 54	11 33	03 05	13 59	29 47	03 12
T	26	2:15:42	02 07	17 46	08 59	26 12	15 43	06 30	29 38	14 37	12 52	01 38	08 56	11 58	03 30	14 18	00 ♏ 18	03 19
W	27	2:19:39	03 07	02 ♊ 46	08 49	27 07	16 41	07 14	29 29	14 33	12 52	01 38	08 58	12 22	03 15	14 37	00 50	03 26
T	28	2:23:35	04 06	17 40	08 41	27 58	17 39	07 58	29 21	14 28	12 52	01 39	09 00	12 46	04 18	14 56	01 22	03 33
F	29	2:27:32	05 06	02 ♋ 20	08 35	28 45	18 38	08 42	29 13	14 23	12 53	01 39	09 02	13 10	04 42	15 15	01 53	03 40
S	30	2:31:28	06 06	16 41	08 31	29 28	19 37	09 27	29 05	14 19	12 53	01 40	09 04	13 35	05 06	15 34	02 25	03 47
S	31	2:35:25	07 06	00 ♌ 42	08 29	00 ♐ 06	20 37	10 11	28 57	14 14	12 53	01 40	09 06	13 59	05 29	15 54	02 57	03 54

EPHEMERIS CALCULATED FOR 12 MIDNIGHT GREENWICH MEAN TIME. ALL OTHER DATA AND FACING ASPECTARIAN PAGE IN **EASTERN STANDARD TIME (BOLD)** AND PACIFIC STANDARD TIME (REGULAR).

NOVEMBER 1999

1 MONDAY
☽⚺♀ **9:01 am** 6:01 am
☉⚺♇ **8:36 pm** 5:36 pm
☽△♃ **8:43 pm** 5:43 pm
☽□☿ 10:17 pm
☽⚻♆ 11:12 pm

2 TUESDAY
☽□☿ **1:17 am**
☽⚻♆ **2:12 am**
⚶⚺⚷ **3:22 am** 12:22 am
☽□⚷ **6:48 am** 3:48 am
☽⚹⚶ **6:55 am** 3:55 am
☽⚺♀ **11:01 am** 8:01 am
☽□♇ **4:00 pm** 1:00 pm
☽⚹☉ **5:34 pm** 2:34 pm
☽△♂ **10:07 pm** 7:07 pm
☽⚻♅ **10:52 pm** 7:52 pm
☽△♄ 9:50 pm

3 WEDNESDAY
☽△♄ **12:50 am**
☽☌⚳ **3:20 am** 12:20 am
☽□⚵ **6:31 am** 3:31 am
♂⚺♅ **11:23 am** 8:23 am
☽☌♀ **9:03 pm** 6:03 pm

4 THURSDAY
☽⚻♃ **3:53 am** 12:53 am
☽⚹☿ **10:11 am** 7:11 am
☽△♆ **10:12 am** 7:12 am
☽⚹⚷ **3:28 pm** 12:28 pm
♂△♄ **4:54 pm** 1:54 pm
☿⚹♆ **5:16 pm** 2:16 pm
☽⚺⚶ **5:31 pm** 2:31 pm
☽⚹♀ **9:00 pm** 6:00 pm
☿⚹♆ **9:05 pm** 6:05 pm
☽⚹♇ 9:39 pm

5 FRIDAY
☽⚹♇ **12:39 am**
☽⚺☉ **7:03 am** 4:03 am
☽△♅ **7:39 am** 4:39 am
☽⚻♄ **9:16 am** 6:16 am
☽□♂ **10:26 am** 7:26 am
☽⚺⚳ **2:05 pm** 11:05 am
☉□♅ **2:43 pm** 11:43 am
☽⚹⚵ **5:05 pm** 2:05 pm

6 SATURDAY
☉☍♄ **8:52 am** 5:52 am
☽⚺♀ **11:50 am** 8:50 am
☽☍♃ **1:01 pm** 10:01 am
☽⚺☿ **7:37 pm** 4:37 pm
☽□♆ **8:11 pm** 5:11 pm
♀⚻♃ 9:18 pm
☽⚺⚷ 11:08 pm

7 SUNDAY
♀⚻♃ **12:18 am**
☽⚺⚷ **2:08 am**
☽☌⚶ **6:18 am** 3:18 am
☽□♀ **8:59 am** 5:59 am
☽⚺♇ **11:11 am** 8:11 am
☽□♅ **6:17 pm** 3:17 pm
☽☍♄ **7:30 pm** 4:30 pm
☽☌☉ **10:53 pm** 7:53 pm
☽⚹♂ 9:57 pm
☽⚹⚳ 11:48 pm

8 MONDAY
☽⚹♂ **12:57 am**
☽⚹⚳ **2:48 am**
☽⚺⚵ **5:35 am** 2:35 am
☽⚻♃ **11:48 pm** 8:48 pm

9 TUESDAY
☿⚹♀ **4:31 am** 1:31 am
☽☌☿ **4:52 am** 1:52 am
☽⚹♀ **4:55 am** 1:55 am
☽⚹♆ **7:50 am** 4:50 am
☽☌⚷ **2:30 pm** 11:30 am
☽⚺⚶ **8:56 pm** 5:56 pm
☽△♀ **10:39 pm** 7:39 pm
☽☌♇ **11:20 pm** 8:20 pm

10 WEDNESDAY
☽⚹♅ **6:29 am** 3:29 am
☽⚻♄ **7:15 am** 4:15 am
♂△⚳ **12:00 pm** 9:00 am
♀△♆ **1:59 pm** 10:59 am
☽⚺☉ **4:42 pm** 1:42 pm
☽□⚳ **5:08 pm** 2:08 pm
☽⚺♂ **5:18 pm** 2:18 pm
☽☌⚵ **7:43 pm** 4:43 pm
☉⚹⚳ 9:38 pm
♇△♀ 11:30 pm

11 THURSDAY
☉⚹⚳ **12:38 am**
♇△♀ **2:30 am**
☽△♃ **11:53 am** 8:53 am
☽⚺☿ **1:28 pm** 10:28 am
☉⚹♂ **7:09 pm** 4:09 pm
☽⚺♆ **8:43 pm** 5:43 pm
☽□♀ **11:45 pm** 8:45 pm

12 FRIDAY
☽⚺⚷ **4:01 am** 1:01 am
♇⚺⚶ **6:25 am** 3:25 am
☿⚻♃ **8:49 am** 5:49 am
☽⚺♇ **12:28 pm** 9:28 am
☽⚹⚶ **12:44 pm** 9:44 am
☽⚻♀ **1:18 pm** 10:18 am
☽⚺♅ **7:33 pm** 4:33 pm
☽△♄ **7:49 pm** 4:49 pm
☉⚺⚵ **8:42 pm** 5:42 pm

13 SATURDAY
☽△⚳ **8:08 am** 5:08 am
☽☌♂ **10:25 am** 7:25 am
☽⚺⚵ **10:29 am** 7:29 am
☽⚹☉ **11:20 am** 8:20 am
♂⚺⚵ **12:13 pm** 9:13 am
♀□⚶ **5:59 pm** 2:59 pm
☽⚹☿ **8:49 pm** 5:49 pm
☽□♃ 9:08 pm

14 SUNDAY
☽□♃ **12:08 am**
♀⚹⚷ **3:54 am** 12:54 am
♄□♅ **4:41 am** 1:41 am
☽☌♆ **9:30 am** 6:30 am
☽⚹⚷ **5:11 pm** 2:11 pm
☽△♀ **6:21 pm** 3:21 pm
☽⚹♇ 9:58 pm

15 MONDAY
☽⚹♇ **12:58 am**
☽☍♀ **3:08 am** 12:08 am
☽□⚶ **3:48 am** 12:48 am
☽□♄ **7:31 am** 4:31 am
☽☌♅ **7:44 am** 4:44 am
☿☌☉ **5:04 pm** 2:04 pm
☽⚻⚳ **9:37 pm** 6:37 pm
☽⚹⚵ **11:42 pm** 8:42 pm
☽⚺♂ 10:49 pm
☽□☿ 11:11 pm

16 TUESDAY
☽⚺♂ **1:49 am**
☽□☿ **2:11 am**
☽□☉ **4:04 am** 1:04 am
☿⚹♂ **4:19 am** 1:19 am
☽⚹♃ **10:31 am** 7:31 am
☽⚺♆ **7:57 pm** 4:57 pm
☿⚺⚵ **8:15 pm** 5:15 pm

17 WEDNESDAY
☽□⚷ **3:41 am** 12:41 am
☽⚻♀ **9:34 am** 6:34 am
☽□♇ **10:35 am** 7:35 am
☿⚹⚳ **11:00 am** 8:00 am
☽⚻♀ **1:43 pm** 10:43 am
☽△⚶ **3:29 pm** 12:29 pm
☽⚹♄ **4:11 pm** 1:11 pm
☽⚺♅ **4:49 pm** 1:49 pm
♀⚹♇ **9:59 pm** 6:59 pm

18 THURSDAY
☽△☿ **5:01 am** 2:01 am
♄☍⚶ **6:53 am** 3:53 am
☽☍⚳ **7:14 am** 4:14 am
☽□⚵ **9:02 am** 6:02 am
☽⚹♂ **12:50 pm** 9:50 am
☽△☉ **4:04 pm** 1:04 pm
☽⚺♃ **5:10 pm** 2:10 pm
♅□⚶ 10:59 pm
☽⚹♆ 11:22 pm

19 FRIDAY
♅□⚶ **1:59 am**
☽⚹♆ **2:22 am**
☉⚻♃ **5:34 am** 2:34 am
☽△⚷ **9:54 am** 6:54 am
☽△♇ **3:55 pm** 12:55 pm
☽☍♀ **7:21 pm** 4:21 pm
☽△♀ **7:41 pm** 4:41 pm
☽⚺♄ **8:39 pm** 5:39 pm
☽⚹♅ **9:37 pm** 6:37 pm
☽⚻⚶ **10:20 pm** 7:20 pm
♀⚹♀ 9:48 pm

20 SATURDAY
♀⚹♀ **12:48 am**
☽⚻☿ **5:16 am** 2:16 am
♀⚻♄ **10:59 am** 7:59 am
☽⚻⚳ **12:10 pm** 9:10 am
☽△⚵ **1:46 pm** 10:46 am
☽□♂ **6:51 pm** 3:51 pm
☽☌♃ **7:42 pm** 4:42 pm
☽⚻☉ **10:48 pm** 7:48 pm
♀△♅ 9:41 pm

21 SUNDAY
♀△♅ **12:41 am**
☽□♆ **4:41 am** 1:41 am
♂□♃ **9:43 am** 6:43 am
☽⚻⚷ **12:05 pm** 9:05 am
♄□♀ **1:34 pm** 10:34 am
☽⚻♇ **5:26 pm** 2:26 pm
☽☌♄ **9:31 pm** 6:31 pm
☽□♀ **9:41 pm** 6:41 pm
☽□♅ **10:45 pm** 7:45 pm
☽⚻♀ 9:28 pm
☽☍⚶ 10:08 pm

22 MONDAY
☽⚻♀ **12:28 am**
☽☍⚶ **1:08 am**
☽☍☿ **3:43 am** 12:43 am
☽△⚳ **1:40 pm** 10:40 am
☽⚻⚵ **3:09 pm** 12:09 pm
♀⚺⚶ **5:00 pm** 2:00 pm
☽⚺♃ **7:25 pm** 4:25 pm
☽△♂ **9:24 pm** 6:24 pm
☽☍☉ 11:04 pm

23 TUESDAY
☽☍☉ **2:04 am**
☽△♆ **4:26 am** 1:26 am
☿⚺♀ **9:09 am** 6:09 am
☽☍⚷ **11:57 am** 8:57 am
☽☍♇ **4:55 pm** 1:55 pm
☽⚺♄ **8:35 pm** 5:35 pm
☿☌⚶ **9:25 pm** 6:25 pm
☽⚹♀ **9:43 pm** 6:43 pm
☽△♅ **10:06 pm** 7:06 pm
☽⚻☿ 10:52 pm
☽⚻⚶ 11:05 pm

24 WEDNESDAY
☽⚻☿ **1:52 am**
☽⚻⚶ **2:05 am**
☽△♀ **3:29 am** 12:29 am
☽□⚳ **1:58 pm** 10:58 am
☉⚹♆ **2:33 pm** 11:33 am
☽☍⚵ **3:26 pm** 12:26 pm
☽⚹♃ **6:21 pm** 3:21 pm
☽⚻♂ **11:08 pm** 8:08 pm

25 THURSDAY
♅☍♀ **3:30 am** 12:30 am
☽⚻♆ **3:48 am** 12:48 am
☽⚻☉ **4:44 am** 1:44 am
☽⚻⚷ **11:48 am** 8:48 am
☽⚻♇ **4:36 pm** 1:36 pm
☽⚹♄ **8:01 pm** 5:01 pm
☽⚻♅ **9:54 pm** 6:54 pm
☽⚺♀ **10:08 pm** 7:08 pm
☽△☿ 10:47 pm

26 FRIDAY
☽△☿ **1:47 am**
☽△⚶ **3:43 am** 12:43 am
☽□♀ **7:22 am** 4:22 am
☽⚹⚳ **3:29 pm** 12:29 pm
☽⚻⚵ **5:01 pm** 2:01 pm
☽□♃ **6:35 pm** 3:35 pm
☽☍♂ 11:37 pm

27 SATURDAY
☽☍♂ **2:37 am**
☽☍♆ **4:52 am** 1:52 am
☽△☉ **9:32 am** 6:32 am
☽△⚷ **1:41 pm** 10:41 am
☽△♇ **6:28 pm** 3:28 pm
☽□♄ **9:42 pm** 6:42 pm
☽☍♅ 9:03 pm
☽☌♀ 9:56 pm

28 SUNDAY
☽☍♅ **12:03 am**
☽☌♀ **12:56 am**
☽□☿ **5:26 am** 2:26 am
☽□⚶ **8:10 am** 5:10 am
☽⚹♀ **2:37 pm** 11:37 am
☽⚺⚳ **8:01 pm** 5:01 pm
☽△⚵ **9:42 pm** 6:42 pm
☽△♃ **9:43 pm** 6:43 pm
♂☌♆ **9:58 pm** 6:58 pm
♃△⚵ **10:00 pm** 7:00 pm

29 MONDAY
☽⚻♆ **9:05 am** 6:05 am
☽⚻♂ **9:45 am** 6:45 am
☽□☉ **6:19 pm** 3:19 pm
☽□⚷ **6:56 pm** 3:56 pm
☽□♇ **11:40 pm** 8:40 pm
☽△♄ 11:42 pm

30 TUESDAY
☽△♄ **2:42 am**
☉☌⚷ **3:25 am** 12:25 am
☽⚻♅ **5:37 am** 2:37 am
☽⚺♀ **7:10 am** 4:10 am
☽⚹☿ **2:11 pm** 11:11 am
☽⚹⚶ **4:27 pm** 1:27 pm
☽⚺♀ 11:22 pm

Eastern Standard Time in bold type

NOVEMBER 1999

D Last Aspect / D Ingress

day	EST / hr:mn / PST	asp	sign	day	EST / hr:mn / PST	asp
1	8:43 pm 5:43 pm	△ ♂	♍	1	11:07 pm 8:07 pm	△ ♂
3	9:03 pm 6:03 pm	♂ ♀	≏	4	6:56 am 3:56 am	♂ ♀
6	1:01 pm 10:01 am	□ ♂	M,	6	4:45 pm 1:45 pm	
	9:57 pm		✗	9	4:15 am 1:15 am	
8	12:57 am		✗	9	4:15 am 1:15 am	
11	11:53 am 8:53 am		ᏉᏒ	11	5:00 pm 2:00 pm	
13	9:08 pm		≈	14	5:46 am 2:46 am	
14	12:08 am		≈	14	5:46 am 2:46 am	
16	10:31 am 7:31 am		✗	16	4:21 pm 1:21 pm	
18	4:04 pm 1:04 pm		♈	18	10:58 pm 7:58 pm	

D Last Aspect / D Ingress

day	EST / hr:mn / PST	asp	sign	day	EST / hr:mn / PST	asp
20	7:42 am 4:42 am		♉	20	11:26 am	
20	7:42 am 4:42 am		♊	22	1:14 am	
22	9:24 am 6:24 am		♊	22	1:14 am	
24	9:24 am 6:24 am		♋	25	2:29 am	
24	6:21 am 3:21 pm		♋	25	2:29 am	
24	6:21 am 3:21 pm		♌	27	1:18 am	
24	6:35 pm 3:35 pm		♌	27	1:18 am	
26	6:35 pm 3:35 pm		♍	29	5:11 am 2:11 am	
28	9:43 pm 6:43 pm		≏	12/1	12:29 pm 9:29 pm	
30	2:11 pm 11:11 am					

D Phases & Eclipses

phase	day	EST / hr:mn / PST
New Moon	7	10:53 pm 7:53 pm
2nd Quarter	16	4:04 am 1:04 am
Full Moon	22	11:04 pm
Full Moon	23	2:04 am
4th Quarter	29	6:19 am 3:19 am

Planet Ingress

	day	EST / hr:mn / PST
♀ ≏	8	9:19 pm 6:19 pm
☿ M,	9	3:12 pm 12:12 pm
⊙ ✗	22	1:25 pm 10:25 am
☿ ✗	25	1:56 am
♂ ≈	26	10:56 pm

Planetary Motion

	day	EST / hr:mn / PST
☿ R	4	9:51 pm 6:51 pm
☿ D	24	10:53 pm 7:53 pm

Ephemeris Table

DATE		SID.TIME	SUN	MOON	NODE	MERCURY	VENUS	MARS	JUPITER	SATURN	URANUS	NEPTUNE	PLUTO	CERES	PALLAS	JUNO	VESTA	CHIRON
M	1	2:39:22	08 ♏ 16	14 ♍ 23	08 ♍ 26	00 ♏ 44	21 ♍ 57	10 ✗ 56	28 ♈ 49	14 ♉ 09	12 ≈ 54	01 ≈ 57	09 ✗ 41	14 ♍ 57	05 ≏ 52	16 ♊ 13	03 ♏ 51	04 ✗ 02
T	2	2:43:18	09	27 44		01	23								15	06	16	04	09
W	3	2:47:15	10	11 ≏ 50		01	24								15	06	17	04	16
T	4	2:51:11	11	25 41		01 R	25								16	07	17	04	23
F	5	2:55:08	13	09 M, 18		01	26								16	07	17	04	31
S	6	2:59:04	14	22 40		00	27								17	08	18	04	38
S	7	3:03:01	15	05 ✗ 46		29 ≏ 40	28								17	08	18	05	45
M	8	3:06:57	16	18 38		29	29								18	09	19	05	52
T	9	3:10:54	17	01 ᏉᏒ 17		28	01 ≏								18	09	19	05	00
W	10	3:14:51	18	13 44		28	02								19	10	20	05	07
T	11	3:18:47	19	26 02		28	04								19	10	20	06	14
F	12	3:22:44	20	08 ≈ 11		28	05								20	11	21	06	22
S	13	3:26:40	21	20 12		28	07								20	11	21	06	29
S	14	3:30:37	22	02 ✗ 07		28	09								21	12	22	06	37
M	15	3:34:33	23	13 58		28 R	10								21	12	22	06	44
T	16	3:38:30	24	25 48		28	12								22	13	23	07	52
W	17	3:42:26	25	07 ♈ 42		28	13								22	13	24	07	59
T	18	3:46:23	26	19 45		27	15								23	14	24	07	07
F	19	3:50:20	27	02 ♉ 02		27	16								23	14	25	07	14
S	20	3:54:16	28	14 37		26	18								23	15	25	07	22
S	21	3:58:13	29	27 36		25	20								24	15	26	07	29
M	22	4:02:09	00 ✗	11 ♊ 03		24	21								24	16	26	07	37
T	23	4:06:06	01	25 01		24	23								24	17	26	07	44
W	24	4:10:02	02	09 ♋ 30		24	25								25	17	27	07	52
T	25	4:13:59	03	24 26		24	26								25	18	27	07	59
F	26	4:17:55	04	09 ♌ 42		24	28								25	18	27	08	07
S	27	4:21:52	05	25 06		24 R	00 M,								26	19	28	08	15
S	28	4:25:49	06	10 ♍ 25		24	01								26	19	28	08	22
M	29	4:29:45	07	25 29		24	03								27	20	28	08	30
T	30	4:33:42	08	10 ≏ 09		24	05								27	20	28	08	38

EPHEMERIS CALCULATED FOR 12 MIDNIGHT GREENWICH MEAN TIME. ALL OTHER DATA AND FACING ASPECTARIAN PAGE IN **EASTERN STANDARD TIME (BOLD)** AND PACIFIC STANDARD TIME (REGULAR).

DECEMBER 1999

1 WEDNESDAY
2:22 am
4:15 am — 1:15 am
4:16 am — 1:16 am
4:46 am — 1:46 am
6:08 am — 3:08 am
4:45 pm — 1:45 pm
8:56 pm — 5:56 pm
10:30 pm — 7:30 pm

2 THURSDAY
3:37 am — 12:37 am
7:08 am — 4:08 am
7:20 am — 4:20 am
8:13 am — 5:13 am
10:55 am — 7:55 am
2:27 pm — 11:27 am
4:40 pm — 1:40 pm
6:37 pm — 3:37 pm

3 FRIDAY
3:56 am — 12:56 am
4:15 am — 1:15 am
11:10 am — 8:10 am
1:03 pm — 10:03 am
1:45 pm — 10:45 am
3:38 pm — 12:38 pm
5:43 pm — 2:43 pm
6:04 pm — 3:04 pm
9:56 pm

4 SATURDAY
12:56 am
3:08 am — 12:08 am
11:20 am — 8:20 am
2:54 pm — 11:54 am
7:14 pm — 4:14 pm
9:31 pm — 6:31 pm
11:32 pm — 8:32 pm
10:39 pm

5 SUNDAY
1:39 am
4:25 am — 1:25 am
6:26 am — 3:26 am
9:30 am — 6:30 am
10:09 pm
10:20 pm

6 MONDAY
1:09 am
1:20 am
5:01 am — 2:01 am
7:21 am — 4:21 am
12:17 pm — 9:17 am
3:15 pm — 12:15 pm

7 TUESDAY
3:38 am — 12:38 am
3:45 am — 12:45 am
5:43 am — 2:43 am
7:43 am — 4:43 am
7:49 am — 4:49 am
9:31 am — 6:31 am
11:12 am
3:32 pm — 12:32 pm
5:23 pm — 2:23 pm
5:32 pm — 2:32 pm
7:11 pm — 4:11 pm

8 WEDNESDAY
9:53 am — 6:53 am
1:36 pm — 10:36 am
5:21 pm — 2:21 pm
7:25 pm — 4:25 pm
10:00 pm — 7:00 pm

9 THURSDAY
4:12 am — 1:12 am
7:44 am — 4:44 am
4:47 am — 1:47 am
5:16 pm — 2:16 pm
8:45 pm — 5:45 pm
8:48 pm — 5:48 pm
9:31 pm — 6:31 pm
10:07 pm — 7:07 pm

10 FRIDAY
3:18 am — 12:18 am
6:41 am — 3:41 am
12:09 pm — 9:09 am
4:23 pm — 1:23 pm
11:41 pm — 8:41 pm
10:35 pm
11:14 pm

11 SATURDAY
1:35 am
2:14 am

12 SUNDAY
2:58 am
6:24 am — 3:24 am
9:26 am — 6:26 am
10:15 am — 7:15 am
1:19 pm — 10:19 am
3:47 pm — 12:47 pm
5:08 pm — 2:08 pm
7:09 pm — 4:09 pm

13 MONDAY
5:42 am — 2:42 am
5:48 am — 2:48 am
3:56 pm — 12:56 pm
7:41 pm — 4:41 pm
10:41 pm — 7:45 pm

14 TUESDAY
1:45 am
4:18 am — 1:18 am
5:59 am — 2:59 am
8:42 am — 5:42 am
5:30 pm — 2:30 pm
7:41 pm — 4:41 pm
7:59 pm — 4:59 pm
8:21 pm — 5:21 pm
10:52 pm — 7:52 pm
11:01 pm
11:33 pm

15 WEDNESDAY
2:01 am
2:33 am
5:07 am — 2:07 am
7:50 pm — 4:50 pm
10:25 pm — 7:50 pm
11:58 pm

16 THURSDAY
2:58 am
8:12 am — 5:12 am
10:13 am — 7:13 am
11:22 am — 8:22 am

17 FRIDAY
12:59 am
2:56 am
3:49 am — 12:49 am
5:28 am — 2:28 am
7:43 am — 4:43 am
8:34 am — 5:34 am
11:15 am — 8:15 am
3:46 pm — 12:46 pm
6:00 pm — 3:00 pm
7:08 pm — 4:08 pm
9:12 pm

18 SATURDAY
12:12 am
5:03 am — 2:03 am
9:03 am — 6:03 am
9:34 am — 6:34 am
10:41 am — 7:41 am
12:27 pm — 9:27 am
4:19 pm — 1:19 pm
11:52 pm — 8:52 pm

19 SUNDAY
4:27 am — 1:27 am
5:41 am — 2:41 am
5:57 am — 2:57 am
7:53 am — 4:53 am
11:14 am — 8:14 am
1:29 pm — 10:29 am
2:43 pm — 11:43 am
5:46 pm — 2:46 pm

20 MONDAY
4:41 am — 1:41 am
9:53 am — 6:53 am
12:21 pm — 9:21 am
3:09 pm — 12:09 pm
5:05 pm — 2:05 pm
5:53 pm — 2:53 pm
6:34 pm — 3:34 pm

21 TUESDAY
4:57 am — 1:57 am
5:37 am — 2:37 am
6:08 am — 3:08 am
1:03 pm — 10:03 am
1:05 pm — 10:05 am
1:17 pm — 10:17 am
6:29 pm — 3:29 pm
7:57 pm — 4:57 pm

22 WEDNESDAY
4:03 am — 1:03 am
12:31 am
1:15 am
3:12 pm — 12:12 pm
4:22 pm — 1:22 pm
6:54 pm — 3:54 pm

23 THURSDAY
4:28 am — 1:28 am
4:38 am — 1:38 am
5:23 am — 2:23 am
7:27 am
10:32 am — 7:32 am
12:01 pm — 9:01 am
5:28 pm — 2:28 pm
9:07 pm — 6:07 pm
9:40 pm — 6:40 pm
9:48 pm — 6:48 pm
9:49 pm — 6:49 pm

24 FRIDAY
3:31 am — 12:31 am
2:43 pm — 11:43 am
3:44 pm — 12:44 pm
3:49 pm — 12:49 pm
4:17 pm — 1:17 pm
5:21 pm — 2:21 pm
8:02 pm — 5:02 pm
9:01 pm

25 SATURDAY
12:01 am
12:19 pm — 9:19 am
5:10 am — 2:10 am
5:51 am — 2:51 am
11:17 am — 8:17 am
12:19 pm — 9:19 am
11:35 pm — 8:31 pm

26 SUNDAY
12:16 am
3:34 am — 12:34 am
5:07 am — 2:07 am
1:59 am
6:46 am — 3:46 am
6:56 am — 3:56 am
7:04 am — 4:04 am
9:58 am — 6:58 am
10:04 am — 7:04 am
9:03 pm
10:04 pm

27 MONDAY
1:04 am
4:16 am — 1:16 am
7:57 am — 4:57 am
9:18 am — 6:18 am
3:10 pm — 12:10 pm
3:37 pm — 12:37 pm
9:39 pm — 6:39 pm

28 TUESDAY
9:57 am — 6:57 am
10:15 am — 7:15 am
11:54 am — 8:54 am
1:52 pm — 10:52 am
3:01 pm — 12:01 pm
3:15 pm — 12:15 pm
8:59 pm — 5:59 pm
9:59 pm
11:11 pm

29 WEDNESDAY
12:59 am
3:18 am — 12:19 am
9:08 am — 6:08 am
2:52 pm — 11:52 am
4:35 pm — 1:35 pm
10:31 pm — 7:31 pm
10:56 pm — 7:56 pm

30 THURSDAY
3:59 am — 12:59 am
7:13 am — 4:13 am
10:35 am — 7:35 am
9:16 pm
10:51 pm

31 FRIDAY
5:02 am — 2:02 am
5:08 am — 2:08 am
8:31 am — 5:31 am
10:51 am — 7:51 am
1:04 pm — 10:04 am
3:44 pm — 12:44 pm
8:04 pm — 5:04 pm
9:35 pm
10:11 pm

Eastern Standard Time in bold type
Pacific Standard Time in medium type

DECEMBER 1999

☽ Last Aspect day	EST / hr:mn	PST	asp	☽ Ingress sign	day	EST / hr:mn	PST
30	**2:11 pm**	11:11 am	✶ ☿	♎	1	**12:29 pm**	9:29 am
3	**6:04 pm**	3:04 pm	☌ ♀	♏	3	**10:36 pm**	7:36 pm
5	**9:30 pm**	6:30 pm	☌ ☿	♐	6	**10:28 am**	7:28 am
8	**1:36 pm**	10:36 am	△ ♃	♑	8	**11:14 pm**	8:14 pm
10		11:14 pm	□ ♃	♒	11	**11:59 am**	8:59 am
11	**2:14 am**		□ ♃	♒	11	**11:59 am**	8:59 am
13	**1:46 pm**	10:46 am	✶ ♃	♓	13	**11:18 pm**	8:18 pm
15	**7:50 pm**	4:50 pm	□ ☉	♈	16	**7:30 am**	4:30 am
18	**5:03 am**	2:03 am	△ ☉	♉	18	**11:45 am**	8:45 am
19	**5:46 pm**	2:46 pm	□ ♂	♊	20	**12:39 pm**	9:39 am
22	**4:03 am**	1:03 am	✶ ♃	♋	22	**11:52 am**	8:52 am
24	**3:31 am**	12:31 am	□ ♃	♌	24	**11:32 am**	8:32 am
26	**5:07 am**	2:07 am	△ ♃	♍	26	**1:34 pm**	10:34 am
28	**1:52 pm**	10:52 am	✶ ♀	♎	28	**7:15 pm**	4:15 pm
30	**10:35 pm**	7:35 pm	△ ♂	♏	30	**4:37 am**	1:37 am

☽ Phases & Eclipses phase	day	EST / hr:mn	PST
New Moon	7	**5:32 pm**	2:32 pm
2nd Quarter	15	**7:50 pm**	4:50 pm
Full Moon	22	**12:31 pm**	9:31 am
4th Quarter	29	**9:05 am**	6:05 am

Planet Ingress	day	EST / hr:mn	PST
♀ ♏	5	**5:41 pm**	2:41 pm
⚵ ♑	10	**2:09 pm**	11:09 am
☿ ♐	10	**9:09 pm**	6:09 pm

Planet Ingress	day	EST / hr:mn	PST
⚳ ♎	14		9:16 pm
⚳ ♎	15	**12:16 am**	
⚶ ♐	20	**8:55 pm**	5:55 pm
☉ ♑	21		11:44 pm
☉ ♑	22	**2:44 am**	
♀ ♐	30	**11:54 pm**	8:54 pm
☿ ♑	30		10:48 pm
☿ ♑	31	**1:48 am**	

Planetary Motion	day	EST / hr:mn	PST
⚴ ℞	15	**5:56 pm**	2:56 pm
♃ D	20	**10:23 am**	7:23 am

DATE		SID.TIME	SUN	MOON	NODE	MERCURY	VENUS	MARS	JUPITER	SATURN	URANUS	NEPTUNE	PLUTO	CERES	PALLAS	JUNO	VESTA	CHIRON
W	1	4:37:38	08 ♐ 19	20 ♍ 42	05 ♌ ℞ 32	18 ♏ 16	24 ♎ 17	03 ♒ 37	25 ♈ ℞ 40	11 ♉ ℞ 50	13 ♒ 30	02 ♒ 13	10 ♐ 16	25 ♍ 31	14 ♌ 24	26 ♐ 28	19 ♏ 23	07 ♐ 45
T	2	4:41:35	09 20	03 ♎ 25	05 30	19 09	25 26	04 23	25 37	11 46	13 31	02 14	10 18	25 51	14 34	26 50	19 55	07 53
F	3	4:45:31	10 21	15 54	05 25	20 07	26 35	05 09	25 33	11 42	13 33	02 16	10 20	26 11	14 43	27 11	20 27	08 00
S	4	4:49:28	11 22	28 11	05 17	21 09	27 45	05 55	25 29	11 38	13 35	02 18	10 23	26 31	14 51	27 33	20 59	08 08
S	5	4:53:24	12 23	10 ♏ 18	05 08	22 16	28 54	06 41	25 26	11 34	13 37	02 19	10 25	26 50	14 59	27 54	21 31	08 16
M	6	4:57:21	13 24	22 18	04 58	23 26	00 ♏ 04	07 27	25 23	11 31	13 40	02 21	10 27	27 10	15 06	28 16	22 02	08 23
T	7	5:01:18	14 24	04 ♐ 14	04 48	24 38	01 14	08 13	25 20	11 27	13 42	02 23	10 30	27 29	15 12	28 37	22 34	08 31
W	8	5:05:14	15 25	16 06	04 39	25 54	02 24	09 00	25 17	11 23	13 44	02 24	10 32	27 48	15 18	28 59	23 06	08 38
T	9	5:09:11	16 26	27 55	04 31	27 12	03 34	09 46	25 15	11 20	13 46	02 26	10 35	28 07	15 23	29 21	23 38	08 46
F	10	5:13:07	17 27	09 ♑ 44	04 26	28 31	04 44	10 32	25 12	11 16	13 48	02 28	10 37	28 26	15 28	29 43	24 09	08 53
S	11	5:17:04	18 28	21 35	04 D 23	29 53	05 54	11 19	25 10	11 13	13 51	02 29	10 39	28 44	15 31	00 ♑ 04	24 41	09 01
S	12	5:21:00	19 29	03 ♒ 30	04 23	01 ♐ 15	07 05	12 05	25 08	11 10	13 53	02 31	10 41	29 02	15 35	00 26	25 13	09 08
M	13	5:24:57	20 30	15 32	04 24	02 39	08 16	12 51	25 07	11 07	13 55	02 33	10 44	29 21	15 37	00 48	25 45	09 16
T	14	5:28:54	21 31	27 47	04 26	04 04	09 26	13 38	25 05	11 04	13 58	02 35	10 46	29 38	15 39	01 10	26 16	09 23
W	15	5:32:50	22 32	10 ♓ 18	04 27	05 30	10 37	14 24	25 04	11 01	14 00	02 37	10 48	29 56	15 40	01 32	26 48	09 31
T	16	5:36:47	23 33	23 09	04 ℞ 28	06 57	11 48	15 11	25 03	10 58	14 03	02 38	10 51	00 ♎ 14	15 40	01 54	27 20	09 38
F	17	5:40:43	24 35	06 ♈ 25	04 27	08 24	12 59	15 57	25 02	10 55	14 05	02 40	10 53	00 31	15 ℞ 40	02 16	27 51	09 46
S	18	5:44:40	25 36	20 08	04 25	09 53	14 11	16 43	25 01	10 52	14 08	02 42	10 55	00 48	15 39	02 38	28 23	09 53
S	19	5:48:36	26 37	04 ♉ 20	04 21	11 21	15 22	17 30	25 01	10 49	14 10	02 44	10 58	01 05	15 37	03 00	28 54	10 00
M	20	5:52:33	27 38	18 59	04 17	12 50	16 33	18 16	25 01	10 47	14 13	02 46	11 00	01 21	15 34	03 22	29 26	10 08
T	21	5:56:29	28 39	04 ♊ 00	04 11	14 20	17 45	19 03	25 D 01	10 44	14 16	02 48	11 02	01 38	15 31	03 44	29 57	10 15
W	22	6:00:26	29 40	19 15	04 06	15 50	18 57	19 49	25 01	10 42	14 18	02 50	11 04	01 54	15 27	04 06	00 ♐ 29	10 22
T	23	6:04:23	00 ♑ 41	04 ♋ 32	04 02	17 20	20 08	20 36	25 01	10 40	14 21	02 52	11 07	02 09	15 23	04 28	01 00	10 30
F	24	6:08:19	01 42	19 42	03 59	18 51	21 20	21 22	25 02	10 38	14 24	02 54	11 09	02 25	15 17	04 50	01 32	10 37
S	25	6:12:16	02 43	04 ♌ 36	03 D 57	20 22	22 32	22 09	25 03	10 36	14 27	02 56	11 11	02 40	15 11	05 13	02 03	10 44
S	26	6:16:12	03 44	19 06	03 57	21 53	23 44	22 55	25 04	10 34	14 30	02 58	11 13	02 56	15 04	05 35	02 35	10 51
M	27	6:20:09	04 45	03 ♍ 08	03 57	23 24	24 56	23 42	25 05	10 32	14 32	03 00	11 15	03 10	14 57	05 57	03 06	10 58
T	28	6:24:05	05 46	16 43	03 58	24 56	26 08	24 28	25 06	10 30	14 35	03 02	11 18	03 ℞ 25	14 48	06 19	03 38	11 06
W	29	6:28:02	06 48	29 52	03 ℞ 59	26 28	27 20	25 15	25 08	10 29	14 38	03 04	11 20	03 20	14 18	06 42	04 03	11 13
T	30	6:31:58	07 49	12 ♎ 38	03 59	28 01	28 33	26 01	25 10	10 27	14 41	03 06	11 22	03 16	13 49	07 08	04 28	11 20
F	31	6:35:55	08 50	25 05	03 58	29 34	29 45	26 48	25 12	10 26	14 44	03 08	11 24	04 D 14	13 23	07 31	04 54	11 27

EPHEMERIS CALCULATED FOR 12 MIDNIGHT GREENWICH MEAN TIME. ALL OTHER DATA AND FACING ASPECTARIAN PAGE IN **EASTERN STANDARD TIME (BOLD)** AND PACIFIC STANDARD TIME (REGULAR).

JANUARY 2000

Eastern Standard Time in bold type
Pacific Standard Time in medium type

1 SATURDAY
10:11 pm
11:18 pm

6 THURSDAY
12:13 am
1:11 am
2:18 am
4:56 am
6:04 am
7:33 am
9:22 am
11:54 am
1:14 pm
3:42 pm

10 MONDAY
9:56 am
11:48 am
2:39 pm
3:02 pm
5:09 pm

15 SATURDAY
12:32 am
2:03 am
4:59 am
7:47 am
11:04 am
11:15 am
1:20 pm
1:23 pm
1:49 pm
4:10 pm
6:19 pm
6:40 pm
6:43 pm
8:19 pm
10:22 pm

19 WEDNESDAY
5:11 am
8:06 am
11:06 am
3:32 pm
6:38 pm
8:45 pm
10:54 pm
11:53 pm

29 SATURDAY
4:14 am
4:55 am
6:31 am
11:58 am
4:13 pm
7:16 pm
7:56 pm
10:23 pm
11:57 pm

7 FRIDAY
9:00 am
11:48 am
2:06 pm
3:12 pm
10:40 pm

2 SUNDAY
3:33 am
7:02 am
9:27 am
4:14 pm
11:07 pm
11:52 pm

11 TUESDAY
12:47 am
1:24 am
3:18 am
3:38 am
5:25 am
7:19 am
10:23 am
11:27 am
4:05 pm
7:58 pm
9:23 pm

20 THURSDAY
12:16 am
3:07 am
5:36 am
11:40 am

24 MONDAY
2:48 am
3:31 am
4:23 am
6:26 am
7:08 am
8:18 am
10:59 am

30 SUNDAY
2:11 am
3:35 am
5:56 am
6:38 pm

8 SATURDAY
6:00 am
8:48 am
9:06 am
10:12 am
7:40 pm
9:13 pm
11:21 pm

3 MONDAY
2:01 am
2:21 am
4:52 am
6:42 am
6:42 am
10:20 am
1:30 pm
3:54 pm
4:38 pm
6:41 pm
7:54 pm
10:50 pm

12 WEDNESDAY
6:12 am
6:50 am
3:37 pm
4:32 pm
8:28 pm

16 SUNDAY
5:19 am
11:26 am
3:51 pm
4:14 pm
4:47 pm
4:50 pm
9:51 pm

21 FRIDAY
1:05 am
5:18 am
5:50 am
11:33 am
5:36 pm
8:40 pm

25 TUESDAY
5:30 am
11:33 am
1:20 pm
4:37 pm
7:00 pm
8:55 pm
11:12 pm

31 MONDAY
12:15 am
12:17 am
4:59 am
8:39 am
1:09 pm
1:22 pm
2:26 pm
6:50 pm
6:58 pm
9:22 pm

9 SUNDAY
12:04 am
6:34 am
3:36 pm
4:14 pm
5:50 pm

4 TUESDAY
4:39 am
6:27 am
8:06 am

13 THURSDAY
2:05 am
2:54 am
8:38 am
9:48 am
11:28 am
12:44 pm
5:57 pm
8:23 pm

17 MONDAY
4:38 am
5:28 am
10:25 am
2:10 pm
3:19 pm
3:51 pm
6:02 pm
8:20 pm
9:36 pm
10:08 pm

22 SATURDAY
12:30 am
12:48 am
1:57 am
2:54 am
4:12 pm
6:53 pm
8:30 pm

26 WEDNESDAY
2:27 am
3:17 am
6:09 am
8:19 am
9:48 am
12:06 pm
12:14 pm
2:55 pm
10:02 pm

5 WEDNESDAY
4:24 am
7:36 am
12:11 pm
7:41 pm
9:04 pm
10:22 pm

14 FRIDAY
6:41 am
8:34 am

18 TUESDAY
12:02 pm
10:55 am
5:21 pm
8:13 pm
11:44 pm

23 SUNDAY
4:36 am
5:17 am
6:53 pm
10:03 pm

27 THURSDAY
1:36 am
6:59 am
7:36 am
8:06 am
11:51 am

28 FRIDAY
12:48 am
2:57 am

Additional columns (right):
5:41 pm
5:57 pm
9:47 pm
11:03 pm
2:11 pm
8:06 pm
10:20 pm
12:30 pm
12:32 pm
3:38 pm
7:45 pm
8:54 pm
9:16 pm

1:59 am
4:47 am
8:15 am
10:23 am
1:10 pm
3:19 pm
3:40 pm
5:19 pm
7:22 pm

2:19 am
8:26 am
12:51 pm
1:14 pm
1:47 pm
1:50 pm
6:51 pm

1:28 pm
5:20 pm
7:25 pm
11:10 pm
12:51 pm
3:02 pm
6:36 pm
9:02 pm

7:55 am
2:21 pm
5:13 pm
8:44 pm

9:39 pm
12:07 pm
2:36 pm
8:40 pm
10:05 pm

12:31 pm
3:26 pm
1:42 pm
5:18 pm
7:59 pm

12:17 pm
3:09 pm
6:48 pm
9:06 am
9:14 am
11:55 am
7:02 pm
10:36 pm

3:59 pm
4:36 pm
5:06 pm
9:48 pm
11:57 pm

1:38 pm
3:17 pm
3:53 pm
7:03 pm

1:14 am
1:55 am
5:31 am
8:58 am
4:16 pm
4:56 pm
7:23 pm
8:57 pm
11:11 pm

12:35 pm
2:56 pm
3:38 pm

4:55 am
6:59 am
11:06 am
1:25 pm
3:18 pm
5:28 pm
5:46 pm
7:28 pm
9:15 pm
9:17 pm

1:59 am
5:39 am
8:39 am
10:09 am
11:26 am
10:22 am
3:50 pm
3:58 pm
6:22 pm

JANUARY 2000

☽ Last Aspect day	EST / hr:mn / PST		asp	☽ Ingress sign	day	EST / hr:mn / PST	
2	**2:28 pm**	11:28 am	□♂	♐	2	**4:32 pm**	1:32 pm
4	**8:06 pm**	5:06 pm	△♃	♑	5	**5:24 am**	2:24 am
7	**9:00 am**	6:00 am	□♃	♒	7	**5:53 pm**	2:53 pm
9	**8:41 pm**	5:41 pm	⚹♃	♓	10	**4:59 am**	1:59 am
11	**9:23 pm**	6:23 pm	⚹☉	♈	12	**1:48 pm**	10:48 am
14	**12:47 pm**	9:47 am	☌♃	♉	14	**7:38 pm**	4:38 pm
16	**4:50 pm**	1:50 pm	△☿	♊	16	**10:25 pm**	7:25 pm
18	**5:21 pm**	2:21 pm	⚹♃	♋	18	**11:01 pm**	8:01 pm
20	**5:36 pm**	2:36 pm	□♃	♌	20	**10:58 pm**	7:58 pm
22	**8:30 pm**	5:30 pm	△♀	♍	22		9:07 pm
22	**8:30 pm**	5:30 pm	△♀	♍	23	**12:07 am**	
23		11:48 pm	☍♂	♎	25	**4:09 am**	1:09 am
24	**2:48 am**		☍♂	♎	25	**4:09 am**	1:09 am
27	**6:59 am**	3:59 am	☍♃	♏	27	**12:01 pm**	9:01 am
28		11:11 pm	△♂	♐	29	**11:17 pm**	8:17 pm
29	**2:11 am**		△♂	♐	29	**11:17 pm**	8:17 pm

☽ Phases & Eclipses phase	day	EST / hr:mn / PST	
New Moon	6	**1:14 pm**	10:14 am
2nd Quarter	14	**8:34 am**	5:34 am
Full Moon	20	**11:40 pm**	8:40 pm
●	20	**11:44 pm**	8:44 pm
4th Quarter	27		11:57 pm
4th Quarter	28	**2:57 am**	

Planet Ingress		day	EST / hr:mn / PST	
♂	♓	3	**10:01 pm**	7:01 pm
☿	♒	18	**5:20 pm**	2:20 pm
☉	♒	20	**1:23 pm**	10:23 am
♀	♑	24	**2:52 pm**	11:52 am

Planetary Motion		day	EST / hr:mn / PST	
♄	D	11	**11:59 pm**	8:59 pm

DATE		SID.TIME	SUN	MOON	NODE	MERCURY	VENUS	MARS	JUPITER	SATURN	URANUS	NEPTUNE	PLUTO	CERES	PALLAS	JUNO	VESTA	CHIRON
Sat	1	6:39:51	09 ♑ 51 33	07 ♏ 18	03 ♌ ℞ 59	01 ♑ 07	00 ♐ 58	27 ♒ 35	25 ♈ 14	10 ♉ ℞ 24	14 ♒ 47	03 ♒ 11	11 ♐ 26	04 ♎ 21	14 ♌ ℞ 08	07 ♑ 49	05 ♐ 42	11 ♐ 34
Sun	2	6:43:48	10 52 43	19 19	03 55	02 40	02 10	28 21	25 16	10 23	14 50	03 13	11 28	04 34	13 56	08 11	06 14	11 41
Mon	3	6:47:44	11 53 53	01 ♐ 13	03 51	04 14	03 23	29 08	25 19	10 22	14 53	03 15	11 30	04 47	13 44	08 33	06 45	11 48
Tue	4	6:51:41	12 55 04	13 04	03 48	05 48	04 36	29 54	25 22	10 21	14 56	03 17	11 32	05 00	13 31	08 56	07 16	11 54
Wed	5	6:55:38	13 56 15	24 53	03 44	07 22	05 48	00 ♓ 41	25 25	10 20	14 59	03 19	11 35	05 12	13 17	09 18	07 47	12 01
Thu	6	6:59:34	14 57 25	06 ♑ 43	03 41	08 57	07 01	01 27	25 28	10 19	15 02	03 21	11 37	05 24	13 03	09 40	08 18	12 08
Fri	7	7:03:31	15 58 36	18 36	03 40	10 32	08 14	02 14	25 32	10 19	15 06	03 24	11 39	05 36	12 48	10 03	08 49	12 14
Sat	8	7:07:27	16 59 47	00 ♒ 34	03 D 39	12 07	09 27	03 00	25 35	10 18	15 09	03 26	11 41	05 47	12 32	10 25	09 20	12 21
Sun	9	7:11:24	18 00 57	12 38	03 39	13 43	10 40	03 47	25 39	10 18	15 12	03 28	11 43	05 58	12 16	10 48	09 51	12 28
Mon	10	7:15:20	19 02 07	24 52	03 40	15 20	11 53	04 33	25 43	10 18	15 15	03 30	11 45	06 09	12 00	11 10	10 22	12 34
Tue	11	7:19:17	20 03 16	07 ♓ 16	03 41	16 56	13 06	05 20	25 47	10 17	15 18	03 32	11 47	06 19	11 43	11 32	10 53	12 41
Wed	12	7:23:13	21 04 25	19 55	03 43	18 34	14 19	06 06	25 52	10 D 17	15 22	03 35	11 48	06 29	11 26	11 55	11 24	12 47
Thu	13	7:27:10	22 05 34	02 ♈ 49	03 44	20 11	15 32	06 53	25 56	10 17	15 25	03 37	11 50	06 39	11 08	12 17	11 54	12 53
Fri	14	7:31:07	23 06 42	16 03	03 ℞ 44	21 49	16 45	07 39	26 01	10 17	15 28	03 39	11 52	06 48	10 49	12 40	12 25	13 00
Sat	15	7:35:03	24 07 49	29 38	03 44	23 28	17 58	08 26	26 06	10 18	15 31	03 41	11 54	06 57	10 31	13 02	12 56	13 06
Sun	16	7:39:00	25 08 55	13 ♉ 36	03 44	25 07	19 12	09 12	26 11	10 18	15 35	03 44	11 56	07 06	10 12	13 25	13 26	13 12
Mon	17	7:42:56	26 10 01	27 56	03 43	26 46	20 25	09 59	26 17	10 19	15 38	03 46	11 58	07 14	09 53	13 47	13 57	13 18
Tue	18	7:46:53	27 11 06	12 ♊ 35	03 42	28 26	21 38	10 45	26 22	10 19	15 41	03 48	12 00	07 22	09 33	14 09	14 27	13 24
Wed	19	7:50:49	28 12 11	27 29	03 42	00 ♒ 07	22 52	11 31	26 28	10 20	15 45	03 50	12 01	07 29	09 13	14 32	14 58	13 30
Thu	20	7:54:46	29 13 14	12 ♋ 31	03 41	01 48	24 05	12 18	26 34	10 21	15 48	03 53	12 03	07 36	08 53	14 54	15 28	13 36
Fri	21	7:58:42	00 ♒ 14 17	27 32	03 D 41	03 30	25 19	13 04	26 40	10 22	15 52	03 55	12 05	07 43	08 33	15 17	15 59	13 42
Sat	22	8:02:39	01 15 19	12 ♌ 23	03 41	05 12	26 32	13 50	26 46	10 23	15 55	03 57	12 07	07 49	08 13	15 39	16 29	13 48
Sun	23	8:06:36	02 16 21	26 56	03 41	06 54	27 46	14 37	26 52	10 24	15 58	03 59	12 08	07 55	07 52	16 02	16 59	13 54
Mon	24	8:10:32	03 17 22	11 ♍ 07	03 ℞ 41	08 37	28 59	15 23	26 59	10 25	16 02	04 02	12 10	08 01	07 32	16 24	17 29	14 00
Tue	25	8:14:29	04 18 22	24 52	03 41	10 21	00 ♑ 13	16 09	27 05	10 27	16 05	04 04	12 11	08 06	07 11	16 46	18 00	14 05
Wed	26	8:18:25	05 19 22	08 ♎ 11	03 41	12 05	01 26	16 56	27 12	10 28	16 09	04 06	12 13	08 11	06 51	17 09	18 30	14 11
Thu	27	8:22:22	06 20 21	21 05	03 41	13 49	02 40	17 42	27 19	10 30	16 12	04 09	12 15	08 15	06 31	17 31	19 00	14 16
Fri	28	8:26:18	07 21 20	03 ♏ 37	03 D 41	15 34	03 54	18 28	27 27	10 31	16 16	04 11	12 16	08 19	06 10	17 54	19 30	14 22
Sat	29	8:30:15	08 22 18	15 51	03 41	17 18	05 07	19 14	27 34	10 33	16 19	04 13	12 18	08 23	05 50	18 16	19 59	14 27
Sun	30	8:34:11	09 23 15	27 52	03 41	19 03	06 21	20 00	27 41	10 35	16 22	04 15	12 19	08 26	05 30	18 38	20 29	14 33
Mon	31	8:38:08	10 24 12	09 ♐ 45	03 42	20 48	07 35	20 46	27 49	10 37	16 26	04 18	12 21	08 29	05 10	19 01	20 59	14 38

EPHEMERIS CALCULATED FOR 12 MIDNIGHT GREENWICH MEAN TIME. ALL OTHER DATA AND FACING ASPECTARIAN PAGE IN **EASTERN STANDARD TIME (BOLD)** AND PACIFIC STANDARD TIME (REGULAR).

FEBRUARY 2000

1 TUESDAY

☽ △ ♃	**8:08 am**	5:08 am
☉ ✶ ♇	**6:00 pm**	3:00 pm
☽ ⚺ ♆	**9:02 pm**	6:02 pm
☽ ⚻ ⚴	**9:16 pm**	6:16 pm

2 WEDNESDAY

♆ ☍ ⚴	**4:56 am**	1:56 am
☽ □ ⚳	**5:31 am**	2:31 am
♀ △ ♄	**8:07 am**	5:07 am
☽ △ ♄	**9:52 am**	6:52 am
☽ ☌ ♀	**10:04 am**	7:04 am
☽ ⚺ ♇	**1:18 pm**	10:18 am
☽ ⚺ ☉	**3:03 pm**	12:03 pm
☽ ⚺ ⚷	**6:17 pm**	3:17 pm
☽ ⚺ ♅	**9:46 pm**	6:46 pm

3 THURSDAY

☽ ☌ ⚵	**5:07 am**	2:07 am
☽ ⚺ ⚶	**10:07 am**	7:07 am
☽ ✶ ♂	**11:48 am**	8:48 am
♀ ⚺ ♇	**5:45 pm**	2:45 pm
☽ ⚺ ☿	**8:10 pm**	5:10 pm
☽ □ ♃	**9:16 pm**	6:16 pm

4 FRIDAY

☿ ✶ ♃	**4:31 am**	1:31 am
☽ ☍ ⚴	**7:53 am**	4:53 am
☉ ✶ ⚷	**7:59 am**	4:59 am
☽ ☌ ♆	**9:22 am**	6:22 am
☽ △ ⚳	**5:30 pm**	2:30 pm
☽ □ ♄	**9:52 pm**	6:52 pm
☽ ✶ ♇		10:06 pm

5 SATURDAY

☽ ✶ ♇	**1:06 am**	
☽ ⚺ ♀	**4:31 am**	1:31 am
☽ ✶ ⚷	**6:13 am**	3:13 am
☽ ☌ ☉	**8:03 am**	5:03 am
☽ ☌ ♅	**9:28 am**	6:28 am
☽ ⚺ ⚵	**6:08 pm**	3:08 pm
♀ ⚺ ⚷	**10:28 pm**	7:28 pm
☽ ✶ ⚶	**11:33 pm**	8:33 pm
☉ ☌ ♅		11:14 pm
☽ ⚺ ♂		11:38 pm

6 SUNDAY

☉ ☌ ♅	**2:14 am**	
☽ ⚺ ♂	**2:38 am**	
☽ ✶ ♃	**8:34 am**	5:34 am
☽ ☌ ☿	**3:52 pm**	12:52 pm
☽ ⚻ ⚴	**4:47 pm**	1:47 pm
☽ ⚺ ♆	**7:43 pm**	4:43 pm
☿ ⚻ ⚴	**10:00 pm**	7:00 pm

7 MONDAY

☽ ⚻ ⚳	**3:22 am**	12:22 am
☽ ✶ ♄	**7:47 am**	4:47 am
♀ ⚺ ♅	**8:10 am**	5:10 am
☽ □ ♇	**10:47 am**	7:47 am
☽ □ ⚷	**3:58 pm**	12:58 pm
☽ ⚺ ♅	**7:00 pm**	4:00 pm
☽ ✶ ♀	**8:05 pm**	5:05 pm
☽ ⚺ ☉	**10:17 pm**	7:17 pm
☿ ⚺ ♆	**10:48 pm**	7:48 pm

8 TUESDAY

☽ ✶ ⚵	**4:44 am**	1:44 am
☽ □ ⚶	**10:28 am**	7:28 am
☽ ☌ ♂	**2:46 pm**	11:46 am
☽ ⚺ ♃	**5:34 pm**	2:34 pm
☽ △ ⚴	**11:38 pm**	8:38 pm

9 WEDNESDAY

☽ ✶ ♆	**3:48 am**	12:48 am
☽ ⚺ ☿	**7:33 am**	4:33 am
☽ ☍ ⚳	**10:54 am**	7:54 am
☽ ⚺ ♄	**3:26 pm**	12:26 pm
☽ △ ♇	**6:11 pm**	3:11 pm
☽ △ ⚷	**11:24 pm**	8:24 pm
☽ ✶ ♅		11:14 pm

10 THURSDAY

☽ ✶ ♅	**2:14 am**	
☽ □ ♀	**8:37 am**	5:37 am
☽ ✶ ☉	**9:39 am**	6:39 am
☽ □ ⚵	**12:54 pm**	9:54 am
☿ ⚻ ⚳	**1:10 pm**	10:10 am
☽ △ ⚶	**6:53 pm**	3:53 pm
☽ ⚺ ♂		9:14 pm
☽ ☌ ♃		9:19 pm
♂ ⚺ ♃		10:59 pm

11 FRIDAY

☽ ⚺ ♂	**12:14 am**	
☽ ☌ ♃	**12:19 am**	
♂ ⚺ ♃	**1:59 am**	
☽ □ ⚴	**4:29 am**	1:29 am
☽ □ ♆	**9:40 am**	6:40 am
☽ ⚻ ⚳	**4:13 pm**	1:13 pm
☽ ✶ ☿	**7:18 pm**	4:18 pm
☽ ☌ ♄	**8:56 pm**	5:56 pm
☽ ⚻ ♇	**11:26 pm**	8:26 pm

12 SATURDAY

☽ ⚻ ⚷	**4:40 am**	1:40 am
☽ □ ♅	**7:20 am**	4:20 am
☿ ✶ ♄	**1:28 pm**	10:28 am
☉ ⚺ ♀	**6:06 pm**	3:06 pm
☽ □ ☉	**6:21 pm**	3:21 pm
☽ △ ♀	**6:22 pm**	3:22 pm
☽ △ ⚵	**6:48 pm**	3:48 pm
☽ ⚻ ⚶		10:00 pm
♀ ☌ ⚵		10:17 pm

13 SUNDAY

☽ ⚻ ⚶	**1:00 am**	
♀ ☌ ⚵	**1:17 am**	
☉ ⚺ ⚵	**3:46 am**	12:46 am
☽ ⚺ ♃	**4:58 am**	1:58 am
☽ ✶ ♂	**7:17 am**	4:17 am
☽ ✶ ⚴	**7:31 am**	4:31 am
♂ △ ⚴	**10:45 am**	7:45 am
☽ △ ♆	**1:33 pm**	10:33 am
☿ □ ♇	**6:23 pm**	3:23 pm
☽ △ ⚳	**7:33 pm**	4:33 pm
☽ ⚺ ♄		9:30 pm
☽ ☍ ♇		11:46 pm

14 MONDAY

☽ ⚺ ♄	**12:30 am**	
☽ ☍ ♇	**2:46 am**	
☽ □ ☿	**3:28 am**	12:28 am
☽ ☍ ⚷	**8:01 am**	5:01 am
☽ △ ♅	**10:34 am**	7:34 am
☽ ⚻ ⚵	**10:47 pm**	7:47 pm
☽ △ ☉		9:51 pm
☽ ⚻ ♀		10:47 pm

15 TUESDAY

☽ △ ☉	**12:51 am**	
☽ ⚻ ♀	**1:47 am**	
☽ ☍ ⚶	**5:13 am**	2:13 am
☽ ✶ ♃	**7:55 am**	4:55 am
☽ ⚺ ⚴	**9:04 am**	6:04 am
☽ □ ♂	**12:24 pm**	9:24 am
☽ ⚻ ♆	**3:50 pm**	12:50 pm
☽ □ ⚳	**9:20 pm**	6:20 pm
☽ ✶ ♄		11:37 pm

16 WEDNESDAY

☽ ✶ ♄	**2:37 am**	
☽ ⚻ ♇	**4:41 am**	1:41 am
☽ △ ☿	**8:46 am**	5:46 am
☽ ⚻ ⚷	**10:00 am**	7:00 am
☽ ⚻ ♅	**12:28 pm**	9:28 am
☽ ☍ ⚵		10:36 pm

17 THURSDAY

☽ ☍ ⚵	**1:36 am**	
♃ □ ⚴	**4:55 am**	1:55 am
☽ ⚻ ☉	**6:02 am**	3:02 am
☽ ☍ ♀	**7:51 am**	4:51 am
☽ ⚻ ⚶	**8:20 am**	5:20 am
☽ ☌ ⚴	**9:48 am**	6:48 am
☽ □ ♃	**9:56 am**	6:56 am
☿ □ ⚷	**12:35 pm**	9:35 am
☽ △ ♂	**4:31 pm**	1:31 pm
♀ ⚺ ⚶	**4:49 pm**	1:49 pm
☽ ☍ ♆	**5:21 pm**	2:21 pm
☽ ✶ ⚳	**10:26 pm**	7:26 pm

18 FRIDAY

♀ ☍ ⚴	**4:10 am**	1:10 am
☽ □ ♄	**4:12 am**	1:12 am
☽ △ ♇	**6:07 am**	3:07 am
♂ ✶ ♆	**9:07 am**	6:07 am
☽ △ ⚷	**11:37 am**	8:37 am
♀ □ ♃	**12:04 pm**	9:04 am
☽ ⚻ ☿	**12:25 pm**	9:25 am
☽ ☍ ♅	**2:05 pm**	11:05 am
⚴ ⚻ ⚶	**5:24 pm**	2:24 pm

19 SATURDAY

☽ ⚻ ⚵	**4:27 am**	1:27 am
☉ ⚻ ⚴	**4:33 am**	1:33 am
☽ ⚺ ⚴	**10:53 am**	7:53 am
☽ ☍ ☉	**11:27 am**	8:27 am
☽ △ ⚶	**11:42 am**	8:42 am
☽ △ ♃	**12:15 pm**	9:15 am
☽ ⚻ ♀	**2:13 pm**	11:13 am
☉ ✶ ⚶	**5:57 pm**	2:57 pm
☽ ⚻ ♆	**7:21 pm**	4:21 pm
☽ ⚻ ♂	**9:12 pm**	6:12 pm
☽ ⚺ ⚳		9:06 pm
☉ ✶ ♃		9:57 pm

20 SUNDAY

☽ ⚺ ⚳	**12:06 am**	
☉ ✶ ♃	**12:57 am**	
☽ △ ♄	**6:39 am**	3:39 am
☽ □ ♇	**8:26 am**	5:26 am
♃ △ ⚶	**1:54 pm**	10:54 am
☽ □ ⚷	**2:18 pm**	11:18 am
☽ ☍ ☿	**3:59 pm**	12:59 pm
☽ ⚻ ♅	**4:51 pm**	1:51 pm

21 MONDAY

☽ △ ⚵	**9:00 am**	6:00 am
☽ ✶ ⚴	**1:44 pm**	10:44 am
☽ ⚻ ♃	**4:27 pm**	1:27 pm
☽ □ ⚶	**5:02 pm**	2:02 pm
☽ ⚻ ☉	**7:04 pm**	4:04 pm
♂ ☍ ⚳	**9:12 pm**	6:12 pm
☽ △ ♀	**11:02 pm**	8:02 pm
☽ △ ♆	**11:24 pm**	8:24 pm

22 TUESDAY

♀ ☌ ♆	**3:06 am**	12:06 am
☽ ☌ ⚳	**3:51 am**	12:51 am
☽ ☍ ♂	**4:19 am**	1:19 am
☽ ⚻ ♄	**11:29 am**	8:29 am
☽ ✶ ♇	**1:09 pm**	10:09 am
☽ ✶ ⚷	**7:33 pm**	4:33 pm
☽ ⚻ ☿	**8:49 pm**	5:49 pm
☽ △ ♅	**10:15 pm**	7:15 pm

23 WEDNESDAY

☽ □ ⚵	**4:49 pm**	1:49 pm
☽ □ ⚴	**7:42 pm**	4:42 pm
♀ △ ⚳	**11:09 pm**	8:09 pm
☽ ☍ ♃	**11:59 pm**	8:59 pm
☽ ✶ ⚶		10:54 pm

24 THURSDAY

☽ ✶ ⚶	**1:54 am**	
☽ △ ☉	**6:45 am**	3:45 am
☽ □ ♆	**6:46 am**	3:46 am
☉ ⚺ ♆	**7:06 am**	4:06 am
☿ □ ⚷	**10:32 am**	7:32 am
☽ ⚺ ⚳	**10:50 am**	7:50 am
☽ □ ♀	**12:15 pm**	9:15 am
☽ ⚻ ♂	**3:27 pm**	12:27 pm
☽ ☍ ♄	**7:52 pm**	4:52 pm
☽ ⚺ ♇	**9:22 pm**	6:22 pm

25 FRIDAY

☽ △ ☿	**3:33 am**	12:33 am
☽ ⚺ ⚷	**4:24 am**	1:24 am
☽ □ ♅	**7:18 am**	4:18 am

26 SATURDAY

☉ ⚻ ⚳	**4:09 am**	1:09 am
☽ ✶ ⚵	**4:33 am**	1:33 am
☽ △ ⚴	**5:16 am**	2:16 am
☽ ⚻ ♃	**11:15 am**	8:15 am
☽ ⚺ ⚶	**2:42 pm**	11:42 am
☽ ✶ ♆	**5:41 pm**	2:41 pm
☽ ✶ ⚳	**9:06 pm**	6:06 pm
☽ □ ☉	**10:53 pm**	7:53 pm
⚴ ☍ ⚵	**11:43 pm**	8:43 pm

27 SUNDAY

☽ ✶ ♀	**6:06 am**	3:06 am
☽ △ ♂	**6:39 am**	3:39 am
☽ ⚻ ♄	**7:39 am**	4:39 am
☽ ☌ ♇	**8:54 am**	5:54 am
☽ □ ☿	**11:43 am**	8:43 am
☽ ☌ ⚷	**4:25 pm**	1:25 pm
♀ ✶ ♂	**6:29 pm**	3:29 pm
☽ ✶ ♅	**7:28 pm**	4:28 pm
♀ □ ♄	**9:57 pm**	6:57 pm
♂ ⚺ ♄		9:25 pm

28 MONDAY

♂ ⚺ ♄	**12:25 am**	
♀ ✶ ♇	**9:06 am**	6:06 am
☿ ⚺ ♀	**3:21 pm**	12:21 pm
☽ ⚻ ⚴	**5:21 pm**	2:21 pm
♂ △ ♇	**6:35 pm**	3:35 pm
☽ ⚺ ⚵	**6:58 pm**	3:58 pm
☿ ⚺ ♂	**9:11 pm**	6:11 pm
☿ □ ♇	**11:07 pm**	8:07 pm
☽ △ ♃		9:53 pm

29 TUESDAY

☽ △ ♃	**12:53 am**	
☽ ☌ ⚶	**5:50 am**	2:50 am
☽ ⚺ ♆	**6:37 am**	3:37 am
☽ □ ⚳	**9:07 am**	6:07 am
☿ ✶ ♄	**10:06 am**	7:06 am
☽ ✶ ☉	**5:21 pm**	2:21 pm
☽ ✶ ☿	**8:01 pm**	5:01 pm
☽ △ ♄	**8:56 pm**	5:56 pm
☽ ⚺ ♇	**9:48 pm**	6:48 pm
☽ □ ♂	**11:38 pm**	8:38 pm
☽ ⚺ ♀		11:02 pm

Eastern Standard Time in bold type

Pacific Standard Time in medium type

FEBRUARY 2000

☽ Last Aspect day	EST	hr:mn / PST	asp	☽ Ingress sign	day	EST	hr:mn / PST
1	**8:08 am**	5:08 am	△ ♃	♑	1	**12:10 pm**	9:10 am
3	**9:16 pm**	6:16 pm	□ ♄	♒	3		9:31 pm
3	**9:16 pm**	6:16 pm	□ ♄	♒	4	**12:31 am**	
6	**8:34 am**	5:34 am	⚹ ♄	♓	6	**11:02 am**	8:02 am
8	**2:46 pm**	11:46 am	☌ ♂	♈	8	**7:17 pm**	4:17 pm
10		9:19 pm	☌ ♄	♉	10		10:21 pm
11	**12:19 am**		☌ ♄	♉	10	**1:21 am**	
12	**6:22 pm**	3:22 pm	△ ♀	♊	13	**5:23 am**	2:23 am
14		9:51 pm	△ ☉	♋	15	**7:45 am**	4:45 am
15	**12:51 am**		△ ☉	♋	15	**7:45 am**	4:45 am
17	**7:51 am**	4:51 am	☍ ♀	♌	17	**9:11 am**	6:11 am
18	**2:05 pm**	11:05 am	☍ ♅	♍	19	**10:53 am**	7:53 am
20	**3:59 pm**	12:59 pm	☍ ☿	♎	21	**2:21 pm**	11:21 am
22	**10:15 pm**	7:15 pm	△ ♅	♏	23	**8:58 pm**	5:58 pm
25	**7:18 am**	4:18 am	□ ♅	♐	26	**7:10 am**	4:10 am
27	**7:28 pm**	4:28 pm	⚹ ♅	♑	28	**7:45 pm**	4:45 pm
29	**11:38 pm**	8:38 pm	□ ♂	♒	2	**8:14 am**	5:14 am

☽ Phases & Eclipses phase	day	EST	hr:mn / PST
● (eclipse)	5	**7:49 am**	4:49 am
New Moon	5	**8:03 am**	5:03 am
2nd Quarter	12	**6:21 pm**	3:21 pm
Full Moon	19	**11:27 am**	8:27 am
4th Quarter	26	**10:53 pm**	7:53 pm

Planet Ingress	day	EST	hr:mn / PST
☿ ♓	5	**3:08 am**	12:08 am
♂ ♈	11	**8:04 pm**	5:04 pm
♄ ♉	14	**4:39 pm**	1:39 pm
♀ ♒	17	**11:43 pm**	8:43 pm
⚶ ♑	18	**10:57 am**	7:57 am
☉ ♓	19	**3:33 am**	12:33 am
⚴ ♋	19	**10:17 am**	7:17 am
⚵ ♒	29	**9:03 pm**	6:03 pm

Planetary Motion	day	EST	hr:mn / PST
⚳ ℞	5	**1:26 pm**	10:26 am
☿ ℞	21	**7:47 am**	4:47 am

DATE		SID.TIME	SUN	MOON	NODE	MERCURY	VENUS	MARS	JUPITER	SATURN	URANUS	NEPTUNE	PLUTO	CERES	PALLAS	JUNO	VESTA	CHIRON
Tue	1	8:42:05	11 ♒ 25 08	21 ♐ 33	03 ♌ 42	22 ♒ 33	08 ♑ 49	21 ♓ 33	27 ♈ 57	10 ♉ 39	16 ♒ 29	04 ♒ 20	12 ♐ 22	08 ♎ 31	04 ♌ ℞ 50	19 ♑ 23	21 ♐ 29	14 ♐ 43
Wed	2	8:46:01	12 26 04	03 ♑ 22	03 43	24 17	10 02	22 19	28 05	10 41	16 33	04 22	12 24	08 33	04 31	19 45	21 58	14 48
Thu	3	8:49:58	13 26 58	15 15	03 44	26 01	11 16	23 05	28 13	10 44	16 36	04 24	12 25	08 34	04 12	20 07	22 28	14 53
Fri	4	8:53:54	14 27 51	27 14	03 ℞ 45	27 44	12 30	23 51	28 21	10 46	16 40	04 27	12 26	08 35	03 53	20 30	22 57	14 58
Sat	5	8:57:51	15 28 44	09 ♒ 21	03 45	29 26	13 44	24 37	28 30	10 49	16 43	04 29	12 28	08r 36	03 35	20 52	23 27	15 03
Sun	6	9:01:47	16 29 35	21 40	03 44	01 ♓ 06	14 58	25 23	28 38	10 52	16 47	04 31	12 29	08 36	03 17	21 14	23 56	15 08
Mon	7	9:05:44	17 30 25	04 ♓ 11	03 43	02 45	16 12	26 09	28 47	10 54	16 50	04 33	12 30	08 36	02 59	21 36	24 25	15 13
Tue	8	9:09:40	18 31 14	16 54	03 41	04 21	17 26	26 55	28 56	10 57	16 54	04 36	12 31	08 35	02 42	21 59	24 54	15 17
Wed	9	9:13:37	19 32 01	29 51	03 38	05 55	18 40	27 40	29 05	11 00	16 57	04 38	12 33	08 34	02 25	22 21	25 24	15 22
Thu	10	9:17:34	20 32 47	13 ♈ 01	03 36	07 25	19 54	28 26	29 14	11 03	17 01	04 40	12 34	08 32	02 09	22 43	25 52	15 26
Fri	11	9:21:30	21 33 31	26 25	03 34	08 51	21 07	29 12	29 23	11 06	17 04	04 42	12 35	08 30	01 53	23 05	26 21	15 31
Sat	12	9:25:27	22 34 14	10 ♉ 03	03 D 33	10 13	22 21	29 58	29 32	11 10	17 08	04 45	12 36	08 28	01 38	23 27	26 50	15 35
Sun	13	9:29:23	23 34 55	23 56	03 32	11 29	23 35	00 ♈ 44	29 42	11 13	17 11	04 47	12 37	08 25	01 23	23 49	27 19	15 39
Mon	14	9:33:20	24 35 34	08 ♊ 02	03 33	12 40	24 49	01 29	29 51	11 16	17 15	04 49	12 38	08 21	01 09	24 11	27 48	15 43
Tue	15	9:37:16	25 36 12	22 20	03 34	13 44	26 03	02 15	00 ♉ 01	11 20	17 18	04 51	12 39	08 17	00 55	24 33	28 16	15 48
Wed	16	9:41:13	26 36 48	06 ♋ 48	03 35	14 40	27 17	03 01	00 11	11 24	17 22	04 53	12 40	08 13	00 42	24 55	28 45	15 52
Thu	17	9:45:09	27 37 23	21 22	03 ℞ 37	15 28	28 31	03 46	00 21	11 27	17 25	04 55	12 41	08 08	00 30	25 17	29 13	15 55
Fri	18	9:49:06	28 37 55	05 ♌ 58	03 37	16 08	29 45	04 32	00 31	11 31	17 29	04 58	12 42	08 03	00 18	25 39	29 41	15 59
Sat	19	9:53:03	29 38 26	20 29	03 36	16 38	00 ♒ 59	05 18	00 41	11 35	17 32	05 00	12 43	07 58	00 07	26 01	00 ♑ 09	16 03
Sun	20	9:56:59	00 ♓ 38 56	04 ♍ 49	03 34	16 59	02 14	06 03	00 51	11 39	17 35	05 02	12 44	07 52	29 ♋ 56	26 22	00 38	16 07
Mon	21	10:00:56	01 39 23	18 54	03 30	17r 09	03 28	06 48	01 02	11 43	17 39	05 04	12 45	07 45	29 46	26 44	01 05	16 10
Tue	22	10:04:52	02 39 50	02 ♎ 38	03 26	17 10	04 42	07 34	01 12	11 48	17 42	05 06	12 45	07 39	29 37	27 06	01 33	16 14
Wed	23	10:08:49	03 40 14	15 59	03 21	17 00	05 56	08 19	01 23	11 52	17 46	05 08	12 46	07 32	29 28	27 28	02 01	16 17
Thu	24	10:12:45	04 40 38	28 57	03 16	16 40	07 10	09 05	01 34	11 56	17 49	05 10	12 47	07 24	29 20	27 49	02 29	16 20
Fri	25	10:16:42	05 41 00	11 ♏ 34	03 12	16 11	08 24	09 50	01 45	12 01	17 52	05 12	12 48	07 16	29 12	28 11	02 56	16 24
Sat	26	10:20:38	06 41 20	23 52	03 10	15 34	09 38	10 35	01 55	12 05	17 56	05 14	12 48	07 08	29 06	28 32	03 24	16 27
Sun	27	10:24:35	07 41 39	05 ♐ 55	03 D 09	14 49	10 52	11 20	02 07	12 10	17 59	05 16	12 49	06 59	28 59	28 54	03 51	16 30
Mon	28	10:28:32	08 41 57	17 49	03 09	13 57	12 06	12 06	02 18	12 15	18 02	05 18	12 49	06 50	28 54	29 15	04 18	16 33
Tue	29	10:32:28	09 42 14	29 38	03 11	13 00	13 20	12 51	02 29	12 20	18 06	05 20	12 50	06 40	28 49	29 37	04 46	16 35

EPHEMERIS CALCULATED FOR 12 MIDNIGHT GREENWICH MEAN TIME. ALL OTHER DATA AND FACING ASPECTARIAN PAGE IN **EASTERN STANDARD TIME (BOLD)** AND PACIFIC STANDARD TIME (REGULAR).

MARCH 2000

1 WEDNESDAY

☽ ⊻ ♀	**2:02 am**	
♆ ⊻ ⚶	**4:02 am**	1:02 am
☽ ⊻ ⚷	**5:31 am**	2:31 am
☽ ⊻ ♅	**8:35 am**	5:35 am
☉ ☌ ☿	**10:10 am**	7:10 am

2 THURSDAY

☽ ☍ ♀	**5:33 am**	2:33 am
☽ ☌ ⚵	**9:18 am**	6:18 am
♀ ⚹ ⚷	**12:31 pm**	9:31 am
☽ □ ♃	**2:13 pm**	11:13 am
☉ ⚹ ♄	**3:19 pm**	12:19 pm
☽ ☌ ♆	**6:59 pm**	3:59 pm
☽ ⊻ ⚶	**8:22 pm**	5:22 pm
☽ △ ⚳	**8:25 pm**	5:25 pm
⚳ □ ⚶	**9:20 pm**	6:20 pm
☉ □ ♇	**10:25 pm**	7:25 pm

3 FRIDAY

☽ ⊻ ☿	**3:06 am**	12:06 am
☽ □ ♄	**9:06 am**	6:06 am
☽ ⚹ ♇	**9:34 am**	6:34 am
☽ ⊻ ☉	**10:32 am**	7:32 am
☽ ⚹ ♂	**3:08 pm**	12:08 pm
☽ ⚹ ⚷	**5:08 pm**	2:08 pm
♀ ☌ ♅	**7:39 pm**	4:39 pm
☽ ☌ ♅	**8:09 pm**	5:09 pm
☽ ☌ ♀	**8:12 pm**	5:12 pm

4 SATURDAY

☽ ⊼ ♀	**3:45 pm**	12:45 pm
☽ ⊻ ⚵	**9:11 pm**	6:11 pm
☽ ⚹ ♃		10:06 pm
♂ △ ⚷		10:54 pm

5 SUNDAY

☽ ⚹ ♃	**1:06 am**	
♂ △ ⚷	**1:54 am**	
☽ ⊻ ♆	**4:53 am**	1:53 am
☽ ⊼ ⚳	**5:17 am**	2:17 am
☽ ⚹ ⚶	**8:06 am**	5:06 am
☽ ☌ ☿	**8:19 am**	5:19 am
☿ ⚹ ⚶	**10:17 am**	7:17 am
☽ ⚹ ♄	**6:32 pm**	3:32 pm
☽ □ ♇	**6:37 pm**	3:37 pm
☽ ☌ ☉		9:17 pm
☽ □ ⚷		10:57 pm

6 MONDAY

☽ ☌ ☉	**12:17 am**	
☽ □ ⚷	**1:57 am**	
☽ ⊻ ♂	**3:20 am**	12:20 am
♆ △ ⚳	**4:12 am**	1:12 am
☽ ⊻ ♅	**4:53 am**	1:53 am
♄ ⊼ ♇	**6:56 am**	3:56 am
☽ ⊻ ♀	**10:35 am**	7:35 am
☉ □ ⚷	**10:48 pm**	7:48 pm
☽ △ ♀	**11:13 pm**	8:13 pm

7 TUESDAY

☽ ⚹ ⚵	**5:57 am**	2:57 am
♂ ⚹ ♅	**8:06 am**	5:06 am
☽ ⊻ ♃	**9:01 am**	6:01 am
☿ ⊻ ♆	**10:01 am**	7:01 am
☽ ☍ ⚳	**11:23 am**	8:23 am
☽ ⊻ ☿	**11:49 am**	8:49 am
☽ ⚹ ♆	**11:55 am**	8:55 am
☽ □ ⚶	**4:43 pm**	1:43 pm
☿ ⊼ ⚳	**10:30 pm**	7:30 pm
☽ △ ♇		9:56 pm
☽ ⊻ ♄		10:13 pm

8 WEDNESDAY

☽ △ ♇	**12:56 am**	
☽ ⊻ ♄	**1:13 am**	
☽ △ ⚷	**8:06 am**	5:06 am
☽ ⊻ ☉	**10:39 am**	7:39 am
☽ ⚹ ♅	**10:58 am**	7:58 am
☽ ☌ ♂	**12:25 pm**	9:25 am
☉ ⊻ ♅	**3:19 pm**	12:19 pm
☽ ⚹ ♀	**9:34 pm**	6:34 pm

9 THURSDAY

☽ □ ♀	**4:26 am**	1:26 am
☿ ⚹ ♃	**6:05 am**	3:05 am
☽ □ ⚵	**12:18 pm**	9:18 am
☽ ⚹ ☿	**2:13 pm**	11:13 am
☽ ☌ ♃	**2:41 pm**	11:41 am
☽ ⊼ ⚳	**3:26 pm**	12:26 pm
☽ □ ♆	**4:49 pm**	1:49 pm
☽ △ ⚶	**11:03 pm**	8:03 pm

10 FRIDAY

☽ ⊼ ♇	**5:22 am**	2:22 am
☽ ☌ ♄	**5:58 am**	2:58 am
☽ ⊼ ⚷	**12:26 pm**	9:26 am
☽ □ ♅	**3:20 pm**	12:20 pm
♃ ⊼ ⚳	**4:13 pm**	1:13 pm
☽ ⚹ ☉	**6:50 pm**	3:50 pm
☽ ⊻ ♂	**7:29 pm**	4:29 pm
☿ ⊻ ⚵	**9:41 pm**	6:41 pm

11 SATURDAY

☽ □ ♀	**6:31 am**	3:31 am
☽ ⚹ ♀	**8:20 am**	5:20 am
☽ □ ☿	**4:18 pm**	1:18 pm
☽ △ ⚵	**5:16 pm**	2:16 pm
☽ △ ⚳	**6:16 pm**	3:16 pm
☽ ⊻ ♃	**7:03 pm**	4:03 pm
☽ △ ♆	**8:31 pm**	5:31 pm

12 SUNDAY

♀ ⊼ ♀	**3:38 am**	12:38 am
☽ ⊼ ⚶	**4:09 am**	1:09 am
☉ ⊻ ♂	**4:37 am**	1:37 am
☽ ☍ ♇	**8:47 am**	5:47 am
☽ ⊻ ♄	**9:43 am**	6:43 am
☽ ☍ ⚷	**3:51 pm**	12:51 pm
⚳ △ ⚵	**6:46 pm**	3:46 pm
☽ △ ♅	**6:48 pm**	3:48 pm
☽ ⚹ ♂		10:34 pm
☽ □ ☉		10:59 pm

13 MONDAY

☽ ⚹ ♂	**1:34 am**	
☽ □ ☉	**1:59 am**	
☽ ⊻ ♀	**11:36 am**	8:36 am
☽ △ ♀	**2:33 pm**	11:33 am
☽ △ ☿	**6:38 pm**	3:38 pm
☽ □ ⚳	**8:32 pm**	5:32 pm
☽ ⊼ ⚵	**9:35 pm**	6:35 pm
☽ ⚹ ♃	**10:50 pm**	7:50 pm
☽ ⊼ ♆	**11:38 pm**	8:38 pm

14 TUESDAY

☽ ☍ ⚶	**8:41 am**	5:41 am
☽ ⊼ ♇	**11:44 am**	8:44 am
☽ ⚹ ♄	**1:01 pm**	10:01 am
☽ ⊼ ⚷	**6:51 pm**	3:51 pm
☽ ⊼ ♅	**9:53 pm**	6:53 pm

15 WEDNESDAY

☽ □ ♂	**7:16 am**	4:16 am
☽ △ ☉	**8:43 am**	5:43 am
☿ ☌ ♀	**1:23 pm**	10:23 am
☽ ☌ ♀	**2:42 pm**	11:42 am
☽ ⊼ ☿	**9:34 pm**	6:34 pm
☽ ⊼ ♀	**10:17 pm**	7:17 pm
☽ ⚹ ⚳	**10:36 pm**	7:36 pm
♀ ⊼ ⚳		10:29 pm
☽ ☍ ⚵		10:42 pm
☽ □ ♃		11:28 pm
☽ ☍ ♆		11:36 pm

16 THURSDAY

♀ ⊼ ⚳	**1:29 am**	
☽ ☍ ⚵	**1:42 am**	
☽ □ ♃	**2:28 am**	
☽ ☍ ♆	**2:36 am**	
♃ □ ♆	**12:15 pm**	9:15 am
☽ ⊼ ⚶	**1:07 pm**	10:07 am
☽ △ ♇	**2:37 pm**	11:37 am
☽ □ ♄	**4:16 pm**	1:16 pm
☽ △ ⚷	**9:51 pm**	6:51 pm
☽ ☍ ♅		10:00 pm

17 FRIDAY

☽ ☍ ♅	**1:00 am**	
☿ ⊼ ⚳	**9:14 am**	6:14 am
☽ △ ♂	**1:07 pm**	10:07 am
☽ ⊼ ☉	**3:37 pm**	12:37 pm
☽ ⊻ ♀	**6:05 pm**	3:05 pm
♆ ☌ ⚵	**6:10 pm**	3:10 pm
♀ ⊻ ♆		9:43 pm
☽ ⊻ ⚳		9:57 pm
☽ ☍ ☿		10:32 pm
♀ ⊻ ⚵		12:00 pm

18 SATURDAY

♀ ⊻ ♆	**12:43 am**	
☽ ⊻ ⚳	**12:57 am**	
☽ ☍ ☿	**1:32 am**	
♀ ⊻ ⚵	**3:00 am**	
☽ ⊼ ♆	**5:55 am**	2:55 am
☽ ⊼ ⚵	**6:11 am**	3:11 am
☽ ☍ ♀	**6:24 am**	3:24 am
☽ △ ♃	**6:28 am**	3:28 am
♀ ⚹ ♃	**7:20 am**	4:20 am
♇ ⊻ ⚶	**5:02 pm**	2:02 pm
☽ □ ♇	**6:02 pm**	3:02 pm
☽ △ ⚶	**6:04 pm**	3:04 pm
☽ △ ♄	**8:06 pm**	5:06 pm
☽ □ ⚷		10:28 pm

19 SUNDAY

☽ □ ⚷	**1:28 am**	
☽ ⊼ ♅	**4:49 am**	1:49 am
☉ △ ♀	**5:46 am**	2:46 am
♃ □ ⚵	**2:59 pm**	11:59 am
☽ ⊼ ♂	**8:02 pm**	5:02 pm
☽ ⚹ ♀	**10:33 pm**	7:33 pm
☽ ☍ ☉	**11:44 pm**	8:44 pm

20 MONDAY

☽ ☌ ⚳	**4:23 am**	1:23 am
☽ ⊼ ☿	**7:31 am**	4:31 am
☽ △ ♆	**10:29 am**	7:29 am
☽ ⊼ ♃	**11:49 am**	8:49 am
☽ △ ⚵	**12:01 pm**	9:01 am
☽ ⊼ ♀	**4:13 pm**	1:13 pm
☽ ⚹ ♇	**10:58 pm**	7:58 pm
☽ □ ⚶		9:40 pm
☽ ⊼ ♄		10:33 pm

21 TUESDAY

☽ □ ⚶	**12:40 am**	
☽ ⊼ ♄	**1:33 am**	
☽ ⚹ ⚷	**6:47 am**	3:47 am
☽ △ ♅	**10:25 am**	7:25 am

22 WEDNESDAY

♂ □ ♀	**3:08 am**	12:08 am
☉ ☍ ⚳	**4:03 am**	1:03 am
☽ □ ♀	**5:20 am**	2:20 am
☽ ☍ ♂	**5:26 am**	2:26 am
☽ ⊻ ⚳	**10:00 am**	7:00 am
☽ ⊼ ☉	**10:37 am**	7:37 am
♄ △ ⚶	**4:23 pm**	1:23 pm
☽ △ ☿	**4:54 pm**	1:54 pm
☽ □ ♆	**5:30 pm**	2:30 pm
☽ ☍ ♃	**7:45 pm**	4:45 pm
☽ □ ⚵	**8:29 pm**	5:29 pm

23 THURSDAY

☿ ⊻ ♆	**4:27 am**	1:27 am
☽ △ ♀	**5:26 am**	2:26 am
☽ ⊻ ♇	**6:33 am**	3:33 am
☽ ☍ ♄	**9:47 am**	6:47 am
☽ ⚹ ⚶	**10:11 am**	7:11 am
☽ ⊻ ⚷	**2:53 pm**	11:53 am
♀ □ ♇	**4:52 pm**	1:52 pm
☽ □ ♅	**6:53 pm**	3:53 pm

24 FRIDAY

☽ △ ♀	**3:20 pm**	12:20 pm
☽ ⊼ ♂	**6:29 pm**	3:29 pm
☽ ⚹ ⚳	**6:34 pm**	3:34 pm
♂ ⊼ ⚳	**7:25 pm**	4:25 pm
☽ △ ☉		10:24 pm

25 SATURDAY

☽ △ ☉	**1:24 am**	
☽ ⚹ ♆	**3:40 am**	12:40 am
♀ ⚹ ♄	**5:31 am**	2:31 am
☽ □ ☿	**6:45 am**	3:45 am
☽ ⊼ ♃	**7:00 am**	4:00 am
☽ ⚹ ⚵	**8:20 am**	5:20 am
☿ ⚹ ♃	**11:33 am**	8:33 am
☽ ☌ ♇	**5:16 pm**	2:16 pm
☽ ⊼ ♄	**9:13 pm**	6:13 pm
☽ □ ♀	**10:52 pm**	7:52 pm
☽ ⊻ ⚶	**11:05 pm**	8:05 pm
♀ ⚹ ⚶		11:01 pm
☽ ☌ ⚷		11:02 pm

26 SUNDAY

♀ ⚹ ⚶	**2:01 am**	
☽ ☌ ⚷	**2:02 am**	
☉ ⚹ ♆	**5:38 am**	2:38 am
☽ ⚹ ♅	**6:26 am**	3:26 am
☿ ⊻ ⚵	**5:20 pm**	2:20 pm

27 MONDAY

☽ ⊼ ♀	**4:15 am**	1:15 am
☽ □ ⚳	**5:38 am**	2:38 am
♀ □ ⚷	**5:38 am**	2:38 am
☽ △ ♂	**10:41 am**	7:41 am
☽ ⊻ ♆	**4:15 pm**	1:15 pm
☽ □ ☉	**7:21 pm**	4:21 pm
☽ △ ♃	**8:42 pm**	5:42 pm
☽ ⊻ ⚵	**10:37 pm**	7:37 pm
☽ ⚹ ☿		9:16 pm

28 TUESDAY

☽ ⚹ ☿	**12:16 am**	
☽ ⊻ ♇	**5:57 am**	2:57 am
☽ △ ♄	**10:34 am**	7:34 am
☽ ☌ ⚶	**1:55 pm**	10:55 am
☽ ⊻ ⚷	**2:51 pm**	11:51 am
☉ ⊻ ♃	**3:49 pm**	12:49 pm
☽ ⚹ ♀	**6:43 pm**	3:43 pm
☽ ⊻ ♅	**7:30 pm**	4:30 pm
⚳ ⚹ ♀	**11:00 pm**	8:00 pm
♀ ⊻ ♅		11:24 pm

29 WEDNESDAY

♀ ⊻ ♅	**2:24 am**	
☽ △ ⚳	**5:14 pm**	2:14 pm
☽ ☍ ♀	**5:50 pm**	2:50 pm
⚷ ⊻ ⚶	**7:38 pm**	4:38 pm

30 THURSDAY

☽ □ ♂	**3:13 am**	12:13 am
☉ ⚹ ⚵	**3:56 am**	12:56 am
☽ ☌ ♆	**4:51 am**	1:51 am
☽ □ ♃	**10:13 am**	7:13 am
☽ ☌ ⚵	**12:36 pm**	9:36 am
☽ ⚹ ☉	**1:07 pm**	10:07 am
☿ □ ♇	**5:25 pm**	2:25 pm
☽ ⚹ ♇	**6:02 pm**	3:02 pm
☽ ⊻ ☿	**6:06 pm**	3:06 pm
☽ □ ♄	**11:04 pm**	8:04 pm
☽ ⚹ ⚷		11:38 pm

31 FRIDAY

☽ ⚹ ⚷	**2:38 am**	
☽ ⊻ ⚶	**3:37 am**	12:37 am
♂ □ ♆	**7:11 am**	4:11 am
☽ ☌ ♅	**7:19 am**	4:19 am
☽ ⊻ ♀	**12:58 pm**	9:58 am
☽ ⊼ ⚳		11:50 pm

Eastern Standard Time in bold type
Pacific Standard Time in medium type

MARCH 2000

☽ Last Aspect day	EST / hr:mn / PST	asp	☽ Ingress sign day	EST / hr:mn / PST
29	**11:38 pm** 8:38 pm	□♂	♒ 2	**8:14 am** 5:14 am
3	**8:12 pm** 5:12 pm	☌♀	♓ 4	**6:30 pm** 3:30 pm
5	9:17 pm	☌☉	♈ 6	10:54 pm
6	**12:17 am**	☌☉	♈ 7	**1:54 am**
8	**9:34 pm** 6:34 pm	⚹♀	♉ 9	**7:01 am** 4:01 am
11	**6:31 am** 3:31 am	□♀	♊ 11	**10:46 am** 7:46 am
12	10:59 pm	□☉	♋ 13	**1:51 pm** 10:51 am
13	**1:59 am**	□☉	♋ 13	**1:51 pm** 10:51 am
15	**8:43 am** 5:43 am	△☉	♌ 15	**4:43 pm** 1:43 pm
17	**1:07 pm** 10:07 am	△♂	♍ 17	**7:48 pm** 4:48 pm
19	**11:44 pm** 8:44 pm	☍☉	♎ 19	**11:57 pm** 8:57 pm
22	**5:26 am** 2:26 am	☍♂	♏ 22	**6:17 am** 3:17 am
23	**6:53 pm** 3:53 pm	□♅	♐ 24	**3:43 pm** 12:43 pm
26	**6:26 am** 3:26 am	⚹♅	♑ 27	**3:51 am** 12:51 am
28	**6:43pm** 3:43 pm	⚹♀	♒ 29	**4:34 pm** 1:34 pm
31	**7:19 am** 4:19 am	☌♅	♓ 4/1	**3:12 am** 12:12 am

☽ Phases & Eclipses phase	day	EST / hr:mn / PST
New Moon	5	9:17 pm
New Moon	6	**12:17 am**
2nd Quarter	12	10:59 pm
2nd Quarter	13	**1:59 am**
Full Moon	19	**11:44 pm** 8:44 pm
4th Quarter	27	**7:21 pm** 4:21 pm

Planet Ingress	day	EST / hr:mn / PST
♀ ♓	13	**6:36 am** 3:36 am
☉ ♈	19	11:35 pm
☉ ♈	20	**2:35 am**
♂ ♉	22	**8:25 pm** 5:25 pm
♀ ♌	25	**10:06 pm** 7:06 pm
⚳ ♍	31	**4:58 am** 1:58 am

Planetary Motion	day	EST / hr:mn / PST
♀ D	7	**1:08 pm** 10:08 am
☿ D	14	**3:40 pm** 12:40 pm
♇ ℞	14	9:32 pm
♇ ℞	15	**12:32 am**
⚷ ℞	27	**5:36 pm** 2:36 pm

DATE		SID.TIME	SUN	MOON	NODE	MERCURY	VENUS	MARS	JUPITER	SATURN	URANUS	NEPTUNE	PLUTO	CERES	PALLAS	JUNO	VESTA	CHIRON
Wed	1	10:36:25	10 ♓ 42 28	11 ♑ 27	03 ♌ 13	12 ♓ ℞ 00	14 ♒ 34	13 ♈ 36	02 ♉ 40	12 ♉ 24	18 ♒ 09	05 ♒ 22	12 ♐ 50	06 ♎ ℞ 31	28 ♋ ℞ 44	29 ♑ 58	05 ♑ 13	16 ♐ 38
Thu	2	10:40:21	11 42 42	23 22	03 ℞ 14	10 57	15 49	14 21	02 52	12 29	18 12	05 24	12 51	06 20	28 40	00 ♒ 20	05 39	16 41
Fri	3	10:44:18	12 42 53	05 ♒ 26	03 14	09 54	17 03	15 06	03 03	12 34	18 16	05 26	12 51	06 10	28 37	00 41	06 06	16 43
Sat	4	10:48:14	13 43 03	17 43	03 13	08 52	18 17	15 51	03 15	12 40	18 19	05 28	12 52	05 59	28 35	01 02	06 33	16 46
Sun	5	10:52:11	14 43 11	00 ♓ 16	03 10	07 53	19 31	16 36	03 27	12 45	18 22	05 30	12 52	05 48	28 33	01 23	06 59	16 48
Mon	6	10:56:07	15 43 18	13 05	03 05	06 56	20 45	17 21	03 38	12 50	18 25	05 31	12 53	05 37	28 32	01 44	07 26	16 50
Tue	7	11:00:04	16 43 22	26 11	02 58	06 04	21 59	18 06	03 50	12 55	18 28	05 33	12 53	05 25	28 D 31	02 05	07 52	16 53
Wed	8	11:04:01	17 43 25	09a 33	02 50	05 18	23 13	18 51	04 02	13 01	18 32	05 35	12 53	05 13	28 31	02 26	08 18	16 55
Thu	9	11:07:57	18 43 26	23 08	02 43	04 37	24 28	19 35	04 14	13 06	18 35	05 37	12 53	05 01	28 31	02 47	08 44	16 57
Fri	10	11:11:54	19 43 24	06 ♉ 54	02 35	04 02	25 42	20 20	04 27	13 12	18 38	05 39	12 54	04 48	28 32	03 08	09 10	16 58
Sat	11	11:15:50	20 43 21	20 49	02 30	03 34	26 56	21 05	04 39	13 18	18 41	05 40	12 54	04 36	28 34	03 29	09 36	17 00
Sun	12	11:19:47	21 43 15	04 ♊ 49	02 26	03 12	28 10	21 49	04 51	13 23	18 44	05 42	12 54	04 23	28 36	03 50	10 01	17 02
Mon	13	11:23:43	22 43 08	18 54	02 D 25	02 58	29 24	22 34	05 03	13 29	18 47	05 44	12 54	04 10	28 38	04 10	10 27	17 03
Tue	14	11:27:40	23 42 57	03d 02	02 25	02 D 49	00 ♓ 38	23 19	05 16	13 35	18 50	05 46	12 54	03 57	28 42	04 31	10 52	17 05
Wed	15	11:31:36	24 42 45	17 11	02 26	02 47	01 52	24 03	05 28	13 41	18 53	05 47	12r 54	03 44	28 45	04 52	11 17	17 06
Thu	16	11:35:33	25 42 31	01 ♌ 21	02 ℞ 27	02 51	03 07	24 48	05 41	13 47	18 56	05 49	12 54	03 30	28 50	05 12	11 42	17 07
Fri	17	11:39:30	26 42 14	15 28	02 26	03 00	04 21	25 32	05 54	13 53	18 59	05 50	12 54	03 17	28 54	05 32	12 07	17 09
Sat	18	11:43:26	27 41 55	29 32	02 23	03 15	05 35	26 16	06 06	13 59	19 02	05 52	12 54	03 03	29 00	05 53	12 31	17 10
Sun	19	11:47:23	28 41 33	13 ♍ 27	02 18	03 36	06 49	27 01	06 19	14 05	19 05	05 54	12 54	02 49	29 06	06 13	12 56	17 11
Mon	20	11:51:19	29 41 10	27 12	02 10	04 01	08 03	27 45	06 32	14 11	19 08	05 55	12 54	02 36	29 12	06 33	13 20	17 11
Tue	21	11:55:16	00 ♈ 40 44	10 ♎ 41	02 00	04 31	09 17	28 29	06 45	14 18	19 10	05 57	12 54	02 22	29 19	06 53	13 44	17 12
Wed	22	11:59:12	01 40 17	23 54	01 50	05 05	10 31	29 13	06 58	14 24	19 13	05 58	12 53	02 08	29 26	07 13	14 08	17 13
Thu	23	12:03:09	02 39 48	06 ♏ 47	01 39	05 44	11 45	29 57	07 11	14 30	19 16	06 00	12 53	01 54	29 33	07 33	14 32	17 13
Fri	24	12:07:05	03 39 17	19 22	01 30	06 26	12 59	00 ♉ 41	07 24	14 37	19 19	06 01	12 53	01 40	29 41	07 53	14 56	17 14
Sat	25	12:11:02	04 38 44	01 ♐ 40	01 23	07 12	14 14	01 26	07 37	14 43	19 21	06 02	12 53	01 27	29 50	08 13	15 19	17 14
Sun	26	12:14:58	05 38 09	13 44	01 18	08 02	15 28	02 09	07 50	14 50	19 24	06 04	12 52	01 13	29 59	08 33	15 43	17 14
Mon	27	12:18:55	06 37 32	25 38	01 15	08 55	16 42	02 53	08 03	14 56	19 27	06 05	12 52	00 59	00 ♌ 08	08 52	16 06	17 ℞ 15
Tue	28	12:22:52	07 36 54	07 ♑ 28	01 D 15	09 50	17 56	03 37	08 17	15 03	19 29	06 07	12 51	00 46	00 18	09 12	16 29	17 15
Wed	29	12:26:48	08 36 14	19 17	01 15	10 49	19 10	04 21	08 30	15 10	19 32	06 08	12 51	00 32	00 28	09 31	16 51	17 15
Thu	30	12:30:45	09 35 32	01 ♒ 13	01 ℞ 15	11 50	20 24	05 05	08 44	15 16	19 35	06 09	12 51	00 19	00 39	09 50	17 14	17 14
Fri	31	12:34:41	10 34 49	13 20	01 15	12 54	21 38	05 49	08 57	15 23	19 37	06 10	12 50	00 05	00 50	10 10	17 36	17 14

EPHEMERIS CALCULATED FOR 12 MIDNIGHT GREENWICH MEAN TIME. ALL OTHER DATA AND FACING ASPECTARIAN PAGE IN **EASTERN STANDARD TIME (BOLD)** AND PACIFIC STANDARD TIME (REGULAR).

APRIL 2000

1 SATURDAY

☽ ⚻ ⚳	**2:50 am**	
☽ ⚻ ⚴	**5:17 am**	2:17 am
☽ ⚺ ♆	**2:55 pm**	11:55 am
☽ ⚹ ♂	**4:46 pm**	1:46 pm
☽ ⚹ ♃	**8:54 pm**	5:54 pm
☽ ⚺ ⚵	**11:35 pm**	8:35 pm
☉ △ ♇		10:18 pm

2 SUNDAY

☉ △ ♇	**1:18 am**	
☽ □ ♇	**3:12 am**	12:12 am
☽ ⚺ ☉	**3:21 am**	12:21 am
☿ ⚹ ♄	**5:19 am**	2:19 am
☽ ⚹ ♄	**8:28 am**	5:28 am
☽ ☌ ☿	**8:45 am**	5:45 am
☽ □ ⚷	**11:17 am**	8:17 am
☽ ⚹ ⚶	**1:51 pm**	10:51 am
☽ ⚺ ♅	**3:53 pm**	12:53 pm
☽ ☌ ♀		11:44 pm

3 MONDAY

☽ ☌ ♀	**2:44 am**	
☽ ☍ ⚳	**9:09 am**	6:09 am
☿ □ ⚷	**12:00 pm**	9:00 am
☽ △ ⚴	**1:09 pm**	10:09 am
☽ ⚹ ♆	**9:26 pm**	6:26 pm
☽ ⚺ ♂		11:09 pm

4 TUESDAY

☽ ⚺ ♂	**2:09 am**	
☽ ⚺ ♃	**3:54 am**	12:54 am
☽ ⚹ ⚵	**6:46 am**	3:46 am
☽ △ ♇	**8:53 am**	5:53 am
☽ ☌ ☉	**1:12 pm**	10:12 am
☽ ⚺ ♄	**2:21 pm**	11:21 am
☽ △ ⚷	**4:31 pm**	1:31 pm
☽ ⚺ ☿	**7:22 pm**	4:22 pm
☽ □ ⚶	**8:23 pm**	5:23 pm
☽ ⚹ ♅	**9:04 pm**	6:04 pm

5 WEDNESDAY

☉ ⚺ ♄	**7:30 am**	4:30 am
☿ ⚹ ⚶	**10:15 am**	7:15 am
☽ ⚺ ♀	**12:16 pm**	9:16 am
☽ ⚻ ⚳	**12:35 pm**	9:35 am
☿ ⚺ ♅	**2:13 pm**	11:13 am
♀ ☍ ⚳	**3:28 pm**	12:28 pm
☽ □ ⚴	**5:56 pm**	2:56 pm
☽ □ ♆		10:09 pm
♂ ☌ ♃		10:41 pm
♅ ⚺ ⚶		11:17 pm

6 THURSDAY

☽ □ ♆	**1:09 am**	
♂ ☌ ♃	**1:41 am**	
♅ ⚺ ⚶	**2:17 am**	
☽ ☌ ♃	**8:09 am**	5:09 am
☽ ☌ ♂	**8:23 am**	5:23 am
☽ □ ⚵	**11:13 am**	8:13 am
☉ △ ⚷	**11:17 am**	8:17 am
☽ ⚻ ♇	**12:04 pm**	9:04 am
☽ ☌ ♄	**5:50 pm**	2:50 pm
☽ ⚻ ⚷	**7:27 pm**	4:27 pm
☽ ⚺ ☉	**8:04 pm**	5:04 pm
☽ □ ♅		9:04 pm
☽ △ ⚶		9:32 pm

7 FRIDAY

☽ □ ♅	**12:04 am**	
☽ △ ⚶	**12:32 am**	
☽ ⚹ ☿	**3:24 am**	12:24 am
☽ △ ⚳	**2:25 pm**	11:25 am
☽ ⚹ ♀	**7:33 pm**	4:33 pm
☽ ⚹ ⚴	**9:11 pm**	6:11 pm
♇ ⚹ ⚵		10:19 pm

8 SATURDAY

♇ ⚹ ⚵	**1:19 am**	
☽ △ ♆	**3:33 am**	12:33 am
☽ ⚺ ♃	**11:15 am**	8:15 am
☽ ⚺ ♂	**1:20 pm**	10:20 am
☽ ☍ ♇	**2:17 pm**	11:17 am
☽ △ ⚵	**2:35 pm**	11:35 am
♀ △ ⚴	**6:42 pm**	3:42 pm
☽ ⚺ ♄	**8:29 pm**	5:29 pm
☽ ☍ ⚷	**9:37 pm**	6:37 pm
☽ ⚹ ☉		11:00 pm
☽ △ ♅		11:25 pm

9 SUNDAY

☽ ⚹ ☉	**2:00 am**	
☽ △ ♅	**2:25 am**	
☽ ⚻ ⚶	**3:59 am**	12:59 am
♂ ⚻ ♇	**7:52 am**	4:52 am
☉ ⚹ ♅	**8:09 am**	5:09 am
☽ □ ☿	**11:01 am**	8:01 am
☽ □ ⚳	**4:03 pm**	1:03 pm
☽ ⚺ ⚴		9:22 pm
☽ □ ♀		11:38 pm

10 MONDAY

☽ ⚺ ⚴	**12:22 am**	
☽ □ ♀	**2:38 am**	
☽ ⚻ ♆	**6:00 am**	3:00 am
♂ □ ⚵	**6:58 am**	3:58 am
☽ ⚹ ♃	**2:34 pm**	11:34 am
☽ ⚻ ♇	**4:45 pm**	1:45 pm
☽ ⚻ ⚵	**6:12 pm**	3:12 pm
☽ ⚹ ♂	**6:33 pm**	3:33 pm
☉ □ ⚶	**8:42 pm**	5:42 pm
☽ ⚹ ♄	**11:32 pm**	8:32 pm
☽ ⚻ ⚷		9:10 pm

11 TUESDAY

☽ ⚻ ⚷	**12:10 am**	
☽ ⚻ ♅	**5:15 am**	2:15 am
☿ ☍ ⚳	**7:54 am**	4:54 am
☽ ☍ ⚶	**7:57 am**	4:57 am
☽ □ ☉	**8:30 am**	5:30 am
♀ ⚹ ♆	**5:45 pm**	2:45 pm
☽ ⚹ ⚳	**6:22 pm**	3:22 pm
☽ △ ☿	**7:45 pm**	4:45 pm

12 WEDNESDAY

☽ ☌ ⚴	**4:23 am**	1:23 am
☽ ☍ ♆	**9:15 am**	6:15 am
☽ △ ♀	**10:45 am**	7:45 am
☽ □ ♃	**6:49 pm**	3:49 pm
☽ △ ♇	**8:08 pm**	5:08 pm
☽ ☍ ⚵	**10:47 pm**	7:47 pm
☽ □ ♂		9:50 pm

13 THURSDAY

☽ □ ♂	**12:50 am**	
☽ □ ♄	**3:33 am**	12:33 am
☽ △ ⚷	**3:39 am**	12:39 am
☽ ☍ ♅	**9:03 am**	6:03 am
♄ ⚻ ⚷	**12:55 pm**	9:55 am
☽ ⚻ ⚶	**12:56 pm**	9:56 am
☽ △ ☉	**4:14 pm**	1:14 pm
☽ ⚺ ⚳	**9:43 pm**	6:43 pm

14 FRIDAY

☽ ⚻ ☿	**6:14 am**	3:14 am
☽ ⚺ ⚴	**9:35 am**	6:35 am
☽ ⚻ ♆	**1:36 pm**	10:36 am
☽ ⚻ ♀	**8:17 pm**	5:17 pm
☽ △ ♃		9:15 pm
☽ □ ♇		9:36 pm

15 SATURDAY

☽ △ ♃	**12:15 am**	
☽ □ ♇	**12:36 am**	
☽ ⚻ ⚵	**4:33 am**	1:33 am
♂ ⚻ ⚷	**5:13 am**	2:13 am
☽ □ ⚷	**8:16 am**	5:16 am
☽ △ ♂	**8:26 am**	5:26 am
☽ △ ♄	**8:45 am**	5:45 am
☽ ⚻ ♅	**2:01 pm**	11:01 am
♂ ☌ ♄	**3:28 pm**	12:28 pm
☿ △ ⚴	**4:32 pm**	1:32 pm
☽ △ ⚶	**7:08 pm**	4:08 pm
♃ ⚻ ♇	**7:41 pm**	4:41 pm
☽ ⚻ ☉		10:26 pm
☽ ☌ ⚳		11:16 pm

16 SUNDAY

☽ ⚻ ☉	**1:26 am**	
☽ ☌ ⚳	**2:16 am**	
☉ ⚻ ⚳	**11:36 am**	8:36 am
☽ ⚹ ⚴	**4:10 pm**	1:10 pm
☽ ☍ ☿	**6:52 pm**	3:52 pm
♀ △ ♇	**7:08 pm**	4:08 pm
☽ △ ♆	**7:15 pm**	4:15 pm
☿ ⚹ ♆	**9:55 pm**	6:55 pm
♀ ⚺ ♃		10:02 pm

17 MONDAY

♀ ⚺ ♃	**1:02 am**	
☽ ⚹ ♇	**6:28 am**	3:28 am
☽ ⚻ ♃	**7:08 am**	4:08 am
☽ ☍ ♀	**7:39 am**	4:39 am
☽ △ ⚵	**11:49 am**	8:49 am
☽ ⚹ ⚷	**2:18 pm**	11:18 am
☽ ⚻ ♄	**3:27 pm**	12:27 pm
☽ ⚻ ♂	**5:45 pm**	2:45 pm
☽ △ ♅	**8:30 pm**	5:30 pm
☽ □ ⚶		11:58 pm

18 TUESDAY

☽ □ ⚶	**2:58 am**	
☽ ⚺ ⚳	**8:29 am**	5:29 am
☽ ☍ ☉	**12:41 pm**	9:41 am
☽ □ ⚴		9:44 pm
☽ □ ♆		11:45 pm

19 WEDNESDAY

☽ □ ⚴	**12:44 am**	
☽ □ ♆	**2:45 am**	
☽ ⚻ ☿	**10:39 am**	7:39 am
☽ ⚺ ♇	**2:18 pm**	11:18 am
♀ ⚹ ⚵	**3:59 pm**	12:59 pm
☽ ☍ ♃	**4:09 pm**	1:09 pm
☽ □ ⚵	**9:16 pm**	6:16 pm
☽ ⚻ ♀	**9:43 pm**	6:43 pm
♂ □ ♅	**9:59 pm**	6:59 pm
☽ ⚺ ⚷	**10:25 pm**	7:25 pm
☽ ☍ ♄		9:20 pm

20 THURSDAY

☽ ☍ ♄	**12:20 am**	
♀ △ ⚷	**4:35 am**	1:35 am
☽ □ ♅	**5:11 am**	2:11 am
☽ ☍ ♂	**5:36 am**	2:36 am
☽ ⚹ ⚶	**1:11 pm**	10:11 am
☿ △ ♇	**1:20 pm**	10:20 am
☽ ⚹ ⚳	**5:00 pm**	2:00 pm
☽ ⚻ ☉		11:56 pm

21 FRIDAY

☽ ⚻ ☉	**2:56 am**	
♀ ⚺ ♄	**3:02 am**	12:02 am
☿ ⚺ ♃	**8:26 am**	5:26 am
☽ △ ⚴	**11:58 am**	8:58 am
☽ ⚹ ♆	**12:44 pm**	9:44 am
⚷ ⚹ ⚵	**6:38 pm**	3:38 pm
☽ ☌ ♇		9:40 pm

22 SATURDAY

☽ ☌ ♇	**12:40 am**	
☽ ⚻ ♃	**3:52 am**	12:52 am
☽ △ ☿	**6:45 am**	3:45 am
☽ ☌ ⚷	**9:02 am**	6:02 am
☽ ⚹ ⚵	**9:25 am**	6:25 am
☽ ⚻ ♄	**11:51 am**	8:51 am
☽ △ ♀	**3:14 pm**	12:14 pm
☽ ⚹ ♅	**4:25 pm**	1:25 pm
♆ ☍ ⚴	**8:25 pm**	5:25 pm
☽ ⚻ ♂	**8:28 pm**	5:28 pm
☿ △ ⚷	**9:54 pm**	6:54 pm
☽ ⚺ ⚶		11:02 pm
♀ ⚹ ♅		11:54 pm

23 SUNDAY

☽ ⚺ ⚶	**2:02 am**	
♀ ⚹ ♅	**2:54 am**	
☿ ⚹ ⚵	**3:31 am**	12:31 am
☽ □ ⚳	**4:03 am**	1:03 am
☿ ⚺ ♄	**7:06 pm**	4:06 pm
☽ △ ☉	**8:14 pm**	5:14 pm
☽ ⚺ ♆		10:00 pm
☽ ⚻ ⚴		10:44 pm

24 MONDAY

☽ ⚺ ♆	**1:00 am**	
☽ ⚻ ⚴	**1:44 am**	
☽ ⚺ ♇	**1:07 pm**	10:07 am
☽ △ ♃	**5:43 pm**	2:43 pm
☽ ⚺ ⚷	**9:32 pm**	6:32 pm
☿ ⚹ ♅	**11:29 pm**	8:29 pm
☽ ⚺ ⚵	**11:34 pm**	8:34 pm
☽ △ ♄		10:16 pm

25 TUESDAY

☽ △ ♄	**1:16 am**	
☽ ⚺ ♅	**5:21 am**	2:21 am
☽ □ ☿	**6:26 am**	3:26 am
☽ □ ♀	**11:07 am**	8:07 am
☽ △ ♂	**1:12 pm**	10:12 am
☽ ☌ ⚶	**4:20 pm**	1:20 pm
☽ △ ⚳	**4:29 pm**	1:29 pm
⚳ △ ⚶	**9:07 pm**	6:07 pm

26 WEDNESDAY

☉ □ ♆	**6:35 am**	3:35 am
☽ ☌ ♆	**1:52 pm**	10:52 am
☽ □ ☉	**2:30 pm**	11:30 am
☽ ☍ ⚴	**4:08 pm**	1:08 pm
☽ ⚹ ♇		10:38 pm

27 THURSDAY

☽ ⚹ ♇	**1:38 am**	
☽ □ ♃	**7:26 am**	4:26 am
♀ ⚺ ♂	**7:33 am**	4:33 am
☽ ⚹ ⚷	**9:43 am**	6:43 am
♀ ⚻ ⚳	**11:57 am**	8:57 am
☽ ☌ ⚵	**1:15 pm**	10:15 am
☽ □ ♄	**2:12 pm**	11:12 am
♂ △ ⚳	**2:56 pm**	11:56 am
☽ ☌ ♅	**5:39 pm**	2:39 pm
☿ ⚻ ⚳	**7:09 pm**	4:09 pm
☉ □ ⚴	**7:18 pm**	4:18 pm
☿ ⚺ ♂	**9:50 pm**	6:50 pm
♀ □ ⚶		10:05 pm

28 FRIDAY

♀ □ ⚶	**1:05 am**	
☽ ⚻ ⚳	**3:53 am**	12:53 am
☿ □ ⚶	**4:10 am**	1:10 am
☽ □ ♂	**4:44 am**	1:44 am
☽ ⚺ ⚶	**5:22 am**	2:22 am
☽ ⚹ ☿	**5:33 am**	2:33 am
☽ ⚹ ♀	**5:44 am**	2:44 am
☿ ☌ ♀	**8:27 am**	5:27 am
♂ △ ⚶	**9:06 pm**	6:06 pm
☽ ⚺ ♆		9:38 pm

29 SATURDAY

☽ ⚺ ♆	**12:38 am**	
☽ ⚻ ⚴	**4:14 am**	1:14 am
☽ ⚹ ☉	**6:05 am**	3:05 am
☽ □ ♇	**11:37 am**	8:37 am
☽ ⚹ ♃	**6:14 pm**	3:14 pm
☽ □ ⚷	**7:05 pm**	4:05 pm
☽ ⚺ ⚵	11:46 pm	8:46 pm
☽ ⚹ ♄		9:03 pm
☽ ⚺ ♅		11:48 pm

30 SUNDAY

☽ ⚹ ♄	**12:03 am**	
☽ ⚺ ♅	**2:48 am**	
☽ ☍ ⚳	**12:01 pm**	9:01 am
☽ ⚹ ⚶	**2:41 pm**	11:41 am
☽ ⚹ ♂	**4:13 pm**	1:13 pm
☽ ⚺ ♀	**7:43 pm**	4:43 pm
☽ ⚺ ☿	**11:35 pm**	8:35 pm

Eastern Standard Time in bold type

Pacific Standard Time in medium type

APRIL 2000

☽ Last Aspect day	EST / hr:mn / PST		asp	☽ Ingress sign day	EST / hr:mn / PST	
31	**7:19 am**	4:19 am	☌♅	♓ 1	**3:12 am**	12:12 am
2		11:44 pm	☌♀	♈ 3	**10:22 am**	7:22 am
3	**2:44 am**		☌♀	♈ 3	**10:22 am**	7:22 am
4	**9:04 pm**	6:04 pm	⚹♅	♉ 5	**2:29 pm**	11:29 am
7	**3:24 am**	12:24 am	⚹☿	♊ 7	**4:58 pm**	1:58 pm
9	**11:01 am**	8:01 am	□☿	♋ 9	**7:16 pm**	4:16 pm
11	**7:45 pm**	4:45 pm	△☿	♌ 11	**10:16 pm**	7:16 pm
13	**4:14 pm**	1:14 pm	△☉	♍ 13		11:19 pm
13	**4:14 pm**	1:14 pm	△☉	♍ 14	**2:19 am**	
15	**8:45 am**	5:45 am	△♄	♎ 16	**7:36 am**	4:36 am
18	**12:41 pm**	9:41 am	☍☉	♏ 18	**2:35 pm**	11:35 pm
20	**5:36 am**	2:36 am	☍♂	♐ 20	**11:58 pm**	8:58 pm
22	**4:25 pm**	1:25 pm	⚹♅	♑ 23	**11:47 am**	8:47 am
25	**1:12 pm**	10:12 am	△♂	♒ 25		9:42 pm
25	**1:12 pm**	10:12 am	△♂	♒ 26	**12:43 am**	
28	**5:44 am**	2:44 am	⚹♀	♓ 28	**12:06 pm**	9:06 am
30	**4:13 pm**	1:13 pm	⚹♂	♈ 30	**7:54 pm**	4:54 pm

☽ Phases & Eclipses phase	day	EST / hr:mn / PST	
New Moon	4	**1:12 pm**	10:12 am
2nd Quarter	11	**8:30 am**	5:30 am
Full Moon	18	**12:41 pm**	9:41 am
4th Quarter	26	**2:30 pm**	11:30 am

Planet Ingress	day	EST / hr:mn / PST	
♀ ♈	6	**1:37 pm**	10:37 am
☿ ♈	12	**7:17 pm**	4:17 pm
☉ ♉	19	**1:39 pm**	10:39 am
☿ ♉	29	**10:53 pm**	7:53 pm
♀ ♉	30	**9:49 pm**	6:49 pm

Planetary Motion	day	EST / hr:mn / PST

DATE		SID.TIME	SUN	MOON	NODE	MERCURY	VENUS	MARS	JUPITER	SATURN	URANUS	NEPTUNE	PLUTO	CERES	PALLAS	JUNO	VESTA	CHIRON
Sat	1	12:38:38	11 ♈ 34 03	25 ♒ 42	01 ♌ ℞ 12	14 ♓ 01	22 ♓ 52	06 ♉ 32	09 ♉ 11	15 ♉ 30	19 ♒ 40	06 ♒ 12	12 ♐ ℞ 50	29 ♍ ℞ 52	01 ♌ 01	10 ♒ 29	17 ♑ 58	17 ♐ ℞ 14
Sun	2	12:42:34	12 33 16	08 ♓ 24	01 07	15 10	24 06	07 16	09 24	15 37	19 42	06 13	12 49	29 39	01 13	10 48	18 20	17 13
Mon	3	12:46:31	13 32 27	21 27	00 59	16 21	25 20	08 00	09 38	15 44	19 44	06 14	12 48	29 27	01 25	11 07	18 42	17 13
Tue	4	12:50:27	14 31 35	04 ♈ 52	00 49	17 34	26 34	08 43	09 51	15 51	19 47	06 15	12 48	29 14	01 37	11 26	19 03	17 12
Wed	5	12:54:24	15 30 42	18 38	00 38	18 49	27 48	09 27	10 05	15 58	19 49	06 16	12 47	29 02	01 50	11 44	19 25	17 11
Thu	6	12:58:21	16 29 47	02 ♉ 40	00 26	20 06	29 03	10 10	10 19	16 05	19 51	06 17	12 46	28 50	02 03	12 03	19 46	17 10
Fri	7	13:02:17	17 28 50	16 53	00 15	21 26	00 ♈ 17	10 54	10 32	16 12	19 54	06 18	12 46	28 38	02 16	12 22	20 06	17 10
Sat	8	13:06:14	18 27 50	01 ♊ 13	00 06	22 47	01 31	11 37	10 46	16 19	19 56	06 19	12 45	28 27	02 30	12 40	20 27	17 08
Sun	9	13:10:10	19 26 49	15 33	00 00	24 10	02 45	12 21	11 00	16 26	19 58	06 20	12 44	28 15	02 44	12 58	20 47	17 07
Mon	10	13:14:07	20 25 45	29 51	29 ♋ 57	25 34	03 59	13 04	11 14	16 33	20 00	06 21	12 43	28 04	02 58	13 16	21 08	17 06
Tue	11	13:18:03	21 24 39	14 ♋ 02	29 D 56	27 01	05 13	13 47	11 28	16 41	20 02	06 22	12 43	27 54	03 13	13 34	21 27	17 05
Wed	12	13:22:00	22 23 30	28 06	29 ℞ 55	28 29	06 27	14 30	11 42	16 48	20 04	06 23	12 42	27 43	03 28	13 52	21 47	17 03
Thu	13	13:25:56	23 22 20	12 ♌ 02	29 55	29 59	07 41	15 13	11 56	16 55	20 06	06 24	12 41	27 33	03 43	14 10	22 06	17 02
Fri	14	13:29:53	24 21 06	25 50	29 53	01 ♈ 30	08 55	15 56	12 10	17 03	20 08	06 25	12 40	27 24	03 59	14 28	22 26	17 00
Sat	15	13:33:50	25 19 51	09 ♍ 29	29 49	03 04	10 09	16 40	12 24	17 10	20 10	06 25	12 39	27 14	04 14	14 45	22 44	16 59
Sun	16	13:37:46	26 18 33	22 59	29 42	04 39	11 23	17 23	12 38	17 17	20 12	06 26	12 38	27 05	04 30	15 03	23 03	16 57
Mon	17	13:41:43	27 17 13	06 ♎ 19	29 32	06 15	12 37	18 05	12 52	17 25	20 14	06 27	12 37	26 57	04 47	15 20	23 21	16 55
Tue	18	13:45:39	28 15 52	19 27	29 20	07 53	13 51	18 48	13 06	17 32	20 16	06 27	12 36	26 48	05 03	15 37	23 40	16 53
Wed	19	13:49:36	29 14 28	02 ♏ 21	29 07	09 33	15 04	19 31	13 20	17 40	20 17	06 28	12 35	26 40	05 20	15 54	23 57	16 51
Thu	20	13:53:32	00 ♉ 13 02	15 02	28 54	11 14	16 18	20 14	13 34	17 47	20 19	06 29	12 34	26 33	05 37	16 11	24 15	16 49
Fri	21	13:57:29	01 11 35	27 28	28 42	12 58	17 32	20 57	13 48	17 55	20 21	06 29	12 33	26 26	05 54	16 28	24 32	16 47
Sat	22	14:01:25	02 10 05	09 ♐ 40	28 32	14 42	18 46	21 39	14 02	18 02	20 22	06 30	12 32	26 19	06 12	16 45	24 49	16 44
Sun	23	14:05:22	03 08 34	21 41	28 25	16 29	20 00	22 22	14 16	18 10	20 24	06 30	12 31	26 13	06 29	17 01	25 06	16 42
Mon	24	14:09:19	04 07 02	03 ♑ 34	28 21	18 17	21 14	23 05	14 31	18 17	20 26	06 31	12 29	26 07	06 47	17 17	25 22	16 39
Tue	25	14:13:15	05 05 27	15 22	28 19	20 07	22 28	23 47	14 45	18 25	20 27	06 31	12 28	26 01	07 05	17 34	25 38	16 37
Wed	26	14:17:12	06 03 52	27 11	28 18	21 58	23 42	24 30	14 59	18 32	20 28	06 32	12 27	25 56	07 24	17 50	25 54	16 34
Thu	27	14:21:08	07 02 14	09 ♒ 06	28 18	23 51	24 56	25 12	15 13	18 40	20 30	06 32	12 26	25 51	07 42	18 05	26 10	16 32
Fri	28	14:25:05	08 00 35	21 13	28 18	25 46	26 10	25 55	15 27	18 48	20 31	06 33	12 25	25 47	08 01	18 21	26 25	16 29
Sat	29	14:29:01	08 58 54	03 ♓ 36	28 15	27 43	27 24	26 37	15 42	18 55	20 32	06 33	12 23	25 43	08 20	18 37	26 39	16 26
Sun	30	14:32:58	09 57 12	16 20	28 11	29 41	28 37	27 19	15 56	19 03	20 34	06 33	12 22	25 39	08 39	18 52	26 54	16 23

EPHEMERIS CALCULATED FOR 12 MIDNIGHT GREENWICH MEAN TIME. ALL OTHER DATA AND FACING ASPECTARIAN PAGE IN **EASTERN STANDARD TIME (BOLD)** AND PACIFIC STANDARD TIME (REGULAR).

MAY 2000

1 MONDAY

	5:56 am
	6:34 am
	8:51 am
	12:14 pm
	4:46 pm
	5:41 pm

2 TUESDAY

	12:31 am
	12:51 am
	5:20 am
	5:50 am
	6:03 am
	7:59 am
	4:21 pm
	7:51 pm
	9:51 pm

3 WEDNESDAY

	4:31 am
	4:37 am
	10:53 am
	11:57 am
	8:21 pm
	11:12 pm

4 THURSDAY

	2:45 am
	4:05 am
	8:27 am
	9:04 am
	10:07 am
	6:00 pm
	10:12 pm

5 FRIDAY

	12:03 am
	12:08 am
	11:27 am
	12:05 pm
	6:40 pm
	9:12 pm

6 SATURDAY

	1:57 am
	3:29 am
	3:36 am
	5:47 am
	5:57 am
	9:45 am
	10:43 am
	11:31 am
	11:43 am

7 SUNDAY

	6:27 am
	7:00 am
	1:01 am
	3:03 pm
	3:52 pm
	8:52 pm
	10:16 pm
	11:08 pm

8 MONDAY

	4:29 am
	6:54 am
	7:51 am
	8:19 am
	12:26 pm
	12:53 pm
	1:53 pm
	8:21 pm
	10:49 pm

9 TUESDAY

	2:06 am
	3:10 am
	3:11 am
	7:46 pm
	10:57 pm

10 WEDNESDAY

	12:34 am
	12:39 am
	3:50 am
	6:59 am
	11:35 am
	2:45 pm
	3:00 pm
	3:00 pm
	3:31 pm
	4:46 pm
	6:01 pm
	7:11 pm
	10:16 pm
	11:45 pm

11 THURSDAY

	12:03 am
	5:44 am
	7:17 am
	11:06 pm

12 FRIDAY

	12:20 am
	3:54 am
	4:51 am
	5:19 am
	8:31 am
	11:31 am
	5:31 pm
	8:37 pm
	8:41 pm
	10:50 pm
	11:54 pm

13 SATURDAY

	12:17 am
	3:34 am
	5:20 am
	10:57 am
	12:44 pm
	2:15 pm
	10:30 pm

14 SUNDAY

	1:30 am
	2:57 am
	2:42 am
	6:06 pm
	9:12 pm

15 MONDAY

	1:38 am
	3:55 am
	4:22 am
	7:01 am
	12:08 pm
	1:02 pm
	9:11 pm

16 TUESDAY

	12:52 am
	6:21 am
	6:03 am
	9:45 am
	2:33 pm
	8:06 pm

17 WEDNESDAY

	1:09 am
	2:42 am
	4:10 am
	5:30 am
	11:54 am
	12:28 pm
	2:14 pm
	5:19 pm
	7:39 pm
	10:54 pm

18 THURSDAY

	2:34 am
	7:40 am
	7:56 am
	8:03 pm
	11:15 pm

19 FRIDAY

	4:15 am
	4:37 am

20 SATURDAY

	12:21 am
	12:30 am
	2:12 am
	5:43 am
	6:33 am
	8:16 am
	10:54 am
	3:24 pm
	7:34 pm
	8:07 pm

21 SUNDAY

	3:05 am
	8:15 am
	9:53 am
	7:01 pm
	8:48 pm

22 MONDAY

	1:35 am
	2:46 am
	3:37 am
	4:29 am
	4:45 am
	1:20 pm
	2:24 pm
	3:42 pm
	7:32 pm

23 TUESDAY

	12:18 am
	2:31 am
	9:35 am
	1:57 pm
	9:12 pm

24 WEDNESDAY

	7:49 am
	11:23 am
	2:26 pm
	7:15 pm
	11:56 pm

25 THURSDAY

	1:58 am
	2:17 am
	4:13 am
	4:56 am
	7:35 am
	8:53 am
	1:11 pm
	9:34 pm
	10:00 pm

26 FRIDAY

	2:13 am
	6:55 am
	1:40 pm
	1:45 pm
	6:49 pm

27 SATURDAY

	12:34 am
	3:39 am
	6:38 am
	7:36 am
	12:07 pm
	3:18 pm
	3:23 pm
	7:20 pm
	10:23 pm
	11:11 pm
	11:17 pm

28 SUNDAY

	7:07 am
	1:04 pm
	12:19 pm
	4:52 pm
	7:33 pm

29 MONDAY

	2:07 am
	7:18 am
	1:18 pm
	3:38 pm
	6:15 pm
	9:52 pm
	10:09 pm

30 TUESDAY

	1:32 am
	5:02 am
	11:18 am
	1:04 pm
	6:03 pm
	8:54 pm
	9:38 pm

31 WEDNESDAY

	3:08 am
	5:28 am
	6:30 pm
	7:35 pm
	8:39 pm

(24 WEDNESDAY cont.)

	4:49 am
	8:23 am
	10:26 am
	11:05 am
	10:58 am
	11:17 pm

(25 THURSDAY cont.)

	1:13 pm
	1:31 am
	1:56 am
	4:35 am
	5:53 am
	6:34 pm
	7:00 pm
	11:13 pm

(26 FRIDAY cont.)

	3:55 am
	5:46 am
	3:49 pm
	9:34 pm

(27 SATURDAY cont.)

	12:39 pm
	3:38 pm
	4:35 pm
	9:07 pm
	10:20 pm
	12:28 pm
	4:20 pm
	7:23 pm
	8:11 pm
	8:17 pm

(28 SUNDAY cont.)

	4:07 pm
	8:04 pm
	9:19 am
	1:52 pm
	4:33 pm
	11:07 pm

(29 MONDAY cont.)

	4:18 pm
	10:18 pm
	12:38 pm
	3:15 pm
	6:52 pm
	7:09 pm
	10:32 pm

(30 TUESDAY cont.)

	2:02 am
	8:18 am
	9:00 am
	10:04 am
	3:03 pm
	5:54 pm
	6:38 pm

(31 WEDNESDAY cont.)

	12:08 am
	2:28 am
	7:09 am
	3:30 pm
	4:35 pm
	5:39 pm
	9:30 pm
	10:08 pm

MAY 2000

☽ Last Aspect				☽ Ingress			
day	EST / hr:mn / PST		asp	sign	day	EST / hr:mn / PST	
2	**7:59 am**	4:59 am	⚹ ♅	♉	2	**11:54 pm**	8:54 pm
4	**10:07 am**	7:07 am	□ ♅	♊	4		10:23 pm
4	**10:07 am**	7:07 am	□ ♅	♊	5	**1:23 am**	10:23 pm
6	**11:01 am**	8:01 am	△ ♅	♋	6		11:14 pm
6	**11:01 am**	8:01 am	△ ♅	♋	7	**2:14 am**	
8	**11:31 am**	8:31 am	⚹ ♄	♌	9	**4:01 am**	1:01 am
10	**7:11 pm**	4:11 pm	□ ☿	♍	11	**7:41 am**	4:41 am
13	**10:57 am**	7:57 am	△ ☿	♎	13	**1:27 pm**	10:27 am
15	**3:55 am**	12:55 am	△ ♅	♏	15	**9:16 pm**	6:16 pm
18		11:34 pm	☍ ☉	♐	18	**7:09 am**	4:09 am

☽ Last Aspect				☽ Ingress			
day	EST / hr:mn / PST		asp	sign	day	EST / hr:mn / PST	
18	**2:34 pm**		☍ ☉	♐	18	**7:09 am**	4:09 am
19		9:30 pm	⚹ ♅	♑	20	**7:01 pm**	4:01 pm
20	**12:30 am**		⚹ ♅	♑	20	**7:01 pm**	4:01 pm
22		11:31 pm	△ ♀	♒	23	**8:00 am**	5:00 am
23	**2:31 am**		△ ♀	♒	23	**8:00 am**	5:00 am
25	**4:56 am**	1:56 am	□ ♄	♓	25	**8:07 pm**	5:07 pm
27	**11:17 pm**	8:17 pm	□ ☿	♈	28	**5:08 am**	2:08 am
29	**6:15 pm**	3:15 pm	⚹ ♅	♉	30	**10:02 am**	7:02 am
31		11:09 pm	☌ ♃	♊	1	**11:34 am**	8:34 am

☽ Phases & Eclipses			
phase	day	EST / hr:mn / PST	
New Moon	3	**11:12 pm**	8:12 pm
2nd Quarter	10	**3:00 pm**	12:00 pm
Full Moon	17		11:34 pm
Full Moon	18	**2:34 am**	
4th Quarter	26	**6:55 am**	3:55 am

Planet Ingress			
	day	EST / hr:mn / PST	
♂ ♊	3	**2:18 pm**	11:18 am
☿ ♊	13		11:10 pm
☿ ♊	14	**2:10 am**	
⚶ ♒	16	**6:00 am**	3:00 am
☉ ♊	20	**12:49 pm**	9:49 am
♀ ♊	25	**7:15 am**	4:15 am
☿ ♋	29	**11:27 pm**	8:27 pm

Planetary Motion			
	day	EST / hr:mn / PST	
⚳ D	7	**5:09 pm**	2:09 pm
♆ ℞	7		9:18 pm
♆ ℞	8	**12:18 am**	
♅ ℞	24	**11:29 pm**	8:29 pm

DATE		SID.TIME	SUN	MOON	NODE	MERCURY	VENUS	MARS	JUPITER	SATURN	URANUS	NEPTUNE	PLUTO	CERES	PALLAS	JUNO	VESTA	CHIRON
Mon	1	14:36:54	10 ♉ 55 28	29 ♓ 30	28 ♋℞ 04	01 ♉ 41	29 ♈ 51	28 ♉ 02	16 ♉ 10	19 ♉ 11	20 ♒ 35	06 ♒ 33	12 ♐℞ 21	25 ♍℞ 36	08 ♌ 58	19 ♒ 07	27 ♑ 08	16 ♐℞ 20
Tue	2	14:40:51	11 53 43	13 ♈ 05	27 55	03 42	01 ♉ 05	28 44	16 24	19 18	20 36	06 34	12 19	25 34	09 18	19 22	27 22	16 17
Wed	3	14:44:47	12 51 56	27 06	27 44	05 45	02 19	29 26	16 39	19 26	20 37	06 34	12 18	25 31	09 38	19 37	27 35	16 14
Thu	4	14:48:44	13 50 07	11 ♉ 28	27 33	07 49	03 33	00 ♊ 08	16 53	19 34	20 38	06 34	12 17	25 29	09 57	19 52	27 48	16 11
Fri	5	14:52:41	14 48 17	26 05	27 22	09 55	04 47	00 50	17 07	19 41	20 39	06 34	12 15	25 28	10 17	20 06	28 01	16 08
Sat	6	14:56:37	15 46 25	10 ♊ 50	27 14	12 02	06 01	01 32	17 22	19 49	20 40	06 34	12 14	25 27	10 38	20 21	28 14	16 04
Sun	7	15:00:34	16 44 32	25 35	27 08	14 10	07 14	02 14	17 36	19 57	20 41	06 34	12 12	25 D 26	10 58	20 35	28 26	16 01
Mon	8	15:04:30	17 42 36	10 ♋ 12	27 05	16 19	08 28	02 56	17 50	20 05	20 42	06 ℞ 34	12 11	25 26	11 18	20 49	28 37	15 57
Tue	9	15:08:27	18 40 39	24 38	27 D 04	18 29	09 42	03 38	18 04	20 12	20 43	06 34	12 10	25 26	11 39	21 02	28 48	15 54
Wed	10	15:12:23	19 38 39	08 ♌ 49	27 ℞ 04	20 40	10 56	04 20	18 19	20 20	20 44	06 34	12 08	25 27	12 00	21 16	28 59	15 50
Thu	11	15:16:20	20 36 38	22 45	27 04	22 50	12 10	05 02	18 33	20 28	20 44	06 34	12 07	25 28	12 21	21 29	29 10	15 47
Fri	12	15:20:17	21 34 35	06f 25	27 03	25 01	13 24	05 44	18 47	20 35	20 45	06 34	12 05	25 30	12 42	21 42	29 20	15 43
Sat	13	15:24:13	22 32 30	19 50	27 00	27 11	14 37	06 26	19 02	20 43	20 46	06 34	12 04	25 31	13 03	21 55	29 30	15 39
Sun	14	15:28:10	23 30 23	03 ♎ 02	26 55	29 21	15 51	07 07	19 16	20 51	20 46	06 34	12 02	25 34	13 25	22 08	29 39	15 36
Mon	15	15:32:06	24 28 14	16 01	26 47	01 ♊ 30	17 05	07 49	19 30	20 59	20 47	06 34	12 01	25 36	13 46	22 20	29 48	15 32
Tue	16	15:36:03	25 26 04	28 48	26 37	03 38	18 19	08 30	19 44	21 06	20 47	06 33	11 59	25 39	14 08	22 33	29 56	15 28
Wed	17	15:39:59	26 23 52	11 ♏ 23	26 27	05 45	19 32	09 12	19 58	21 14	20 48	06 33	11 58	25 43	14 29	22 45	00 ♒ 04	15 24
Thu	18	15:43:56	27 21 39	23 47	26 16	07 50	20 46	09 53	20 13	21 22	20 48	06 33	11 56	25 47	14 51	22 56	00 12	15 20
Fri	19	15:47:52	28 19 24	06 ♐ 01	26 06	09 53	22 00	10 35	20 27	21 29	20 48	06 33	11 54	25 51	15 13	23 08	00 19	15 16
Sat	20	15:51:49	29 17 08	18 04	25 58	11 55	23 14	11 16	20 41	21 37	20 49	06 32	11 53	25 55	15 35	23 19	00 26	15 12
Sun	21	15:55:45	00 ♊ 14 51	00 ♑ 00	25 53	13 53	24 27	11 58	20 55	21 45	20 49	06 32	11 51	26 00	15 57	23 31	00 32	15 08
Mon	22	15:59:42	01 12 33	11 49	25 50	15 50	25 41	12 39	21 09	21 52	20 49	06 31	11 50	26 06	16 20	23 41	00 38	15 04
Tue	23	16:03:39	02 10 13	23 36	25 D 48	17 44	26 55	13 20	21 24	22 00	20 49	06 31	11 48	26 11	16 42	23 52	00 44	15 00
Wed	24	16:07:35	03 07 52	05 ♒ 25	25 49	19 35	28 09	14 02	21 38	22 08	20 49	06 31	11 47	26 17	17 05	24 02	00 49	14 56
Thu	25	16:11:32	04 05 31	17 20	25 50	21 24	29 22	14 43	21 52	22 15	20 ℞ 49	06 30	11 45	26 24	17 27	24 13	00 53	14 52
Fri	26	16:15:28	05 03 08	29 26	25 ℞ 51	23 09	00 ♊ 36	15 24	22 06	22 23	20 49	06 29	11 43	26 30	17 50	24 22	00 57	14 48
Sat	27	16:19:25	06 00 44	11 ♓ 48	25 51	24 52	01 50	16 05	22 20	22 31	20 49	06 29	11 42	26 37	18 13	24 32	01 01	14 44
Sun	28	16:23:21	06 58 20	24 31	25 49	26 32	03 04	16 46	22 34	22 38	20 49	06 28	11 40	26 45	18 36	24 41	01 04	14 40
Mon	29	16:27:18	07 55 54	07 ♈ 39	25 46	28 09	04 17	17 27	22 48	22 46	20 49	06 28	11 38	26 53	18 59	24 50	01 06	14 35
Tue	30	16:31:14	08 53 28	21 15	25 41	29 43	05 31	18 08	23 02	22 53	20 49	06 27	11 37	27 01	19 22	24 59	01 09	14 31
Wed	31	16:35:11	09 51 00	05b 18	25 34	01 ♋ 14	06 45	18 49	23 16	23 01	20 49	06 26	11 35	27 09	19 45	25 08	01 10	14 27

EPHEMERIS CALCULATED FOR 12 MIDNIGHT GREENWICH MEAN TIME. ALL OTHER DATA AND FACING ASPECTARIAN PAGE IN **EASTERN STANDARD TIME (BOLD)** AND PACIFIC STANDARD TIME (REGULAR).

JUNE 2000

1 THURSDAY

12:30	am	
2:48	am	
4:00	am	1:00 am
7:20	am	4:20 am
1:17	pm	10:17 am
6:06	pm	3:06 pm
9:53	pm	6:53 pm

2 FRIDAY

3:01	am	
6:03	am	3:03 am
7:14	am	4:14 am
10:26	am	7:26 am
11:13	am	8:13 am
4:35	pm	1:35 pm
8:50	pm	5:50 pm
9:03	pm	6:03 pm
9:06	pm	6:06 pm
		9:01 pm
		10:01 pm
		10:59 pm

3 SATURDAY

12:01	am	
1:01	am	
1:59	am	
4:27	am	1:27 am
7:49	am	4:49 am
11:59	am	8:59 am
1:25	pm	10:25 am
3:30	pm	12:30 pm
9:41	pm	6:41 pm
10:36	pm	7:36 pm

4 SUNDAY

5:48	am	2:48 am
6:17	am	3:17 am
7:07	am	4:07 am
10:04	am	7:04 am
10:20	am	7:20 am
10:47	am	7:47 am
10:23	pm	7:23 pm
11:19	pm	8:19 pm
		10:27 pm
		11:48 pm

5 MONDAY

1:27	am	
2:48	am	
4:56	am	1:56 am
8:32	am	5:32 am
1:40	pm	10:40 am
5:17	pm	2:17 pm
10:12	pm	7:12 pm

6 TUESDAY

3:36	am	12:36 am
6:33	am	3:33 am
12:34	pm	9:34 am
		7:50 am
10:13	pm	7:13 pm
		10:21 pm

7 WEDNESDAY

3:23	am	12:23 am
3:35	am	12:35 am
5:32	am	2:22 am
7:10	am	4:10 am
11:13	am	5:04 am
3:51	pm	12:51 pm
5:22	pm	2:22 pm
		9:53 pm

8 THURSDAY

12:53	am	
9:40	am	6:40 am
11:03	am	8:03 am
2:01	pm	11:01 am
9:16	pm	6:16 pm
10:29	pm	7:29 pm
		11:17 pm

9 FRIDAY

2:17	am	
7:14	am	4:14 am
8:29	am	5:29 am
10:36	am	7:36 am
10:48	am	7:48 am
12:11	pm	9:11 am
4:26	pm	1:26 pm
4:50	pm	1:50 pm
8:47	pm	5:47 pm

10 SATURDAY

2:20	am	
6:28	am	3:28 am
3:43	pm	12:43 pm
8:08	pm	5:08 pm
9:33	pm	6:33 pm
		7:00 pm

11 SUNDAY

3:12	am	12:12 am
3:36	am	12:36 am
3:43	am	12:43 am
9:18	am	6:18 am
9:48	am	6:48 am
9:54	am	6:54 am
4:23	pm	1:23 pm
4:25	pm	1:25 pm
5:26	pm	2:26 pm
7:20	pm	4:20 pm
9:14	pm	6:14 pm
		10:33 pm

12 MONDAY

1:33	am	
4:31	am	1:31 am
2:54	pm	11:54 am
		9:31 pm

13 TUESDAY

12:31	am	
4:56	am	1:56 am
10:40	am	7:40 am
6:55	pm	3:55 pm
		9:24 pm
		11:04 pm
		11:58 pm

14 WEDNESDAY

12:24	am	
2:04	am	
2:58	am	
4:21	am	1:21 am
6:31	am	3:31 am
6:36	am	3:36 am
10:49	am	7:49 am
11:49	am	8:49 am
12:55	pm	9:55 am
1:02	pm	10:02 am
2:33	pm	11:33 am
		10:37 pm

15 THURSDAY

1:37	am	
10:55	am	7:55 am
11:31	am	8:31 am
1:23	pm	10:23 am
3:52	pm	12:52 pm
		10:05 pm
		10:21 pm

16 FRIDAY

1:05	am	
1:21	am	
7:01	am	4:01 am
3:27	pm	12:27 pm
5:27	pm	2:27 pm
5:38	pm	2:38 pm
6:25	pm	3:25 pm
6:52	pm	3:52 pm
7:39	pm	4:39 pm
8:50	pm	5:50 pm
9:22	pm	6:22 pm
		11:11 pm
		11:18 pm
		11:31 pm

17 SATURDAY

2:11	am	
2:11	am	
2:18	am	
2:31	am	
9:27	am	6:27 am
11:59	am	8:59 am
1:40	pm	10:40 am
1:56	pm	10:56 am
11:58	pm	8:58 pm

18 SUNDAY

4:11	am	1:11 am
4:19	am	1:19 am
4:28	am	1:28 am
7:16	am	4:16 am
8:12	am	5:12 am

19 MONDAY

4:59	am	1:59 am
8:03	am	5:03 am
9:34	am	6:34 am
9:46	am	6:46 am
10:56	am	7:56 am

20 TUESDAY

2:51	am	
12:49	pm	9:49 am
4:48	pm	1:48 pm
6:05	pm	3:05 pm

21 WEDNESDAY

6:33	am	3:33 am
8:45	am	5:45 am
7:58	am	4:58 am
2:27	pm	11:27 am
6:12	pm	3:12 pm
11:25	pm	8:25 pm
		9:14 pm
		11:15 pm

22 THURSDAY

12:14	am	
2:15	am	
5:59	am	2:59 am
11:00	am	8:00 am
12:03	pm	9:03 am
2:38	pm	11:38 am
2:50	pm	11:50 am
		9:28 pm

23 FRIDAY

12:26	am	
4:06	am	1:06 am
3:12	pm	12:12 pm
5:50	pm	2:50 pm
6:51	pm	3:51 pm
7:17	pm	4:17 pm

24 SATURDAY

5:14	am	2:14 am
7:10	am	4:10 am
11:38	am	8:38 am
12:24	pm	9:24 am
5:01	pm	2:01 pm
8:00	pm	5:00 pm
11:45	pm	8:45 pm

25 SUNDAY

12:08	am	
6:56	am	3:56 am
8:10	am	5:10 am
12:25	pm	9:25 am
6:52	pm	3:52 pm
		9:59 pm
		11:23 pm

26 MONDAY

12:59	pm	9:36 am
2:23	am	
12:36	pm	9:36 am
1:56	pm	10:56 am
5:25	pm	2:25 pm
6:04	pm	3:04 pm
8:31	pm	5:31 pm
		9:09 pm
		11:48 pm

27 TUESDAY

12:09	am	
2:48	am	
5:39	am	2:39 am
5:52	am	2:52 am
8:04	am	5:04 am
1:27	pm	10:27 am
2:03	pm	11:03 am
2:06	pm	11:03 am
4:56	pm	1:56 pm

28 WEDNESDAY

3:51	am	12:51 am
6:04	am	3:04 am
4:06	pm	1:06 pm
4:54	pm	1:54 pm
7:34	pm	4:34 pm
9:34	pm	6:34 pm
		9:37 pm

29 THURSDAY

12:37	am	
3:27	am	12:27 am
7:37	am	4:37 am
12:19	pm	9:19 am
		11:21 am
3:33	pm	12:33 pm
6:10	pm	3:10 pm

30 FRIDAY

3:26	am	12:26 am
6:47	am	3:47 am
4:49	am	1:49 am
5:08	pm	2:08 pm
7:11	pm	4:11 pm
10:26	pm	7:26 pm
		11:04 pm

JUNE 2000

D Last Aspect

day	EST / hr:mn / PST	asp
1	1:08 am	
2	9:03 am 6:03 pm	♂♂
2	11:48 pm	
4	2:48 am	
7	5:22 am	
7	10:48 am	
11	9:14 pm	
11	9:14 pm	
14	6:31 am 3:31 am	
16	8:50 pm 5:50 pm	

D Ingress

sign	day	EST / hr:mn / PST	asp
♊	1	11:34 am 8:34 am	
⊗	3	11:30 am 8:30 am	
♌	5	11:45 am 8:45 am	
♍	7	1:58 pm 10:58 am	
♎	9	6:58 pm 3:58 pm	
♏	11	11:55 pm	
♐	12	2:55 am	
♑	14	1:18 pm 10:18 am	
♒	16	5:50 pm	

D Last Aspect

day	EST / hr:mn / PST	asp	sign	day	EST / hr:mn / PST	asp
16	8:50 pm	5:50 pm		♒ 17	1:26 am	
19	9:46 am	6:46 am		♓ 19	2:26 am	11:26 am
21	11:25 pm		♈ 21	11:52 pm	
24	11:25 pm	8:25 pm		♉ 21	2:52 am	
24	11:23 pm		♉ 23	9:55 am	
25	2:23 am		♊ 26	7:19 am	4:19 am
28	9:34 pm	6:34 pm		⊗ 26	7:19 am	4:19 am
30	6:47 am	3:47 am		♌ 28	9:59 pm	6:59 pm
			♍ 30	10:09 pm	7:09 pm

D Phases & Eclipses

phase	day	EST / hr:mn / PST
New Moon	2	7:14 am 4:14 am
2nd Quarter	8	10:29 pm 7:29 pm
Full Moon	16	5:27 pm 2:15 pm
4th Quarter	24	8:00 pm 5:00 pm

Planet Ingress

	day	EST / hr:mn / PST
☿ ♎	2	10:46 am 7:46 am
♀ ⊗	16	7:30 am 4:30 am
☉ ⊗	18	5:15 pm 2:15 pm
♀ ♌	19	11:34 pm 8:34 pm
♂ ♉	20	8:48 pm 5:48 pm
♀ ♍	25	4:29 am 1:29 am
♂ ♊	30	2:34 am

Planetary Motion

	day	EST / hr:mn / PST
♇ R	2	4:53 am 1:53 pm
♀ R	23	3:32 am 12:32 am
♆ R	24	4:59 am 1:59 am

DATE	SID.TIME	SUN	MOON	NODE	MERCURY	VENUS	MARS	JUPITER	SATURN	URANUS	NEPTUNE	PLUTO	CERES	PALLAS	JUNO	VESTA	CHIRON

(detailed daily ephemeris data follows)

EPHEMERIS CALCULATED FOR 12 MIDNIGHT GREENWICH MEAN TIME. ALL OTHER DATA AND FACING ASPECTARIAN PAGE IN **EASTERN STANDARD TIME (BOLD)** AND PACIFIC STANDARD TIME (REGULAR).

JULY 2000

1 SATURDAY
```
2:04 am
4:20 am          1:20 pm
7:26 am          4:26 pm
10:50 am         7:50 pm
2:16 pm          11:16 pm
2:20 pm          11:20 pm
3:11 pm
5:38 pm          2:38 pm
11:56 pm         8:56 pm
                 10:06 pm
                 10:23 pm
```

2 SUNDAY
```
1:06 am
1:23 am          12:30 am
3:30 am          3:11 am
6:11 am          7:35 am
10:35 am         7:35 am
12:39 pm         9:39 am
4:27 pm          1:27 pm
4:36 pm          1:36 pm
6:00 pm          3:00 pm
10:34 pm         7:34 pm
                 11:57 pm
```

3 MONDAY
```
2:57 am
4:12 am          1:12 am
6:11 am          3:11 am
6:55 am          3:55 am
1:58 pm          10:58 am
4:43 pm          1:43 pm
5:26 pm          2:26 pm
5:49 pm          2:49 pm
12:00 am         9:00 pm
```

4 TUESDAY
```
4:45 am          1:45 am
4:10 am          1:10 am
5:12 am          2:12 am
5:17 pm          2:17 pm
11:31 pm         8:31 pm
```

5 WEDNESDAY
```
3:25 am          12:25 am
5:22 am          2:22 am
6:46 am          3:46 am
7:57 am          4:57 am
10:34 am         7:34 am
4:15 pm          1:15 pm
6:41 pm          3:41 pm
8:12 pm          5:12 pm
10:34 pm         7:34 pm
11:25 pm         8:25 pm
```

6 THURSDAY
```
6:36 am          3:36 am
8:30 am          5:30 am
8:25 am          5:25 am
7:33 pm          4:33 pm
8:08 pm          5:08 pm
8:57 pm          5:57 pm
```

7 FRIDAY
```
4:21 am          1:21 am
6:08 am          3:08 am
9:08 am          6:08 am
11:00 am         8:00 am
11:58 am         8:58 am
11:59 am         8:59 am
9:30 pm          6:30 pm
8:52 pm          5:52 pm
11:20 pm         8:20 pm
```

8 SATURDAY
```
2:15 am
3:59 am          12:59 am
7:53 am          4:53 am
2:13 pm          11:13 am
3:54 pm          12:54 pm
11:10 pm         8:10 pm
                 10:47 pm
                 10:48 pm
```

9 SUNDAY
```
1:47 am
1:48 am          12:43 am
3:43 am          9:26 am
4:05 am          4:34 pm
12:26 pm         5:36 pm
8:36 pm          6:02 pm
9:02 pm
```

10 MONDAY
```
12:30 am         3:08 pm
5:03 am          6:55 pm
7:33 am          7:37 pm
8:26 am          8:14 pm
3:53 pm          11:28 pm
9:37 pm          11:36 pm
11:22 pm         12:29 pm
```

11 TUESDAY
```
6:08 am          4:31 pm
9:55 am          8:52 pm
10:37 am
11:14 am
2:28 pm
2:36 pm
3:29 pm
7:31 pm
11:52 pm
```

12 WEDNESDAY
```
6:14 am          3:14 pm
8:00 am          6:25 pm
9:25 am          6:37 pm
9:37 am          1:08 pm
4:08 pm          2:38 pm
5:38 pm          3:36 pm
6:36 pm
```

13 THURSDAY
```
6:58 am          3:58 pm
11:02 am         8:02 pm
2:37 pm          11:37 am
9:34 pm          6:34 pm
10:49 pm         7:49 pm
```

14 FRIDAY
```
3:21 am          12:21 am
10:46 am         7:46 am
1:20 pm          10:20 am
6:41 pm          3:41 pm
11:42 pm         8:42 pm
                 9:33 pm
```

15 SATURDAY
```
12:33 am         1:47 am
4:47 am          1:59 am
4:59 am          9:26 am
12:26 pm         12:33 pm
7:34 pm          6:01 pm
9:01 pm
                 4:09 pm
                 12:33 pm
```

16 SUNDAY
```
5:29 am          2:29 pm
8:55 am          5:55 pm
9:19 am          6:19 pm
11:07 am         9:57 pm
12:57 pm         1:48 pm
4:48 pm
```

17 MONDAY
```
3:18 am          12:18 am
6:48 am          3:48 am
7:30 am          4:30 am
8:49 am          5:49 am
1:30 pm          10:30 am
2:18 pm          11:18 am
5:28 pm          2:28 pm
5:35 pm          2:35 pm
7:49 pm          4:49 pm
```

18 TUESDAY
```
10:05 am         7:05 am
12:17 pm         9:17 am
3:37 pm          12:37 pm
8:38 pm          5:38 pm
10:51 pm         7:51 pm
                 11:38 pm
```

19 WEDNESDAY
```
2:38 am
5:37 am          2:37 am
4:13 pm          1:13 pm
4:22 pm          1:22 pm
7:24 pm          4:24 pm
                 10:35 pm
```

20 THURSDAY
```
1:35 am          12:48 pm
3:48 am          2:16 pm
5:16 am          2:46 pm
5:46 am          2:59 pm
5:59 am          4:20 pm
7:20 am          4:38 pm
11:18 pm         8:18 pm
```

21 FRIDAY
```
3:42 am          12:42 am
5:57 am          2:57 am
6:24 am          3:24 am
```

22 SATURDAY
```
12:39 am         12:18 pm
3:18 am          2:15 pm
5:15 am          5:20 pm
8:20 am          6:28 pm
9:28 am          11:54 pm
2:54 pm          12:18 pm
3:33 pm          12:33 pm
4:37 pm          1:37 pm
5:16 pm          2:16 pm
5:24 pm          2:24 pm
6:07 pm          3:07 pm
                 11:59 pm
```

23 SUNDAY
```
2:59 am          4:47 am
7:47 am          10:41 am
1:41 pm          1:18 pm
4:18 pm          2:11 pm
5:11 pm          9:37 pm
```

24 MONDAY
```
12:37 am         3:02 am
11:09 am         8:09 am
9:07 pm          9:09 am
10:43 pm         6:07 pm
10:50 pm         7:43 pm
                 7:50 pm
                 10:21 pm
                 11:09 pm
```

25 TUESDAY
```
1:21 am          12:20 am
2:09 am          2:02 am
3:20 am          10:04 am
5:02 am          2:54 pm
1:04 pm
5:54 pm
```

26 WEDNESDAY
```
12:36 am         2:20 am
1:52 am          10:52 am
3:35 am          12:35 pm
3:47 pm          2:47 pm
                 10:52 pm
```

27 THURSDAY
```
12:18 am         12:05 am
3:05 am          11:54 am
6:23 am          3:23 am
8:13 am          5:13 am
12:29 pm         9:29 am
3:18 pm          12:18 pm
5:49 pm          2:49 pm
7:15 pm          4:15 pm
8:41 pm          5:41 pm
9:49 pm          6:49 pm
```

28 FRIDAY
```
4:40 am          1:40 am
7:09 am          4:09 am
4:47 pm          1:47 pm
5:15 pm          2:15 pm
6:24 pm          3:24 pm
9:00 pm          6:00 pm
                 10:01 pm
                 11:30 pm
```

29 SATURDAY
```
1:01 pm          1:53 am
2:30 am          4:56 am
4:53 am          9:19 am
7:56 am          12:26 pm
12:19 pm         2:08 pm
5:08 pm          3:45 pm
6:45 pm          6:16 pm
9:16 pm
```

30 SUNDAY
```
6:47 am          3:47 am
7:18 am          4:18 am
10:21 am         7:21 am
4:30 pm          1:30 pm
```

31 MONDAY
```
12:43 am         2:45 am
2:10 am          6:07 am
5:45 am          10:01 am
9:07 am          2:06 pm
4:22 pm          1:22 pm
5:55 pm          2:55 pm
8:26 pm          5:26 pm
9:14 pm          6:14 pm
```

Eastern Standard Time in bold type
Pacific Standard Time in medium type

JULY 2000

☽ Last Aspect day	EST / hr:mn / PST		asp	☽ Ingress sign day	EST / hr:mn / PST	
2	**4:36 pm**	1:36 pm	⚹♄	♌ 2	**9:38 pm**	6:38 pm
4	**5:26 pm**	2:26 pm	□♄	♍ 4	**10:19 pm**	7:19 pm
6	**8:57 pm**	5:57 pm	△♄	♎ 6		10:47 pm
6	**8:57 pm**	5:57 pm	△♄	♎ 7	**1:47 am**	
8	**11:10 pm**	8:10 pm	□♀	♏ 9	**8:48 am**	5:48 am
11	**3:29 pm**	12:29 pm	△♀	♐ 11	**7:06 pm**	4:06 pm
13	**11:02 am**	8:02 am	⚹♅	♑ 14	**7:27 am**	4:27 am
16	**4:48 pm**	1:48 pm	△♄	♒ 16	**8:27 pm**	5:27 pm
19	**5:37 am**	2:37 am	□♄	♓ 19	**8:44 am**	5:44 am
21	**6:08 pm**	3:08 pm	△☉	♈ 21	**7:09 pm**	4:09 pm
23	**5:11 pm**	2:11 pm	□♂	♉ 23		11:44 pm
23	**5:11 pm**	2:11 pm	□♂	♉ 23	**2:44 am**	
26	**5:20 am**	2:20 am	☌♄	♊ 26	**7:01 am**	4:01 am
27	**3:18 pm**	12:18 pm	△♅	♋ 28	**8:30 am**	5:30 am
30	**7:18 am**	4:18 am	⚹♄	♌ 30	**8:23 am**	5:23 am

☽ Phases & Eclipses phase	day	EST / hr:mn / PST	
New Moon	1	**2:20 pm**	11:20 am
●	1	**2:33 pm**	11:33 am
2nd Quarter	8	**7:53 am**	4:53 am
Full Moon	16	**8:55 am**	5:55 am
●	16	**8:56 am**	5:56 am
4th Quarter	24	**6:02 am**	3:02 am
●	30	**9:13 pm**	6:13 pm
New Moon	30	**9:25 pm**	6:25 pm

Planet Ingress	day	EST / hr:mn / PST	
♀ ♌	13	**3:02 am**	12:02 am
☉ ♌	22	**7:43 am**	4:43 am
♂ ♌	31	**8:21 pm**	5:21 pm

Planetary Motion	day	EST / hr:mn / PST	
☿ D	17	**8:20 am**	5:20 am

DATE		SID.TIME	SUN	MOON	NODE	MERCURY	VENUS	MARS	JUPITER	SATURN	URANUS	NEPTUNE	PLUTO	CERES	PALLAS	JUNO	VESTA	CHIRON
Sat	1	18:37:24	09 ♋ 28 02	28 ♊ 00	24 ♋ ℞ 37	17 ♋ ℞ 54	14 ♋ 50	09 ♋ 40	00 ♊ 09	26 ♉ 39	20 ♒ ℞ 18	05 ♒ ℞ 53	10 ♐ ℞ 47	03 ♎ 48	02 ♍ 21	26 ♒ ℞ 50	28 ♑ ℞ 08	12 ♐ ℞ 23
Sun	2	18:41:21	10 25 15	13 ♋ 12	24 D 36	17 23	16 04	10 19	00 21	26 45	20 17	05 51	10 46	04 04	02 46	26 47	27 55	12 19
Mon	3	18:45:17	11 22 29	28 21	24 36	16 49	17 18	10 59	00 33	26 51	20 15	05 50	10 45	04 21	03 11	26 44	27 43	12 16
Tue	4	18:49:14	12 19 43	13 ♌ 20	24 37	16 14	18 31	11 39	00 46	26 57	20 13	05 48	10 43	04 38	03 37	26 41	27 30	12 13
Wed	5	18:53:11	13 16 56	28 00	24 37	15 37	19 45	12 18	00 58	27 04	20 12	05 47	10 42	04 55	04 02	26 37	27 16	12 09
Thu	6	18:57:07	14 14 09	12 ♍ 18	24 38	15 00	20 59	12 58	01 10	27 10	20 10	05 45	10 41	05 12	04 28	26 33	27 03	12 06
Fri	7	19:01:04	15 11 22	26 10	24 39	14 23	22 13	13 38	01 22	27 16	20 08	05 44	10 39	05 30	04 53	26 28	26 49	12 03
Sat	8	19:05:00	16 08 35	09 ♎ 36	24 ℞ 39	13 46	23 26	14 17	01 34	27 22	20 06	05 42	10 38	05 48	05 19	26 23	26 35	12 00
Sun	9	19:08:57	17 05 47	22 39	24 39	13 11	24 40	14 57	01 46	27 28	20 04	05 41	10 37	06 05	05 44	26 18	26 21	11 57
Mon	10	19:12:53	18 02 59	05 ♏ 21	24 39	12 38	25 54	15 36	01 58	27 34	20 03	05 39	10 36	06 23	06 10	26 12	26 07	11 54
Tue	11	19:16:50	19 00 11	17 46	24 39	12 07	27 08	16 16	02 10	27 39	20 01	05 38	10 35	06 42	06 36	26 06	25 53	11 51
Wed	12	19:20:46	19 57 24	29 57	24 38	11 40	28 22	16 55	02 22	27 45	19 59	05 36	10 33	07 00	07 01	26 00	25 38	11 49
Thu	13	19:24:43	20 54 36	11i 58	24 38	11 16	29 35	17 35	02 33	27 51	19 57	05 35	10 32	07 18	07 27	25 53	25 24	11 46
Fri	14	19:28:40	21 51 48	23 51	24 37	10 56	00 ♌ 49	18 14	02 45	27 56	19 55	05 33	10 31	07 37	07 53	25 45	25 09	11 43
Sat	15	19:32:36	22 49 01	05 ♑ 41	24 37	10 40	02 03	18 53	02 56	28 02	19 53	05 32	10 30	07 56	08 19	25 38	24 55	11 41
Sun	16	19:36:33	23 46 14	17 29	24 D 37	10 30	03 17	19 33	03 08	28 07	19 51	05 30	10 29	08 15	08 44	25 30	24 40	11 38
Mon	17	19:40:29	24 43 27	29 17	24 ℞ 37	10 D 24	04 30	20 12	03 19	28 13	19 49	05 28	10 28	08 34	09 10	25 21	24 25	11 36
Tue	18	19:44:26	25 40 40	11 ♒ 09	24 37	10 24	05 44	20 51	03 30	28 18	19 46	05 27	10 27	08 53	09 36	25 13	24 11	11 33
Wed	19	19:48:22	26 37 54	23 06	24 37	10 29	06 58	21 30	03 41	28 23	19 44	05 25	10 26	09 13	10 02	25 04	23 56	11 31
Thu	20	19:52:19	27 35 09	05 ♓ 11	24 36	10 40	08 12	22 10	03 52	28 29	19 42	05 24	10 25	09 32	10 28	24 54	23 42	11 29
Fri	21	19:56:15	28 32 24	17 27	24 36	10 56	09 25	22 49	04 03	28 34	19 40	05 22	10 24	09 52	10 54	24 44	23 27	11 27
Sat	22	20:00:12	29 29 40	29 55	24 35	11 18	10 39	23 28	04 14	28 39	19 38	05 20	10 23	10 12	11 20	24 34	23 13	11 25
Sun	23	20:04:09	00 ♌ 26 57	12 ♈ 40	24 35	11 46	11 53	24 07	04 25	28 44	19 36	05 19	10 22	10 31	11 46	24 24	22 59	11 23
Mon	24	20:08:05	01 24 14	25 43	24 D 35	12 20	13 07	24 46	04 35	28 49	19 33	05 17	10 21	10 52	12 12	24 13	22 45	11 21
Tue	25	20:12:02	02 21 33	09 ♉ 08	24 35	13 00	14 21	25 25	04 46	28 54	19 31	05 16	10 21	11 12	12 38	24 02	22 31	11 19
Wed	26	20:15:58	03 18 52	22 56	24 35	13 45	15 34	26 04	04 56	28 58	19 29	05 14	10 20	11 32	13 04	23 50	22 17	11 18
Thu	27	20:19:55	04 16 12	07 ♊ 08	24 36	14 36	16 48	26 43	05 07	29 03	19 27	05 12	10 19	11 52	13 31	23 38	22 04	11 16
Fri	28	20:23:51	05 13 34	21 41	24 37	15 32	18 02	27 22	05 17	29 08	19 24	05 11	10 18	12 13	13 57	23 26	21 51	11 15
Sat	29	20:27:48	06 10 56	06 ♋ 32	24 37	16 34	19 16	28 01	05 27	29 12	19 22	05 09	10 17	12 34	14 23	23 14	21 38	11 13
Sun	30	20:31:44	07 08 20	21 34	24 ℞ 38	17 41	20 30	28 40	05 37	29 17	19 20	05 07	10 17	12 55	14 49	23 01	21 25	11 12
Mon	31	20:35:41	08 05 44	06 ♌ 40	24 38	18 54	21 43	29 19	05 47	29 21	19 17	05 06	10 16	13 15	15 16	22 49	21 12	11 11

EPHEMERIS CALCULATED FOR 12 MIDNIGHT GREENWICH MEAN TIME. ALL OTHER DATA AND FACING ASPECTARIAN PAGE IN **EASTERN STANDARD TIME (BOLD)** AND PACIFIC STANDARD TIME (REGULAR).

AUGUST 2000

1 TUESDAY
7:26 am · 4:26 am
7:34 am · 4:34 am
9:00 am · 6:00 am
4:41 pm · 1:41 pm
6:25 pm · 3:25 pm
9:53 pm
10:14 pm
10:16 pm
11:43 pm

2 WEDNESDAY
12:53 am
1:14 am
1:16 am
2:43 am
6:29 am · 3:29 am
7:42 am · 4:42 am
11:32 am · 8:32 am
4:07 pm · 1:07 pm
6:32 pm · 3:32 pm
9:05 pm · 6:05 pm
10:54 pm · 7:54 pm
11:03 pm · 8:03 pm

3 THURSDAY
3:24 am · 12:24 am
9:50 am · 6:50 am
11:15 am · 8:15 am
1:33 pm · 10:33 am
7:09 pm · 4:09 pm
9:41 pm · 6:41 pm

4 FRIDAY
4:20 am · 1:20 am
5:53 am · 2:53 am
8:16 am · 5:16 am
12:41 pm · 9:41 am
5:08 pm · 2:08 pm
8:08 pm · 5:08 pm
10:11 pm · 7:11 pm
9:44 pm

5 SATURDAY
12:44 am
11:03 am · 8:03 am
1:56 pm · 10:56 am
3:36 pm · 12:36 pm
4:37 am
7:27 am
1:48 pm · 10:48 am
11:29 pm · 8:29 pm

6 SUNDAY
10:10 pm · 7:10 pm
10:15 pm
1:15 am
4:45 am · 1:45 am
8:25 am · 5:25 am
9:51 am · 6:51 am
12:51 pm · 9:51 am
9:51 pm · 6:51 pm
10:29 pm · 7:20 pm

7 MONDAY
3:02 am · 12:02 am
4:02 am · 1:02 am
5:38 am · 2:38 am
8:04 am · 5:04 am
10:17 pm
11:34 pm

8 TUESDAY
1:17 am
2:34 am
4:53 am · 1:53 am
5:40 am · 2:40 am
5:51 am · 2:51 am
6:04 am · 3:04 am
9:22 am · 6:22 am
11:07 am · 8:07 am
3:41 pm · 12:41 pm
9:44 pm · 6:44 pm
11:29 pm · 8:29 pm

9 WEDNESDAY
10:07 am · 7:07 am
10:51 am · 7:51 am
12:13 pm · 9:13 am
3:33 pm · 12:33 pm
4:22 pm · 1:22 pm
4:41 pm · 1:41 pm
6:28 pm · 3:28 pm

10 THURSDAY
7:37 am · 4:37 am

11 FRIDAY
12:53 am
12:26 pm · 9:26 am
12:44 pm · 9:44 am
1:02 pm · 10:02 am
3:14 pm · 12:14 pm
5:02 pm · 2:02 pm
5:58 pm · 2:58 pm
9:41 pm · 6:41 pm
10:26 pm · 7:26 pm
10:43 pm

12 SATURDAY
1:43 am
3:08 am
3:59 am · 12:59 am
4:38 am · 1:38 am
6:12 am · 3:12 am
6:32 am · 3:32 am
8:01 am · 5:01 am
8:14 am · 5:14 am
6:58 pm · 3:58 pm
7:50 pm · 4:50 pm
7:51 pm · 4:51 pm
8:50 pm · 5:50 pm

13 SUNDAY
3:04 am · 12:04 am
3:08 pm · 12:08 pm
6:37 pm · 3:37 pm
7:35 pm · 4:35 pm
8:56 pm · 5:56 pm
11:12 pm · 8:12 pm
10:00 pm

14 MONDAY
1:00 am
6:53 am · 3:53 am
4:12 pm · 1:12 pm
4:17 pm · 1:17 pm
4:32 pm · 1:32 pm
5:27 pm · 2:27 pm
6:55 pm · 3:55 pm
6:57 pm · 3:57 pm
10:44 pm · 7:44 pm

15 TUESDAY
12:13 am
12:53 am
12:28 pm · 9:28 am
3:17 pm · 12:17 pm
4:52 pm · 1:52 pm
11:51 pm · 8:51 pm

16 WEDNESDAY
6:47 am · 3:47 am
10:21 am · 7:21 am
10:34 am · 7:34 am
12:21 pm · 9:21 am
1:43 pm · 10:43 am
1:50 pm · 10:50 am
2:34 pm · 11:34 am
2:58 pm · 11:58 am
3:48 pm · 12:48 pm
6:26 pm · 3:26 pm

17 THURSDAY
12:26 am
2:56 am
3:06 am
4:52 pm · 1:52 pm
5:34 pm · 2:34 pm
8:30 pm · 5:30 pm
11:30 pm · 8:30 pm

18 FRIDAY
1:02 am
1:31 am
4:48 pm · 1:48 pm
7:52 pm · 4:52 pm
9:37 pm · 6:37 pm
10:41 pm · 7:41 pm
11:47 pm

19 SATURDAY
9:13 pm
9:53 pm
2:47 am
6:07 am · 3:07 am
10:42 am · 7:42 am
11:13 am · 8:13 am
11:26 am · 8:26 am
3:09 pm · 12:09 pm
9:48 pm · 6:48 pm
9:31 pm

20 SUNDAY
12:31 am
4:14 am · 1:14 am
9:27 am · 6:27 am
4:46 pm · 1:46 pm
11:13 pm · 8:13 pm
9:25 pm
11:51 pm

21 MONDAY
12:25 am
2:51 am
4:34 am · 1:34 am
8:17 am · 5:17 am
9:25 am · 6:25 am
12:28 pm · 9:28 am
4:06 pm · 1:06 pm
5:18 pm · 2:18 pm
5:35 pm · 2:35 pm
6:07 pm · 3:07 pm
8:05 pm · 5:05 pm
10:52 pm · 7:52 pm

22 TUESDAY
5:29 am · 2:29 am
10:23 am · 7:23 am
1:51 pm · 10:51 am
2:57 pm · 11:57 am
3:22 pm · 12:22 pm
9:43 pm · 6:43 pm

23 WEDNESDAY
5:33 am · 2:33 am
6:16 am · 3:16 am
7:27 am · 4:27 am
9:09 am · 6:09 am
3:08 pm · 12:08 pm
7:15 pm · 4:15 pm
9:05 pm · 6:05 pm
9:23 pm · 6:23 pm
11:57 pm

24 THURSDAY
2:57 am
4:01 am · 1:01 am
10:34 am · 7:34 am
11:46 am · 8:46 am
6:07 pm · 3:07 pm
8:35 pm · 5:35 pm
8:38 pm · 5:38 pm
9:24 pm
11:22 pm

25 FRIDAY
12:24 am
2:22 am
8:24 am · 5:24 am
9:50 am · 6:50 am
11:32 am · 8:32 am
7:31 pm · 4:31 pm
8:26 pm · 5:26 pm
10:53 pm · 7:53 pm
11:09 pm · 8:09 pm

26 SATURDAY
7:02 am · 4:02 am
9:10 am · 6:10 am
11:12 am · 8:12 am
10:50 am
1:35 pm · 10:35 am
7:28 pm · 4:28 pm
10:13 pm
10:25 pm
11:31 pm

27 SUNDAY
1:13 am
1:25 am
2:31 am
9:41 am · 6:41 am
10:40 am · 7:40 am
10:45 am · 7:45 am
11:23 am · 8:23 am
12:29 pm · 9:29 am
10:28 pm · 7:28 pm
11:44 pm · 8:44 pm
10:12 pm

28 MONDAY
1:12 am
9:01 am · 6:01 am

29 TUESDAY
2:01 am
5:22 am · 2:19 am
5:19 am · 7:46 am
10:46 am · 8:33 am
11:33 am · 10:22 am
12:22 pm · 2:46 pm
5:46 pm · 3:33 pm
6:33 pm · 5:41 pm
8:41 pm · 9:38 pm
10:43 pm
2:14 pm · 11:14 am
3:44 pm · 12:44 pm
8:12 pm · 5:12 pm
11:56 pm · 8:56 pm
11:01 pm

30 WEDNESDAY
12:36 am
12:38 am
1:43 am
9:53 am · 6:53 am
10:50 am · 7:50 am
11:41 am · 8:41 am
6:51 pm · 3:51 pm
9:21 pm · 5:21 pm
9:58 pm · 6:58 pm

31 THURSDAY
3:52 am · 12:52 am
11:07 am · 8:07 am
1:27 pm · 10:27 am
1:56 pm · 10:56 am
3:21 pm · 12:21 pm
3:55 pm · 12:56 pm
8:24 pm · 3:24 pm
7:26 pm · 4:26 pm
10:47 pm · 7:47 pm

Eastern Standard Time in bold type
Pacific Standard Time in medium type

AUGUST 2000

☽ Last Aspect day	EST	hr:mn / PST	asp	☽ Ingress sign	day	EST	hr:mn / PST
1	**7:34 am**	4:34 am	□♄	♍	1	**8:27 am**	5:27 am
3	**9:50 am**	6:50 am	△♄	♎	3	**10:31 am**	7:31 am
5	**1:56 pm**	10:56 am	⚹♀	♏	5	**4:04 pm**	1:04 pm
7		10:17 pm	☍♄	♐	7		10:30 pm
8	**1:30 am**		☍♄	♐	8	**1:17 am**	
9	**3:15 pm**	12:15 pm	⚹♅	♑	10	**1:44 pm**	10:44 am
10		10:02 pm	△♀	♒	12		11:43 pm
11	**1:02 am**		△♀	♒	13	**2:43 am**	
14		9:13 pm	☍☉	♓	15	**2:41 pm**	11:41 am
15	**12:13 am**		☍☉	♓	15	**2:41 pm**	11:41 am

☽ Last Aspect day	EST	hr:mn / PST	asp	☽ Ingress sign	day	EST	hr:mn / PST
16	**2:58 pm**	11:58 am	☍♀	♈	17		9:44 pm
16	**2:58 pm**	11:58 am	☍♀	♈	18	**12:44 am**	
20	**4:14 am**	1:14 am	△☉	♉	20	**8:31 am**	5:31 am
22	**1:51 pm**	10:51 am	□☉	♊	22	**1:55 pm**	10:55 am
23		11:57 pm	□♀	♋	24	**4:59 pm**	1:59 pm
24	**2:57 am**		□♀	♋	24	**4:59 pm**	1:59 pm
26	**9:10 am**	6:10 am	⚹♀	♌	26	**6:17 pm**	3:17 pm
27	**11:44 pm**	8:44 pm	☍♅	♍	28	**6:55 pm**	3:55 pm
30	**8:21 pm**	5:21 pm	☌♀	♎	30	**8:33 pm**	5:33 pm

☽ Phases & Eclipses phase	day	EST	hr:mn / PST
2nd Quarter	6	**8:02 pm**	5:02 pm
Full Moon	14		9:13 pm
Full Moon	15	**12:13 am**	
4th Quarter	22	**1:51 pm**	10:51 am
New Moon	29	**5:19 am**	2:19 am

Planet Ingress		day	EST	hr:mn / PST
♀	♍	6	**12:32 pm**	9:32 am
☿	♌	6		9:42 pm
☿	♌	7	**12:42 am**	
♄	♊	9	**9:25 pm**	6:25 pm
☿	♍	22	**5:11 am**	2:11 am
☉	♍	22	**2:48 pm**	11:48 am
♀	♎	30	**10:35 pm**	7:35 pm

Planetary Motion		day	EST	hr:mn / PST
⚷	D	12	**11:02 am**	8:02 am
♇	D	20	**2:16 pm**	11:16 am
⚵	D	28	**11:31 am**	8:31 am

DATE		SID.TIME	SUN	MOON	NODE	MERCURY	VENUS	MARS	JUPITER	SATURN	URANUS	NEPTUNE	PLUTO	CERES	PALLAS	JUNO	VESTA	CHIRON
Tue	1	20:39:38	09 ♌ 03 09	21 ♌ 41	24 ♋ ℞ 37	20 ♋ 12	22 ♌ 57	29 ♋ 58	05 ♊ 57	29 ♉ 25	19 ♒ ℞ 15	05 ♒ ℞ 04	10 ♐ ℞ 15	13 ♎ 36	15 ♍ 42	22 ♒ ℞ 35	21 ♑ ℞ 00	11 ♐ ℞ 10
Wed	2	20:43:34	10 00 35	06 ♍ 28	24 35	21 34	24 11	00e 37	06 06	29 29	19 13	05 03	10 15	13 58	16 08	22 22	20 48	11 08
Thu	3	20:47:31	10 58 01	20 53	24 33	23 02	25 25	01 16	06 16	29 33	19 10	05 01	10 14	14 19	16 35	22 09	20 37	11 08
Fri	4	20:51:27	11 55 29	04 ♎ 54	24 31	24 34	26 39	01 54	06 25	29 37	19 08	04 59	10 14	14 40	17 01	21 55	20 26	11 07
Sat	5	20:55:24	12 52 56	18 28	24 29	26 10	27 52	02 33	06 35	29 41	19 06	04 58	10 13	15 02	17 27	21 41	20 15	11 06
Sun	6	20:59:20	13 50 25	01 ♏ 35	24 28	27 51	29 06	03 12	06 44	29 45	19 03	04 56	10 13	15 23	17 54	21 27	20 04	11 05
Mon	7	21:03:17	14 47 54	14 18	24 D 27	29 35	00 ♍ 20	03 51	06 53	29 49	19 01	04 54	10 12	15 45	18 20	21 13	19 54	11 05
Tue	8	21:07:13	15 45 24	26 41	24 28	01 ♌ 22	01 34	04 29	07 02	29 53	18 58	04 53	10 12	16 07	18 47	20 58	19 45	11 04
Wed	9	21:11:10	16 42 55	08i 49	24 29	03 13	02 47	05 08	07 11	29 56	18 56	04 51	10 11	16 29	19 13	20 44	19 35	11 04
Thu	10	21:15:07	17 40 27	20 46	24 30	05 06	04 01	05 47	07 19	00 ♊ 00	18 54	04 50	10 11	16 51	19 40	20 29	19 27	11 03
Fri	11	21:19:03	18 38 00	02 ♑ 36	24 32	07 02	05 15	06 25	07 28	00 03	18 51	04 48	10 11	17 13	20 06	20 15	19 18	11 03
Sat	12	21:23:00	19 35 33	14 23	24r 33	09 00	06 29	07 04	07 36	00 06	18 49	04 47	10 10	17 35	20 33	20 00	19 10	11 D 03
Sun	13	21:26:56	20 33 08	26 12	24 34	10 59	07 42	07 42	07 45	00 10	18 47	04 45	10 10	17 57	20 59	19 45	19 03	11 03
Mon	14	21:30:53	21 30 44	08 ♒ 04	24 33	12 59	08 56	08 21	07 53	00 13	18 44	04 43	10 10	18 19	21 26	19 31	18 56	11 03
Tue	15	21:34:49	22 28 21	20 04	24 31	15 01	10 10	08 59	08 01	00 16	18 42	04 42	10 10	18 42	21 52	19 16	18 49	11 03
Wed	16	21:38:46	23 25 59	02 ♓ 12	24 27	17 02	11 24	09 38	08 09	00 19	18 39	04 40	10 09	19 04	22 19	19 01	18 43	11 04
Thu	17	21:42:42	24 23 38	14 30	24 23	19 04	12 37	10 16	08 17	00 21	18 37	04 39	10 09	19 27	22 46	18 46	18 37	11 04
Fri	18	21:46:39	25 21 19	26 59	24 18	21 06	13 51	10 55	08 24	00 24	18 35	04 37	10 09	19 50	23 12	18 31	18 32	11 04
Sat	19	21:50:36	26 19 01	09 ♈ 41	24 13	23 08	15 05	11 33	08 32	00 27	18 32	04 36	10 09	20 12	23 39	18 17	18 27	11 05
Sun	20	21:54:32	27 16 45	22 37	24 08	25 09	16 18	12 12	08 39	00 29	18 30	04 34	10 D 09	20 35	24 05	18 02	18 22	11 06
Mon	21	21:58:29	28 14 30	05 ♉ 47	24 05	27 10	17 32	12 50	08 46	00 32	18 28	04 33	10 09	20 58	24 32	17 48	18 19	11 06
Tue	22	22:02:25	29 12 17	19 13	24 D 03	29 09	18 46	13 29	08 53	00 34	18 25	04 31	10 09	21 21	24 59	17 33	18 15	11 07
Wed	23	22:06:22	00 ♍ 10 06	02 ♊ 56	24 02	01 ♍ 08	20 00	14 07	09 00	00 36	18 23	04 30	10 09	21 44	25 26	17 19	18 12	11 08
Thu	24	22:10:18	01 07 57	16 56	24 03	03 06	21 13	14 45	09 07	00 38	18 21	04 29	10 09	22 07	25 52	17 05	18 10	11 09
Fri	25	22:14:15	02 05 49	01 ♋ 12	24 05	05 03	22 27	15 24	09 13	00 40	18 18	04 27	10 09	22 30	26 19	16 51	18 08	11 10
Sat	26	22:18:11	03 03 43	15 44	24 ℞ 06	06 58	23 41	16 02	09 20	00 42	18 16	04 26	10 09	22 54	26 46	16 37	18 06	11 12
Sun	27	22:22:08	04 01 39	00 ♌ 27	24 06	08 53	24 54	16 40	09 26	00 44	18 14	04 24	10 10	23 17	27 13	16 23	18 05	11 13
Mon	28	22:26:05	04 59 37	15 15	24 04	10 46	26 08	17 18	09 32	00 46	18 11	04 23	10 10	23 40	27 39	16 10	18 D 05	11 14
Tue	29	22:30:01	05 57 36	00 ♍ 03	24 01	12 37	27 22	17 57	09 38	00 47	18 09	04 22	10 10	24 04	28 06	15 57	18 05	11 16
Wed	30	22:33:58	06 55 37	14 42	23 55	14 28	28 35	18 35	09 44	00 49	18 07	04 20	10 10	24 28	28 33	15 44	18 05	11 17
Thu	31	22:37:54	07 53 39	29 05	23 49	16 17	29 49	19 13	09 50	00 50	18 05	04 19	10 11	24 51	29 00	15 31	18 06	11 19

EPHEMERIS CALCULATED FOR 12 MIDNIGHT GREENWICH MEAN TIME. ALL OTHER DATA AND FACING ASPECTARIAN PAGE IN **EASTERN STANDARD TIME (BOLD)** AND PACIFIC STANDARD TIME (REGULAR).

SEPTEMBER 2000

1 FRIDAY
☽△♅ **3:36 am** 12:36 am
☽□⚴ **3:46 am** 12:46 am
☽⚺☿ **5:00 am** 2:00 am
☽⚹♂ **7:23 am** 4:23 am
☽☌⚳ **5:02 pm** 2:02 pm
☉□♃ **11:46 pm** 8:46 pm
☽⚺♀ 9:55 pm
☽⚻♄ 11:31 pm

2 SATURDAY
☽⚺♀ **12:55 am**
☽⚻♄ **2:31 am**
☉□♇ **4:01 am** 1:01 am
☽⚺♀ **6:04 am** 3:04 am
☿⚺♂ **8:19 am** 5:19 am
☽□♆ **8:40 am** 5:40 am
☽⚻♃ **7:23 pm** 4:23 pm
☽⚺♇ **7:35 pm** 4:35 pm
☽⚹☉ **8:50 pm** 5:50 pm
☽⚺⚷ **9:50 pm** 6:50 pm

3 SUNDAY
☽□⚵ **4:13 am** 1:13 am
♀△♆ **9:36 am** 6:36 am
☽□♅ **10:04 am** 7:04 am
☽⚹⚴ **10:35 am** 7:35 am
☉□⚷ **10:41 am** 7:41 am
☽□♂ **5:13 pm** 2:13 pm
☽⚹☿ **8:34 pm** 5:34 pm
♄△♀ 11:06 pm
☽⚺⚳ 11:30 pm

4 MONDAY
♄△♀ **2:06 am**
☽⚺⚳ **2:30 am**
♃☍♇ **5:53 am** 2:53 am
☽☍♄ **10:56 am** 7:56 am
☽⚹♀ **11:15 am** 8:15 am
☽⚹♆ **5:21 pm** 2:21 pm
☽⚹♀ **8:56 pm** 5:56 pm

5 TUESDAY
☽☌♇ **5:09 am** 2:09 am
☽☍♃ **5:17 am** 2:17 am
☽☌⚷ **7:41 am** 4:41 am
☽□☉ **11:27 am** 8:27 am
☽⚹⚵ **1:25 pm** 10:25 am
☽⚹♅ **8:21 pm** 5:21 pm
☽⚺⚴ **9:19 pm** 6:19 pm

6 WEDNESDAY
☿⚺⚳ **3:37 am** 12:37 am
☽△♂ **7:22 am** 4:22 am
☉⚻⚵ **8:28 am** 5:28 am
☽⚹⚳ **3:54 pm** 12:54 pm
☽□☿ **5:26 pm** 2:26 pm
☽⚻♄ **10:43 pm** 7:43 pm
☽□♀ 10:20 pm

7 THURSDAY
☽□♀ **1:20 am**
☽⚺♆ **5:14 am** 2:14 am
☽□♀ **4:02 pm** 1:02 pm
☽⚺♇ **5:35 pm** 2:35 pm
☽⚻♃ **6:03 pm** 3:03 pm
☽⚺⚷ **8:20 pm** 5:20 pm
☽⚺⚵ 10:09 pm

8 FRIDAY
☽⚺⚵ **1:09 am**
☽△☉ **5:27 am** 2:27 am
♀⚹♇ **7:04 am** 4:04 am
☿△♄ **7:27 am** 4:27 am
☽⚺♅ **8:55 am** 5:55 am
☽☌⚴ **10:28 am** 7:28 am
♀△♃ **12:29 pm** 9:29 am
☽⚻♂ **11:43 pm** 8:43 pm

9 SATURDAY
☽□⚳ **7:00 am** 4:00 am
♀⚹⚷ **10:51 am** 7:51 am
☽△♄ **11:42 am** 8:42 am
☽△☿ **4:10 pm** 1:10 pm
☽△♀ **4:41 pm** 1:41 pm
☽☌♆ **6:05 pm** 3:05 pm
☿☌♀ **9:10 pm** 6:10 pm
☉⚻♅ **10:19 pm** 7:19 pm

10 SUNDAY
☿△♆ **6:09 am** 3:09 am
☽⚹♇ **6:26 am** 3:26 am
☽△♃ **7:11 am** 4:11 am
☽⚹⚷ **9:19 am** 6:19 am
☽△♀ **11:47 am** 8:47 am
☽☌⚵ **1:03 pm** 10:03 am
☽☌♅ **9:17 pm** 6:17 pm
♀△⚵ **10:58 pm** 7:58 pm
☽⚻☉ **11:21 pm** 8:21 pm
☽⚺⚴ **11:26 pm** 8:26 pm
☉△⚴ 9:23 pm

11 MONDAY
☉△⚴ **12:23 am**
♆△♀ **4:24 am** 1:24 am
☽☍♂ **3:09 pm** 12:09 pm
☽△⚳ **8:57 pm** 5:57 pm
☽□♄ **11:29 pm** 8:29 pm

12 TUESDAY
☽⚺♆ **5:32 am** 2:32 am
☽⚻♀ **6:31 am** 3:31 am
☽⚻☿ **12:33 pm** 9:33 am
☽□♇ **5:34 pm** 2:34 pm
☽□♃ **6:30 pm** 3:30 pm
☽□⚷ **8:30 pm** 5:30 pm
☽⚺⚵ **11:12 pm** 8:12 pm

13 WEDNESDAY
☽⚻♀ **5:02 am** 2:02 am
☽⚺♅ **7:36 am** 4:36 am
☽⚹⚴ **10:20 am** 7:20 am
☽☍☉ **2:37 pm** 11:37 am

14 THURSDAY
☽⚻♂ **3:52 am** 12:52 am
☿⚹♇ **5:18 am** 2:18 am
♀△♅ **6:53 am** 3:53 am
☽⚻⚳ **8:18 am** 5:18 am
☽⚹♄ **8:50 am** 5:50 am
☿△♃ **2:03 pm** 11:03 am
☽⚹♆ **2:33 pm** 11:33 am
☽☍♀ **5:37 pm** 2:37 pm
♄⚻⚳ 9:38 pm
☽△♇ 11:12 pm

15 FRIDAY
♄⚻⚳ **12:38 am**
☽△♇ **2:12 am**
☽⚹♃ **3:16 am** 12:16 am
☽☍☿ **4:57 am** 1:57 am
☽△⚷ **5:11 am** 2:11 am
☽⚹⚵ **7:01 am** 4:01 am
☿⚹⚷ **7:01 am** 4:01 am
☽⚹♅ **3:28 pm** 12:28 pm
♀□⚴ **5:10 pm** 2:10 pm
☽□⚴ **6:45 pm** 3:45 pm
☽☍♀ **6:54 pm** 3:54 pm
☿△⚵ **9:45 pm** 6:45 pm
☽⚻☉ 11:46 pm

16 SATURDAY
☽⚻☉ **2:46 am**
☽△♂ **1:50 pm** 10:50 am
☽⚺♄ **3:49 pm** 12:49 pm
☽☍⚳ **5:05 pm** 2:05 pm
☽□♆ **9:18 pm** 6:18 pm
☽⚻♀ 11:13 pm

17 SUNDAY
☽⚻♀ **2:13 am**
☽⚻♇ **8:40 am** 5:40 am
☽⚺♃ **9:48 am** 6:48 am
☽⚻⚷ **11:42 am** 8:42 am
☽□⚵ **12:49 pm** 9:49 am
☽⚻☿ **5:58 pm** 2:58 pm
☽□♅ **9:19 pm** 6:19 pm
☽△⚴ 10:11 pm

18 MONDAY
☽△⚴ **1:11 am**
☽⚻♀ **6:05 am** 3:05 am
♂□♄ **7:18 am** 4:18 am
☽△☉ **12:31 pm** 9:31 am
☽☌♄ **9:01 pm** 6:01 pm
☽□♂ **9:41 pm** 6:41 pm
☽⚻⚳ **11:55 pm** 8:55 pm
☿△♅ 9:38 pm
☽△♆ 11:19 pm

19 TUESDAY
☿△♅ **12:38 am**
☽△♆ **2:19 am**
☽△♀ **8:56 am** 5:56 am
☽☍♇ **1:30 pm** 10:30 am
☽☌♃ **2:40 pm** 11:40 am
☽☍⚷ **4:36 pm** 1:36 pm
☽△⚵ **5:07 pm** 2:07 pm
☽△♅ 10:39 pm

20 WEDNESDAY
☽△♅ **1:39 am**
☽△☿ **4:34 am** 1:34 am
☽⚻⚴ **6:07 am** 3:07 am
☽△♀ **3:19 pm** 12:19 pm
☽□☉ **8:28 pm** 5:28 pm
☿□⚴ **9:41 pm** 6:41 pm
☽⚺♄ 9:49 pm

21 THURSDAY
☽⚺♄ **12:49 am**
☽⚹♂ **3:57 am** 12:57 am
☽△⚳ **5:15 am** 2:15 am
☽⚻♆ **6:00 am** 3:00 am
☽□♀ **2:12 pm** 11:12 am
☽⚻♇ **5:01 pm** 2:01 pm
☽⚺♃ **6:13 pm** 3:13 pm
☽⚻⚷ **8:12 pm** 5:12 pm
☽⚻⚵ **8:13 pm** 5:13 pm
⚷⚹⚵ **10:13 pm** 7:13 pm

22 FRIDAY
☽⚻♅ **4:45 am** 1:45 am
♆□⚳ **5:45 am** 2:45 am
☽☍⚴ **9:50 am** 6:50 am
☽□☿ **1:15 pm** 10:15 am
☽□♀ **10:58 pm** 7:58 pm
♂⚻♆ 9:49 pm
☽⚹☉ 11:59 pm

23 SATURDAY
♂⚻♆ **12:49 am**
☽⚹☉ **2:59 am**
☽⚹♄ **3:28 am** 12:28 am
☽☍♆ **8:34 am** 5:34 am
☽⚺♂ **8:56 am** 5:56 am
☽□⚳ **9:23 am** 6:23 am
☉△♄ **9:43 am** 6:43 am
☽⚹♀ **6:18 pm** 3:18 pm
☽△♇ **7:30 pm** 4:30 pm
☽⚹♃ **8:42 pm** 5:42 pm
☽☍⚵ **10:22 pm** 7:22 pm
☽△⚷ **10:47 pm** 7:47 pm

24 SUNDAY
☽☍♅ **6:54 am** 3:54 am
☽⚻⚴ **12:39 pm** 9:39 am
♂⚹⚳ **2:36 pm** 11:36 am
☽⚹☿ **8:33 pm** 5:33 pm
♀⚻♄ 11:45 pm

25 MONDAY
♀⚻♄ **2:45 am**
☽□♄ **5:24 am** 2:24 am
☽⚹♀ **5:40 am** 2:40 am
☽⚺☉ **8:40 am** 5:40 am
♇⚹♀ **10:29 am** 7:29 am
☽⚻♆ **10:31 am** 7:31 am
☽⚹⚳ **12:52 pm** 9:52 am
☽☌♂ **1:13 pm** 10:13 am
☽□♇ **9:33 pm** 6:33 pm
☽⚺♀ **9:54 pm** 6:54 pm
☽□♃ **10:44 pm** 7:44 pm
☽⚻⚵ 9:13 pm
☽□⚷ 10:01 pm

26 TUESDAY
☽⚻⚵ **12:13 am**
☽□⚷ **1:01 am**
☽⚻♅ **8:52 am** 5:52 am
☉△♆ **11:40 am** 8:40 am
☽△⚴ **3:26 pm** 12:26 pm
♃△♀ 10:14 pm

27 WEDNESDAY
♃△♀ **1:14 am**
☽⚺☿ **3:49 am** 12:49 am
☽△♄ **7:41 am** 4:41 am
☽⚺♀ **12:49 pm** 9:49 am
☽△♆ **12:58 pm** 9:58 am
♀□♆ **2:34 pm** 11:34 am
☽☌☉ **2:53 pm** 11:53 am
☽⚺⚳ **4:57 pm** 1:57 pm
☽⚺♂ **6:07 pm** 3:07 pm
☽⚹♇ 9:25 pm
☽△♃ 10:35 pm
☽☌♀ 11:23 pm
☽△⚵ 11:58 pm

28 THURSDAY
☽⚹♇ **12:25 am**
☽△♃ **1:35 am**
☽☌♀ **2:23 am**
☽△⚵ **2:58 am**
☽⚹⚷ **4:09 am** 1:09 am
☽△♅ **11:57 am** 8:57 am
♀△⚵ **7:28 pm** 4:28 pm
☽□⚴ **7:40 pm** 4:40 pm
☿⚻♄ **10:39 pm** 7:39 pm

29 FRIDAY
☽⚻♄ **11:46 am** 8:46 am
☽☌☿ **1:06 pm** 10:06 am
☉⚺⚳ **4:31 pm** 1:31 pm
☽□♆ **5:24 pm** 2:24 pm
☽☌♀ **10:35 pm** 7:35 pm
☽☌⚳ **11:21 pm** 8:21 pm
☽⚺☉ **11:40 pm** 8:40 pm
☽⚹♂ 10:31 pm

30 SATURDAY
☽⚹♂ **1:31 am**
☽⚺♇ **5:37 am** 2:37 am
☽⚻♃ **6:47 am** 3:47 am
☽□⚵ **8:11 am** 5:11 am
☽⚺♀ **9:32 am** 6:32 am
☽⚺⚷ **9:48 am** 6:48 am
♀☌⚳ **10:53 am** 7:53 am
☽□♅ **5:42 pm** 2:42 pm
⚷⚹♀ **6:57 pm** 3:57 pm
☽⚹⚴ 11:57 pm

Eastern Standard Time in bold type
Pacific Standard Time in medium type

SEPTEMBER 2000

☽ Last Aspect day	EST / hr:mn / PST		asp	☽ Ingress sign	day	EST / hr:mn / PST	
1	**7:23 am**	4:23 am	⚹♂	♏	1		9:55 pm
1	**7:23 am**	4:23 am	⚹♂	♏	2	**12:55 am**	
3	**8:34 pm**	5:34 pm	⚹☿	♐	4	**9:08 am**	6:08 am
6	**5:26 pm**	2:26 pm	□☿	♑	6	**8:47 pm**	5:47 pm
8	**5:27 am**	2:27 am	△☉	♒	9	**9:44 am**	6:44 am
11	**3:09 pm**	12:09 pm	☍♂	♓	11	**9:34 pm**	6:34 pm
13	**2:37 pm**	11:37 am	☍☉	♈	14	**7:00 am**	4:00 am
16	**1:50 pm**	10:50 am	△♂	♉	16	**2:05 pm**	11:05 am
18	**12:31 pm**	9:31 am	△☉	♊	18	**7:22 pm**	4:22 pm
20	**8:28 pm**	5:28 pm	□☉	♋	20	**11:16 pm**	8:16 pm

☽ Last Aspect day	EST / hr:mn / PST		asp	☽ Ingress sign	day	EST / hr:mn / PST	
22	**10:58 pm**	7:58 pm	□♀	♌	22		11:00 pm
22	**10:58 pm**	7:58 pm	□♀	♌	23	**2:00 am**	
24	**8:33 pm**	5:33 pm	⚹☿	♍	25	**4:02 am**	1:02 am
25	**10:44 pm**	7:44 pm	□♃	♎	27	**6:22 am**	3:22 am
28	**11:57 am**	8:57 am	△♅	♏	29	**10:30 am**	7:30 am
30	**5:42 pm**	2:42 pm	□♅	♐	1	**5:50 pm**	2:50 pm

☽ Phases & Eclipses phase	day	EST / hr:mn / PST	
2nd Quarter	5	**11:27 am**	8:27 am
Full Moon	13	**2:37 pm**	11:37 am
4th Quarter	20	**8:28 pm**	5:28 pm
New Moon	27	**2:53 pm**	11:53 am

Planet Ingress		day	EST / hr:mn / PST	
♀	♎	1		9:52 pm
♀	♎	2	**12:52 am**	
☿	♎	7	**5:22 pm**	2:22 pm
⚳	♏	12	**3:21 pm**	12:21 pm
♂	♍	16	**7:19 pm**	4:19 am
☉	♎	22	**12:28 pm**	9:28 am
♀	♏	24	**10:26 am**	7:26 am
☿	♏	28	**8:28 am**	5:28 am

Planetary Motion		day	EST / hr:mn / PST	
♄	℞	12	**5:14am**	2:14 am
♃	℞	29	**7:13 am**	4:13 am
⚵	D	30		11:31 pm

DATE		SID.TIME	SUN	MOON	NODE	MERCURY	VENUS	MARS	JUPITER	SATURN	URANUS	NEPTUNE	PLUTO	CERES	PALLAS	JUNO	VESTA	CHIRON
Fri	1	22:41:51	08 ♍ 51 43	13 ♎ 06	23 ♋ ℞ 41	18 ♍ 05	01 ♎ 03	19 ♌ 51	09 ♊ 55	00 ♊ 52	18 ♒ ℞ 02	04 ♒ ℞ 18	10 ♐ 11	25 ♎ 15	29 ♍ 27	15 ♒ ℞ 19	18 ♑ 07	11 ♐ 21
Sat	2	22:45:47	09 49 49	26 43	23 35	19 52	02 16	20 29	10 00	00 53	18 00	04 17	10 11	25 39	29 53	15 06	18 09	11 23
Sun	3	22:49:44	10 47 55	09 ♏ 53	23 29	21 37	03 30	21 08	10 05	00 54	17 58	04 15	10 12	26 02	00 ♎ 20	14 55	18 11	11 25
Mon	4	22:53:40	11 46 04	22 39	23 25	23 22	04 43	21 46	10 10	00 55	17 56	04 14	10 12	26 26	00 47	14 43	18 14	11 27
Tue	5	22:57:37	12 44 14	05 ♐ 04	23 D 23	25 05	05 57	22 24	10 15	00 56	17 54	04 13	10 13	26 50	01 14	14 32	18 17	11 29
Wed	6	23:01:34	13 42 25	17 11	23 23	26 47	07 11	23 02	10 20	00 56	17 52	04 12	10 13	27 14	01 41	14 21	18 21	11 31
Thu	7	23:05:30	14 40 38	29 07	23 24	28 27	08 24	23 40	10 24	00 57	17 50	04 11	10 14	27 38	02 08	14 10	18 25	11 33
Fri	8	23:09:27	15 38 52	10 ♑ 56	23 25	00 ♎ 07	09 38	24 18	10 28	00 58	17 48	04 10	10 14	28 02	02 35	14 00	18 29	11 36
Sat	9	23:13:23	16 37 08	22 44	23r 26	01 45	10 51	24 56	10 32	00 58	17 46	04 08	10 15	28 27	03 02	13 51	18 34	11 38
Sun	10	23:17:20	17 35 25	04 ♒ 35	23 25	03 22	12 05	25 34	10 36	00 58	17 44	04 07	10 16	28 51	03 28	13 41	18 40	11 41
Mon	11	23:21:16	18 33 44	16 33	23 22	04 58	13 18	26 12	10 40	00 59	17 42	04 06	10 16	29 15	03 55	13 32	18 45	11 43
Tue	12	23:25:13	19 32 04	28 41	23 17	06 33	14 32	26 50	10 44	00r 59	17 40	04 05	10 17	29 39	04 22	13 23	18 52	11 46
Wed	13	23:29:09	20 30 27	11 ♓ 02	23 10	08 07	15 45	27 28	10 47	00 59	17 38	04 04	10 18	00 ♏ 04	04 49	13 15	18 58	11 49
Thu	14	23:33:06	21 28 51	23 37	23 00	09 40	16 59	28 06	10 50	00 59	17 36	04 03	10 19	00 28	05 16	13 07	19 05	11 52
Fri	15	23:37:02	22 27 17	06 ♈ 26	22 50	11 11	18 12	28 44	10 53	00 58	17 34	04 02	10 19	00 53	05 43	13 00	19 13	11 55
Sat	16	23:40:59	23 25 45	19 29	22 40	12 42	19 26	29 22	10 56	00 58	17 32	04 01	10 20	01 17	06 10	12 53	19 21	11 58
Sun	17	23:44:56	24 24 15	02 ♉ 44	22 30	14 11	20 39	29 59	10 58	00 58	17 31	04 01	10 21	01 42	06 37	12 46	19 29	12 01
Mon	18	23:48:52	25 22 47	16 10	22 22	15 39	21 53	00 ♍ 37	11 01	00 57	17 29	04 00	10 22	02 06	07 04	12 40	19 38	12 05
Tue	19	23:52:49	26 21 21	29 47	22 17	17 07	23 06	01 15	11 03	00 56	17 27	03 59	10 23	02 31	07 31	12 34	19 47	12 08
Wed	20	23:56:45	27 19 57	13 ♊ 34	22 14	18 33	24 19	01 53	11 05	00 56	17 26	03 58	10 24	02 56	07 58	12 29	19 56	12 11
Thu	21	0:00:42	28 18 36	27 31	22 D 13	19 58	25 33	02 31	11 07	00 55	17 24	03 57	10 25	03 20	08 25	12 24	20 06	12 15
Fri	22	0:04:38	29 17 17	11 ♋ 36	22 ℞ 14	21 21	26 46	03 09	11 08	00 54	17 22	03 56	10 26	03 45	08 52	12 20	20 16	12 19
Sat	23	0:08:35	00 ♎ 16 00	25 50	22 14	22 44	28 00	03 46	11 10	00 53	17 21	03 56	10 27	04 10	09 19	12 16	20 27	12 22
Sun	24	0:12:31	01 14 46	10 ♌ 10	22 13	24 05	29 13	04 24	11 11	00 52	17 19	03 55	10 28	04 35	09 46	12 12	20 37	12 26
Mon	25	0:16:28	02 13 34	24 35	22 09	25 26	00 ♏ 26	05 02	11 12	00 50	17 18	03 54	10 29	05 00	10 13	12 09	20 49	12 30
Tue	26	0:20:25	03 12 24	08 ♍ 59	22 03	26 44	01 40	05 40	11 13	00 49	17 16	03 54	10 30	05 24	10 40	12 06	21 00	12 34
Wed	27	0:24:21	04 11 16	23 17	21 54	28 02	02 53	06 17	11 13	00 47	17 15	03 53	10 32	05 49	11 07	12 04	21 12	12 38
Thu	28	0:28:18	05 10 10	07 ♎ 24	21 43	29 18	04 06	06 55	11 14	00 46	17 14	03 52	10 33	06 14	11 34	12 02	21 24	12 42
Fri	29	0:32:14	06 09 06	21 15	21 31	00 ♏ 33	05 19	07 33	11 ℞ 14	00 44	17 12	03 52	10 34	06 39	12 01	12 01	21 37	12 46
Sat	30	0:36:11	07 08 04	04 ♏ 45	21 20	01 46	06 33	08 10	11 14	00 42	17 11	03 51	10 35	07 05	12 27	12 00	21 50	12 50

EPHEMERIS CALCULATED FOR 12 MIDNIGHT GREENWICH MEAN TIME. ALL OTHER DATA AND FACING ASPECTARIAN PAGE IN **EASTERN STANDARD TIME (BOLD)** AND PACIFIC STANDARD TIME (REGULAR).

OCTOBER 2000

1 SUNDAY
- 2:57 am
- 1:27 am 10:27 am
- 7:03 am 4:03 pm
- 10:11 pm
- 11:22 pm

2 MONDAY
- 1:11 am
- 2:22 am
- 6:45 am 3:45 am
- 9:32 am 6:32 am
- 12:46 pm 9:46 am
- 12:54 pm 9:54 am
- 12:54 pm 9:54 am
- 3:28 pm 12:28 pm
- 4:51 pm 1:51 pm
- 5:01 pm 2:01 pm
- 7:04 pm 4:04 pm
- 8:36 pm 5:36 pm

3 TUESDAY
- 3:03 am 12:03 am
- 4:00 am 1:00 am
- 9:12 am 6:12 am
- 2:06 pm 11:06 am
- 2:38 pm 11:38 am
- 6:55 pm 3:55 pm
- 10:08 pm 7:08 pm

4 WEDNESDAY
- 5:49 am 2:49 am
- 6:59 am 3:59 am
- 12:24 pm 9:24 am
- 2:28 pm 11:28 am
- 6:49 pm 3:49 pm
- 7:40 pm 4:40 pm
- 11:23 pm 8:23 pm
- 11:20 pm

5 THURSDAY
- 5:17 am 2:17 am
- 4:02 am 1:02 am
- 5:05 am 2:05 am
- 5:59 am 2:59 am

6 FRIDAY
- 6:45 am 3:45 am
- 7:29 am 4:29 am
- 11:04 am 8:04 am
- 3:16 pm 12:16 pm
- 10:21 pm

7 SATURDAY
- 1:02 am
- 1:21 am
- 1:10 am 1:00 am
- 2:31 am 3:28 pm
- 10:17 pm
- 8:10 am
- 11:31 am
- 1:03 pm
- 3:28 pm
- 5:13 pm
- 5:43 pm
- 9:19 pm
- 11:13 pm

8 SUNDAY
- 12:19 am
- 1:43 am
- 2:13 am
- 3:18 am 12:18 am
- 3:55 am 12:55 am
- 6:23 am 3:23 am
- 8:05 am 5:05 am
- 9:19 am 6:19 am
- 3:26 pm 12:26 pm
- 4:23 pm 1:23 pm
- 5:40 pm 2:46 pm

9 MONDAY
- 6:16 am 3:16 am
- 6:53 am 3:53 am
- 5:10 pm 2:10 pm
- 1:02 pm 10:02 am
- 7:28 pm 4:28 pm
- 10:09 pm 7:09 pm
- 11:39 pm

10 TUESDAY
- 2:39 am
- 3:02 am 12:02 am
- 3:02 am 12:48 am
- 4:25 am 1:25 pm
- 5:29 am 2:29 pm
- 5:32 am 2:32 pm
- 8:03 am 5:03 pm
- 10:18 am 7:18 pm
- 2:26 pm 11:26 am
- 3:03 pm 12:03 pm
- 4:04 pm 1:04 pm
- 8:09 pm 5:09 pm

11 WEDNESDAY
- 4:53 am 1:53 am
- 3:16 pm 12:16 pm
- 5:44 pm 5:52 pm

12 THURSDAY
- 9:04 am 6:04 am
- 10:52 am 7:52 am
- 10:57 am 7:57 am
- 1:42 pm 10:42 am
- 3:39 pm 12:39 pm
- 4:13 pm 1:13 pm
- 4:30 pm 1:30 pm
- 8:44 pm 5:44 pm
- 9:52 pm 6:52 pm 9:25 pm

13 FRIDAY
- 12:25 am
- 3:24 am 12:24 am
- 3:53 am 12:53 am
- 8:50 am 5:50 am
- 12:46 pm 9:46 am
- 8:20 pm 5:20 pm
- 9:17 pm 6:17 pm

14 SATURDAY
- 3:47 am 12:47 am
- 4:08 am 1:08 am
- 4:20 am 1:20 am
- 7:22 am 4:22 am
- 8:39 am 5:39 am
- 9:43 am 6:43 am
- 11:36 pm 8:36 pm
- 11:46 pm

15 SUNDAY
- 2:46 am
- 4:14 am 1:14 am
- 7:03 am 4:03 am
- 12:40 pm 9:40 am
- 4:48 pm 1:48 pm
- 6:20 pm 3:20 pm
- 6:26 pm 10:17 pm

16 MONDAY
- 4:50 am
- 7:50 am 12:51 am
- 3:51 am 12:51 am
- 7:42 am 4:42 am
- 8:13 am 5:13 am
- 11:28 am 8:28 am
- 10:42 pm
- 10:57 pm

17 TUESDAY
- 1:42 am
- 1:57 am
- 4:14 am 1:14 am
- 6:19 am 3:19 am
- 10:11 am 7:11 am
- 12:15 pm 9:15 am
- 8:01 pm 5:01 pm
- 10:49 pm 7:49 pm
- 11:40 pm

18 WEDNESDAY
- 2:40 am
- 4:23 am 1:23 am
- 11:05 am 8:05 am
- 9:46 am 6:46 am
- 10:40 am 7:40 am
- 11:29 am 8:29 am

19 THURSDAY
- 3:04 am 12:04 am
- 5:11 am 2:11 am
- 6:41 am 3:41 am
- 7:25 am 4:25 am
- 9:25 am 6:25 am
- 3:39 pm 12:39 pm
- 5:02 pm 2:02 pm
- 9:14 pm
- 11:59 pm

20 FRIDAY
- 12:14 am
- 2:59 am
- 3:02 am 12:02 am
- 3:59 am 12:59 am
- 7:15 am 4:15 am
- 10:34 am 7:34 am
- 2:10 pm 11:10 am
- 10:30 pm
- 11:41 pm

21 SATURDAY
- 1:30 am
- 2:41 am
- 6:40 am 3:40 am
- 8:37 am 5:37 am
- 9:33 am 6:33 am
- 11:23 am 8:23 am
- 12:31 pm 9:31 am
- 9:08 pm 6:08 pm
- 9:51 pm 6:51 pm

22 SUNDAY
- 4:31 am 1:31 am
- 7:21 am 4:21 am
- 7:53 am 4:53 am
- 10:12 am 7:12 am
- 12:05 pm 9:05 am
- 5:23 pm 2:23 pm
- 6:36 pm 3:36 pm
- 9:18 pm

23 MONDAY
- 12:18 am
- 4:30 am 1:30 am
- 6:05 am 3:05 am
- 10:31 am 7:31 am
- 12:18 pm 9:18 am
- 12:51 pm 9:51 am
- 3:56 pm 12:56 pm
- 4:21 pm 1:21 pm
- 11:59 pm

24 TUESDAY
- 2:59 am
- 3:00 am 12:00 am
- 4:31 am 1:31 am
- 12:09 pm 9:09 am
- 1:34 pm 10:34 am

25 WEDNESDAY
- 5:40 am 2:40 am
- 9:08 am 6:08 am
- 3:21 am 12:21 am
- 8:08 am 5:08 am
- 10:10 am 7:10 am
- 11:49 am 8:49 am
- 3:14 pm 12:14 pm
- 4:47 pm 1:47 pm
- 8:03 pm 5:03 pm
- 10:16 pm 7:16 pm

26 THURSDAY
- 8:22 am 5:22 am
- 9:19 am 6:19 am
- 10:02 am 7:02 am
- 1:25 pm 10:25 am
- 5:54 pm 2:54 pm
- 6:09 pm 3:09 pm
- 6:18 pm 3:18 pm
- 11:17 pm
- 11:58 pm

27 FRIDAY
- 2:17 am
- 2:58 am
- 6:17 am 3:17 am
- 9:20 am 6:20 am
- 12:54 pm 9:54 am
- 1:20 pm 10:20 am
- 1:22 pm 10:22 am
- 2:08 pm 11:08 am
- 3:58 pm 12:58 pm
- 9:51 pm 6:51 pm
- 11:09 pm 8:09 pm
- 11:10 pm

28 SATURDAY
- 2:10 am
- 6:20 am 3:20 am
- 10:32 am 7:32 am
- 6:03 pm 3:03 pm
- 7:37 pm 4:37 pm
- 10:04 pm

29 SUNDAY
- 1:04 am
- 3:02 am 12:02 am
- 9:59 am 6:59 am
- 3:29 pm 12:29 pm
- 4:25 pm 1:25 pm

30 MONDAY
- 12:32 am
- 4:33 am 1:33 am
- 7:31 am 4:31 am
- 8:27 am 5:27 am
- 11:11 am 8:11 am
- 5:38 pm 2:38 pm

31 TUESDAY
- 8:43 am 5:43 am
- 10:59 am 7:59 am
- 3:08 pm 12:08 pm
- 4:19 pm 1:19 pm
- 8:45 pm 5:45 pm
- 9:53 pm 6:53 pm
- 11:42 pm 8:42 pm

Eastern Standard Time in bold type
Pacific Standard Time in medium type

OCTOBER 2000

☽ Last Aspect day	EST / hr:mn / PST		asp	☽ Ingress sign	day	EST / hr:mn / PST	
30	**5:42 pm**	2:42 pm	□ ♅	♐	1	**5:50 pm**	2:50 pm
3	**3:03 am**	12:03 am	⚹ ♅	♑	4	**4:42 am**	1:42 am
5	**7:34 am**	4:34 am	⚹ ♀	♒	6	**5:33 pm**	2:33 pm
8	**3:55 am**	12:55 am	☌ ♅	♓	9	**5:36 am**	2:36 am
10	**8:09 pm**	5:09 pm	△ ♀	♈	11	**2:51 pm**	11:51 am
13	**3:53 am**	12:53 am	☍ ☉	♉	13	**9:06 pm**	6:06 pm
15		10:17 pm	☌ ♄	♊	15		10:19 pm
16	**1:17 am**		☌ ♄	♊	16	**1:19 am**	
17	**8:01 pm**	5:01 pm	△ ☉	♋	18	**4:37 am**	1:37 am
20	**7:15 am**	4:15 am	⚹ ♄	♌	20	**7:42 am**	4:42 am
22	**10:12 am**	7:12 am	□ ♄	♍	22	**10:52 am**	7:52 am
24	**1:34 pm**	10:34 am	△ ♄	♎	24	**2:30 pm**	11:30 am
25	**8:03 pm**	5:03 pm	△ ♅	♏	26	**7:23 pm**	4:23 pm
28		10:04 pm	☍ ♄	♐	28		11:40 pm
29	**1:04 am**		☍ ♄	♐	29	**2:40 am**	
31	**8:43 am**	5:43 am	□ ♂	♑	31	**1:01 pm**	10:01 am

☽ Phases & Eclipses phase	day	EST / hr:mn / PST	
2nd Quarter	5	**5:59 am**	2:59 am
Full Moon	13	**3:53 am**	12:53 am
4th Quarter	19		11:59 pm
4th Quarter	20	**2:59 am**	
New Moon	26		11:58 pm
New Moon	27	**2:58 am**	

Planet Ingress	day	EST / hr:mn / PST	
♄ ♉	15	**7:46 pm**	4:46 pm
♀ ♐	18		10:18 pm
♀ ♐	19	**1:18 am**	
☉ ♏	22	**9:47 pm**	6:47 pm
⚶ ♒	28	**1:30 pm**	10:30 am

Planetary Motion	day	EST / hr:mn / PST	
⚵ D	1	**2:31 am**	
♆ D	15	**6:24 am**	3:24 am
♅ D	26	**7:59 am**	4:59 am
☿ ℞	18	**8:35 am**	5:35 am

DATE		SID.TIME	SUN	MOON	NODE	MERCURY	VENUS	MARS	JUPITER	SATURN	URANUS	NEPTUNE	PLUTO	CERES	PALLAS	JUNO	VESTA	CHIRON
Sun	1	0:40:07	08 ♎ 07 03	17 ♏ 52	21 ♋℞ 10	02 ♏ 57	07 ♏ 46	08 ♍ 48	11 ♊℞ 14	00 ♊℞ 40	17 ♒℞ 10	03 ♒℞ 51	10 ♐ 37	07 ♏ 30	12 ♎ 54	12 ♒ 00	22 ♑ 03	12 ♐ 54
Mon	2	0:44:04	09 06 05	00 ♐ 37	21 02	04 07	08 59	09 26	11 13	00 38	17 09	03 50	10 38	07 55	13 21	12 00	22 17	12 59
Tue	3	0:48:00	10 05 09	13 01	20 57	05 14	10 12	10 03	11 13	00 36	17 07	03 50	10 39	08 20	13 48	12 00	22 31	13 03
Wed	4	0:51:57	11 04 14	25 09	20 54	06 20	11 26	10 41	11 12	00 34	17 06	03 50	10 41	08 45	14 15	12 01	22 45	13 08
Thu	5	0:55:54	12 03 22	07 ♑ 05	20 D 53	07 23	12 39	11 18	11 11	00 32	17 05	03 49	10 42	09 10	14 42	12 03	22 59	13 12
Fri	6	0:59:50	13 02 31	18 55	20 ℞ 53	08 24	13 52	11 56	11 10	00 29	17 04	03 49	10 44	09 36	15 09	12 05	23 14	13 17
Sat	7	1:03:47	14 01 41	00 ♒ 43	20 53	09 23	15 05	12 33	11 08	00 27	17 03	03 49	10 45	10 01	15 36	12 07	23 29	13 22
Sun	8	1:07:43	15 00 54	12 35	20 51	10 18	16 18	13 11	11 07	00 24	17 02	03 48	10 46	10 26	16 03	12 10	23 45	13 26
Mon	9	1:11:40	16 00 08	24 37	20 48	11 11	17 31	13 48	11 05	00 21	17 01	03 48	10 48	10 52	16 30	12 13	24 00	13 31
Tue	10	1:15:36	16 59 24	06 ♓ 52	20 41	12 00	18 44	14 26	11 03	00 19	17 01	03 48	10 50	11 17	16 57	12 17	24 16	13 36
Wed	11	1:19:33	17 58 42	19 24	20 32	12 45	19 57	15 03	11 01	00 16	17 00	03 48	10 51	11 42	17 24	12 21	24 32	13 41
Thu	12	1:23:29	18 58 02	02 ♈ 14	20 21	13 27	21 10	15 41	10 58	00 13	16 59	03 48	10 53	12 08	17 51	12 25	24 49	13 46
Fri	13	1:27:26	19 57 24	15 23	20 08	14 04	22 23	16 18	10 56	00 10	16 58	03 48	10 54	12 33	18 18	12 30	25 06	13 51
Sat	14	1:31:23	20 56 48	28 49	19 55	14 36	23 36	16 56	10 53	00 07	16 58	03 47	10 56	12 59	18 45	12 36	25 22	13 56
Sun	15	1:35:19	21 56 14	12 ♉ 29	19 43	15 03	24 49	17 33	10 50	00 03	16 57	03 D 47	10 58	13 24	19 11	12 41	25 40	14 02
Mon	16	1:39:16	22 55 42	26 20	19 33	15 24	26 02	18 10	10 47	00 00	16 57	03 47	10 59	13 49	19 38	12 48	25 57	14 07
Tue	17	1:43:12	23 55 12	10 ♊ 19	19 26	15 39	27 15	18 48	10 44	29 ♉ 57	16 56	03 47	11 01	14 15	20 05	12 54	26 15	14 12
Wed	18	1:47:09	24 54 45	24 22	19 22	15 ℞ 47	28 28	19 25	10 40	29 53	16 56	03 48	11 03	14 40	20 32	13 01	26 33	14 18
Thu	19	1:51:05	25 54 20	08 ♋ 27	19 D 21	15 47	29 41	20 02	10 36	29 50	16 55	03 48	11 05	15 06	20 59	13 08	26 51	14 23
Fri	20	1:55:02	26 53 57	22 32	19 ℞ 20	15 40	00 ♐ 54	20 40	10 32	29 46	16 55	03 48	11 06	15 32	21 26	13 16	27 09	14 29
Sat	21	1:58:58	27 53 37	06 ♌ 38	19 20	15 24	02 07	21 17	10 28	29 42	16 55	03 48	11 08	15 57	21 52	13 24	27 28	14 34
Sun	22	2:02:55	28 53 19	20 43	19 19	15 00	03 19	21 54	10 24	29 39	16 54	03 48	11 10	16 23	22 19	13 33	27 47	14 40
Mon	23	2:06:52	29 53 03	04 ♍ 45	19 15	14 26	04 32	22 31	10 19	29 35	16 54	03 48	11 12	16 48	22 46	13 42	28 06	14 46
Tue	24	2:10:48	00 ♏ 52 49	18 43	19 09	13 44	05 45	23 09	10 15	29 31	16 54	03 49	11 14	17 14	23 13	13 51	28 25	14 51
Wed	25	2:14:45	01 52 38	02 ♎ 36	18 59	12 53	06 58	23 46	10 10	29 27	16 54	03 49	11 16	17 40	23 40	14 01	28 45	14 57
Thu	26	2:18:41	02 52 29	16 18	18 48	11 54	08 10	24 23	10 05	29 23	16 D 54	03 49	11 17	18 05	24 06	14 11	29 04	15 03
Fri	27	2:22:38	03 52 21	29 47	18 35	10 49	09 23	25 00	10 00	29 19	16 54	03 50	11 19	18 31	24 33	14 22	29 24	15 09
Sat	28	2:26:34	04 52 16	13 ♏ 00	18 23	09 37	10 36	25 37	09 54	29 14	16 54	03 50	11 21	18 57	25 00	14 32	29 44	15 15
Sun	29	2:30:31	05 52 12	25 56	18 12	08 22	11 48	26 15	09 49	29 10	16 54	03 50	11 23	19 22	25 26	14 44	00 ♒ 05	15 21
Mon	30	2:34:27	06 52 11	08 ♐ 33	18 03	07 04	13 01	26 52	09 43	29 06	16 54	03 51	11 25	19 48	25 53	14 55	00 25	15 27
Tue	31	2:38:24	07 52 11	20 54	17 57	05 48	14 13	27 29	09 37	29 02	16 54	03 51	11 27	20 14	26 20	15 07	00 46	15 33

EPHEMERIS CALCULATED FOR 12 MIDNIGHT GREENWICH MEAN TIME. ALL OTHER DATA AND FACING ASPECTARIAN PAGE IN **EASTERN STANDARD TIME (BOLD)** AND PACIFIC STANDARD TIME (REGULAR).

NOVEMBER 2000

1 WEDNESDAY
☽ ⚹ ☉ **7:53 am** 4:53 am
☽ ⚻ ♃ **8:00 am** 5:00 am
☉ ⚻ ♃ **9:10 am** 6:10 am
☿ □ ♆ **9:29 am** 6:29 am
☽ ⚺ ♇ **12:08 pm** 9:08 am
☽ ⚺ ⚵ **8:17 pm** 5:17 pm
☽ ⚺ ⚷ **8:43 pm** 5:43 pm
☽ ⚺ ♀ **10:55 pm** 7:55 pm
☽ ⚺ ♅ **11:04 pm** 8:04 pm
♀ ⚹ ♅ 9:25 pm
☿ △ ♀ 9:41 pm

2 THURSDAY
♀ ⚹ ♅ **12:25 am**
♂ △ ♄ **12:41 am**
☽ ⚹ ⚳ **8:00 am** 5:00 am
☽ □ ♀ **8:59 pm** 5:59 pm
☽ △ ♄ **11:13 pm** 8:13 pm
☽ △ ♂ 9:37 pm

3 FRIDAY
☽ △ ♂ **12:37 am**
☽ ☌ ⚴ **5:42 am** 2:42 am
☽ □ ☿ **5:46 am** 2:46 am
☿ □ ⚴ **6:26 am** 3:26 am
☽ ☌ ♆ **9:36 am** 6:36 am
☉ ⚺ ♇ **11:59 am** 8:59 am
⚷ ⚹ ⚵ **5:19 pm** 2:19 pm
☽ △ ♃ **8:24 pm** 5:24 pm
☽ ⚹ ♇ 10:16 pm
☽ □ ☉ 11:27 pm

4 SATURDAY
☽ ⚹ ♇ **1:16 am**
☽ □ ☉ **2:27 am**
☽ ⚹ ⚷ **10:13 am** 7:13 am
☽ ☌ ⚵ **10:23 am** 7:23 am
☽ ☌ ♅ **12:03 pm** 9:03 am
☽ ⚹ ♀ **6:44 pm** 3:44 pm
☽ □ ⚳ **11:08 pm** 8:08 pm
♄ ⚻ ♀ **11:53 pm** 8:53 pm
☿ ⚺ ♂ 10:05 pm

5 SUNDAY
☿ ⚺ ♂ **1:05 am**
☽ □ ♄ **11:26 am** 8:26 am
☽ △ ♀ **11:56 am** 8:56 am
☽ △ ☿ **3:04 pm** 12:04 pm
☽ ⚻ ♂ **4:25 pm** 1:25 pm
☽ ⚺ ⚴ **7:58 pm** 4:58 pm
☽ ⚺ ♆ **9:58 pm** 6:58 pm

6 MONDAY
☽ □ ♃ **7:47 am** 4:47 am
☽ □ ♇ **1:10 pm** 10:10 am
☽ △ ☉ **7:22 pm** 4:22 pm
☽ □ ⚷ **10:03 pm** 7:03 pm
☽ ⚺ ⚵ **10:51 pm** 7:51 pm
☽ ⚺ ♅ **11:20 pm** 8:20 pm

7 TUESDAY
☽ □ ♀ **11:51 am** 8:51 am
☽ △ ⚳ **11:52 am** 8:52 am
♀ ⚺ ⚳ **12:09 pm** 9:09 am
☽ ⚹ ♄ **9:04 pm** 6:04 pm
☿ ☌ ♀ **10:49 pm** 7:49 pm
☽ ⚻ ☿ **11:56 pm** 8:56 pm
☽ ⚻ ♀ **11:58 pm** 8:58 pm
♅ ☌ ⚵ 9:34 pm

8 WEDNESDAY
♅ ☌ ⚵ **12:34 am**
☽ ☍ ♂ **5:00 am** 2:00 am
☽ ⚹ ⚴ **7:08 am** 4:08 am
☽ ⚹ ♆ **7:23 am** 4:23 am
☉ ⚺ ⚷ **8:15 am** 5:15 am
☽ ⚹ ♃ **4:02 pm** 1:02 pm
♆ ☌ ⚴ **4:11 pm** 1:11 pm
☉ □ ♅ **8:57 pm** 5:57 pm
☽ △ ♇ **9:43 pm** 6:43 pm

9 THURSDAY
☉ □ ⚵ **3:23 am** 12:23 am
☽ △ ⚷ **6:20 am** 3:20 am
☽ ⚹ ♅ **7:07 am** 4:07 am
☽ ⚹ ⚵ **7:40 am** 4:40 am
☽ ⚻ ☉ **7:56 am** 4:56 am
☽ ⚻ ⚳ **8:36 pm** 5:36 pm
☽ △ ♀ 9:07 pm

10 FRIDAY
☽ △ ♀ **12:07 am**
☽ ⚺ ♄ **3:06 am** 12:06 am
☽ ☍ ☿ **6:59 am** 3:59 am
☽ ☍ ♀ **7:55 am** 4:55 am
♂ △ ♆ **8:14 am** 5:14 am
☽ □ ♆ **1:08 pm** 10:08 am
☽ ⚻ ♂ **1:21 pm** 10:21 am
☽ □ ⚴ **2:20 pm** 11:20 am
☽ ⚺ ♃ **8:46 pm** 5:46 pm
☽ ⚻ ♇ 11:43 pm

11 SATURDAY
☽ ⚻ ♇ **2:43 am**
♀ ⚻ ♄ **8:01 am** 5:01 am
☽ ⚻ ⚷ **11:07 am** 8:07 am
☽ □ ♅ **11:31 am** 8:31 am
☽ □ ⚵ **12:58 pm** 9:58 am
☽ ☍ ☉ **4:15 pm** 1:15 pm
☽ ☍ ⚳ 10:53 pm

12 SUNDAY
☽ ☍ ⚳ **1:53 am**
☽ ☌ ♄ **6:12 am** 3:12 am
☽ ⚻ ♀ **8:22 am** 5:22 am
☽ ⚻ ☿ **12:23 pm** 9:23 am
☽ ⚻ ♀ **12:44 pm** 9:44 am
☽ △ ♆ **4:10 pm** 1:10 pm
☽ △ ♂ **6:37 pm** 3:37 pm
☽ △ ⚴ **6:39 pm** 3:39 pm
♂ △ ⚴ **9:32 pm** 6:32 pm
☽ ☌ ♃ **11:03 pm** 8:03 pm
☿ ☌ ♀ 11:34 pm

13 MONDAY
☿ ☌ ♀ **2:34 am**
☽ ☍ ♇ **5:22 am** 2:22 am
☽ ☍ ⚷ **1:48 pm** 10:48 am
☽ △ ♅ **1:51 pm** 10:51 am
☽ △ ⚵ **4:11 pm** 1:11 pm
♅ ⚹ ⚷ **8:43 pm** 5:43 pm
☽ ⚻ ☉ **10:10 pm** 7:10 pm

14 TUESDAY
☽ ⚻ ⚳ **5:24 am** 2:24 am
☽ ⚺ ♄ **7:52 am** 4:52 am
☽ ☍ ♀ **2:47 pm** 11:47 am
☽ △ ♀ **4:09 pm** 1:09 pm
☽ △ ☿ **5:25 pm** 2:25 pm
☽ ⚻ ♆ **6:04 pm** 3:04 pm
☽ ⚻ ⚴ **9:50 pm** 6:50 pm
☽ □ ♂ **10:38 pm** 7:38 pm
☽ ⚺ ♃ 9:24 pm
☿ □ ♆ 11:58 pm

15 WEDNESDAY
☽ ⚺ ♃ **12:24 am**
☿ □ ♆ **2:58 am**
☽ ⚻ ♇ **7:16 am** 4:16 am
☽ ⚻ ♅ **3:42 pm** 12:42 pm
♀ ⚹ ♀ **3:47 pm** 12:47 pm
☽ ⚻ ⚷ **3:59 pm** 12:59 pm
☽ ⚻ ⚵ **6:57 pm** 3:57 pm

16 THURSDAY
☽ △ ☉ **3:46 am** 12:46 am
♀ ⚺ ♆ **6:50 am** 3:50 am
☽ △ ⚳ **8:50 am** 5:50 am
☽ ⚹ ♄ **9:30 am** 6:30 am
♂ △ ♃ **9:38 am** 6:38 am
☽ □ ♀ **7:45 pm** 4:45 pm
☽ ☍ ♆ **8:11 pm** 5:11 pm
☽ ⚻ ♀ **9:23 pm** 6:23 pm
☽ □ ☿ **11:33 pm** 8:33 pm
☽ ☍ ⚴ 10:21 pm
☽ ⚹ ♃ 11:07 pm

17 FRIDAY
☽ ☍ ⚴ **1:21 am**
☽ ⚹ ♃ **2:07 am**
☽ ⚹ ♂ **3:00 am** 12:00 am
♄ ☍ ⚳ **3:38 am** 12:38 am
☽ △ ♇ **9:41 am** 6:41 am
♆ □ ♀ **10:10 am** 7:10 am
☽ ☍ ♅ **6:12 pm** 3:12 pm
☽ △ ⚷ **6:50 pm** 3:50 pm
♃ △ ⚴ **10:08 pm** 7:08 pm
☽ ☍ ⚵ **10:32 pm** 7:32 pm

18 SATURDAY
☿ ⚻ ♃ **3:14 am** 12:14 am
☿ □ ⚴ **6:24 am** 3:24 am
☽ □ ☉ **10:24 am** 7:24 am
☽ □ ♄ **12:03 pm** 9:03 am
☽ □ ⚳ **1:17 pm** 10:17 am
☽ ⚻ ♆ **11:22 pm** 8:22 pm
☽ ⚹ ♀ 9:31 pm
♀ ⚻ ♃ 9:33 pm

19 SUNDAY
☽ ⚹ ♀ **12:31 am**
♀ ⚻ ♃ **12:33 am**
☽ □ ♃ **4:54 am** 1:54 am
☽ △ ♀ **5:21 am** 2:21 am
☽ ⚻ ⚴ **6:06 am** 3:06 am
☉ ☍ ♄ **7:41 am** 4:41 am
☽ ⚹ ☿ **7:45 am** 4:45 am
☽ ⚺ ♂ **8:40 am** 5:40 am
☽ □ ♇ **1:17 pm** 10:17 am
♀ ⚺ ⚴ **5:59 pm** 2:59 pm
☽ ⚻ ♅ **9:59 pm** 6:59 pm
☽ □ ⚷ **10:59 pm** 7:59 pm
☿ ⚺ ♂ 10:07 pm

20 MONDAY
☿ ⚺ ♂ **1:07 am**
☽ ⚻ ⚵ **3:31 am** 12:31 am
☽ △ ♄ **3:57 pm** 12:57 pm
☽ ⚹ ☉ **6:45 pm** 3:45 pm
☽ ⚹ ⚳ **7:13 pm** 4:13 pm

21 TUESDAY
☽ △ ♆ **3:58 am** 12:58 am
☉ ☌ ⚳ **5:18 am** 2:18 am
☽ ⚺ ♀ **6:50 am** 3:50 am
☽ △ ♃ **9:05 am** 6:05 am
☽ △ ⚴ **2:27 pm** 9:27 am
☽ □ ♀ **3:12 pm** 12:12 pm
☽ ☌ ♂ **4:00 pm** 1:00 pm
☿ ⚺ ♇ **6:07 pm** 3:07 pm
☽ ⚹ ♇ **6:24 pm** 3:24 pm
☽ ⚺ ☿ **6:26 pm** 3:26 pm

22 WEDNESDAY
☽ △ ♅ **3:18 am** 12:18 am
☽ ⚹ ⚷ **4:42 am** 1:42 am
♀ □ ♂ **8:43 am** 5:43 am
☽ △ ⚵ **10:11 am** 7:11 am
☽ ⚻ ♄ **9:26 pm** 6:26 pm
☽ ⚺ ⚳ 11:57 pm

23 THURSDAY
☽ ⚺ ⚳ **2:57 am**
♀ ⚺ ♇ **4:12 am** 1:12 am
☽ ⚺ ☉ **5:09 am** 2:09 am
☽ □ ♆ **10:17 am** 7:17 am
♃ ⚻ ♀ **12:34 pm** 9:34 am
☽ ⚻ ♃ **2:55 pm** 11:55 am
☽ ☌ ♀ **3:02 pm** 12:02 pm
☽ □ ⚴ **8:43 pm** 5:43 pm
♂ ⚹ ♇ 9:03 pm
☽ ⚺ ♇ 10:18 pm
☽ ⚺ ♂ 10:22 pm

24 FRIDAY
♂ ⚹ ♇ **12:03 am**
☽ ⚺ ♇ **1:18 am**
☽ ⚺ ♂ **1:22 am**
☽ ⚹ ♀ **3:23 am** 12:23 am
☽ ☌ ☿ **8:00 am** 5:00 am
☽ □ ♅ **10:28 am** 7:28 am
☽ ⚺ ⚷ **12:19 pm** 9:19 am
☽ □ ⚵ **6:57 pm** 3:57 pm

25 SATURDAY
☽ ☍ ♄ **4:52 am** 1:52 am
☿ □ ♅ **6:02 am** 3:02 am
☽ ☌ ⚳ **12:56 pm** 9:56 am
☽ ☌ ☉ **6:11 pm** 3:11 pm
☽ ⚹ ♆ **6:42 pm** 3:42 pm
☽ ☍ ♃ **10:50 pm** 7:50 pm
☿ ⚺ ⚷ 9:29 pm
☉ ⚹ ♆ 9:38 pm
☽ ⚺ ♀ 10:35 pm

26 SUNDAY
☿ ⚺ ⚷ **12:29 am**
☉ ⚹ ♆ **12:38 am**
☽ ⚺ ♀ **1:35 am**
☽ ⚹ ⚴ **7:25 am** 4:25 am
☽ ☌ ♇ **10:27 am** 7:27 am
☽ ⚹ ♂ **1:17 pm** 10:17 am
☽ ⚺ ♀ **6:31 pm** 3:31 pm
☽ ⚹ ♅ **7:57 pm** 4:57 pm
☽ ☌ ⚷ **10:18 pm** 7:18 pm
☽ ⚺ ☿ 10:06 pm

27 MONDAY
☽ ⚺ ☿ **1:06 am**
☽ ⚹ ⚵ **6:17 am** 3:17 am
♀ ⚺ ♅ **9:40 am** 6:40 am
☽ ⚻ ♄ **2:39 pm** 11:39 am
☉ ☍ ♃ **9:12 pm** 6:12 pm
☽ ⚺ ⚳ 10:36 pm

28 TUESDAY
☽ ⚺ ⚳ **1:36 am**
☽ ⚺ ♆ **5:34 am** 2:34 am
☽ ⚻ ♃ **9:05 am** 6:05 am
☽ ⚺ ☉ **10:20 am** 7:20 am
♀ ⚺ ⚷ **1:30 pm** 10:30 am
☽ ⚹ ♀ **2:48 pm** 11:48 am
☽ ⚺ ⚴ **8:48 pm** 5:48 pm
☽ ⚺ ♇ **10:01 pm** 7:01 pm

29 WEDNESDAY
☽ □ ♂ **3:57 am** 12:57 am
☿ □ ⚵ **5:40 am** 2:40 am
☽ ⚺ ♅ **7:49 am** 4:49 am
☽ ⚺ ⚷ **10:42 am** 7:42 am
☽ ☌ ♀ **12:49 pm** 9:49 am
☽ ⚺ ⚵ **8:07 pm** 5:07 pm
☽ ⚹ ☿ **9:47 pm** 6:47 pm
☽ △ ♄ 11:34 pm

30 THURSDAY
☽ △ ♄ **2:34 am**
♇ ⚹ ⚴ **10:48 am** 7:48 am
☽ ⚹ ⚳ **4:28 pm** 1:28 pm
☽ ☌ ♆ **6:22 pm** 3:22 pm
☽ △ ♃ **9:08 pm** 6:08 pm

Eastern Standard Time in bold type
Pacific Standard Time in medium type

NOVEMBER 2000

☽ Last Aspect day	EST / hr:mn / PST	asp	☽ Ingress sign day	EST / hr:mn / PST
2	9:37 pm	△♂	♒ 2	10:41 pm
3	**12:37 am**	△♂	♒ 3	**1:41 am**
5	**11:26 am** 8:26 am	□♄	♓ 5	**2:13 pm** 11:13 am
7	**9:04 pm** 6:04 pm	⚹♄	♈ 7	9:02 pm
7	**9:04 pm** 6:04 pm	⚹♄	♈ 8	**12:02 am**
9	9:07 pm	△♀	♉ 10	**6:12 am** 3:12 am
10	**12:07 am**	△♀	♉ 10	**6:12 am** 3:12 am
12	**6:12 am** 3:12 am	☌♄	♊ 12	**9:27 am** 6:27 am
13	**1:51 pm** 10:51 am	△♅	♋ 14	**11:21 am** 8:21 am
16	**9:30 am** 6:30 am	⚹♄	♌ 16	**1:19 pm** 10:19 am
18	**12:03 pm** 9:03 am	□♄	♍ 18	**4:15 pm** 1:15 pm
20	**6:45 pm** 3:45 pm	⚹☉	♎ 20	**8:35 pm** 5:35 pm
22	**3:18 am** 12:18 am	△♅	♏ 22	11:33 pm
22	**3:18 am** 12:18 am	△♅	♏ 23	**2:33 am**
25	**4:52 am** 1:52 am	☍♄	♐ 25	**10:33 am** 7:33 am
26	**7:57 pm** 4:57 pm	⚹♅	♑ 27	**8:57 pm** 5:57 pm
29	11:34 pm	△♄	♒ 30	**9:26 am** 6:26 am
30	**2:34 am**	△♄	♒ 30	**9:26 am** 6:26 am

☽ Phases & Eclipses phase	day	EST / hr:mn / PST
2nd Quarter	3	11:27 pm
2nd Quarter	4	**2:27 am**
Full Moon	11	**4:15 pm** 1:15 pm
4th Quarter	18	**10:24 am** 7:24 am
New Moon	25	**6:11 pm** 3:11 pm

Planet Ingress	day	EST / hr:mn / PST
♂ ♎	3	**9:00 pm** 6:00 pm
☿ ♎	6	11:28 pm
☿ ♎	7	**2:28 am**
♀ ♏	7	11:02 pm
♀ ♏	8	**2:02 am**
☿ ♏	8	**4:43 pm** 1:43 pm
♀ ♑	12	**9:14 pm** 6:14 pm
☉ ♐	21	**7:19 pm** 4:19 pm
⚳ ♐	22	**2:26 pm** 11:26 am

Planetary Motion	day	EST / hr:mn / PST
☿ D	7	**9:26 pm** 6:26 pm

DATE		SID.TIME	SUN	MOON	NODE	MERCURY	VENUS	MARS	JUPITER	SATURN	URANUS	NEPTUNE	PLUTO	CERES	PALLAS	JUNO	VESTA	CHIRON
Wed	1	2:42:20	08 ♏ 52 13	03 ♑ 00	17 ♋ ℞ 54	04 ♏ ℞ 34	15 ♐ 26	28 ♍ 06	09 ♊ ℞ 31	28 ♉ ℞ 57	16 ♒ 54	03 ♒ 52	11 ♐ 29	20 ♏ 39	26 ♎ 46	15 ♒ 19	01 ♒ 07	15 ♐ 39
Thu	2	2:46:17	09 52 17	14 55	17 D 53	03 26	16 38	28 43	09 25	28 53	16 55	03 53	11 31	21 05	27 13	15 32	01 28	15 45
Fri	3	2:50:14	10 52 22	26 43	17 53	02 25	17 51	29 20	09 19	28 48	16 55	03 53	11 33	21 31	27 40	15 45	01 49	15 51
Sat	4	2:54:10	11 52 29	08 ♒ 31	17 ℞ 54	01 33	19 03	29 57	09 12	28 44	16 56	03 54	11 36	21 56	28 06	15 58	02 10	15 58
Sun	5	2:58:07	12 52 37	20 23	17 53	00 52	20 16	00 ♎ 34	09 06	28 39	16 56	03 54	11 38	22 22	28 33	16 12	02 32	16 04
Mon	6	3:02:03	13 52 47	02 ♓ 25	17 51	00 22	21 28	01 11	08 59	28 34	16 56	03 55	11 40	22 48	28 59	16 26	02 54	16 10
Tue	7	3:06:00	14 52 59	14 42	17 47	00 03	22 40	01 48	08 52	28 30	16 57	03 56	11 42	23 14	29 26	16 40	03 16	16 16
Wed	8	3:09:56	15 53 11	27 19	17 41	29 ♎ D 56	23 53	02 25	08 45	28 25	16 58	03 57	11 44	23 39	29 52	16 54	03 38	16 23
Thu	9	3:13:53	16 53 26	10 ♈ 17	17 32	00 ♏ 01	25 05	03 02	08 38	28 20	16 58	03 57	11 46	24 05	00 ♏ 19	17 09	04 00	16 29
Fri	10	3:17:49	17 53 42	23 38	17 22	00 16	26 17	03 38	08 31	28 16	16 59	03 58	11 48	24 31	00 45	17 24	04 22	16 36
Sat	11	3:21:46	18 54 00	07 ♉ 22	17 12	00 41	27 29	04 15	08 24	28 11	17 00	03 59	11 50	24 57	01 11	17 40	04 45	16 42
Sun	12	3:25:43	19 54 19	21 25	17 02	01 15	28 41	04 52	08 17	28 06	17 01	04 00	11 53	25 22	01 38	17 56	05 08	16 49
Mon	13	3:29:39	20 54 40	05 ♊ 42	16 55	01 58	29 53	05 29	08 09	28 01	17 01	04 01	11 55	25 48	02 04	18 12	05 30	16 55
Tue	14	3:33:36	21 55 03	20 08	16 49	02 47	01 ♑ 05	06 06	08 02	27 56	17 02	04 02	11 57	26 14	02 30	18 28	05 53	17 02
Wed	15	3:37:32	22 55 28	04 ♋ 37	16 D 46	03 43	02 17	06 42	07 54	27 52	17 03	04 03	11 59	26 39	02 57	18 45	06 16	17 09
Thu	16	3:41:29	23 55 54	19 03	16 46	04 45	03 29	07 19	07 46	27 47	17 04	04 04	12 01	27 05	03 23	19 02	06 40	17 15
Fri	17	3:45:25	24 56 22	03 ♌ 23	16 47	05 52	04 41	07 56	07 39	27 42	17 05	04 05	12 04	27 31	03 49	19 19	07 03	17 22
Sat	18	3:49:22	25 56 53	17 34	16 ℞ 48	07 03	05 53	08 33	07 31	27 37	17 06	04 06	12 06	27 57	04 15	19 36	07 27	17 29
Sun	19	3:53:19	26 57 25	01 ♍ 36	16 48	08 17	07 04	09 09	07 23	27 32	17 08	04 07	12 08	28 22	04 42	19 54	07 50	17 35
Mon	20	3:57:15	27 57 58	15 27	16 46	09 35	08 16	09 46	07 15	27 27	17 09	04 08	12 10	28 48	05 08	20 12	08 14	17 42
Tue	21	4:01:12	28 58 34	29 06	16 43	10 55	09 28	10 23	07 07	27 22	17 10	04 10	12 13	29 14	05 34	20 30	08 38	17 49
Wed	22	4:05:08	29 59 11	12 ♎ 35	16 37	12 18	10 39	10 59	06 59	27 17	17 11	04 11	12 15	29 39	06 00	20 49	09 02	17 56
Thu	23	4:09:05	00 ♐ 59 50	25 52	16 29	13 42	11 51	11 36	06 51	27 12	17 13	04 12	12 17	00 ♐ 05	06 26	21 08	09 26	18 02
Fri	24	4:13:01	02 00 31	08 ♏ 56	16 21	15 08	13 02	12 12	06 43	27 08	17 14	04 13	12 20	00 31	06 52	21 27	09 50	18 09
Sat	25	4:16:58	03 01 13	21 48	16 13	16 36	14 14	12 49	06 34	27 03	17 16	04 15	12 22	00 56	07 18	21 46	10 15	18 16
Sun	26	4:20:54	04 01 56	04 ♐ 25	16 06	18 04	15 25	13 25	06 26	26 58	17 17	04 16	12 24	01 22	07 43	22 06	10 39	18 23
Mon	27	4:24:51	05 02 41	16 49	16 00	19 34	16 36	14 02	06 18	26 53	17 19	04 17	12 26	01 47	08 09	22 25	11 04	18 30
Tue	28	4:28:47	06 03 28	29 01	15 57	21 04	17 47	14 38	06 10	26 48	17 20	04 19	12 29	02 13	08 35	22 45	11 29	18 37
Wed	29	4:32:44	07 04 15	11 ♑ 02	15 D 55	22 34	18 58	15 15	06 02	26 43	17 22	04 20	12 31	02 39	09 01	23 06	11 54	18 44
Thu	30	4:36:41	08 05 03	22 54	15 55	24 06	20 09	15 51	05 53	26 39	17 24	04 21	12 33	03 04	09 27	23 26	12 18	18 51

EPHEMERIS CALCULATED FOR 12 MIDNIGHT GREENWICH MEAN TIME. ALL OTHER DATA AND FACING ASPECTARIAN PAGE IN **EASTERN STANDARD TIME (BOLD)** AND PACIFIC STANDARD TIME (REGULAR).

DECEMBER 2000

1 FRIDAY
	EST	PST
	4:50 am	1:50 am
	5:57 am	2:57 am
	9:07 am	6:07 am
	11:10 am	8:10 am
	11:59 am	8:59 am
	8:16 pm	5:16 pm
	9:00 pm	6:00 pm
		9:20 pm
		11:32 pm

2 SATURDAY
	EST	PST
	12:15 am	
	2:32 am	
	6:38 am	5:38 am
	10:01 am	8:01 am
	3:10 pm	12:10 pm
	7:51 pm	4:51 pm
		9:15 pm

3 SUNDAY
	EST	PST
	1:20 am	
	2:32 am	
	7:18 am	4:18 am
	7:32 am	4:32 am
	9:12 am	6:12 am
	8:41 pm	5:41 pm
	10:55 pm	7:55 pm
	11:44 pm	8:44 pm
		11:30 pm

4 MONDAY
	EST	PST
	2:30 am	
	9:03 am	6:03 am
	9:12 am	6:12 am
	11:27 am	8:27 am
	12:50 pm	9:50 am
	7:52 pm	4:52 pm
	10:54 pm	7:54 pm
		9:15 pm
		11:05 pm
		11:26 pm

5 TUESDAY
	EST	PST
	12:15 am	
	2:05 am	
	2:26 am	

---

6 WEDNESDAY
	EST	PST
	8:16 am	5:16 am
	9:21 am	6:21 am
	11:18 am	8:18 am
	1:41 pm	10:41 am
	1:49 pm	10:49 am
	6:09 pm	3:09 pm
	8:10 pm	5:10 pm
	9:15 pm	6:15 pm
	10:30 pm	7:15 pm
		7:50 pm

7 THURSDAY
	EST	PST
	4:17 am	1:17 am
	9:26 am	6:26 am
	9:36 am	6:36 am
	3:22 pm	12:22 pm
	8:01 pm	5:01 pm
	8:49 pm	5:49 pm
		9:30 pm
		9:52 pm

8 FRIDAY
	EST	PST
	12:30 am	
	3:52 am	12:52 am
	4:05 am	1:05 am
	4:49 am	1:49 am
	2:57 pm	11:57 am
	3:31 pm	12:27 pm
	8:31 pm	5:35 pm
	11:08 pm	8:08 pm
		11:56 pm

9 SATURDAY
	EST	PST
	2:56 am	
	5:41 am	2:41 am
	6:20 am	3:20 am
	9:14 am	6:14 am
	1:00 pm	10:00 am
	2:49 pm	11:49 am
	11:21 pm	8:21 pm

---

10 SUNDAY
	EST	PST
	3:07 pm	12:07 pm
	5:50 pm	2:55 pm
	6:55 pm	3:55 pm
	7:58 pm	4:58 pm
	10:05 pm	7:05 pm

11 MONDAY
	EST	PST
	3:19 am	12:19 am
	3:31 am	12:31 am
	5:19 am	2:19 am
	1:31 pm	10:31 am
	7:03 pm	4:03 pm
	11:54 pm	8:54 pm
		10:00 pm

12 TUESDAY
	EST	PST
	1:00 am	
	4:03 am	1:03 am
	4:55 am	1:55 am
	9:15 am	6:15 am
	1:58 pm	10:58 am
	5:15 pm	2:15 pm
	6:18 pm	3:18 pm
	8:16 pm	5:16 pm
		10:11 pm

13 WEDNESDAY
	EST	PST
	1:11 am	
	3:40 am	12:40 am
	4:21 am	1:21 am
	4:22 am	1:22 am
	4:24 am	1:24 am
	10:22 am	7:22 am
	5:49 pm	2:49 pm
	7:42 pm	4:42 pm
	8:53 pm	5:53 pm
		10:30 pm
		10:44 pm

14 THURSDAY
	EST	PST
	1:30 am	
	1:44 am	
	5:39 am	2:39 am
	7:56 am	4:56 am
	10:37 am	7:37 am
	11:36 am	8:36 am
	2:03 pm	11:03 am
	6:52 pm	3:52 pm

---

15 FRIDAY
	EST	PST
	2:10 am	
	2:24 am	
	4:02 am	1:02 am
	4:24 am	1:24 am
	6:55 am	3:55 am
	12:35 pm	9:35 am
	2:45 pm	11:45 am
	2:57 pm	11:57 am
	6:54 pm	3:54 pm
	9:33 pm	6:33 pm
		10:32 pm

16 SATURDAY
	EST	PST
	1:32 am	
	4:49 am	1:49 am
	6:36 am	3:36 am
	3:06 pm	12:06 pm
	3:43 pm	12:43 pm
	8:18 pm	5:18 pm
	8:53 pm	5:53 pm
		10:27 pm
		11:43 pm
		11:54 pm

17 SUNDAY
	EST	PST
	1:27 am	
	2:43 am	
	2:54 am	
	5:06 am	2:06 am
	8:19 am	5:19 am
	10:06 am	7:06 am
	5:51 pm	2:51 pm
	7:41 pm	4:41 pm
	8:13 pm	5:13 pm
		11:35 pm

18 MONDAY
	EST	PST
	2:35 am	
	8:13 am	5:13 am
	10:39 am	7:39 am
	12:08 pm	9:08 am
	9:49 pm	6:49 pm
		9:23 pm
		10:42 pm

---

19 TUESDAY
	EST	PST
	12:23 am	
	1:42 am	
	10:22 am	6:34 am
	3:26 pm	12:26 pm
	4:07 pm	1:07 pm
	8:15 pm	5:15 pm
	11:22 pm	8:22 pm
	11:48 pm	8:48 pm

20 WEDNESDAY
	EST	PST
	4:41 am	1:41 am
	6:07 am	3:07 am
	11:23 am	8:33 am
	1:59 pm	10:59 am
	2:15 pm	11:15 am
	5:24 pm	2:24 pm

21 THURSDAY
	EST	PST
	6:51 am	3:51 am
	9:13 am	6:13 am
	1:09 pm	10:09 am
	6:19 pm	3:19 pm
	7:10 pm	4:10 pm
		9:29 pm
		10:30 pm

22 FRIDAY
	EST	PST
	12:29 am	
	1:30 am	
	4:07 pm	1:21 pm
	4:50 pm	1:50 pm
	7:46 pm	4:41 pm
		5:13 pm
		11:35 pm

23 SATURDAY
	EST	PST
	2:42 am	
	6:34 am	3:34 am
	7:11 am	4:11 am
		9:52 pm
		11:45 pm

24 SUNDAY
	EST	PST
	12:52 am	

---

25 MONDAY
	EST	PST
	6:05 am	3:05 am
	9:25 am	6:25 am
	10:38 am	7:38 am
	12:15 pm	9:15 am
	12:22 pm	9:22 am
	2:07 pm	11:07 am
	2:23 pm	11:23 am
	6:03 pm	3:03 pm
	8:12 pm	5:12 pm

26 TUESDAY
	EST	PST
	2:35 am	
	7:07 am	4:07 am
	8:27 am	5:27 am
	9:42 am	6:42 am
	9:30 pm	6:30 pm
	11:22 pm	8:22 pm
		9:10 pm

27 WEDNESDAY
	EST	PST
	1:46 am	
	5:52 am	2:52 am
	8:42 am	5:42 am
	5:00 pm	2:00 pm
	9:34 pm	6:34 pm
	9:50 pm	6:50 pm
		10:34 pm

28 THURSDAY
	EST	PST
	1:34 am	
	3:00 am	12:00 am
	6:32 am	3:32 am
	6:47 am	3:47 am
	10:27 am	7:27 am
	11:36 pm	5:15 pm
		8:36 pm

---

29 FRIDAY
	EST	PST
	6:09 am	3:09 am
	12:40 pm	9:40 am
	1:48 pm	10:48 am
	5:35 pm	2:35 pm
	6:40 pm	3:40 pm
	6:47 pm	3:47 pm
	7:31 pm	4:31 pm
	8:16 pm	5:16 pm

30 SATURDAY
	EST	PST
	10:07 am	7:07 am
	2:00 pm	11:00 am
	4:08 pm	1:08 pm
	4:52 pm	1:52 pm
	8:27 pm	5:27 pm
		8:55 pm

31 SUNDAY
	EST	PST
	1:23 am	
	8:47 am	6:08 am
	9:08 am	8:22 am
	11:22 am	8:55 am
	11:55 am	11:23 am
	2:23 pm	3:53 pm
	6:53 pm	10:23 pm
		11:39 pm

Eastern Standard Time in **bold type**
Pacific Standard Time in medium type

DECEMBER 2000

D Last Aspect

day	EST / hr:mn / PST	asp
2	7:51 pm 4:51 pm	□ ♀
4	11:26 pm	✶ ♀
5	2:26 am	✶ ♂
6	3:22 pm 12:22 pm	□ ♀
9	1:00 pm 10:00 am	♂ ♄
11	9:15 am 6:15 am	△ ♀
13	2:03 pm 11:03 am	✶ ♄
15	2:57 pm 11:57 am	□ ♄
17	7:41 pm 4:41 pm	□ ⊙
17	7:41 pm 4:41 pm	□ ⊙

D Ingress

sign day	EST / hr:mn / PST
♓ 2	10:23 pm 7:23 pm
♈ 5	9:17 am 6:17 am
♉ 7	9:17 am 6:17 am
♊ 9	4:26 pm 1:26 pm
♋ 11	7:50 am 4:50 pm
♌ 13	8:48 pm 5:48 pm
♍ 15	9:09 pm 6:09 pm
♍ 15	10:30 pm 7:30 pm
⚖ 18	1101 pm
⚖ 18	2:01 am

D Last Aspect

day	EST / hr:mn / PST	asp
20	6:07 am 3:07 am	✶ ⊙
22	7:28 am 4:28 am	♂ ♀
24	5:03 am 2:03 am	□ ♀
27	5:52 am 2:52 am	△ ♀
29	6:47 pm 3:47 pm	♂ ♀

D Ingress

sign day	EST / hr:mn / PST
♍ 20	8:12 am 5:12 am
⚖ 22	4:57 pm 1:57 pm
♏ 25	3:54 am 12:54 am
♐ 27	4:25 pm 1:25 pm
♑ 30	5:27 pm 2:27 pm

Planetary Motion

day	EST / hr:mn / PST

Planet Ingress

	day	EST / hr:mn / PST
♀ ♐	3	3:26 pm 12:26 pm
♀ ✕	8	3:48 am 12:48 am
✶ ♑	17	7:32 am 4:32 am
⊙ ♑	21	8:37 pm 5:37 pm
♀ ♏	22	9:03 pm 6:03 pm
♂ ♏	23	9:37 pm 6:37 pm

D Phases & Eclipses

phase	day	EST / hr:mn / PST
2nd Quarter	3	10:55 pm 7:55 pm
Full Moon	11	4:03 am 1:03 am
4th Quarter	17	7:41 pm 4:41 pm
New Moon	25	12:22 pm 9:22 am
	25	12:35 pm 9:35 am

Main Ephemeris

DATE	SID.TIME	SUN	MOON	NODE	MERCURY	VENUS	MARS	JUPITER	SATURN	URANUS	NEPTUNE	PLUTO	CERES	PALLAS	JUNO	VESTA	CHIRON
Fri 1	4:40:37	09 ♐ 05 53	04 ≈ 44	15 ⊗ 42	25 ♏ 56	21 ♑ 37	16 ⚖ 20	05 ♉ 45	26 ♉ 34	17 ≈ 25	04 ≈ 04	12 ♐ 36	03 ✕ 30	09 ♏ 52	23 ≈ 47	12 ≈ 44	18 ✕ 58
Sat 2	4:44:34	10 06 16	16 58	16 38	27 58	22 52	16 37	05 42	26 25	17 25	04 04	12 37	03 55	09 58	23 55	12 18	18 04
Sun 3	4:48:30	11 07 34	28 56	16 34	00 ♐ 01	24 09	17 40	05 38	26 15	17 26	04 04	12 40	04 21	10 04	24 02	13 34	19 11
Mon 4	4:52:27	12 08 27	10 ✕ 48	16 31	02 04	25 26	18 18	05 35	26 06	17 26	04 04	12 40	04 46	10 09	24 09	13 50	19 18
Tue 5	4:56:23	13 09 18	22 39	16 34	04 05	26 45	18 52	05 31	25 57	17 26	04 04	12 42	05 11	10 13	24 16	14 05	19 25
Wed 6	5:00:20	14 10 13	05 ♈ 37	16 38	06 03	28 05	19 25	05 27	25 48	17 27	04 04	12 44	05 36	10 17	24 23	14 21	19 32
Thu 7	5:04:17	15 11 08	18 08	16 39	07 59	29 25	19 57	05 22	25 39	17 27	04 04	12 45	06 01	10 22	24 30	14 37	19 39
Fri 8	5:08:13	16 12 05	00 ♉ 27	16 37	09 51	00 ✕ 46	20 29	05 18	25 30	17 27	04 04	12 47	06 25	10 25	24 36	14 53	19 46
Sat 9	5:12:10	17 12 59	12 51	16 34	11 38	02 07	21 00	05 13	25 21	17 28	04 04	12 49	06 50	10 29	24 43	15 08	19 53
Sun 10	5:16:06	18 13 54	25 29	16 30	13 21	03 29	21 30	05 08	25 12	17 28	04 04	12 50	07 14	10 31	24 49	15 24	20 00
Mon 11	5:20:03	19 14 51	08 ♊ 14	16 27	14 59	04 51	21 59	05 03	25 04	17 29	04 04	12 52	07 38	10 33	24 56	15 40	20 07
Tue 12	5:23:59	20 15 49	21 24	16 25	16 31	06 13	22 27	04 58	24 55	17 29	04 04	12 54	08 01	10 34	25 02	15 55	20 14
Wed 13	5:27:56	21 16 48	04 ♋ 53	16 24	17 57	07 36	22 55	04 53	24 47	17 30	04 04	12 56	08 24	10 35	25 09	16 11	20 21
Thu 14	5:31:52	22 17 47	18 42	16 24	19 16	08 59	23 21	04 48	24 39	17 30	04 04	12 58	08 47	10 36	25 15	16 26	20 28
Fri 15	5:35:49	23 18 48	02 ♌ 53	16 24 D	20 27	10 22	23 47	04 42	24 31	17 31	04 05	13 00	09 09	10 37	25 21	16 42	20 35
Sat 16	5:39:46	24 19 49	17 20	16 25	21 31	11 46	24 12	04 37	24 24	17 31	04 05	13 02	09 31	10 38 R	25 27	16 57	20 42
Sun 17	5:43:42	25 20 52	02 ♍ 01	16 25	22 24	13 10	24 35	04 32	24 16	17 32	04 05	13 04	09 52	10 37	25 34	17 12	20 49
Mon 18	5:47:39	26 21 55	16 50	16 24	23 08	14 34	24 58	04 26	24 09	17 33	04 05	13 06	10 12	10 37	25 40	17 28	20 56
Tue 19	5:51:35	27 23 00	01 ⚖ 42	16 22	23 39	15 58	25 20	04 20	24 02	17 34	04 05	13 08	10 32	10 36	25 46	17 43	21 03
Wed 20	5:55:32	28 24 06	16 28	16 19	23 59	17 23	25 40	04 15	23 55	17 35	04 05	13 10	10 51	10 35	25 52	17 58	21 10
Thu 21	5:59:28	29 25 12	01 ♏ 01	16 16	24 04	18 48	26 00	04 09	23 49	17 36	04 05	13 12	11 10	10 33	25 58	18 14	21 17
Fri 22	6:03:25	00 ♑ 26 19	15 14	16 14	23 55	20 13	26 18	04 03	23 42	17 37	04 05	13 14	11 28	10 31	26 03	18 29	21 24
Sat 23	6:07:21	01 27 26	29 05	16 13	23 31	21 38	26 35	03 57	23 36	17 38	04 05	13 16	11 46	10 28	26 09	18 44	21 31
Sun 24	6:11:18	02 28 42	12 ♐ 32	16 13	22 51	23 04	26 51	03 51	23 30	17 39	04 05	13 18	12 03	10 25	26 14	18 59	21 38
Mon 25	6:15:15	03 29 51	25 36	16 14	21 59	24 30	27 06	03 45	23 24	17 40	04 05	13 20	12 20	10 21	26 20	19 15	21 45
Tue 26	6:19:11	04 31 00	08 ♑ 20	16 15	20 58	25 57	27 19	03 39	23 19	17 41	04 06	13 22	12 36	10 17	26 25	19 30	21 52
Wed 27	6:23:08	05 32 09	20 47	16 14	19 52	27 23	27 31	03 32	23 13	17 42	04 06	13 24	12 52	10 12	26 30	19 45	21 58
Thu 28	6:27:04	06 33 20	03 ≈ 00	16 12	18 44	28 50	27 43	03 26	23 08	17 43	04 06	13 26	13 07	10 07	26 35	20 00	22 05
Fri 29	6:31:01	07 34 31	15 03	16 09	17 39	00 ♑ 18	27 53	03 19	23 03	17 44	04 06	13 28	13 22	10 02	26 40	20 15	22 12
Sat 30	6:34:57	08 35 41	26 58	16 06	16 41	01 46	28 02	03 12	22 59	17 46	04 06	13 30	13 36	09 56	26 45	20 30	22 19
Sun 31	6:38:54	09 36 51	08 ✕ 49	16 04	15 55	03 14	28 09	03 06	22 54	17 47	04 06	13 32	13 49	09 51	26 50	20 45	22 25

EPHEMERIS CALCULATED FOR 12 MIDNIGHT GREENWICH MEAN TIME. ALL OTHER DATA AND FACING ASPECTARIAN PAGE IN **EASTERN STANDARD TIME (BOLD)** AND PACIFIC STANDARD TIME (REGULAR).

Llewellyn Computerized Astrological Services

Simple Natal Chart

Learn the locations of your midpoints and aspects, elements, and more. Discover your planets and house cusps, retrogrades, and other valuable data necessary to make a complete interpretation. .... APS03-119 (2 pages) $5

Personality Profile

Our most popular report! What makes you tick? This profile describes your "astrological self"—from habits to secret drives! .. APS03-503 (13 pages) $20

Life Progression

As you progress through life, so does your horoscope. Discover what awaits you in the next 12 months. This report forecasts your best bets for success in love, career, health and money. Specify current residence ...... APS03-507 (15 pages) $20

Compatibility Profile

What do the stars say about the two of you? Obtain startling revelations about the strengths, trouble spots and unique dynamics within your relationship. Send birth data for both persons. Indicate each person's gender and type of relationship (romance, business, etc.) .... APS03-504 (18 pages) $30

Personal Relationship Interpretation

What do you need and want from your relationships? Find out why certain people attract you and others leave you cold. Uncover your ideal partner in any relationship—work, family, friends, or romantic APS03-506 $20

Ultimate Astro-Profile

Our most deluxe report is the closest thing to having your own personal astrologer! Your personal qualities, talents, drives and needs unfold in a 50-page booklet all about you! .... APS03-505 (50 pages) $40

Transit Report

What is the best day to ask for that raise? Take your dream vacation? Are you due for a cash windfall—or a new romance? This report helps you pinpoint your best dates for doing just about anything. Specify your present residence.

APS03-500 – 3-month report (8 pages) $12

APS03-501 – 6-month report (16 pages) $20

APS03-502 – 1-year report (25 pages) $30

Biorhythm Report

One day you have unlimited energy, the next day you feel sluggish and awkward. These cycles are called biorhythms. When you know how you'll feel, you can plan each day to the fullest. This report maps your daily biorhythms completely.

APS03-515 – 3-month report (8 pages) $12

APS03-516 – 6-month report (16 pages) $18

APS03-517 – 1-year report (25 pages) $25

Tarot Reading

Find out what the cards have in store for you with this 12-page report that features a 10-card "Celtic Cross" spread selected especially for you. For every card that turns up there is a detailed corresponding explanation of what it means for you. Indicate the number of shuffles you want APS03-120 $10

Lucky Lotto Report (State Lottery Report)

If you play the state lottery, you can increase your chances of winning when you locate your personal lucky numbers and the best days to play them. Give full birth date and middle name. Tell us how many numbers your state lottery requires in sequence, and the highest possible numeral. Indicate the month you want to start.

APS03-512 – 3-month report (9 pages) $10

APS03-513 – 6-month report (15 pages) $15

APS03-514 – 1-year report (25 pages) $25

Numerology Report

Are you a mystic "seven" ... or an independent "one"? What triumphs and challenges await you in the coming months? Your special numbers foreshadow important trends in your life and alert you to upcoming events. Please indicate your full birth name.

APS03-508 – 3-month report (19 pages) $12

APS03-509 – 6-month report (27 pages) $18

APS03-510 – 1-year report (37 pages) $25

ASTROLOGICAL SERVICES ORDER FORM

Be sure to give accurate birth data including exact time, date, and place of birth. (Check your birth certificate for this information!) Noon will be used as your birthtime if you don't provide an exact time. Llewellyn will not be responsible for mistakes that result from inaccurate information.

1. Name and number of desired service

Full name (first, middle, last)

Birthplace (city, county, state, country)

Birthday (month, day, year)   Birthtime   ❏ a.m. ❏ p.m

2. Name and number of desired service

Full name (first, middle, last)

Birthplace (city, county, state, country)

Birthday (month, day, year)   Birthtime   ❏ a.m. ❏ p.m

Billing Information

Name

Address

City, State, Zip

Daytime phone:

Make check or money order payable to Llewellyn Publications, or charge it!
Check one: ❏ Visa ❏ MasterCard ❏ American Express

Account Number   Expiration Date

Cardholder Signature

Mail this form and payment to:
Llewellyn's Personal Services • P.O. Box 64383 • St. Paul, MN 55164-0383
Allow 4 to 6 weeks for delivery